Debating austerity in Ireland: crisis, experience and recovery

EDITORS

Emma Heffernan,
John McHale
and Niamh Moore-Cherry

RIA Acadamh Ríoga na hÉireann
Royal Irish Academy

Debating austerity in Ireland: crisis, experience and recovery
First published in 2017 by

Royal Irish Academy
19 Dawson Street,
Dublin 2,
Ireland
www.ria.ie

ISBN 978-1-908997-68-5 (PB)
ISBN 978-1-908997-69-2 (pdf)
ISBN 978-1-908997-70-8 (epub)
ISBN 978-1-908997-71-5 (mobi)

British Library Cataloguing in Publication Data. A CIP catalogue record for this
book is available from the British Library.

Printed in Ireland by Sprint-PRINT

10 9 8 7 6 5 4 3 2 1

Sponsors:

Banc Ceannais na hÉireann
Central Bank of Ireland
Eurosystem

Comhairle Chomhairleach Bhuiséadach na hÉirean
Irish Fiscal Advisory Council

Ollscoil na hÉireann
National University of Ireland

UCD College of
Social Sciences and Law

Contents

Part 1: Austerity as concept and practice

Part 2: Experiencing austerity

Part 3: Beyond austerity?
From crisis to recovery

List of figures

List of tables

About the authors

Kieran Allen is a senior lecturer in the School of Sociology in University College Dublin (UCD). He is the author of a number of books on Irish society and its economy. These include *Austerity Ireland: The Failure of Irish Capitalism* (2013), *The Irish Economic Crash* (2009) and *The Corporate Takeover of Ireland* (2007). He advocates radical change and is the author of *Marx and the Alternative to Capitalism* (2011). His latest publication is *1916: Ireland's Revolutionary Tradition*.

Spyros Blavoukos (PhD, Essex) is an assistant professor at Athens University of Economics and Business. His research focuses on the structural features of the international and European political economy system and the international interactions of the EU, especially with other International Organizations. He has published in *Review of International Studies, West European Politics, Cooperation and Conflict, Journal of Common Market Studies, European Journal of Political Research, Journal of Public Policy* and *European Union Politics*.

Seamus Coffey is a lecturer in economics in University College Cork (UCC). His teaching includes microeconomics, government and business, advanced microeconomics and econometrics as well as on UCC's MBA programme. His research and writing focuses on the performance of the Irish economy. He is a sometime contributor to print, broadcast and online media relating to the Irish economy, including fiscal outcomes, taxation, debt, national accounts and other issues.

Sebastian Dellepiane-Avellaneda (PhD, Essex) is a senior lecturer in the School of Government and Public Policy at the University of Strathclyde. He studied economics and political science in Buenos Aires, Argentina. He has held research positions in several European universities, including Essex, Antwerp and University College Dublin. He teaches regularly at the Essex Summer School, the Institute of Development Policy and Management in Antwerp, the Maastricht Graduate School of Governance and the German Development Institute in Bonn. His research interests centre on political economy, institutional design and economic development.

Mary Gilmartin is a professor in the Department of Geography at Maynooth University. Her current research interests include contemporary migration to and from Ireland. Her book, *Ireland and Migration in the Twenty First Century*, was published by Manchester University Press in 2015, and her work has also been published in a range of journals, including *Gender, Place & Culture* and *European Urban and Regional Studies*. She is managing editor of *Social & Cultural Geography*.

Niamh Hardiman (DPhil Oxon) is a professor of political science and public policy at University College Dublin (UCD) and director of the interdisciplinary UCD Public Policy Programme, and a research fellow at UCD Geary Institute for Public Policy. She has written extensively on comparative European political economy and on Irish politics and public policy. She is currently co-authoring a book on the political economy of the European periphery, examining the evolution of the pathways to crisis in Ireland, Spain, Portugal and Greece.

Seán Healy is director of Social Justice Ireland. For more than 25 years he has been active on issues of socio-economic policy in Ireland. Before that he worked for more than ten years in Africa. He has been a member of the National Economic and Social Council (NESC) since 1997. He has been a member of Council of Europe working groups and has chaired government working groups, most recently on 'Citizen Engagement with Local Government'. Seán's most recent book (co-author) is *Towards a Just Society*, published April 2015. The most recent book he has co-edited (with Brigid Reynolds) is *Planning and Delivering a Fairer Future*, published November 2014.

Emma Heffernan is currently working in clinical research at St James's Hospital in Dublin. She completed her PhD in anthropology at Maynooth University in 2011 and a Masters in Public Health in University College Dublin in 2013. Emma is also a registered nurse and holds a BSc (Hons) in nursing from RCSI and a Postgraduate Diploma in Specialist Nursing from Trinity College Dublin. Her research interests include social exclusion, global health, social and cultural determinants of health and illness, sexuality and public health.

Niamh Hourigan is senior lecturer and head of the Department of Sociology at University College Cork. Her current book, *Rule-breakers: Why 'being there' trumps 'being fair' in Ireland* (Gill and Macmillan, 2015), examines whether attitudes to rules and relationships in Irish public life have changed as a result of the banking crisis and austerity programme imposed between 2010 and 2013. She has previously published work on social exclusion (*Understanding Limerick*, 2011), media (*Minority Language Media*, 2007), social movements (*Social Movements and Ireland*, 2006) and adult transitions in the Irish Traveller Community (The TEACH Report, 2010).

Ronan Lyons is assistant professor of economics at Trinity College Dublin. His areas of focus include long-run housing markets and sustainable and behavioural aspects of real estate markets. His doctoral thesis at Oxford was on the economics of Ireland's property market bubble and crash. Ronan worked previously as economist to Ireland's National Competitiveness Council and as managing consultant at IBM's Global Centre for Economic Development. He is a frequent contributor to national and international media on the Irish economy and is author of the quarterly Daft.ie reports on the housing market.

Bertrand Maître is a senior research officer at the Economic and Social Research Institute in Dublin. His main research interests focus on multidimensional approaches to poverty, social exclusion and quality of life. He is particularly interested in the development and the use of instruments comprising not only indirect but also direct measures of deprivation, ranging from durable goods to participation in social life, through to housing and environmental conditions.

John McHale is established professor of Economics and dean of the College of Business, Public Policy and Law at National University of Ireland, Galway. He served as chairperson of the Irish Fiscal Advisory Council from 2011 to 2016. He previously held appointments as associate professor of managerial economics at the Queen's School of Business, Ontario and as assistant and associate professor of economics at Harvard University, where he also received his PhD in 1996. He is currently president of the Irish Economics Association.

Julien Mercille is associate professor at the School of Geography, University College Dublin. His research focuses on political economy and the European and Irish economic crisis as well as US foreign policy. In addition to his academic projects, he is a regular contributor to various media outlets in Ireland and abroad. His latest books are *The Political Economy and Media Coverage of the European Economic Crisis: The Case of Ireland* (2014) and *Europe's Treasure Ireland: Deepening Neoliberalism, Austerity, and Crisis* (2015).

Niamh Moore-Cherry is associate professor and deputy head of school in the School of Geography, University College Dublin. She is an urban geographer and her research is focused on understanding how cities are governed; how urban policy is developed; and with what impacts. She is the author of *Dublin Docklands Reinvented* (Four Courts Press, 2008), has co-edited two books and has published papers in national and international journals. She is President of the Geographical Society of Ireland and a member of the Royal Irish Academy Social Sciences Committee.

Fiona Murphy is a research fellow at the Senator George J. Mitchell Institute for Global Peace, Security and Justice. Her research interests include sustainability, business anthropology, migration and indigenous rights.

Brian Nolan is director of the Employment, Equity and Growth Programme at the Institute for New Economic Thinking, Oxford Martin School, professor of social policy at the Department of Social Policy and Intervention and senior research fellow at Nuffield College Oxford. His main areas of research are income inequality, poverty and the economics of social policy. Recent books published by Oxford University Press include *The Handbook of Economic Inequality* (2008), co-edited with W. Salverda and T. Smeeding; *Poverty and Deprivation in Europe* (2011), co-authored with C. T. Whelan; *The Great Recession and the Distribution of Household Income* (2013), co-edited with S. Jenkins, A. Brandolini and J. Micklewright, and two co-edited volumes from the *Growing Inequalities' Impacts* (GINI) EU FP7 project in 2014.

Seán Ó Riain is professor of sociology at Maynooth University. His most recent book is *The Rise and Fall of Ireland's Celtic Tiger: Liberalism, Boom and Bust* (Cambridge, 2014), which explores how Ireland's crisis of 2008 was caused by financialisation, the narrowing of the European integration project and the national politics of economic liberalism. He is currently directing a five-year study of changing workplace bargains in Europe, particularly in Ireland and Denmark. The project is funded by a Starting Investigator grant of the European Research Council. He is an independent member of the National Economic and Social Council in Ireland.

George Pagoulatos (DPhil Oxon) is professor of European politics and economy at the Athens University of Economics & Business (AUEB), and visiting professor at the College of Europe in Bruges. He is a member of the Board of Directors of ELIAMEP and the European Policy Centre (EPC), and a regular columnist in the Sunday edition of Greek daily *Kathimerini*. His publications focus on EMU governance and the EU, and the political economy of Greece and Southern Europe. He has published in leading journals such as *West European Politics, Journal of Common Market Studies, Journal of Public Policy, Public Administration, European Journal of Political Research* and *Government and Opposition*.

Rosalind Pritchard is emeritus professor of education at Ulster University where she was head of the school of education and co-ordinator of research. She is a senior distinguished research fellow of her home institution. She is a member of the Royal Irish Academy and chairperson of its Social Sciences Committee. She has published several books including *Reconstructing Education: East German Schools and Universities after Unification, The End of Elitism? The Democratisation of the West German University System* and *Neoliberal Developments in Higher Education*. She is an honorary member of the British Association for International and Comparative Education and is currently secretary of the European Association for Institutional Research.

Maria Slowey is professor and director of the Higher Education Research Centre, Dublin City University, where she also served as vice-president and academic registrar. She has published widely on the sociology of lifelong learning and higher education and been expert advisor to *inter alia*: OECD, UNESCO, EC, Scottish Parliament, ESRC and several higher education funding councils. She was previously professor of adult education and vice-dean of research, University of Glasgow, and head of the Centre for Widening Access,

Northumbria University. She is an elected academician of the British Academy of Social Sciences and vice-chairperson of the Royal Irish Academy Committee for Social Sciences.

Dorothy Watson is a sociologist and associate research professor at the Economic and Social Research Institute and adjunct at Trinity College Dublin. Her main research focus has been on social exclusion and equality both in Ireland and in a comparative European context. Recent publications include work on childhood economic vulnerability in the recession, household joblessness transitions in Ireland, educational and work circumstances of people with a disability, a comparative European analysis of exposure to workplace risks and developing a multidimensional indicator of quality of life in Europe.

Christopher T. Whelan is an emeritus professor in the School of Sociology and the Geary Institute for Public Policy, University College Dublin, an associate member of Nuffield College, Oxford and a member of the Royal Irish Academy. He was formerly professor of sociology, in the School of Sociology, Social Policy and Social Work, Queen's University Belfast, chairperson of the Standing Committee of the Social Sciences of the European Science Foundation and the European Consortium for Sociological Research. His research interests include the causes and consequences of poverty and inequality, social mobility and inequality. He has published extensively on these topics and on economic and social change in Ireland during bust and boom.

James Williams is a research professor at the Economic and Social Research Institute and adjunct at Trinity College Dublin. He is principal investigator of the Growing Up in Ireland Study. He is responsible for the strategic development and implementation of all aspects of the project with particular responsibility for the project design and methodology. His research interests include child well-being, poverty and social inclusion and survey research methodology.

Simon Wren-Lewis is currently professor of economic policy at the Blavatnik School of Government at Oxford University, having previously been a professor in the Economic Department at Oxford. He is also an emeritus fellow of Merton College. He began his career as an economist in H.M.Treasury, and then moved to the National Institute of Economic and Social Research, where he ended up as head of macroeconomic research. In 1990 he became a professor at Strathclyde University, and from 1995 to 2006 he was a professor at Exeter University. He has published papers on macroeconomics in a wide range of academic journals including the *Economic Journal*, *European Economic Review* and *American Economic Review*. Since becoming an academic he has advised H.M.Treasury, the Bank of England and the Office for Budget Responsibility. In September 2015 he was appointed to the British Labour Party's Economic Advisory Committee. He writes on economic policy issues in various publications and at his blog: mainlymacro.blogspot.com.

Foreword

Patrick Honohan

This cross-disciplinary volume on the sharp adjustments to the public finances from 2008–14, colloquially known as austerity, and their impacts is a timely contribution to a national debate that will continue to define public policy discussions in Ireland for years to come. By concentrating on Ireland, the contributions help to delineate the Irish experience with austerity as a distinct narrative against a background of contrasting contemporary austerities around the world.

The word 'austerity' is one that attracts many rhetorical ambiguities. In some uses, austerity is an *ideology*: an approach to economic policy that squeezes the role of government to the minimum and calls on individuals and firms to be self-reliant and disciplined in their financial planning as a supposed prerequisite for successful long-term economic performance. For some, austerity is a *tool* of economic management that imagines hard constraints as essential in combating waste and moral hazard and expects bankruptcies and recession to be cathartic and cleansing of the economic system. Neither of these perspectives—the first overblown, the second insufficiently cognizant of a century of economic thought—is reflective of widespread opinion in Ireland.

Seen by policymakers in Ireland rarely as either an ideology or a tool, austerity here can only refer in a descriptive way to the cutbacks in spending and tax increases that (in their scale) were an unavoidable *consequence* of earlier errors as the government ran up against an insuperable financing constraint. Indeed, as the almost overwhelming magnitude of the Irish crisis became increasingly clear from October 2008, the task of Irish budgetary policy and bank restructuring was to do as little damage as possible to national living standards and well-being, while slowing and reversing the growth in public debt. Dependent as Ireland was in those years on a sizable annual net injection of resources from abroad, this meant allaying the concerns of foreign lenders and demonstrating the capacity and willingness to restore financial sustainability.

The depth of the Irish crisis is correctly understood by the contributors to this volume as deriving from buccaneering, poorly governed banking and property speculation in an extreme version of the financialised capitalism then prevalent. Apparently regardless of which of the main varieties of capitalism they adhered to, many other countries had also been infected by a precarious financialisation, albeit in most cases to a lesser extent. Observers have also rightly pointed to the inadequacies of official regulation of the banking system and to government policies that had helped stoke the property and construction bubble, using the resources that flowed into the government's coffers to lower income tax rates and boost public spending—including public sector pay rates—unsustainably.

The strategic response was to focus on a strengthening of the regulation of banks while pressing forward decisively on the painful and ultimately unavoidable task of correcting the emerging budget deficit. In official circles there was no questioning of the long-term project of competitive engagement with the globalised economic system. The economic model that had generated the earlier Celtic Tiger period of employment and income growth—driven by an expansion of an internationally competitive export business—remained intact.

The governments' room for manoeuvre was limited; yet correcting the budget deficit could have been carried out in a variety of ways, with different short and long-term consequences. The failure (in 2011 and 2016) of two adjusting governments to win re-election may be attributed as much to the choices they had made in achieving the overall correction, and the limited effectiveness of their attempts to communicate and justify those choices, as to the fact of austerity *per se*. True, the budgetary decisions, and especially the established safety nets that were already in place, had the effect that relative inequality as measured did not widen during the crisis. But with overall decline in living standards, soaring unemployment and the over-indebtedness that had been accumulated by some, large numbers of households slid into poverty and financial distress. The consequences in different dimensions and at the individual level are illustrated throughout this volume.

The policy priority in the crisis years had to be the restoring of confidence (and the clawing back of as much of the prospective banking losses as possible) in order to maximise the continued flow of financial resources on a sustainable basis in order to avoid even more severe austerity. But this need not have been at the expense of realistic communication and public debate on what could be attainable on a lasting basis post-crisis. *Debating austerity in Ireland* provides an excellent foundation for filling that void and helping form a longer-term vision for a post-austerity Ireland.

25 April 2016

Introduction
Austerity in Ireland: a debate

Niamh Moore-Cherry, John McHale and Emma Heffernan

Since the global financial crisis of 2008, much has been written about austerity and its impacts, but there has been a particular emphasis on the impact of the crisis on countries of the European periphery. The combination of global recession, the structure of the European Monetary Union and particular country-specific factors meant that Portugal, Ireland, Greece and Spain became the 'problem children' of Europe. The European experience of the Great Recession is of particular interest given its disproportionate effect in challenging the very stability of the common currency and, some would argue, the European project as a whole. This is a common theme across many of the chapters of this book and sets the scene for the primary discussion on austerity and Ireland.

One of the defining features of the debate to date has been its tendency to polarise opinion and adopt a one-dimensional perspective. This book challenges us to adopt a more nuanced approach to understanding austerity, and by extension the path to recovery. By design, there is no overarching hypothesis, conclusion or endpoint. Rather, the book aims to bring together for the first time a diversity of social science perspectives on this important topic to encourage agonistic readings. Central to the book is debate about whether austerity was indeed necessary or overdone, and our contributors take quite different stances from both ideological and pragmatic perspectives. What alternative strategies might have been employed, how the impact of austerity unfolded and how has it been experienced by different groups within society are key questions that the authors have been invited to address. In our conclusion, we highlight some common themes emerging from the evidence presented throughout the chapters and reflect on what this might mean for Ireland moving forward.

The book originated in a day-long symposium on 'Debating austerity' held at the Royal Irish Academy in October 2015. The goal of the symposium was to invite a plurality of readings on an issue that has generated so much public debate. To date much of the academic literature on the topic has involved specialists debating each other within disciplinary silos, but not across intellectual domains. This may be because of the challenges faced in fostering multidisciplinary discussion; although social scientists often use the same language, different disciplinary lenses will produce multiple interpretations and can often result in people speaking past each other. In this volume, while recognising this challenge, we have tried to encourage authors to engage with each other across disciplinary boundaries. As editors, one of the other challenges in compiling this volume has been the ideologically charged nature of the public debate and media reporting on 'austerity' in Ireland. Although the debate has not been as strident or polarised in Ireland as it has been in other countries such as Spain or Greece, real debate has more often than not been shut down because of ideological divergences. This book tries to counter this trend by highlighting the value of a multiplicity of approaches to understanding the profound changes that Ireland has experienced in recent times.

In this centenary decade, much emphasis has been placed on reflecting how far Ireland has come since 1916, and for perhaps the first time in the history of our state, pluralistic understandings of our national history are being interrogated. We believe that it is precisely this plurality of lenses that can help us to better understand our recent past, our present and our future. All of the contributors in this book accept that austerity measures have produced real harm in Ireland, but whether or not there were policy alternatives—given the broader political-economic context—is one of the key lines of debate in the volume. The contributors are social scientists and activists drawn from across the island of Ireland and further afield, and the majority presented their initial findings at the symposium. Individual chapters question Ireland's recent experiences, the lessons that have or have not been learned and the approaches now needed to build a sustainable and fair recovery for the future. While the emphasis is primarily on Ireland, the situation here is put into a comparative perspective in a number of chapters, and the importance of transnationalism and interdependency are highlighted.

Defining austerity

So what is austerity? Economists would generally define fiscal consolidation as the reining in of spending or the raising of taxes in order to reduce the structural deficit. The *Oxford English Dictionary* (OED) broadly defines austerity as 'difficult economic conditions created by government measures to reduce public expenditure', while Simon Wren-Lewis in the first chapter of this book argues that austerity is defined as fiscal consolidation that causes unemployment to rise in a recession. The distinguishing feature of austerity is the resort to fiscal consolidation at a point in the business cycle that is inappropriate from a cyclical management perspective. A core point of contention among economists is whether other considerations—such as limiting the risk of an even deeper crisis that could follow a default—makes austerity a hugely regrettable but necessary policy response. For social scientists more generally, austerity is broader than these definitions, encompassing wider social, political and cultural attributes. In popular parlance austerity has become shorthand for cuts in public spending during recession, the results of which have been devastating for particular social groups. This is the focus of a number of the chapters in Part 2 of the book.

Since 2008, the word austerity has been increasingly used as an adjective to describe particular types of action across different domains. For example, 'austerity politics' (Newman 2012, Rüdig and Karyotis 2014) describes an approach to governing that has emerged since the global financial crisis, while 'austerity urbanism' (Peck 2012; Tonkiss 2013) is used to describe a new phase in urban policy usually involving minimal, or the total withdrawal of, public funding to urban projects, temporary or 'holding' projects on particular urban sites to allow the property market to bounce back, and those that increasingly push responsibility on to civil actors. In the context of the discussions in this volume, Callan *et al.*'s (2011) work is particularly useful in setting a context for the type of transformation that has occurred recently in Ireland. They use a relative definition, describing 'austerity measures' as:

> (i) reductions in cash benefits and public pensions; (ii) increases in direct taxes and contributions; (iii) increases in indirect taxes; (iv) reductions in public services that have an indirect impact on the welfare of households using them; (v) reductions in public expenditure that cannot be allocated to households (e.g. pure public goods like defence spending) and increases in taxes that are not straightforward to allocate to households; (vi) cuts in public sector pay (vii) cuts in public sector employment' (Callan *et al.*, 2011, p. 4).

Beyond these very tangible indicators of austerity in practice, many writers argue that austerity is also very much an ideological project. Since the Great Recession of 2008, changes to public policy and the transformation of the state as a result of spending cuts have paved the way for increased privatisation of public services and indeed public life. For example, Bramall (2013) describes how the context of austerity has become appropriated and commodified in fashion, culture and the media as something that can enhance self-sufficiency, innovation and entrepreneurialism and is inherently 'anti-statist'. Fraser *et al.* (2013) argue that in Ireland, the government's austerity programme was used as a tool to deliver public sector reform and deepen processes of neoliberalisation. Whether ideologically or pragmatically driven, the outcome has been the creation of new axes of division and polarisation within society. Borooah (2014) argues that at a European level, this has manifested itself in multiple ways, pitting north verus south, Germany versus Greece and 'core' versus 'periphery'. Equally in Ireland, austerity has resulted in increased hardship for some traditionally vulnerable groups and the creation of new axes of division and vulnerability.

Situating austerity in Ireland

From the mid-1990s until the early-2000s, Ireland has been described as a 'flexible developmental state' (O'Riain 2000) with economic policy focusing on creating the conditions to attract increasingly mobile, global capital and foreign direct investment to Ireland. This approach delivered very positive economic and social benefits with real GDP growing on average 6% per annum from 1998–2007, and unemployment falling from 16% in 1994 to 4% in 2000. Low corporation tax rates, combined with generous financial incentives and a business-friendly regulatory climate, led to this rapid economic growth. However, by the early 2000s, productivity was declining and growth was being driven by speculation in the built environment rather than productive investment. By 2007, construction accounted for 13.3% of all employment and almost 23% of GNP with the state precariously reliant on property-based taxation (O'Riain 2014; Finn 2011). When the global financial crisis occurred in 2008 and credit became increasingly squeezed, a number of countries, particularly in the European periphery, came under increasing financial pressure leading to a contraction of their economies. In Ireland, as in Spain and other countries where property-driven speculation had been a key component of the national economy, the credit crunch led to a banking crisis. In Ireland, the contraction of the construction sector compounded by a state guarantee of the banking system, produced not just an economic, but also a massive fiscal crisis (Donovan and Murphy 2013; Healy 2013). The debt-to-GDP ratio rose from a low of just under 25% of GDP to over 120% of GDP at its peak. Even excluding the direct deficit-increasing costs of the banking sector bailout, the deficit rose to 11.5% of GDP. And the State lost its access to borrowing at affordable rates, with the yield on Irish long-term bonds reaching over 14% in mid-2011.

In response to the deteriorating public finances and risk to the stability of the entire Eurozone, the Irish government on 28 November 2010 applied to the EU-IMF for financial support or what has been colloquially termed a 'bailout'. The Department of Finance (n.d) described the objectives of the programme in the following terms: 'The objectives of Ireland's EU-IMF programme were to address financial sector weaknesses, to put Ireland's economy on the path of sustainable growth, to stabilise the public finances and to create jobs, while protecting the poor and most vulnerable'. Official international funding of €67.5 billion was provided contingent upon major restructuring of the public finances, taxation system and public sector and the introduction of significant 'austerity measures' (Callan *et al.* 2011). Many would argue that while austerity measures certainly targeted the health of the economy and public finances, the 'big-bang' approach to austerity in Ireland generated unnecessary hardship for the most vulnerable. It has also been argued that the economic crisis was used as a shield to force through a wide-ranging, ideological and dramatic public sector reform agenda . While we do not specifically focus on this reform agenda in a particular chapter, this does underpin many of the chapters and we do return to it in the conclusion where we attempt to assess the impact of austerity on Ireland's long-term historical record.

As well as significant social implications, the Irish crisis has had profound spatial outcomes. Although not explicit, the socio-spatial dimensions of austerity are drawn out here in chapters by Lyons and Hardiman *et al.*, while the recovery is also showing particular spatial dimensions. Following longer-term patterns of spatial inequity, regional disparities across ireland are clearly evident in the housing market upturn and economic recovery currently taking place, providing a new set of challenges for policymakers moving forward. The 'two-speed' recovery alluded to by Healy in the final chapter of this volume is not just social but also spatial. These transformations over the last decade in Irish society are detailed extensively in the excellent volume by Kearns, Meredith and Morrissey (2014) who highlight the creation of new spaces of disadvantage and exclusion, and new topographies of dereliction and abandonment. How, to where and to whom scarce resources have been distributed during the crisis and period of austerity are extensively detailed in their work, as well as more publicly through blogs like Ireland after NAMA and data resources including those of the All-Ireland Research Observatory (airo.ie). This book takes a complementary perspective to these particular resources and offers itself as a companion to the essays in the *Spatial Justice and the Irish Crisis* volume (Kearns, Meredith and Morrissey 2014) previously published by the Royal Irish Academy.

Structure of the book

The book is organised in three broad parts: austerity as concept in Ireland and beyond; the experience of austerity measures; and a discussion on which direction Irish public policy and society will take as we exit the austerity context. Our goal in Part 1 is to set the broad scene and parameters for the debate about austerity but we do not aim to be entirely comprehensive, given the many other excellent works on the history of austerity (see for example, Allen and O'Boyle 2013;

Drudy and Collins 2011; Fraser *et al.* 2013; Kinsella 2012). As social scientists, our primary focus is on societal challenges, the experiences of societies and the impact of public policy on them and this is extensively the focus of parts two and three.

Part 1: Austerity as concept and practice

This book challenges understandings of austerity and its context, adopting different perspectives on it both in practice but also ideologically. The first part opens with an ambitious attempt by Simon Wren-Lewis to provide a 'General theory of austerity'. Professor Wren-Lewis, who provided the keynote lecture at the October 2015 symposium, questions why global austerity gained such momentum, particularly since 2010, and argues that it was not inevitable. There was no particular economic need for such rapid and sharp fiscal consolidation by various governments, but was more ideological in nature. This is a theme picked up in the chapters by Kieran Allen and Julien Mercille. Allen argues that austerity is so hegemomic that it has been institutionalised in European policy through the Fiscal Compact, limiting and justifying particular policy choices by national governments. He argues that this ideological framing of austerity is re-enforced by pro-austerity economists and other experts who are used by technocrats to justify strongly neoliberal objectives. The importance of governance—not just those formally governing but the broader milieu of influential voices—in the practice of austerity is thus an important theme and is developed further by Mercille, in his analysis of the role of the mainstream media in austerity politics. He outlines the role of particular media channels in sustaining the housing bubble that played a key part in Ireland's economic crisis, but also argues that particular news outlets have provided strong ideological support for austerity.

While Wren-Lewis adopts the perspective of the Euro Area as a whole in considering the necessity of austerity in its periphery, John McHale takes the European policy stance as given in considering the choices facing Irish policy makers. Once the property bubble burst, he argues that the size of the resulting deficit, the exploding debt and the increasing difficulty of accessing funds on international credit markets made policies to lower the deficit unavoidable. He notes that the underlying deficit to be corrected would have been large even without the costs of bailing out the banking system and that the 'troika programme' allowed for a more phased adjustment once Ireland lost access to sovereign credit markets. While the new post-crisis fiscal framework should help reduce the risk of past mistakes being repeated, it will be an ongoing challenge to meet the demands of this framework given the inevitable pressures on spending in the post-crisis economy.

Part 2: Experiencing austerity

In the second part of the book, the focus shifts to examining how austerity has been experienced politically, culturally, and socially both on an aggregate basis and across different social groups. The discussion begins with Hardiman *et al.*, who place the Irish experience of austerity in a European context, particularly alongside that of the other Eurozone periphery countries. The manner in which anti-austerity politics has resulted in fragmentation of the party system in Spain, Portugal, Greece and Ireland and given rise to challenger parties articulating values and priorities that may be difficult to accommodate within the current European policy regime is illustrated. The difficulties of government formation in Ireland following the February 2016 general election mirrors the situation in other European peripheral countries since 2010 and is indicative of a significant legitimacy gap between a large proportion of the electorate and the established political parties. This has become a clear theme in broader studies of austerity within Europe where the mantra 'no taxation without representation' is rearing its head in new ways as issues of democratic accountability and legitimacy come centre stage (Borooah 2014).

The chapter by Christopher Whelan and Brian Nolan also places Ireland in a comparative perspective, discussing the impact of the economic crisis on income levels, poverty and inequality, and also on subjectively assessed economic stress. There has been, and continues to be, considerable disagreement about the degree to which the costs of the recession have been distributed in an equitable manner and whether or not government policy has been progressive or regressive. The findings in the case of Ireland are placed in a comparative perspective; this highlights that the impact of the Great Recession varied even among the hardest-hit countries, and even more so between them and the countries where it represented a less dramatic, though still very substantial, macroeconomic shock.

While these societal shocks and the various measures introduced under structural reform programmes generated protest votes across

Europe, in Ireland this was clearly identifiable in the results of both the 2011 and 2016 Irish general elections. However contrary to some of the early discourse in Ireland, resistance did not just remain confined to the ballot box but also occurred, albeit more sowly than in other contexts in the form of street-level protest organised by the anti-austerity movement. In her chapter, Niamh Hourigan examines the achievements of Irish anti-austerity protesters in light of the substantial theoretical and empirical literature on social movement outcomes. In the aftermath of the Irish bank bailout in 2010, a number of commentators expressed surprise at the relatively subdued protest response to austerity in Ireland particularly when compared with what was happening in other countries of the European periphery, particularly Greece and Spain. Others have suggested that this may be explained by the fact that Ireland was spared the levels of absolute deprivation experienced in places like Greece, the stoic nature of the Irish people but also the inordinate desire of the Irish to be liked, and become the poster child of austerity Europe (Borooah 2014). However, Hourigan suggests that as fiscal consolidation focused on households, through the introduction of local property taxes and water charges—Ireland was a European anomaly in terms of not already having such taxes in place—resistance to austerity policies intensified. She argues that the introduction of water charges in 2013 acted as the key catalyst in galvanizing the Irish anti-austerity movement. The successes and failures of the Irish anti-austerity movement are examined in terms of three criteria: goal attainment, changes to systems of interest representation and value transformation. While the movement has had little immediate success in terms of changing policies linked to austerity, Hourigan highlights the successes of the movement in terms of electoral politics and in reconfiguring a stronger and more radical political left in Ireland that may have more far-reaching and longer-term implications.

These two chapters by Hardiman *et al.* and Hourigan set the scene for the next six chapters that focus on the relationship between austerity and particular public policy choices. Many would argue that one of the key reasons Ireland was so adversely affected by the Global Financial Crisis—and the common thread linking the banking, fiscal crisis and property crises in Ireland—was the housing sector. In his chapter, Ronan Lyons discusses the two-way relationship between housing and austerity. He begins by examining the contribution made by the housing sector to a significant expansion in government spending and thus, by corollary, in austerity, and then assesses the impact austerity had on the housing sector in Ireland. It is widely accepted that Ireland, and in particular Dublin, faces a housing crisis with the wrong types of housing built in the wrong locations and a significant shortage of appropriate supply where it is most needed. Lyons argues that housing needs to be rethought in terms of both efficiency and equity and outlines some key principles that should act as the foundation for housing policy into the future. However, one key theme running through this chapter is that the housing crisis in Ireland is not necessarily a product of the recent economic crash and introduction of austerity politics, but has its roots in government policy even at the height of the Celtic Tiger.

This theme also underlies the chapter by Emma Heffernan in which she examines the impact of recent cuts in government spending on the community and social care sector, using a particular case study of homeless, drug-using women engaged in prostitution in Dublin city. She demonstrates that even during boom times, a significant section of the Irish population was living in consistent poverty, struggling to survive and unable to afford everyday expenses. Following the financial crash, austerity policies have pushed people further into poverty, as well as significantly reducing access to essential public services and supports. Through an ethnographic study of two women, she highlights the consequences of austerity budgets on the lives of the most vulnerable and argues that to create any meaningful change in the lives of the most vulnerable, a holistic approach to policy development is needed, one that considers the multiple and overlapping historical, socio-economic and political and structural processes that shape people's lives.

The disproportionate vulnerability of particular members of society to cuts in social supports and spending is also a key theme explored by Dorothy Watson and colleagues. Using data from the Growing Up in Ireland study, Watson *et al.* examine the changing well-being of families and the consequences for children over the last decade in Ireland. Child poverty is a concern not only because of its immediate consequences for the well-being of children but also because it has potentially long-term negative consequences that persist into adulthood. Their analysis concludes that economic vulnerability increased and that a broader group of families—more couple families and more families with higher levels of education—was drawn into economic vulnerability in the recession. This runs contrary to previous studies on those most vulnerable to experiencing childhood poverty and requires a new policy focus, beyond the traditional focus in welfare policy on income support, to include a broader mix of strategies such as those addressing childcare, housing supply and housing costs. They see the chances of such an integrated approach being adopted as slim given the relatively short-term approach taken to much of Irish public policymaking. This is evidenced, for example, by the way in which resourcing for education was cut as a result of austerity.

Right across the spectrum from primary, through secondary and on to higher education, cutbacks and reduced resourcing have impacted on children and young people. Additional burdens of cost have been transferred onto individuals and families as the education sector tries to balance reduced central government funding through other means. The chapter by Rosalind Pritchard and Maria Slowey, which focuses on higher education, adopts an all-Ireland perspective to investigate whether policies introduced during the period since 2010—including increased cost-sharing in the form of rising student contributions and fees—represents a step-change in direction or just a logical development of several decades of neoliberal policies. They highlight the measures being taken by higher education management to counter the effects of reduced funding and develop institutional resilience. They question whether survival is occurring at the cost of compromising core values and purposes; there is a distinct sense from their analysis that austerity has provided the 'cover' for intensifying shifts in educational provision and resourcing in both the Republic and Northern Ireland.

This sense of continuity and change is a theme picked up by Mary Gilmartin in her discussion of emigration. During the early period of the crisis, one of the most widely discussed social impacts was the return of net emigration with increases in levels of emigration of Irish nationals. Newspapers and broadcast media were replete with images of young, educated Irish people forced to leave because of high unemployment and poor opportunities. However the analysis by Gilmartin illustrates a much more complex story. She shows that while emigration has increased, immigration continues, and new forms of migration have emerged. In this way, the chapter provides evidence for both continuities and changes in the contemporary movements of people from and to Ireland. She considers the experiences of migrants in an era of austerity, with a particular focus on work and the working conditions of migrants and other workers.

In her chapter, Fiona Murphy argues that new articulations of parenting, thrift-culture and sustainability through the lens of the 'austerity myth' do much to help us clarify the mythology of the market economy and the failures therein. She points to the role the austerity myth plays in transforming ordinary citizens into thrifty consumers and questions whether these idioms of thrift and frugality will bring lasting benefits of any kind in our role as parents or citizen-consumers. Murphy argues that when examined through the lens of sustainability politics, one might have a sense that the austerity myth is working to achieve some new-found respect for notions of 'thrift' and 'frugality' which coalesce with forms of sustainable consumption. She further argues this is a thrift culture created by the rolling back of important welfare and institutional supports; a culture grounded in deep societal inequities unmoored from the premises of social justice and thus *not* a progressive form of sustainability politics.

Part 3: Beyond austerity? From crisis to recovery

The final part of the book adopts a more speculative and forward-looking analytical frame. The three papers challenge us to think differently not just about austerity but about the type of future society we wish to develop and the policies required to achieve it. In his chapter, Seán O'Riain begins by exploring the meaning of austerity creating interesting parallels and comparisons with the chapters in the first part of the book. He does this to set the scene for a discussion about the nature of recovery and cautions about the potential dangers that it may bring. He explains how Ireland's recovery is not a break with past practices but is in many ways—for better and for worse—continuous with key historical features of its economy. These include high inequality linked to property and other assets, flexible labour markets, the mobilisation of foreign investment and a tentatively emerging domestic business class across a range of sectors supported by public agencies. The unevenness of the recovery was one of the key points of debate during the February 2015 general election campaign and is thus a key societal challenge facing the country. O'Riain concludes his contribution by arguing that Ireland will once more face important choices previously faced in the late 1980s and late 1990s and that sustained investment and public action is required to deepen and broaden the current uplift.

How this investment might happen and whether the resources exist to maintain it are examined in the chapter by Seamus Coffey. In the first part of the chapter, a detailed analysis is provided of the differences in revenue and expenditure patterns in Ireland and other European countries. Ireland's comparative position is shown to be very different depending on whether revenue and expenditure are expressed as percentages of Gross Domestic Product (GDP), Gross National Product (GNP) or some hybrid of the two. This reflects that large gap between GDP and GNP due to the heavy reliance on multinational investment in Ireland. He also shows that relative expenditure shortfalls in Ireland are largely explained by lower spending on old-age social protection. The enforced austerity in Ireland since 2008 has shown the importance of preparing for the downturns before they arrive. Ireland has successfully closed a huge budget deficit and the second half of the chapter examines a proposal which attempts to reduce the probability of such measures being necessary in the future. One way to do this is to run surpluses in times of growth and expansion. This chapter contains a proposal for a 'stability fund' with contributions based on corporation tax receipts from the multinational corporate (MNC) sector in Ireland and withdrawals based on projections of employment growth. Such a fund would provide surpluses and accumulated savings which can be used to mitigate the fiscal and economic consequences of downturns in the economic cycle.

There has been much discussion about Ireland's focus on austerity as the main means towards addressing the problems it faced following the crash of 2008. Far less attention has been paid to how future policy might move Ireland towards ensuring that the recovery is inclusive and just, both socially and spatially. In the closing chapter of Part 3, Seán Healy sets out a series of key questions that should be at the core of decision-making. He goes on to identify key policy challenges Ireland faces and argues for a balanced and integrated response. A policy framework is proposed that would ensure the development of a vibrant economy, decent services and infrastructure, just taxation, good governance and sustainability. The need for action in all five areas simultaneously, not sequentially, is required.

Conclusion

Austerity is complex. While having its roots in economic discourse, over the last decade it has become the key descriptor of a range of government policies and impacts that have reshaped Irish society fundamentally. It is a disputed issue both conceptually and in practice and has generated highly charged discourse across political, media and the public domain. Much of this discussion has been highly ideologically charged and there has been little room for wide-ranging and reflective debate across disciplinary boundaries about austerity in Ireland. This volume adopts a pluralistic approach, gathering a range of perspectives together in an attempt to move understanding of our recent past forward and to highlight some of the key public policy choices facing Ireland as it moves into recovery mode. Many have argued that we have now reached the 'end of austerity' but whether or not this is true will depend on how we deal with the legacy of the last decade. We do not claim to be entirely comprehensive in our coverage but each of the chapters aims to stimulate evidence-based discussion and to contribute to what needs to be an ongoing debate about where we as a society have come from, are currently placed, and would like to go.

Part 1: Austerity as concept and practice

1. A general theory of austerity

Simon Wren-Lewis

Introduction

This chapter is highly ambitious in scope. It will first look at whether, from a strictly macroeconomic point of view, fiscal austerity was necessary. The conclusions are stark: for the world as a whole austerity could have been easily avoided. In a few Eurozone countries some austerity was inevitable, but unemployment at the levels we have actually seen could almost certainly have been avoided. The macroeconomics needed to establish this proposition are standard and discussed in a later section: the allusion in the title to the General Theory of Keynes is deliberate. The next section of the chapter looks at whether financial market pressures meant that beneficial delays to fiscal consolidation could not have been implemented.

This prompts an obvious question. If austerity was unnecessary, why did it happen? On the one hand it is possible to tell a story about why austerity occurred that depends on two historical accidents: the Greek debt funding crisis and the peculiar diminished role that Keynesian economics plays in German policy discussion, coupled with Germany's central role in reacting to the Greek crisis. For various reasons a story along these lines is seriously incomplete, and in particular cannot play more than a walk-on role in developments in the

US and UK. A general, political economy theory of austerity, involving political opportunism on the right, will be introduced. I will suggest that this opportunism is made possible partly by the delegation of monetary policy to independent central banks. The conclusion summarises the argument, and asks whether austerity is therefore an inevitable consequence of any major recession.

'Austerity' is a widely used word, and is often applied in a way that makes it equivalent to fiscal consolidation—any attempt to reduce the government's deficit by cuts to public spending or higher taxes. In this discussion, I will reserve the term 'fiscal consolidation' to refer to any package to cut spending or raise taxes. Austerity is when that fiscal consolidation leads to significant increases in involuntary unemployment. A more technical definition would be that austerity is fiscal consolidation that leads to a noticeably larger negative output gap. This definition implies that while austerity will always involve fiscal consolidation, fiscal consolidation could occur without austerity.

Why delaying fiscal consolidation can avoid austerity

In 2010, the Eurozone and the United Kingdom switched from fiscal stimulus to fiscal consolidation. A year later the United States followed. It therefore makes sense to first consider what the impact of fiscal consolidation at a global level might be. As nearly all textbooks at undergraduate and graduate level show, for a given stance of monetary policy (and in particular, for a given level of interest rates), fiscal consolidation reduces the total amount of demand in the economy. If the economy is already suffering from a lack of demand, as was the case in 2010, this will make any recession worse. The assumption that monetary policy does not change is critical. Central banks routinely change interest rates to stabilise aggregate demand. Deficient aggregate demand should lead to below-target inflation, and if central banks respond to this by reducing nominal interest rates this will encourage people to save less and spend more, which raises demand, which in turn increases inflation. So when fiscal consolidation reduces aggregate demand, interest rates could be cut to offset this impact. As a result, a policy of fiscal consolidation accompanied by an easing of monetary policy could avoid any need for total output to fall and unemployment to rise. As long as monetary policy is working well, fiscal consolidation does not lead to austerity.

A study of fiscal consolidation in individual economies supports this idea. When some people point to particular periods in individual countries where fiscal consolidation did not lead to austerity, this period also featured an expansionary monetary policy (and/or, in countries with their own exchange rate, a large depreciation). This does not imply, of course, that in these cases fiscal consolidation becomes painless. Raising taxes, cutting transfers or cutting public sector jobs is difficult and can lead to hardship. But if incomes are growing, and for every public sector job lost a private sector job is created, then the hardship brought about by fiscal consolidation can be greatly reduced.

This brings us to the heart of why fiscal consolidation in 2010 had such negative effects on economies as a whole. A distinguishing feature of the recession caused by the financial crisis, often called the Great Recession, is that short-term interest rates were cut very rapidly, and quickly ended up becoming stuck close to zero. Economists often call this the zero lower bound (ZLB) problem, and it is also called a liquidity trap (any subtle differences between the two need not concern us here). Central banks cut interest rates to encourage more spending and less saving. The less you get for saving money, the less saving you will want to do. If interest rates became negative, people would find that by saving they actually lose money. That would be a very strong incentive not to save, but the problem is that most people could avoid these negative interest rates by saving in the form of cash. As a result, central banks are reluctant to push rates much below zero: it would have no impact except to make people hoard cash. That is the ZLB problem.

As an alternative to cutting short-term interest rates, central banks have tried the unconventional form of monetary policy known as quantitative easing (QE). Central banks are in the position of having a large influence on most short interest rates (interest rates on financial assets that are paid back in a matter of months), but normally their impact on longer-term interest rates (on assets that are paid back after a number of years) is only indirect. QE is an attempt to influence these rates more directly, by buying substantial amounts of these assets. To be able to do this, central banks have to create huge amounts of money. Although QE appears to have had some impact in reducing long-term interest rates, and therefore in increasing output, it remains a highly unreliable instrument. As a result, it is far from being a complete solution to the ZLB problem. It was for these reasons that governments in the US, the UK and Germany embarked on fiscal stimulus in 2009. With interest rates stuck at the ZLB, and huge uncertainty about the effectiveness of QE, governments needed to use fiscal policy to help increase demand and reduce unemployment.

For exactly the same reason, when governments turned to fiscal consolidation in 2010, monetary policy was unable to offset the negative impact that this had on demand and unemployment. What this negative impact actually meant depended on the economy. In the US it led to an unusually slow recovery, and unusually persistent unemployment. In the UK a recovery that had just begun in 2010 stalled, and did not resume until 2013. In the Eurozone we had a second recession shortly after the Great Recession. These differences may be easy to explain: in the US fiscal consolidation was delayed until 2011, and in the Eurozone interest rates were mistakenly raised in 2011. But the common feature is that fiscal consolidation increased unemployment substantially compared to what it might have been otherwise. This is the tragedy of austerity. If governments had waited before embarking on fiscal consolidation and, crucially, had undertaken fiscal consolidation when interest rates were no longer at their ZLB, that consolidation need not have led to austerity. Instead interest rates could have been used to offset the negative demand effects of lower public spending or higher taxes. Postponing fiscal consolidation would not just have delayed austerity, but avoided it altogether.

How long would we have had to delay fiscal consolidation to avoid austerity? In a back-of-the-envelope calculation, I looked at the impact of a counterfactual which assumed that government consumption and investment in the US, the UK and the Eurozone had grown at trend rates from 2010 onwards.[1] If government had followed this trend path, by 2013 this spending would have been around 15% higher in the US, a bit less than this in the UK, and about 10% higher in the Eurozone. This indicates the extent of austerity that occurred from 2010 onwards. This would have raised the level of GDP in 2013 by over 4% in the US, over 4.5% in the UK, and nearly 4% in the Eurozone. For the Eurozone these numbers accord with some more elaborate model-based exercises (which include the impact of higher taxes or lower transfers), although others suggest a still greater impact from austerity. This analysis also suggests that without the turn to fiscal consolidation in 2010, it seems highly likely that interest rates would have begun to rise by 2013. As interest rates departing the ZLB are the key to having fiscal consolidation without austerity, this suggests that fiscal consolidation need only have been delayed by around three years to avoid austerity.

The most common argument put forward against delaying fiscal consolidation is that the markets would not have allowed this. I will discuss this in detail in the next section, but the conclusion is that there is no evidence to support this idea, and plenty of reasons to think it is wrong. (The issue is more complex for the periphery Eurozone countries, but here we are talking about the Eurozone as a whole.) Another argument is more political. It suggests that fiscal consolidation is only possible at a time of crisis. If it had been delayed until the recovery had been more complete, it would not have happened at all. This seems very difficult to believe. As a result of the Great Recession, debt levels in all economies rose substantially. Although the recovery itself may have reduced debt-to-GDP ratios compared to their peak following the recession, it still seems probable that they would have been substantially higher by 2013 than before the recession if no consolidation had occurred between 2010 and 2013. It is difficult to imagine that policy makers would have simply ignored this.

If the US, the Eurozone and the UK could have avoided austerity altogether, can the same be said for individual Eurozone economies that had unusually large fiscal problems? The obvious example is Ireland, which had not only bailed out a large financial sector, but also allowed a housing boom which expanded tax receipts to increase public spending beyond a sustainable level. This is discussed in much more detail in Chapter 2. Without prejudice, let us assume that the fiscal consolidation required for Ireland was greater than for the Eurozone as a whole. Could Ireland have also avoided any austerity?

The short answer is no, but the reasons are rather different from those normally put forward, and they in turn imply that the amount of austerity required might have been much less than we actually observed. Interest rates in Ireland are set at the Eurozone level, therefore if Ireland required a period of greater fiscal consolidation than for the Eurozone as a whole, it could not have offset the impact of this on demand in Ireland by reducing interest rates. As a result, for a time unemployment would have had to be higher relative to its 'natural' level.[2] However, higher unemployment relative to its Eurozone partners would have in time reduced inflation in Ireland (again relative to other Eurozone economies), increasing the competitiveness of its traded sector. This in turn would have added to demand, offsetting the negative impact of fiscal consolidation and bringing unemployment back down.

In macroeconomic terms, it is the real exchange rate (competitiveness) rather than real interest rates that adjust to ensure that any austerity is temporary, even if the demand impact of fiscal consolidation is more long-lived. We can think of this in terms of financial balances. The government needs to run a large primary surplus for some time to service a higher level of debt and also to bring debt down. In the medium term this can be matched by a larger current account surplus, generated by increased competitiveness. If Ireland had its own exchange rate, and the foreign exchange markets had behaved as they should, then this adjustment in competitiveness could have happened immediately through a depreciation in the nominal exchange rate. That in turn would have meant no need for additional unemployment to bring this improvement in competitiveness about. In other words, the only reason that austerity is required in Ireland (in the absence of austerity in the Eurozone as a whole) is that Ireland is part of a monetary union.

How much austerity is required to get inflation down and bring about an improvement in competitiveness in a monetary union? That depends on how sensitive domestic inflation is to increases in unemployment, or, as an economist would say, it depends on the slope of the Phillips curve. However we can use basic macroeconomic theory to say something rather important about the speed at which inflation has to fall. Suppose, for the sake of argument, that prices needed to fall by 10% in Ireland relative to its Eurozone neighbours to offset the impact of fiscal consolidation. Suppose the slope of the Phillips curve implied that each 1% increase in unemployment above its natural level would reduce inflation in that year by 1%. At first sight that might suggest you could get prices down by 10% either by raising unemployment by 10% in one year, or (say) by raising unemployment by 2% for five years. That would be wrong, because it ignores a key feature of the Phillips curves commonly used in macroeconomics: inflation this year depends on expected inflation next year as well as unemployment this year.

This means that a more modest increase in unemployment spread over time could achieve the 10% cut in prices. Suppose unemployment increased by just 1% for four years, and assume also that expectations about inflation depended on past inflation. In the first year inflation would be reduced by just 1%. It would be reduced by 2% in the second year (1% because of higher unemployment and 1% because inflation expectations had fallen by 1%), by 3% in the third year and by 4% in the fourth. That produces the required total cut in prices of 10%, but at a substantially smaller total unemployment cost than if everything was done in one year.

Nowadays macroeconomists believe that expectations are formed in a more sophisticated manner than just looking at last year's data. However, if we move to the opposite extreme, where agents' expectations about inflation turn out to be completely correct, we get a very similar result.[3] The point is robust as long as inflation depends on expected inflation. A small increase in unemployment spread over a number of years is much more efficient at bringing about an improvement in competitiveness than a more short lived but larger increase in unemployment.

Without additional assumptions and a great deal of analysis it is difficult to say by how much the path of adjustment followed in Ireland, Portugal and Spain departed from this efficient, gradualist approach, and whether fiscal consolidation should have been delayed to achieve this gradualist path. As with thinking about the Eurozone as a whole, any discussion along these lines is normally pre-empted by claims that any more gradual fiscal consolidation was impossible because of the financial markets. It is to this issue that I now turn.

Financial markets

For the major economies including the Eurozone as a whole, austerity could have been avoided completely by delaying fiscal consolidation by a few years. For individual economies in the Eurozone periphery some austerity was necessary, because a period of below-average inflation was required to improve competitiveness relative to other Eurozone members. It would have been far more efficient to spread the unemployment required to achieve this over time. In each case supporters of austerity would normally argue that neither was possible because of pressure from financial markets. Once again, I will consider each type of economy in turn.

An initial point worth making is that the austerity that followed the Great Recession was unusual compared to previous economic downturns, as Kose *et al.* (2013) show. In the past economic downturns have led to large government budget deficits and rising government debt, but governments have not felt the need to embark on fiscal consolidation the moment the recovery has begun. Markets in the past have not forced such an outcome.

One reason often given for why markets might be unwilling to buy government debt in a recession is that large deficits mean there is more debt that needs to be bought. Yet this argument ignores a basic Keynesian insight. Typically, recessions are caused by people saving more. This increase in saving needs somewhere to go. So although the supply of new government debt might increase in an economic downturn, the number of people wanting to buy financial assets also increases.

There are two key differences between the Great Recession and previous recessions. The first is scale and its global nature. As discussed in the previous section, the depth of the recession was a key reason for the ZLB problem. The second is that the recession was the result of a crisis within the financial sector. Since WWII downturns in most countries have typically reflected the need by governments or central banks to reduce inflation. The main impact of this difference has been that financial institutions have been less willing to lend to consumers or firms after the Great Recession, and those with financial assets have been reluctant to invest in risky assets.

Should these differences make a difference to how the financial markets regard the need for governments to sell more debt? The answer is probably that they should make the markets more interested in buying these assets compared to earlier downturns. Although government deficits have increased by more in the Great Recession compared to earlier downturns because the Great Recession was much deeper, the recession was larger because consumers and firms saved more than in previous downturns. Once again an increased supply of government debt was met by an increase in the amount people wanted to hold. In addition, the flight from risky assets increased the demand for government debt compared to more risky alternatives such as debt issued by firms. So there is no *a priori* reason to believe that governments would not be able to sell the extra debt that arose as a result of the Great Recession.

Indeed, a large literature, associated with the work of Ricardo Caballero, now argues that there remains a shortage of safe assets in the economy as a whole. Caballero writes:[4]

> This shortage of safe assets existed before the crisis, but it is even worse today. The demand for these assets has expanded as a result of the fear triggered by the crisis— as it did for emerging markets after the 1997–1998 crisis. But this time the private sector industry created to supply these safe assets—the securitisation and complex-assets production industry—is severely damaged.

In this context, any additional safe assets in the form of more government debt from the UK, the US or non-periphery Euro countries would be welcomed

How would we be able to tell if the markets were in danger of failing to buy government debt? The first symptom would be a rise in interest rates on government debt, as governments were forced to raise the return from these assets to attract buyers. That is exactly what happened in the case of Eurozone periphery governments. However, everywhere else has seen a steady fall in the interest rate paid on government debt. There is no evidence from the markets themselves that we were close to a global panic in the market for government debt.

This observation may appear to be at variance with evidence from people who work in financial institutions, who typically say that we should worry about what the market will do, and that there is a need for austerity. Unfortunately this source of information lacks authority and has a biased view. To say it lacks authority may seem surprising, given that financial institutions are closely involved in these markets. But where these institutions make money is by predicting day-to-day movements in the market and not from forecasting longer-run trends. Many in the US markets were convinced that interest rates on US government debt were bound to rise substantially after 2010, but they have not risen. They are biased for two reasons. One is simply institutional: a well-known saying is that a bond economist never saw a fiscal contraction they did not like. Another is more subtle, and is discussed later.

A slightly more nuanced version of the argument that austerity was required to prevent a market panic is the idea that, although at a global level the supply of savings had risen to match the additional supply of government debt, this still meant that individual economies that showed no signs of cutting back on spending were vulnerable. Investors could easily move from one government's debt to another's. Again the empirical evidence suggests this argument is wrong. There were two notable major economies that did not switch to austerity in 2010: Canada and Japan. Neither appeared to suffer any adverse market reaction.

In contrast, we have a compelling theory about why the Eurozone periphery countries did suffer at the hands of the markets from 2010 to 2012. That theory was put to the test at the end of 2012 and was vindicated. Unlike normal countries, members of the Eurozone do not have their own central bank. Instead they have the European Central

Bank (ECB). Why does this matter when it comes to how the markets regard government debt? It has to do with the risk of a country being forced to default because it cannot roll over that debt. Most governments have to roll over a substantial proportion of their debt each year. Assuming that a government has no wish to default on its existing debt and that the stock of debt is not increasing, as long as people buy the debt that it needs to roll over each year, it will not default. That debt remains potentially risky for any investor, because the investor has to be sure that there are enough other investors in the market to ensure the government can roll over its debt. Even if an investor is totally confident that the government has no wish to default, they also need to think about what other investors in the market believe. This can quickly lead to self-fulfilling panic. If every investor is worried that other investors will not buy the debt to be rolled over, they themselves will not invest, and the government may be forced to default: particularly if its debt-to-GDP ratio is already high.[5]

This will not happen if the government can create its own currency. If the market did panic in this way, the central bank would simply buy the debt that needed to be rolled over by creating money. Economists call this the central bank acting as a sovereign lender of last resort. This removes the need for an investor to worry about other investors in making a decision to invest. It removes a key source of risk, and makes government debt much safer. This in turn means that in practice the central bank never has to actually intervene in this way. Simply its existence means that self-fulfilling panics are much less likely to occur.

What this analysis suggests is that the debt-funding crisis that began in Greece only spread to other periphery countries because the ECB was not prepared to act as a sovereign lender of last resort. The crisis was never going to spread to countries outside the Eurozone whose governments borrowed mainly in their own currency, because they had their own central banks. This theory was put to the test in September 2012, when the ECB changed its policy. With the Outright Monetary Transactions (OMT) programme, it agreed to act as a sovereign lender of last resort. This support was not unconditional, but it was enough to bring the Eurozone crisis to an end. This provided a clear test of the theory, and the test was passed.[6]

This raises an obvious question that should be of great interest to those in the Eurozone. If the ECB had brought in OMT in 2010 rather than 2012, would the Eurozone crisis have spread beyond

Greece, and would Ireland and Portugal backed by the ECB have retained market access? The only logical reason why market access should not have been retained is if the markets doubted the ECB's resolve to sustain OMT support. Without that doubt, we can then ask whether this market access could have also been retained even if Ireland and Portugal had enacted a more gradual programme of fiscal consolidation, consistent with the analysis outlined earlier, resulting in less austerity? The answer is the same. The only barrier to a more sensible path for fiscal consolidation is the ECB's willingness to support it

A clear example where austerity has gone way beyond what was required for a Eurozone economy is Greece. Even if OMT had been available in 2010, Greece should not have been allowed to participate in this programme for two reasons. First, it had built up such a large amount of government debt and such a large deficit that it was far from clear that it could avoid default. Second, it had deliberately deceived its Eurozone neighbours about the extent of its debts. Without OMT support, Greece would have and should have been forced to completely default on all or most of its debt. Even if this had happened, Greece was still running a large primary deficit (spending was greater than taxes). Without any assistance, Greece would have suffered immediate and acute austerity. The IMF was established to provide conditional funding in cases like this, and this would have allowed Greece to avoid acute austerity. Nevertheless the fiscal adjustment it would have needed to make would have been large.

What actually happened was much worse than this. The rest of the Eurozone initially tried to avoid a Greek default, and then restricted the size of that default, by lending money directly to Greece, assisted by the IMF. It is often said that the Eurozone lent Greece money to give it time to adjust, but this appears false. The amount of money Greece needed to fund its adjustment towards primary surplus is of the same order of magnitude as the amount it received from the IMF. Most of the money lent by the Eurozone went to bailing out those who had lent to the Greek government. The reason for this may be very straightforward: many of those creditors were Eurozone banks, and a Greek default in 2010 might have sparked a Eurozone banking crisis.

In an attempt to allow Greece to repay these loans to the rest of the Eurozone, the Eurozone (with the IMF's unenthusiastic support) imposed an amount of fiscal contraction that went far beyond what any economy could cope with. As a result, Greek GDP declined by a massive 25%. Nevertheless by 2015 Greece had achieved primary surplus, and asked that either further fiscal consolidation should be delayed to allow the economy to recover or restructuring of its debt should occur. The Eurozone refused to do either. The ECB restricted the supply of euros to Greek banks, and forced Greece to either embark on yet more fiscal consolidation or leave the Eurozone. It was an incredible exercise in raw political and economic power at the expense of the Greek people. The immorality of first encouraging Greece to keep its debt for the sake of the Eurozone banking system, and then failing to allow default once that banking system had become healthier, seems lost on those that wielded this power.

Was austerity an unfortunate accident?

Earlier in the chapter, I showed that for the major economies including the Eurozone as a whole, austerity could have been avoided completely by delaying fiscal consolidation by a few years. There was also no evidence that the financial markets had demanded the switch to austerity in 2010. Instead the Eurozone crisis went beyond a crisis for the Greek government because of the ECB's unwillingness until 2012 to act as a sovereign lender of last resort. In other words, austerity at the global level was a huge and avoidable mistake. This naturally leads to the question of why that mistake was made. Is there a general theory of austerity, which might lead us to think that it would occur again following a future global recession, or is it specific to the particular circumstances that occurred in 2010? In this section I will explore the second possibility.

The accident story would run as follows. The first unfortunate accident was Greece, where it became clear to everyone except Eurozone policy makers in 2010 that default was necessary. The second accident was that Greece happened to be inside a Eurozone that was dominated by Germany. The negative influence of Germany was felt in two ways. First, German policy makers were strongly opposed to OMT, which helped delay it until 2012. Second, Germany interpreted the crisis of 2010 as a generalised debt-funding crisis, and so reacted by imposing a modified set of fiscal rules that led to austerity throughout the Eurozone.

There does appear to be something special about macroeconomic beliefs among German policy makers. Elsewhere Keynesian theory is mainstream. Few policy makers in the UK or the US would ever try to argue that Keynesian theory was incorrect, or that a fiscal consolidation would not lead—for a given monetary policy—to a fall in aggregate demand and output. In contrast, the Keynesian position in Germany is clearly a minority view. Among the five members of Germany's Council of Economic Experts, Peter Bofinger is described as 'the Keynesian'. Among any similar group in the UK or the US, someone with anti-Keynesian views would be the exception. From a Keynesian perspective, the dangers to demand and output of reacting to primary deficits by imposing fiscal consolidation would have been recognised. The need to provide central bank support rather than impose draconian austerity on countries having difficulty with market access would also be more easily recognised. Perhaps most importantly, the folly of imposing austerity across the Eurozone when it could not be counteracted by monetary policy would have been understood.

While the unusual position of Keynesian ideas in German policy discourse has been widely recognised, understanding where this comes from is more difficult. Some have argued that it reflects a desire never to repeat the hyperinflation of the Weimar Republic, but this neglects that the recession of the 1930s played a major role in bringing Hitler to power. Some have pointed to language, noting that the German word for debt (*schuld*) is the same as for guilt. But if there was a deep and unusual cultural aversion to debt, you might expect the German government to have a low level of debt by international standards, yet it does not. The economics taught in German universities appears very similar to that taught elsewhere.

A number of authors have focused on the economic doctrine of ordoliberalism. However, you could equally point to the influence of neoliberalism in the UK and USA, which I will discuss further in the next section. To the extent that ordoliberalism differs from neoliberalism in recognising the dangers of market imperfections, this might make it more open to New Keynesian ideas that see demand deficient recessions as also reflecting market imperfections.

One of the distinctive features of institutional arrangements in Germany is that trade union integration within many firms is strong, and unions remain important in setting wages. Another feature of Germany that is absent in many other countries is that Germany has for many years been part of a fixed or quasi-fixed exchange rate system. These two features combine to give Germany an alternative way to stimulate the economy besides fiscal policy, which is through downward pressure on German wages and undercutting Germany's competitors within the fixed exchange rate system. It is a mechanism that employers naturally prefer, but to make it operate they need to dominate the policy debate and sideline Keynesian ideas. It is noticeable, for example, that Germany only recently imposed a national minimum wage; its imposition was opposed by the majority of economists during the public debate, whereas economists' views about the minimum wage in the UK and the US are more evenly divided.

This mechanism can be seen in how wages developed in the Eurozone before the Great Recession. While the overheating and above-average inflation in the periphery countries are well known, the opposite process happened in Germany, with wage increases well below nearly all the other Eurozone countries. This was, at least to some extent, a deliberate strategy by German firms and unions.[7] Germany gained a substantial competitive advantage over its Eurozone neighbours, which together with the impact of the Hartz reforms—a set of reforms of the German labour market named after the head of a commission, Peter Hartz, that proposed them in 2002—has meant that while unemployment has increased substantially in the rest of the Eurozone, it remains very low in Germany. The German current account surplus has ballooned to nearly 8% of GDP.

This position has in turn made Germany less sympathetic to calls for the easing of austerity across the Eurozone. If Germany joined the Eurozone at something close to its equilibrium exchange rate (competitiveness), and if this has not changed significantly over the subsequent 15 years (both suggested by large current account surpluses), then undercutting the rest of the Eurozone before the recession would imply a subsequent period where German inflation would have to exceed the rest of the Eurozone to restore equilibrium. However, above 2% inflation in Germany could be avoided if inflation in the Eurozone as a whole fell well below the ECB's 2% target. As a result, general Eurozone austerity and a resistance to unconventional monetary policy could be seen as simply pursuing Germany's own national interest.

While there is undoubtedly an important element of truth in both the unfortunate timing of the Greek debt crisis and the role of Germany in interpreting and reacting to it, there are three reasons why it cannot explain the dominance of austerity since 2010. First, within the Eurozone it would seem odd that there has been so little resistance to German views. If Germany is so unusual in its attitudes to Keynesian ideas, why did other countries where Keynesian theory is standard not attempt to challenge Germany? Second, while events in Greece and German attitudes clearly had some influence in the US and the UK, it seems incredibly unlikely that this could fully explain the turn to austerity in these countries. Finally, by 2014 the damage done by austerity, and the special nature of the debt funding crisis in the Eurozone, were quite clear to most economists. A report published by the IMF Independent Evaluation Office (2014) came to the following conclusions:

> IMF advocacy of fiscal consolidation proved to be premature for major advanced economies, as growth projections turned out to be optimistic. Moreover, the policy mix of fiscal consolidation coupled with monetary expansion that the IMF advocated for advanced economies since 2010 appears to be at odds with long-standing assessments of the relative effectiveness of these policies in the conditions prevailing after a financial crisis characterized by private debt overhang ... Many analysts and policymakers have argued that expansionary monetary and fiscal policies working together would have been a more effective way to stimulate demand and reduce unemployment—which in turn could have reduced adverse spillovers ... In articulating its concerns [in 2010], the IMF was influenced by the fiscal crises in the euro area periphery economies ... although their experiences were of limited relevance given their inability to conduct independent monetary policy or borrow in their own currencies.

In other words the move to austerity in 2010, although advocated by the IMF, had been a mistake, and a key cause of this mistake had been an incorrect interpretation of the Eurozone crisis. Yet while the IMF's own economists were prepared to make this admission, politicians (including those running the IMF) were not. In 2015 in the UK the Conservatives won an election on a platform promising more austerity, even though UK interest rates remained at 0.5%.

A general theory of austerity

In 2009 every single Republican in the US Congress opposed Obama's plan to use fiscal policy to stimulate the US economy. In that same year the Conservative opposition in the UK opposed similar stimulus measures in the UK. In both cases the political right argued that deficits needed to be brought down more rapidly than the government was planning. On both sides of the Atlantic similar arguments were used: debt needed to be brought down to protect future generations, lower debt would boost confidence which would then stimulate demand ('expansionary fiscal contraction'), and rising debt would lead to higher interest rates because of market concern.

At first this last argument appeared to be vindicated as the Eurozone crisis developed. After the May 2010 election in the UK, this may have been important in persuading the minority party in the coalition government to agree to Conservative plans for more fiscal consolidation. However, by 2012 it was clear that fiscal consolidation was hurting the economy (the Office for Budget Responsibility (OBR) calculated that it had reduced growth by 1% in each of the financial years 2010/11 and 2011/12), that the debt funding crisis in the Eurozone was a purely Eurozone phenomenon, and that there was no evidence of any potential UK or US debt funding crisis. However, the austerity rhetoric continued. Republicans in Congress shut down the government in 2013 to force greater public spending cuts. In 2015 in the UK the Conservatives won an election outright on a programme involving substantial additional fiscal consolidation.

By this time, a growing number of people began to view austerity as a means to use fears about debt as a pretext to reduce the size of the state. In the UK in early 2010, 20 eminent economists and policy makers wrote a letter essentially endorsing the Conservatives' austerity plans. One of those was Lord Turnbull, head of the UK civil service from 2002 to 2005. By 2012, as the damage caused by UK austerity became clear, half those signatories had to varying extents backtracked. In 2015, Lord Turnbull questioned the British Chancellor, George Osborne, in the following terms:[8]

> I think what you are doing actually, is, the real argument
> is you want a smaller state and there are good arguments
> for that and some people don't agree but you don't tell
> people you are doing that. What you tell people is this
> story about the impoverishment of debt which is a
> smokescreen. The urgency of reducing debt, the extent, I
> just can't see the justification for it.

When George Osborne published his fiscal charter in 2015, proposing a new fiscal rule that would require budget surpluses as long as real growth exceeded 1% (and requiring substantial further austerity to achieve that), nearly 80 economists signed a letter stating that this plan had no basis in economics, and it was difficult to find even one economist who would support it. The idea that deficit concern was being used as a pretext to reduce the size of the state, which I will call the deficit deceit hypothesis, is based on two propositions:

1. Political parties on the right wanted a smaller state, but popular support for such a programme was at best mixed.

2. From 2010 there was strong popular support for reducing government deficits.

Political parties of the right repeatedly used simple analogies between household and government budgets to reinforce this second point. The UK, for example, was described as 'maxing out its credit card'. One strong piece of evidence in favour of deficit deceit is the form of austerity imposed. Republicans in the US called for spending cuts to reduce the deficit, while at the same time arguing elsewhere that taxes should be cut. In the UK, over 80% of deficit reduction between 2010 and 2015 came from spending cuts. The further cuts proposed between 2015 and 2020 were entirely on the spending side, in part to pay for income and inheritance tax cuts. At first, France appeared to be an exception, proposing to focus on tax increases to reduce deficits. European Commissioner Olli Rehn was not pleased, saying that 'Budgetary discipline must come from a reduction in public spending and not from new taxes'.[9] Because some of any tax increase is likely to come out of savings, at a time of unemployment *a priori* you might expect fiscal consolidation to focus on tax increases.

An indication of the strength of popular support for cutting budget deficits came from the lack of opposition to these policies from the centre left. In the UK the Labour party has been extremely reluctant to adopt an anti-austerity platform, and centre-left parties in Europe have often helped to enact fiscal consolidation following European fiscal rules even when unemployment has been rising. Opposition to austerity has tended to come from parties outside the political mainstream.

One question the deficit deceit hypothesis has to answer is why we have not seen similar tactics from the political right in earlier recessions. It is true that what economists call 'pro-cyclical fiscal policy' is not a new problem, but before the Great Recession economists were also focused on a problem they called 'deficit bias'—the tendency of government debt to rise over time (Calmfors and Wren-Lewis 2011)—which seems to cast doubt on the generality of the deficit deceit idea. There are two clear answers. First, the size of this recession meant that government debt increased substantially in a relatively short period of time. Second, to the extent that the financial crisis generated what economists call a balance sheet recession, most individuals were in the process of increasing their savings and cutting back on borrowing, so it seemed only right (to them) that the government should be doing the same.

Although politicians on the right repeatedly use analogies with households when discussing government debt, anyone who has completed just one year of undergraduate economics knows that such analogies are false. When an individual cuts back on their spending, the impact on the economy-wide level of aggregate demand is small. When a government cuts back on spending, that either has a direct and noticeable impact on aggregate demand or it influences a large number of other people's incomes, which leads them to cut back on their spending. As this point is both standard among economists and not that difficult to explain, this raises the question as to why the kind of macroeconomic logic outlined in the first two sections has been ineffective as an antidote to deficit deceit.

This issue is addressed elsewhere in detail (Wren-Lewis 2015), but the key points are summarised here. The tendency of economists from the financial sector to favour fiscal consolidation is clear. Perhaps even more important is the interest they have in exaggerating the unpredictability of financial markets, so that they become like high priests to the god of an unpredictable financial market. The bias that financial economists have in favour of austerity, plus this perceived 'high priest' role, matters all the more because of the contacts they have with the media. The bias that the media has in favour of talking to financial sector economists rather than academics about day-to-day market movements is perfectly understandable, but unfortunately too many in the media tend to also rely on financial market economists to talk about longer-term issues like austerity, and here academics have greater expertise. Chapter 4 of this volume, by Mercille, discusses the role of the media in the Irish bubble and bust in more detail.

Perhaps the most interesting argument is that the creation of independent central banks has helped reduce the extent to which policy makers and the media hear about the costs of fiscal consolidation in a liquidity trap (Wren-Lewis 2015). There appear to be two reasons for this. One concerns the expertise in finance ministries. If governments have in effect contracted out the business of macroeconomic stabilisation to central banks, there is less need to retain macroeconomic expertise in these ministries. The second concerns the attitudes of senior figures in central banks to budget deficits.

Mervyn King (1995) once remarked: 'Central banks are often accused of being obsessed with inflation. This is untrue. If they are obsessed with anything, it is with fiscal policy.' This follows from a historic concern that governments will force central banks to monetise debt, which outside of a recession could lead to large increases in inflation. As a result, when policy makers and the media ask central bank governors about the impact of fiscal consolidation, the information they give is likely to be distorted by this primitive fear. They are likely to overplay the financial market risks of high debt, and be over-optimistic about the ability of unconventional monetary policy to overcome the ZLB problem. This is despite the fact that the models the central banks themselves use are Keynesian, and would produce analysis that accords with the logic outlined earlier.

This role of central banks may also help explain two other puzzles discussed earlier. Germany's anti-Keynesian approach may in part reflect the fact that they have had an independent central bank for some time. It may also help explain why deficit deceit has not been so evident in the UK at least in previous recessions.

Conclusion and implications

This chapter has argued that there was no good macroeconomic reason for any austerity at the global level over the past five years, and austerity seen in periphery Eurozone countries could most probably have been significantly milder. Instead, austerity was the result of right-wing opportunism, using voters' instinctive feeling that government should follow them in reducing borrowing to reduce the size of the state. The depressing implication is that the same process might occur in a future liquidity trap recession where consumers are reducing their borrowing. One way to avoid this would be to strengthen the influence of academic economists in policy discussions so that false analogies between consumer and government could be exposed. Another would be to give independent central banks the power to issue 'helicopter money'.

Acknowledgements

I would like to thank John McHale and Karl Whelan for helpful discussions on these issues, but views expressed are entirely my responsibility.

Notes

[1] Published here: http://www.voxeu.org/article/fiscal-policy-explains-weak-recovery

[2] The natural level, sometimes called the NAIRU, is the level at which inflation is constant.

[3] In the previous example inflation would fall by 4% in the first year, 3% in the second, etc. The big difference between the two cases is that with a backward-looking Phillips curve, we would need unemployment to be below its natural rate after four years to bring inflation back up to the average Eurozone level.

[4] Ricardo Caballero, *VoxEU* post, 21 May 2010.

[5] Suppose a fifth of debt has to be rolled over each year, and total debt is equal to the size of GDP. If taxes are around a third of GDP, then to avoid default if the markets refuse to roll over debt would require increasing taxes by 60%.

[6] See, for example, Ana-Maria Fuertes, Elena Kalotychou, Orkun Saka, *VoxEU* post, 26 March 2015.

[7] Peter Bofinger, *VoxEU* post, 30 November 2015.

[8] House of Lords select committee's questioning of George Osborne available here: http://parliamentlive.tv/Event/Index/7407feb6-9b7b-4f41-8fc8-00768eab2869

[9] Quoted by Benjamin Fox in the *EUobserver*, 26 August 2013.

2. Why austerity?

John McHale

Introduction

Ireland has endured a prolonged period of austerity as a result of the economic and financial crisis that erupted in 2008. As explained by Simon Wren-Lewis (Chapter 1, this volume), austerity reflects a period of severe expenditure cuts and tax rises in a recession, leading to a rise in involuntary unemployment. On the face of it, such contractionary policies in a recession go against the principles of sound macroeconomic management, especially where monetary policy is not available as an alternative demand management tool. As discussed in detail in many chapters of this volume, and reviewed in the concluding chapter, these budgetary measures have also caused severe hardship across Irish society. Was this austerity necessary given the circumstances that Irish policy makers faced?

To provide some macroeconomic context for the in-depth studies that follow, I review in this chapter the circumstances that made austerity an unavoidable response to the Irish crisis. The next section briefly reviews the fundamental cause of the crisis as the bursting of a property bubble and its links to an initially 'hidden bubble' in the public finances. The bursting of these bubbles exposed a large structural budget deficit and an explosive debt path that together necessitated extremely difficult adjustment measures to prevent an even greater collapse. The following two sections review the respective roles of the banking bailout and the 'troika' programme in the resulting austerity. The penultimate section reviews the policies that eventually led to the successful resolution of the crisis. Finally, the concluding section offers some thoughts on what we need to do to make sure that we have sufficient fiscal capacity in bad times so that austerity is never necessary again.

Crisis and austerity

The fundamental cause of Ireland's crisis lay in a property bubble. In fact, what we refer to as the property bubble was really three interacting bubbles—a property-price bubble, a credit bubble, and a construction bubble (for broader discussions of the causes of the crisis, see Donovan and Murphy 2013, McHale 2012 and Whelan 2014). The price and credit bubbles interacted directly, with the expectation of rising prices driving the demand for credit from prospective house buyers and developers, and the ample supply of credit provided the means to bid the prices of houses and development land ever higher. In normal circumstances, a strong construction supply response might be expected to temper the price increases. But the force of expectations of ever-rising prices overwhelmed any direct price-reducing effect of rising supply. The strong credit growth also had a critical international dimension, with Irish banks increasingly relying on fragile wholesale funding from abroad rather than traditionally more stable domestic deposits.[1] The inflow of foreign funds was also associated with a sharp deterioration in the current account of the balance of payments and in international competitiveness, as resources were increasingly directed into the construction sector.

When the unsustainable rise in house prices came to an end, the credit flows—and especially the foreign funds being intermediated through the domestic banks—came to a 'sudden stop'. Construction activity collapsed along with prices and credit. The result was a deep recession and severely impaired balance sheets across the financial, household, business, and government sectors of the economy.[2]

Although the cause of Ireland's crisis was not primarily fiscal, the property bubble interacted with a 'hidden bubble' in the public finances. Expansionary fiscal policies in the years preceding the crisis helped fuel the boom, and, even more importantly, the unsustainable boom helped hide a large structural deficit in the public finances.

Figure 2.1

Growth in general government expenditure, consumer prices, gross domestic product, and general government revenue, 2002 to 2007
Source: CSO

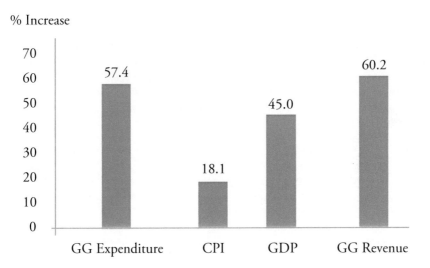

% Increase

Figure 2.1 helps show the way in which the hidden bubble formed. In the period from 2002 to 2007, nominal general government expenditure rose by 57%. Over the same period, cumulative consumer price inflation was 18%, indicating a roughly 40% increase in real expenditure. However, nominal Gross Domestic Product (GDP) rose by 45% so that government expenditure as a share of GDP only rose by only about 3 percentage points. But the main reason that the fragility of the fiscal position was hidden lay with the 60% increase in government revenue. This surge in revenue was driven by the general boom in economic activity and the direct effect of the property boom itself on revenue sources such as stamp duties, VAT on construction activity, and capital gains taxes.

Revenues collapsed when the property bubble deflated. Figure 2.2 shows the broad-based nature of the collapse, which extended well beyond property-related revenue sources. The deteriorating revenue situation was compounded by the global nature of the recession,

Figure 2.2

Annual changes in Exchequer revenue by category

Source: Department of Finance

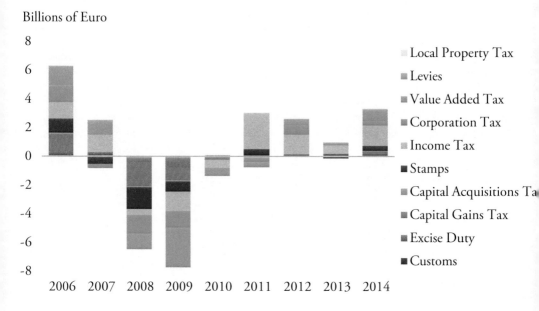

Billions of Euro

Legend:
- Local Property Tax
- Levies
- Value Added Tax
- Corporation Tax
- Income Tax
- Stamps
- Capital Acquisitions Ta
- Capital Gains Tax
- Excise Duty
- Customs

which impacted on the internationally traded sectors of the economy. Although Ireland had being running measured budget surpluses in the years prior to the crisis, Figure 2.3 shows that a massive deficit quickly opened up. Just looking at the underlying deficit that excludes the direct deficit-raising costs of the bank bailout measures, the deficit reached 11.5% of GDP in 2009—well above the 3% Maastricht limit of the Stability and Growth Pact (SGP). Moreover, given the significant downward revisions to estimates of sustainable (or potential) GDP, this deficit was subsequently estimated to be predominantly structural (see Figure 2.4). Although one can quibble with estimates of sustainable GDP made using the harmonised European Union (EU) methodology, it was evident that much of the lost revenue was not coming back any time soon. Recognising the size of the underlying structural deficit and the explosive rise in government debt (see Figure 2.5), there was no way to avoid measures to stabilise the public finances while protecting the solvency of the state.

Figure 2.3

Actual and underlying general government deficit, % of GDP

Sources: CSO; Department of Finance

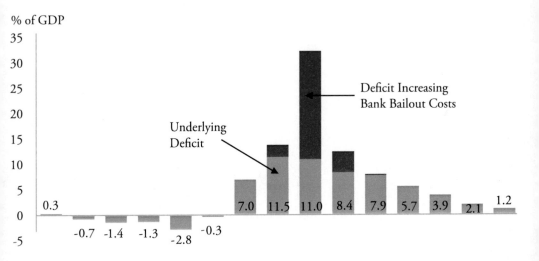

Figure 2.4

Actual general government deficit and structural general government deficit, % of GDP

Source: Department of Finance

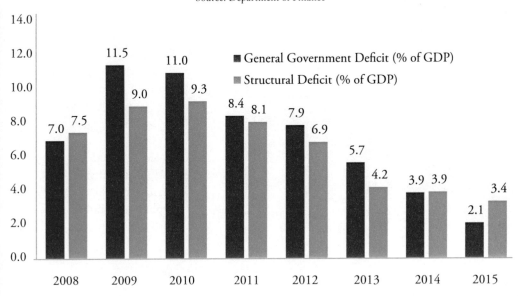

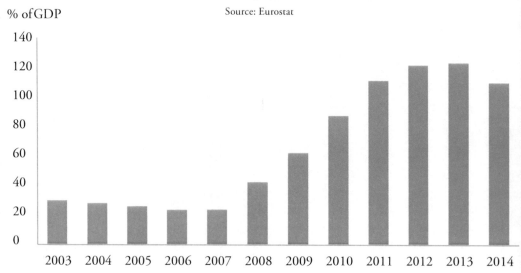

Figure 2.5

Evolution of the debt-to-GDP ratio, % of GDP

Source: Eurostat

% of GDP

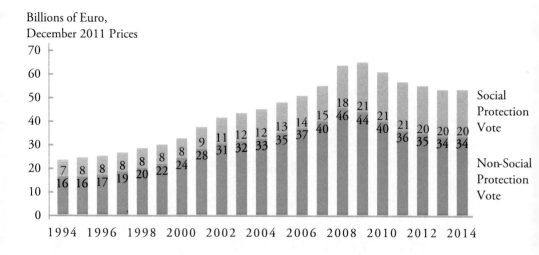

Figure 2.6

Evolution of real social protection and non-social protection expenditure, billions of euro

Source: Department of Public Expenditure and Reform

Billions of Euro,
December 2011 Prices

The programme of austerity began with a budget in October 2008.[3] Cumulatively over the period 2008 to 2014, the announced measures amounted to roughly €30 billion, with a peak annual announced adjustment of €6 billion for 2011. To get a more concrete sense of what this implied on the expenditure side, it is useful to look at the evolution of real voted expenditure outside of the social protection budget (see Figure 2.6). (Social protection spending tends to rise automatically in recessions due to the rising cost of unemployment-related benefits, and so the overall expenditure aggregate can hide the extent of expenditure cuts.) Between 2008 and 2014, this spending fell by €12 billion, bringing it back to roughly 2004 levels. Once further allowance is made for population growth, per capita real spending fell back to 2001 levels, with impacts on practically all categories of spending.

The role of the bank bailouts

A serious complicating factor in the fiscal crisis was the cost of rescuing the banking system. Following large-scale losses on outstanding loans, a series of policies were pursued to preserve a functioning banking system, including liability guarantees, purchases of 'toxic assets' by the National Asset Management Agency (NAMA), and recapitalisations using a combination of direct injections of Exchequer funds, funds from the National Pensions Reserve Fund (NPRF) and the issuance of promissory notes and other government IOUs. A recent estimate by the Comptroller and Auditor General (2015) puts the total gross cost at €66.8 billion.

Between the end of 2007 and the end of 2014, total gross government debt rose by €156 billion. Of this, roughly two-thirds was due to accumulated deficits (including interest costs) and roughly one-third was due to the direct cost of the banking bailout. A further €20.7 billion came from the NPRF.[4] While the deficit was the most important cause of the explosion in outstanding debt, there is no doubt that the direct banking-related component significantly undermined debt sustainability and contributed to the fragility of the state's creditworthiness. This debt in turn limited options in terms of a more gradual phasing of the austerity measures.

A possibly underappreciated feature of the banking rescue is that it was financed at extremely low interest rates. A large part of the rescue involved the cost of the promissory note arrangements used to cover the losses of Anglo Irish Bank and Irish Nationwide Building Society.

Although these notes had a high headline interest rate, the complex circular financing arrangements involving the Exchequer, the Central Bank and the banks meant that the ultimate cost to the state was close to zero (see Barnes and Smyth 2013; Whelan 2012). The benefits of these arrangements were extended when the promissory notes were restructured as part of the liquidation of Irish Bank Resolution Corporation (IBRC) in 2013.[5]

As of 2014, the Comptroller and Auditor General calculates that the total annual Exchequer interest bill due to the bank bailout measures was €0.74 billion. In addition, €0.95 billion in interest was paid on the floating-rate notes issued to the Central Bank as part of the promissory note restructuring. But most of these latter payments were returned to the Exchequer in the form of Central Bank surplus income. Recognising that the need for austerity was primarily driven by the need to close the underlying structural deficit, the relatively limited impact on the deficit of the bailouts means that the bulk of the austerity would have been required even without these costs.

Austerity and the troika

Not surprisingly, the creditworthiness of the state came under severe strain following the eruption of the crisis (see Figure 2.7). However, debt sustainability and creditworthiness were seen as broadly manageable until 2010. Over the course of 2010 a number of events took place that fundamentally complicated the challenge facing the Irish government. In the spring of 2010, Greece was forced to seek a bailout, leading bond market investors to question the capacity of other vulnerable countries to manage without outside assistance. Confidence was also undermined by the drip-feed of bad news on the size of the bank losses and rating agency downgrades. In October, the Deauville Accord between the leaders of France and Germany raised the risk that creditors would be forced to take losses ('bailed-in') in future rescue programmes. The cumulative result was a rise in the risk premium on Irish debt, as investors increasingly feared some form of default (see Figure 2.7). Of even greater urgency, however, was a slow-motion run on the banking system, with foreign lenders in particular pulling deposit funding and refusing to roll over maturing bonds. This loss intensified due to the reaching of the funding cliff associated with the expiry of the original blanket bank liability guarantee at the end of September 2010. The resulting funding shortfall in the banking

Figure 2.7

Evolution of Irish and German 10-year bond yields, monthly averages

Source: ECB

10-Year Bond Yield, %

system was bridged through borrowing from the Eurosystem, including increasing use of Emergency Liquidity Assistance (ELA).

As the situation became unmanageable without outside assistance, Ireland negotiated a programme of official assistance with the European Commission, the International Monetary Fund (IMF) and the European Central Bank (ECB) in November 2010.[6] This assistance included support for the recapitalisation of the banking system and funding to cover the deficit and maturing debt until the end of 2013. Of course, this funding came with conditions, including requirements for fiscal adjustment and the restructuring of the banking system.

However, it would be a mistake to see the troika programme as being responsible for the subsequent austerity. As already noted, the government was forced by the size of the underlying structural deficit and the resulting explosive debt dynamics to pursue a severe austerity programme since 2008. In late 2010, the Fianna Fáil/Green coalition had already published a national recovery plan that targeted adjustments of €15 billion for the period 2011 to 2014, with a substantial front-loaded package of €6 billion announced for 2011. The plan also targeted 2014 as the year in which the deficit would be brought below

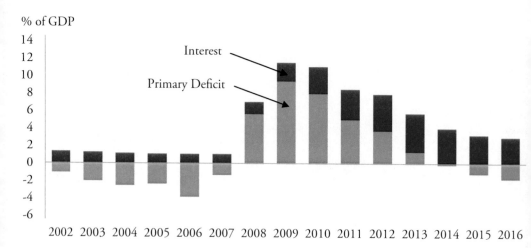

Figure 2.8

Evolution of the primary and total deficit, % of GDP

Source: Department of Finance

3% of GDP under the Excessive Deficit Procedure (EDP) of the SGP. However, the negotiated package extended the target by a year. It is also important to recognise that the underlying primary deficit—the deficit excluding interest costs and the direct deficit-raising costs of bank bailout measures—was €8.5 billion in 2010 (see Figure 2.8). With access to bond market funding at affordable interest rates lost, being forced to close this deficit immediately would have had a catastrophic impact on the economy and society. The first-order effect of the programme, therefore, was to allow much greater phasing of the unavoidable austerity.[7]

Resolving the crisis

Although the programme was agreed in December 2010, the market creditworthiness of the state as measured by secondary market bond yields continued to deteriorate significantly over the first half of 2011 (see Figure 2.7), with rating agencies also further downgrading Ireland's credit ratings. In a critical sense the programme was not working. Investors feared an eventual default, possibly coming as a required debt restructuring as a condition of any extension of the programme. Long-term bond yields peaked at close to 15% in July 2011, with standard calculations suggesting that bond market investors placed a roughly 85% probability on a sovereign default.

A number of uncertainties lay behind this pessimism:

1. There was uncertainty about the prospects for growth, with doubts about the capacity to resume the kind of export-led growth that had fuelled the initial phase of the 'Celtic Tiger' and also concerns that impaired balance sheets across the financial, business, and household sectors would weigh on demand.

2. There were worries that the fiscal adjustment would be 'self-defeating' in terms of bringing down the deficit and stabilising the growth in the debt-to-GDP ratio as austerity measures directly slowed the economy. This was in turn associated with 'multiplier pessimism', with new evidence emerging that multipliers were larger in recessions than previously believed (see e.g. Guajardo *et al.* 2011).

3. There was concern that, after multiple upward revisions, estimates of the size of the ultimate bank losses would continue to rise.

4. As European leaders struggled to get ahead of fast-moving events, there were fears about the inadequate development of European support policies, including the risk that policy would shift towards requiring larger 'bail-ins' of existing creditors.

5. There were doubts about the political capacity of the new centre-right/centre-left coalition to push through the harsh adjustment measures necessary to stabilise the debt and avoid default.

These uncertainties began to subside from the second half of 2011, with ultimately dramatic falls in the risk premium on Irish debt (see Figure 2.7). Compared to other crisis-hit economies, Ireland's export performance was strong. This was supported by notable improvements in competitiveness and a strong performance of the multinational sector of the economy. Improvements in the primary and total deficit reduced fears that the fiscal adjustment would be self-defeating. And although the debt-to-GDP ratio initially continued to rise, projections indicated that the fiscal measures were effective in reducing its rate of increase.

The Prudential Capital Assessment Review published in March 2011 allayed the worst fears about the size of the bank losses and also induced a significant recapitalisation of the banking system. Although the process was sometimes tortuous, European support policies were strengthened following agreements among European governments to strengthen the European fiscal framework. Key developments were the institutionalisation of the European Stability Mechanism (ESM) as a permanent fund and the introduction of the Outright Monetary Transactions (OMT) programme by the ECB. Fears of creditor bail-ins generally subsided despite a large restructuring of Greek sovereign debt. There were also improvements in the Irish programme in relation to the interest rates and maturities of official loans. The restructuring of the promissory note arrangements as part of the liquidation of IBRC was also highly beneficial, with the greatest potential gain being in the case where the cost of borrowing to the state remained high, thereby providing an important form of insurance (see Barnes and Smyth 2013). Finally, the new government demonstrated its capacity to achieve the necessary fiscal adjustments and established the credibility of its commitment to avoid a sovereign default.

Ireland's crisis-resolution strategy of adjustment with outside support is usefully seen as an example of 'catalytic finance', where official support combined with country-level adjustments eventually catalyses private-sector sovereign finance (see e.g. Morris and Shin 2006). Even after entering the programme, Ireland was in a 'bad equilibrium' where potential investors in Irish debt feared the government would not be able to make the adjustments necessary to avoid a future forced restructuring of the privately held debt as a condition of any future support programme. The goal of moving to a 'good equilibrium' therefore involved three sets of actors: official lenders, the government, and private investors. Achieving good equilibrium requires: (i) that official lenders are willing to provide the necessary funding to cover deficits and roll over maturing debt, conditional on a belief that the government will make the agreed adjustments and private investors are (eventually) willing to fund the government at affordable interest rates; (ii) that the government is willing and able to make the necessary adjustments, conditional on the belief that official funders will provide the necessary support without forced 'bail-ins' and private investors are (eventually) willing to fund it at affordable interest rates; and (iii) that private investors are (eventually) willing to provide the necessary funding at affordable interest rates conditional on being convinced that official lenders will not demand bail-ins subject to effective government delivery and that the government is willing and able to meet the conditions for external support without restructuring.

While Ireland appeared to be firmly stuck in the bad equilibrium in the early months of the programme, the flow of news over 2011 and beyond led to the required shift in beliefs that allowed the catalytic finance strategy to work. Ireland successfully exited the programme without requiring additional assistance at the end of 2013. Figure 2.7 confirms the dramatic fall in the expectation that Ireland would default, which was followed with a lag by upgrades from the rating agencies.

We can only speculate on counterfactual scenarios that would have involved an early default on Irish debt. This option had many distinguished adherents as conditions worsened in 2011. However, the chosen catalytic finance strategy not only was successful in securing a return to market creditworthiness, but also was consistent with a dramatic improvement in the condition of the public finances and the return of the economy to growth. While an alternative strategy that involved some form of early default could not be easily dismissed in mid-2011, recognising the observed success of the catalytic finance strategy, it would be hard to argue now that such a default—with all its associated uncertainties—would have been the better course to follow.

Concluding thoughts: preventing future crises

There were no easy choices once the property bubble burst, driving the economy into deep recession and opening up a massive structural budget deficit. The loss of state creditworthiness was not a risk but a fact, making the Irish situation different from some of the other austerity experiences reviewed by Simon Wren-Lewis in Chapter 1. While I believe that a large-scale fiscal adjustment was unavoidable, the challenge was to phase that adjustment as much as possible so as to limit further damage to the economy, to give people time to adjust, and to allow future growth to do part of the heavy lifting. This was ultimately done with the support of outside official funding. While the huge scale of the bank losses certainly compounded the problems and limited options to phase the adjustment, the size of the underlying structural deficit excluding bank-related interest costs meant that a large adjustment would have been necessary even without these costs. Moreover, even though the troika is often associated with austerity, we should not forget that the first-order impact of the official funding programme was avoidance of much more severe austerity, given the size of the primary deficit and the shut-off from market funding.

The crisis underscores the wisdom of avoiding pro-cyclical policies in good times in a volatile global economy (see also Coffey's discussion in Chapter 15). Pro-cyclical credit and budgetary policies at a time of easy financing contributed significantly to the unsustainable boom; once the bubble burst pro-cyclical adjustment could not be avoided in the bust.

A challenge now is to minimise the chances of such a crisis happening again. The banking inquiry has highlighted the substantial changes to financial regulation and supervision that have been implemented—with greatly increased European-level enforcement—and also the new tools of macro-prudential policy to limit credit booms such as loan-to-value and loan-to-disposable income limits. Banks must now be better capitalised, have enhanced tools for risk management, and be subject to orderly resolution outside of bankruptcy and with limited recourse to public funds if they are at risk of failure. These reforms should limit the risk of future credit booms financed by short-term international funding that are prone to 'sudden stops' and can leave huge damage in their wake.

On the fiscal protection side, an enhanced budgetary framework combining complementary European and national elements has been put in place. The peer pressure, surveillance, and ultimate possibility of sanctions under the enhanced SGP gives credibility to the national framework; the national framework helps ensure the domestic ownership of a countercyclical and risk reduction approach to fiscal management. At both levels, there is also a positive interaction between rules, institutions, and procedures for setting fiscal policies. Rather than seeing the framework as something imposed on Ireland to further European-level interests in the context of monetary union, it should be seen as something that is in Ireland's interest insofar as it limits the boom–bust cycle and helps ensure sustainable growth.

At its core, the crisis can be seen as a failure of national macroeconomic risk management. Too much credence was given to arguably plausible central scenarios such as a 'soft landing' and not enough attention to what could go wrong. As a small open economy that is highly integrated through trade and finance into a volatile global economy, Irish policy makers must remain acutely aware of the risks of reversals. We can be almost certain that the next crisis—should it occur—will have different characteristics to what we have just experienced. For example, concerns have risen recently about the sustainability of the poorly understood surge in corporate tax revenues that occurred in 2015. This revenue surge was partly used for in-year increases in spending through the supplementary estimates process, which has echoes of the use of ultimately unsustained property-related revenues to fund permanent increases in spending during the last boom. More generally, Ireland remains exposed to the global business cycle and bouts of international financial instability. There is always a danger that the emphasis on prudence will wane as crisis memories fade. Sound macroeconomic management in the context of sustained commitments to new financial and fiscal frameworks should provide the best defence in an uncertain world.

Notes

[1] The inflow of funds was related to a 'global savings glut' and an excessive degree of belief in the efficiency and stability of even highly leveraged banking systems (see e.g. Wolf, 2014).

[2] Once a crisis is triggered, the economy tends to be subject to a series of 'adverse feedback loops' (or amplification mechanisms) between the financial sector, the public finances, and the real economy. Bank losses, for example, can lead to government bailouts that directly undermine the fiscal position. But a weakening of the fiscal position in turn undermines the credibility of government guarantees of banking-sector liabilities. As the banking sector retrenches, reduced credit availability adds to the contractionary forces on the real economy. But contraction in real activity and falls in asset prices feed back to a further worsening of the balance sheets of the banks. A contracting economy also leads to a further worsening of the public finances. But the effects of austerity measures to stabilise the public finances cause further shrinkage in aggregate demand and the real economy. Policy makers therefore face a hugely challenging task in trying to turn around this downward spiral, with actions on one dimension—e.g. trying to retain a functioning banking system—causing damage along another—e.g. the condition of the public finances.

[3] Budget 2009 was brought forward from December as an emergency measure.

[4] The state's holdings of banking assets were valued at €18.6 billion in 2015.

[5] Anglo Irish Bank and Irish Nationwide Building Society merged to form the IBRC in 2011.

[6] Bilateral assistance was also provided by the governments of Denmark, Sweden and the United Kingdom.

[7] One area in which the troika programme has been criticised is the unwillingness to allow the government to impose losses on remaining unguaranteed and unsecured

senior bondholders. Discussions about the possibility of 'burning' these bondholders took place in November 2010 and again in March 2011. Realistically, the relevant senior bondholders were those in Anglo and Irish Nationwide, which accounted for under €4 billion after the original guarantee expired. Even if substantial losses had been imposed, the resulting impact on the deficit would have been minor and the requirement for austerity only marginally lessened even with large percentage write-downs. The ECB in particular has been severely criticised for its opposition to the imposition of these losses. It also appears that the ECB pushed hardest for a rapid deleveraging of the banking system and a faster fiscal adjustment (see Cardiff 2015). But it is important to view the ECB's role in Ireland's rescue in the round. At its peak, total Eurosystem support to the Irish banking system reached roughly €160 billion—approximately equivalent to Ireland's annual GDP. This funding support came at extremely low interest rates. In the absence of an effective bank resolution regime that allowed for differentiation between non-junior creditors, the ECB was concerned about the implications of setting a precedent for senior creditor losses for the funding of both the Irish and the broader Euro Area banking systems.

3. The ideological project of austerity experts

Kieran Allen

Introduction

By austerity, we mean a discourse that comprises two key policy points, as follows.

1. The principal cause of economic difficulties is over spending by the state sector and a strategy of fiscal retrenchment is required.

2. This debt can be reduced by institutional rules and 'structural reforms'. Elected politicians need to be constrained by independent central banks and independent fiscal councils.

In this chapter, the focus on state spending is explained as growing out of a pre-existing neoliberal model that sought to shrink the state and remove regulations on the freedom of capital (Harvey 2007). In the European Union (EU) a variant of this discourse has been strengthened by the growing hegemony of ordoliberalism, reflecting the increased weight of the German elite within the EU, as discussed by Simon Wren-Lewis in Chapter 1 of this volume. Ordoliberalism differs from the Anglo-American version of neoliberalism, which assumes that the market triumphs naturally provided the state remains passive. Ordoliberalism calls for active state intervention, which seals itself off from democratic pressure, in order to restrict public spending and create the conditions necessary for competitiveness, by means of constitutional rules and supposedly 'independent' institutions that limit the ability of states to borrow or spend.

The German political establishment saw the global crash of 2008 as an opportunity to impose this model on the wider EU. When states adopt this economic philosophy, it is assumed that they will increase market confidence and this will lead to a flow of credit and investment. Ironically, however, the more talk there was about austerity, the more the debt level of the EU rose. Gross government debt in the Eurozone rose from 66% to 92% between 2008 and 2014. (Eurostat 2016). Specific proposals that arise from this approach are usually articulated by economic experts who present them as technical prescriptions that are devoid of any particular bias. They claim that the discipline of economics belongs to a separate sphere from discourses about political choice.

Austerity is also embodied in the institutional framework of the EU. Through the Treaty on Stability, Coordination and Governance (Fiscal Compact Treaty), there is an obligation on countries whose general government debt exceeds the 60% reference value to reduce it at an average rate of one-twentieth per year. This is reinforced by 'Six Pack' rules that stipulate financial sanctions that can be imposed on member states. These rules provide an undemocratic instrument to enforce austerity policies on the EU because 16 countries of the EU-28 have a debt to Gross Domestic Product (GDP) ratio that is higher than 60% (Eurostat 2015). The institutionalisation of austerity rules provides political cover to local elites. It allows them to express sympathy with social suffering but to equally invoke the TINA—There Is No Alternative—mantra. The aim is to draw on a powerful sentiment of fatalism that pervades modern culture. Fatalism is reinforced by apparently neutral technical experts who, consciously or unconsciously, seek to limit political choices. I shall use the term 'austerity experts' to describe this collective body of pro-austerity economists and shall argue that they are engaged in an ideological project.

The term 'ideology' is used in a sociological sense to refer to ways in which particular ideas are connected to the maintenance of power relations. The German sociologist Max Weber provided the classic definition of power when he noted that it was 'the probability that one actor in a social relationship will be in a position to carry out his will despite resistance, regardless of the basis on which this probability exists' (Weber 1978). One possible way of carrying out this 'will' is to get social actors to internalise the viewpoint of dominant actors. In these situations, authority will appear legitimate and there will be less need to rely on force. Ideas can therefore have a strong impact on social relations. When ideas help to uphold the power of dominant groups and when they express their worldview, we refer to them as ideology.

Let me explain with a relatively simple example. The rather awkward and ungainly word 'competitiveness' pervades popular and academic discourse and is largely unquestioned. There is no equivalent term for 'co-operativeness'. This stretching of the English language is interesting because terminology can imply a package of ideas. The popularity of the term 'competitiveness' is linked to an assumption that competition is the most appropriate way to organise an economy and, therefore, that 'entrepreneurs' are best placed to promote it. In this way, the ideas and meanings that lie behind the term 'competitiveness' provide ideological support for a particular social group.

More broadly, ideologies function in a number of ways:

- They present current social relations as natural and ahistorical to convey an impression that they cannot be changed.
- They mask conflicts of interest and invoke terms which convey an impression of common interest.
- They provide partial explanations of the aspects of social reality and avoid drawing links with deeper structures of the social totality.

The manner in which austerity has been justified in Ireland provides an example of an ideological discourse.

The crash

Among the factors that led to the crash of 2008, according to austerity experts, were lax fiscal discipline by the state, reliance on pro-cyclical tax policies, and state incompetence. Types of explanation that fit into this category include the following.

- References to how the Irish state operated too lax a fiscal policy, causing overheating in the economy.

Thus John FitzGerald suggested that 'What should have happened is that from at least 2003, fiscal policy should have been progressively tightened. This would have reduced inflationary pressures in the economy' (FitzGerald 2010, p. 6).

- A failure of the state's fiscal policy to respond in a counter-cyclical manner to the natural rhythms of a capitalist economy. This is the argument often presented by Patrick Honohan, who claimed that there was a 'systematic shift towards cyclically sensitive taxes over the past two decades' (Honohan 2009).
- A general culture of incompetence either among Department of Finance officials or among regulatory agents. Thus the Wright Commission pointed to the extraordinary low number of professional economists working in the Department of Finance and its lack of 'sufficient engagement with the broader economic community' (Wright 2010, pp. 6, 45). This conveniently ignores the fact that very few of the same professional economists had the slightest inkling of the forthcoming crash.

However, such attempts to focus on state spending and the faults of regulatory agents in isolation from the workings of capitalism do not adequately explain the Irish crash. In the first place, the Irish state's spending was by no means out of line with the doyen of ordo-liberalism, Germany, as Table 3.1 illustrates. Hence, on the surface, state spending cannot be described as the main cause of the 2008 crash. In response, austerity economists move to one of two defensive reformulations.

The first is to state that Ireland had a 'structural deficit' even though most observers did not notice it at the time, an argument advanced by John McHale in Chapter 2 of the current volume. Elsewhere he put it like this: 'It was not apparent to the majority of observers that Ireland has a large underlying structural deficit related to the underlying structural imbalances of the bubble-driven economy' (McHale 2012, p. 1225). Even as a concept, the structural deficit appears to have a somewhat shadowy existence. It supposedly refers to the proportion of a budget deficit that arises from structural imbalances that are independent of the economic cycle. But, as economists are singularly

Table 3.1

Government deficit and debt-to-GDP ratio: Germany and Ireland

Source: OECD Country Statistical Profiles: Key Tables.

	2003	2004	2005	2006	2007
German government deficit	−4.0	−3.8	−3.3	−1.6	0.3
German central government debt-to-GDP	65%	68%	71%	69%	69%
Irish government deficit	0.4	1.4	1.6	2.9	0.1
Irish central government debt-to-GDP	34%	33%	335	29%	29%

unable to predict the economic cycles, it is difficult to see how it is a meaningful rather than merely an ideological concept.

The manner in which the concept is used ideologically can be illustrated by the fact that the International Monetary Fund (IMF) issued a report *before* the crash indicating that Ireland's structural deficit was non-existent but *after* the crash claimed it was substantial. In its 2007 report on Ireland, the IMF stated that Ireland's structural budget balance for 2007 stood at 0.7% of GDP, implying a healthy surplus. But its 2009 review revised this figure for 2007 to claim that there was a structural budget deficit of 8.7% of GDP (McArdle 2012). No wonder the Bundesbank has described the procedure for calculating the structural deficit as 'relatively complex, opaque and elastic on account of the numerous discretionary modelling options' (Deutsche Bundesbank 2011, p. 55).

The second defence strategy is to argue that Ireland's healthy fiscal condition was due to an over-reliance on tax revenues from construction or 'cyclically sensitive taxes' (Honohan 2009). Now there is clearly an important degree of truth in this, but it is a partial truth. At the height of the Celtic Tiger boom a full 17% of tax revenues came from property-related taxes (Goodbody Stockbrokers 2006). But this invites the following questions.

- Why did construction feature so heavily in Irish capitalism? Why was so much of the investment made by native Irish capitalism put into this sector—as against manufacturing, for example?

- How was the state's over-reliance on cyclically sensitive taxes related to the manner in which Ireland was marketed as a tax haven?

If about two thirds of capital investment went into construction during the late Celtic Tiger period, the obvious question is why? In other words, we should not start and finish with the issue of state revenue, but ask more fundamentally what it is about Irish capitalism that led it in this disastrous direction.

Framing the question in this manner leads us towards a discussion on the weakness of domestic Irish capitalism, despite the decades of state support it has received. According to the 2004 report of the Enterprise Strategy Group, the contribution of Irish indigenous firms to export growth in the period 1990–2002 was 'negligible' (Enterprise Strategy Group 2004, p. 8). It seeks out protected areas of high profit and tends to favour short-term gains. It looks to markets that can be influenced by state activity or in some cases deliberate non-activity to create sheltered spaces.

If we factor in the enthusiastic embrace of neoliberalism by the Irish state we get some inkling of why so much investment was geared to construction. In 2000, Ireland occupied third place on the 'freedom index' of the neoliberal Heritage Institute precisely because it promoted a light-touch system of regulation (*Irish Times* 2000). Essentially, this meant putting in place a veneer of regulatory control while giving the private sector the maximum level of freedom. In 2004, for example, the White Paper on Better Regulation stated baldly, 'we will regulate as lightly as possible given the circumstances and use more alternatives' (*Regulating Better* 2004, 20–21). This official state policy—which was never fundamentally critiqued by the austerity experts—led to a system of self-regulation of building standards, a failure to substantially tax or control the use of development land, and of course 'light-touch' supervision of banks which enabled them to give huge loans to developers (Allen 2009).

When it comes to the state's over-reliance on cyclically sensitive taxes, there are further fruitful areas of enquiry that should be explored. Ireland is marketed abroad as a respectable tax haven for multinational firms. These are offered some of the lowest effective rates of corporation taxes in the world and are given full freedom to repatriate their profits. The state's strategy of low taxes for global corporations pervades almost every aspect of Irish society. As the boom tightened the labour market, for example, the state embarked on a strategy of cutting income taxes as a device to ease wage pressures. Under a peculiar form of neoliberal social partnership, tax cutting for workers became the mechanism for promoting moderate wage rises. The vast majority of austerity experts who advocate broadening the tax base do so without challenging Ireland's role as a tax haven for corporations. The base they wish to broaden is primarily from Pay As You Earn (PAYE) earners and consumers rather than from corporations.

The central point is this: issues pertaining to the structural weakness of Irish capitalism, the state elite's embrace of neoliberalism, and the niche that the country has secured as a tax haven for global corporations barely feature in the austerity experts' analysis. Ireland's enthusiastic adoption of a neoliberal discourse is not even mentioned as a major contributory factor to the depth of the crisis. Aside from the Telesis report produced by NESC in 1982, there has been no substantial critique of the longer term contradictions in the current development model, which assumes that offering a tax haven for multinationals would cause Irish capitalism to grow (National Economic and Social Council 1982). Yet the difficulties that this model causes for the wider Irish society deserve careful attention (Allen and O'Boyle 2013).

The reasons are ideological. The wider social context is ignored because the austerity experts assume that the workings of capitalism are natural. They therefore attempt explanations of the 2008 crash that bracket out the wider workings of the system. They focus instead on issues that can be dealt with within an intellectual framework that did not foresee the crash. The outcome of this limited analysis is that the failure of regulatory agents or policy makers to properly manage the economy becomes the main causal factor. This is accompanied by a reference to the global 'market failure' seen as an episodic event rather than systemic failure (McHale 2012).

The regulatory agents, however, did not in fact fail, but were rather doing what neoliberal Ireland required them to do. They went through the motions of providing a regulatory environment while turning a blind eye to the actual functioning of private enterprise. Their primary function was to act as ornaments of respectability, not controlling agents that restricted profit making. Historically, the Irish state has provided Irish capitalists—as well as their multinational allies—with high levels of grants and generous tax breaks. Company directors have enjoyed easy access to state officials who pride themselves on a 'frictionless' relationship with business. These wider patterns help to explain why the current crop of state officials were imbued with an ethos of 'supporting the green jersey' by ignoring failures to implement official regulations. The scapegoating of a number of hapless individuals is really an attempt to deflect anger away from the central agencies of the state that promoted a 'light-touch' version of regulation.

Nor was there simply a 'market failure' in the terms typically understood by the austerity experts. Since the 2008 crash, it has become commonplace to discuss the possibility that the global economy is entering a period of secular stagnation (Summers 2014). By this we mean the inability of the industrialised world to grow at satisfactory rates despite very loose monetary policies. Interest rates have been cut in Japan, China, the EU and the United States and major stimulus packages are available, but investment remains stubbornly low, as Figure 3.1 indicates. When the global economy does not rebound after its greatest crash since 1929, it is clear that we are not experiencing a once-off event, but a more fundamental problem.

The fiscal deficit

Once the 2007 crash was analysed in this limited way, the primary issue became how to fix the fiscal deficit. Typically, analysis by the austerity economists was echoed in the mass media discussions which focused on questions of the format: how would you fix the €18 billion black hole in the economy? Other aspects of the crisis such as a €30 billion fall in investment were simply ignored. It is difficult to recall any media discussion where respondents were asked 'How do you intend to fix the problem of falling investment?' The latter framing of the problem might lead to questions about the private control of assets and the manner in which the investment decisions of a handful of people affect the lives of the many. By focusing nearly exclusively on the deficit question, respondents were required to provide an answer that stuck to the framework of the capitalist economy and the media were implicated in the ideological construction of the TINA narrative (see also Mercille, Chapter 4, this volume). In other words, respondents were required to give an answer to a problem caused by the system without questioning the nature of the system itself.

Figure 3.1

Investment and return on equity

Source: Minack Advisors, OECD, MSCI, NBER, June 2015

Return on equity (ROE), %

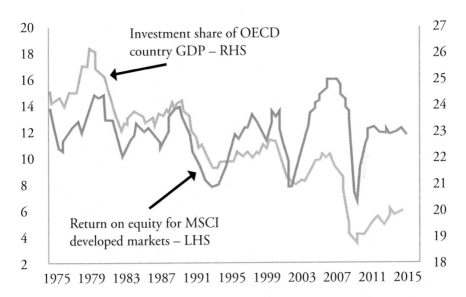

Yet the fiscal deficit is, in fact, a symptom rather than a root cause of the crisis. It was caused in the first instance by the decision to pay off private bank debt. Secondly, it arose from the economic crash itself as capital was destroyed or went on strike to await better investment opportunities. Then as a result of austerity policies, which cut back on domestic demand, many were made redundant and tax revenue fell. These combined problems meant that interest payments on Irish state debt rose from €2 billion in 2008 to €4.9 billion in 2010 to €8.1 billion in 2014.

An obvious answer to the 'black-hole' problem might, therefore, be to halt the repayments of interest to bondholders and default on the bank debt that was imposed on the Irish population by the European Central Bank. Alternatively it could have been suggested that it might be necessary to take control of capital away from the hands of private investors to restart investment. But precisely this type of response was ruled out as 'political ideology' and not a suitable answer to the technical, neutral question. A parameter was set up that dovetails with the interpretations of the political establishment.

The 'How do we fix the fiscal deficit?' question was also used to de-politicise the wider austerity programme by presenting it as a form of good housekeeping, as Simon Wren-Lewis points out in this volume (Chapter 1). No household, it was asserted, could run up debts forever and neither could a country. This clichéd metaphor was originally used by Margaret Thatcher to justify her attack on the welfare state in the 1980s, but her homely image does not stand the test of logic. A society is not like a household because there are different social classes within it. In a household, savings result from a voluntary effort to abstain, but in society the 'savings' extracted from one social group are the result of attacks mounted by another. In a household, the savings of today create extra holidays for tomorrow but in society the money saved in welfare cuts or lost wages is never returned. In a household, savings can be a way of accumulating funds that lead to an increase in wealth. In a society, the money 'saved' from working people simultaneously cuts their demand and so helps push other workers out of their jobs. Concentrating, then, on 'how to get the budget right', as if it were a matter of organising family savings, invariably produces a distorted picture of the fundamental issues at the heart of the crisis.

The medicine

Once the analysis of the economic crash is reduced to an issue of state spending, the way is opened for an austerity strategy. Another ideological device then becomes apparent because this is presented as producing 'sacrifices for all' and, therefore, not contributing to inequality. Alternatively, there is some acknowledgement of a link between austerity and inequality, but this is conceived solely in terms of how particular income groups are disadvantaged. This is seen as an unintended consequence that could be remedied by relatively minor policy changes. There is no examination of how austerity helps to strengthen the power of the dominant social class.

Yet there is clear evidence of a class bias in the pattern of budgetary measures taken since the crisis began. Discussions on who has suffered most tends to focus solely on which income category were most affected. While this is a legitimate and interesting question, it ignores a larger issue: how much extra tax is taken from *income* rather than *capital?* The majority of those who live on an income receive a wage and are taxed as PAYE workers. Others, who are usually more fortunate, live off dividends, rent, property, speculation or profit. As Table 3.2 shows, however, income earners carried the burden of increases in taxation. This is all the more remarkable because the tax hikes on workers occurred when the labour force was in decline and experiencing pay cuts.

The other main area for generating revenue has been indirect taxes. Traditionally, Ireland has relied heavily on indirect taxes rather than taxes on wealth or capital or employers' social insurance. Since the crash, the state has increased its reliance on such taxes through carbon taxes and water charges. However, indirect taxes hit the poorest sections of the population harder. One international study has shown that the poorest 10% pay at least twice as much indirect tax relative to their income as the richest (Decoster *et al.* 2010, p. 335). An Irish study came to a broadly similar conclusion, suggesting that 'indirect tax payments for households in the lowest decile amounted to almost 21 per cent of income—the corresponding figure at the upper end of the distribution was 9.6 per cent' (Barrett and Wall 2006, p. 8).

Reduced public spending has also hit lower income groups harder. Cuts in social protection directly affect lower income groups such as lone parents, the unemployed and short-time workers, the elderly and large families. Lone parents have been a particular target because once

Table 3.2

Percentage of tax revenue, Ireland, 2008–2014 from capital and labour (€ million)

Source: Revenue Commissioners: Revenue Net Receipts by Taxhead on an Annual Basis.

	2008	2014
PAYE + Universal Social Charge (USC)	10,069 (25%)	14,427 (35%)
Corporation plus Capital Gains and Capital Acquisition Tax	6, 838 (16%)	5,512 (13%)
Total net revenue	41,074	41,385

a child reaches the age of seven, his or her parent will be deprived of One Parent Family Allowance. Discrimination against younger people has been hard-wired into the system, as welfare is now related to age, with lower rates for under-25s. The fuel allowance for the elderly has been cut, even though Ireland was reported in 2007 to have one of the highest rates of 'excess deaths', with an estimated 2,800 dying due to hypothermia annually (Public Health Policy Centre 2007).

However, in a broader sense the attacks on public services have a discriminatory effect because the poor and vulnerable are more likely to rely exclusively on these services, as also discussed by Heffernan (Chapter 9, this volume). The numbers on the first time waiting list for outpatient hospital services was 412,422 in April 2015, and it was estimated that half of these would wait for over six months (National Treatment Purchase Fund 2015). Longer waiting lists affect the poorer sections of society most because they already tend to wait longer for hospital services. In 2007, it was estimated that Medical Card holders were three times as likely to be on in-patient waiting lists and twice as likely to be on outpatient waiting lists as privately insured patients (Central Statistics Office 2010, 16). The Expert Group found that 'individuals who can afford private health insurance gain access to some hospital services faster than those with equivalent health needs but who do not have insurance' (*Report of the Expert Group on Resource Allocation and Financing in the Health Sector* 2010, p. 11). As the number of people giving up private health insurance has grown significantly since 2008, this has produced even higher demand for public health services.

The state's policy on housing provides another example of the class bias in austerity policies. State spending on housing has been cut substantially since the crash of 2008 and there is also a distinct bias towards relying on the private sector. There has been a dramatic decline in social housing and a growing use of the private sector to accommodate those in housing need. In 2007, 6,671 new local authority and voluntary non-profit housing units were provided but by 2013, this had declined to just 504. Government policy appeared to be geared towards reviving Ireland's property market. This is evident in an annual expenditure of €498 million to private landlords for rent supplements; the introduction of tax breaks for Real Estate Investment Trusts (REITs) to purchase Irish property; and the failure to introduce rent controls. The result is an escalating housing crisis.

As part of its 'austerity measures' (Callan *et al.* 2011), the state also sought to reduce wage costs for employers. It achieved this, in the first instance, by repeating the mantra that it was not the function of the state to create jobs. High levels of unemployment disadvantaged workers and made them more susceptible to accepting poorer wages and conditions. The state also led the way by introducing the Financial Emergency Measures in the Public Interest (FEMPI) Acts to cut the wages of its own employees. At the start of the crisis, the employers' organisation, Irish Business and Employers Confederation (IBEC), called for a policy of wage cuts but it required state action to turn this call into a determined strategy. By cutting the wages of its own employees by an average of 16%, the state normalised wage cutting and provided an important precedent for private employers. The reduction in public sector numbers was accompanied by a greater reliance on precarious forms of employment, helping to legitimise similar moves throughout the private sector economy. The effects of these policies in shifting the balance of class force can be demonstrated in a number of ways.

First, a growing proportion of Irish workers are employed on low wages as expectations have been reduced. The 2010 *Structure of Earnings Survey* estimated that 20.7% of Irish workers were low paid—defined as those earning two-thirds or less of the national median gross hourly earnings (Eurostat 2010). Data from the Survey on Income and Living Conditions indicates that those at work (the working poor) represent 12.6% of all those at risk of poverty while the real median equivalised income per individual has fallen from €20,681 in 2008 to €17,374 in 2013. (Central Statistics Office 2013) The situation continues to worsen. The most recent OECD employment survey suggests that the number of workers who are classified as low paid has risen from 19% of the workforce in 2003 to 23% in 2013. This makes Ireland the country with the third highest level of low paid workers among OECD countries (Organisation of Economic Co-operation and Development 2015). The shift towards a more low-paid workforce is one of the reasons why the National Competitiveness Council can boast that 'between 2009 and 2011, significant reductions in nominal Irish Unit Labour Costs were recorded while increases were recorded across most of the euro area' (National Competitiveness Council 2015, 33).

Second, there has been a growth in precarious employment. Nine per cent of the workforce are employed in temporary jobs or on contracts of limited duration and 14% are employed for less than a year.

Twenty-three per cent of the workforce are working part time and 36% of these are described as under-employed (Central Statistics Office 2015). There has been a large increase in the numbers of those who are involuntarily working part-time. The most recent OECD employment survey showed that the number in involuntary part-time employment had grown from 2.7% of the workforce in 2000 to 8.9% (OECD 2015).

The result has been a shift in the balance of power between labour and capital. There has been a significant restoration of profits even with a declining workforce, as Table 3.3 indicates.

The austerity experts may claim that the policies they recommend are neutral, technical prescriptions. The evidence, however, shows the contrary. The result of the austerity programme has been to shift the balance of power in favour of capital and away from labour and the poor. Their ideological project has therefore been to use the economic crash of 2008 to strengthen the already dominant economic elite and the subservient state officials who serve their interests.

Table 3.3

Net value added at factor cost and net national income at market prices: domestic trading profits and wage and salaries 2008–2013 (€ million)
Source: Central Statistics Office.

	2008	2009	2010	2011	2012	2013
Domestic trading profits of companies	40,259	36,701	43,962	49,023	49,896	46,925
Wages and salaries	76,235	69,43	64,427	64,151	64,562	66,581

4. Irish media coverage of the housing bubble and austerity

Julien Mercille

Introduction

During the 'Celtic Tiger', from the 1990s until 2007, Irish GDP grew on average by 6% annually in real terms. However, the period was in fact composed of two distinct and successive booms (Kelly 2010). First, an export-based expansion in the 1990s enabled the country to emerge from a lengthy period of economic stagnation. Second, as export growth rates fell significantly after 2000, a credit-fuelled construction boom took over: real residential property prices rose threefold between 1994 and 2006 (Honohan 2010). As discussed in Chapter 1, the bubble started deflating in 2007 and as the housing market collapsed, the government implemented austerity measures (fiscal consolidation) as a response to deteriorating public finances.

The theoretical framework that underpins this chapter's conceptualisation of the media is rooted in political economy but is only sketched briefly here (for a detailed discussion, see Mercille 2013, 2014b, 2015). It notes that mass media outlets either are corporate entities or are owned by the state, with the result that the stories they run tend to reflect the range of interests and viewpoints among political and economic elites, as suggested in Chapter 3 of this volume by Allen. Therefore, while there is diversity in the views presented by the media, it is relatively narrow, being mostly confined to the spectrum of elite viewpoints. State-owned media have their top officers appointed by the government and it is they who set programming guidelines. Private media organisations are integrated in the broader market and need to generate revenues and profits for their shareholders, to invest in new projects and to repay loans to banks. Both private and public media organisations face commercial pressures and the need to raise funds and, for this reason, all operate as profit-making enterprises, at least to some degree. Therefore, media outlets have little incentive to seriously criticise the capitalist system in which they exist and from which they profit. To do so would amount to undermining their own position.

Another key factor that explains media coverage is advertising pressures. Advertising revenues are crucial to today's news industry. They allow newspapers to be sold for a lower price, thus making them more competitive. Media unable to attract ads are at a serious disadvantage in the market and run the risk of bankruptcy. This affects news content because corporate advertisers tend not to support television programmes or news stories that seriously question or attack their own business or the political economic system of which they are part (McChesney 2004).

The Irish media landscape fits within this framework. Independent News & Media (INM) is the dominant conglomerate and is part and parcel of the Irish corporate establishment. It is owned by one of Ireland's richest individuals, Denis O'Brien. *The Irish Times* is considered Ireland's 'newspaper of record' and is of a somewhat less corporate nature than INM, being owned by the Irish Times Trust, whose purpose is to reduce commercial pressures, although the extent to which this actually occurs is not always evident. The newspaper remains subject to significant commercial pressures so that its coverage is largely reflective of elite interests. In particular, its board is replete with individuals linked to the corporate and political establishments.

The influence of advertisers on news content was particularly clear during the housing boom, when the media received a large amount of funding from property advertising. Most newspapers published weekly supplements for commercial and residential property, 'glamorizing the whole sector', while 'glowing editorial pieces about a new housing estate were often miraculously accompanied by a large advertisement plugging the same estate', in the words of Shane Ross, former

Sunday Independent business editor (Ross 2009, p. 157). One Irish media journalist interviewed in an academic study stated that reporters 'were leaned on by their organisations not to talk down the banks [and the] property market because those organisations have a heavy reliance on property advertising' (Fahy *et al.* 2010, 15).

Moreover, in testimony at the Irish Parliament's Banking Inquiry, Geraldine Kennedy, *Irish Times* editor during the bubble years, stated that many telephone calls were made to the newspaper's management office about news coverage and that some individuals in the property sector threatened that *The Irish Times* would never get an advertisement again after an article by Morgan Kelly was published that predicted a collapse of the real estate market (Kennedy 2015).

Such political economic pressures explain why the real estate boom and austerity have not often been challenged or questioned in the mass media. It is because they were advantageous to key sectors of the Irish corporate and political establishment. Before 2008, high rates of economic growth and an overheating property sector directly benefited banks, builders and developers, property firms and the government. The government, led by the Fianna Fáil party, was able to collect large tax revenues from the boom through stamp duty, capital-related taxes and income taxes on construction workers, as well as VAT on construction materials (O'Toole 2009).

Austerity has since provided a tool for elites to 'deepen neoliberalism' (Mercille and Murphy 2015; see also Brenner *et al.* 2010) so as to reinforce their power relative to ordinary people. This has been accomplished by raising regressive taxes, reducing wages, cutting spending on public services on which the majority of the population depends, supporting privatisation, and making the workforce more 'flexible', among other things (Mercille and Murphy 2015, 2016, 2017a, 2017b). In this respect, this chapter concurs with Wren-Lewis's claim (Chapter 1, this volume) that the policy of austerity may be interpreted as a result of 'right-wing opportunism' to further a right-wing agenda, whereas in fact austerity was in many respects unnecessary and was applied too early and too heavily. Moreover, as Allen (Chapter 3, this volume) notes, Irish establishment support for austerity has been reinforced by the fact that European elites have also strongly advocated and implemented it. European institutions have formally integrated austerity rules relative to national budgets and debt, for example. These have acted as additional layers of political, economic and legal justifications for austerity.

Media coverage: housing bubble

The role of the media in Ireland's economic crisis has been discussed in detail in previous publications (Mercille 2014a, 2014b, 2015; Mercille and Murphy 2015; O'Callaghan *et al.* 2014), but this chapter refines and updates earlier conclusions. In particular, it discusses the methodology employed for assessing media coverage of the housing bubble, thereby addressing the queries of some media commentators (O'Brien 2015) who have criticised the lack of detail presented in earlier analyses.

Although hindsight is obviously beneficial, it is possible to identify bubbles with a reasonable degree of confidence before they burst, by comparing average house prices with average incomes or with average rental prices. The *Economist* magazine (2002, 2003) used such measures to warn about global real estate bubbles early on. In Ireland, the commentator David McWilliams (1998) warned unambiguously about the bubble, as did Professor Morgan Kelly (2007a). However, overwhelmingly, Irish analysts and institutions, including the media, maintained that there was no bubble or that if there was one, it would gradually deflate in a 'soft landing'.

The analysis in this chapter is restricted to *The Irish Times* for illustrative purposes but the results are similar for other mass media in Ireland (Mercille 2015). The following search was conducted in the Nexis online newspaper database:

> **Search:** bubble W/s (property OR "real estate" OR hous!) :
> At the Start
> **Duplicate removal:** moderate on
> **Date:** 1 January 1996 to 31 December 2011
> **Source:** Irish Times

Appendix 1 (page 281 of this book) lists the 255 articles returned through the above database search. After removing those that were off topic and readers' letters to the editor, the dataset comprises 165 pieces. The search returned all *Irish Times* articles published between 1 January 1996 and 31 December 2011 that contain the word 'bubble' in the same sentence (operator 'W/s') as one or all of the following words: 'property', 'real estate' or 'house' and its variations (the '!' is the truncation symbol). The 'At the Start' operator is useful because it returns only articles that contain the key words in the title or lead

Figure 4.1

Number of *Irish Times* articles on the housing bubble published by year, 1996–2011

Source: Author calculations based on database search

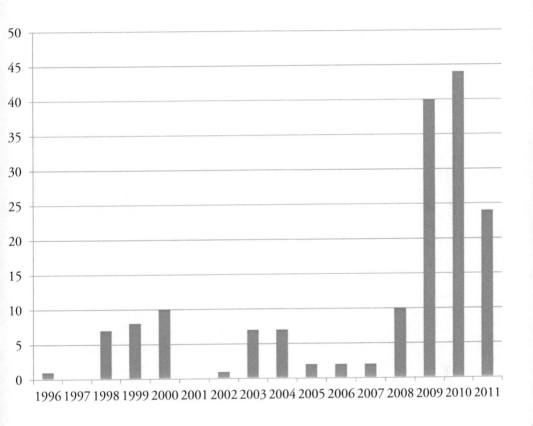

paragraphs. This makes it more likely that the housing bubble will be a central subject in the article.

Figure 4.1 plots the number of articles by year of publication. It shows that in the years prior to the housing crash, *The Irish Times* talked very little about the housing bubble: 57 articles referred to it from 1996 to 2008. Only in 2009 did the phrase started to be used more frequently. It is interesting that even in 2008, the year after the bubble started deflating, news outlets remained relatively quiet about the bubble (the significant drop in 2011 is attributed to the fact that the bubble became a more distant event in time).

Moreover, the few articles that appeared before the crash did not necessarily claim that a dangerous bubble was growing. The nature of the pieces published in 2007 or before was assessed by coding them according to two criteria (Appendix 2). First, does the article acknowledge that a bubble is likely in formation in the market (1 = yes, 2 = no, 3 = neutral/vague)? Second, what are the likely consequences of such a bubble for the Irish economy (1 = dangerous, 2 = not dangerous, 3 = neutral/vague)?

A strong warning from the media corresponds to articles coded 1-1 ('yes' for the first question and 'dangerous' for the second question), namely those that identified the bubble as well as the fact that it constituted a threat to the economy. Conversely, articles coded 2-2 ('no' and 'not dangerous') correspond to a strong denial by the media that the housing market posed a problem: they denied the existence of a bubble and assumed that the economy faced no negative consequences. Articles coded 1-2 ('yes' and 'not dangerous') correspond to a milder denial of the dangers posed by a bubble by acknowledging its existence but claiming that the market would stabilise with no significant negative consequences (e.g. the bubble would deflate slowly, often referred to as a 'soft landing'). Finally, articles remaining vague (coded 3-3) ('neutral/vague' and 'neutral/vague') failed to identify the bubble or warn about its consequences.

Of the 47 articles published between 1996 and 2007, only 10 were coded 1-1 and can thus claim to have warned about the dangers of the bubble. Ten others were coded 2-2 and thus largely denied the existence of a bubble. The remaining articles were either neutral or vague on the existence or consequences of the bubble, or accepted that there was a bubble but sought to reassure readers that there would be a soft landing and that there were no grounds for panic. However, it is important to note that whatever the number of articles warning about a bubble, strongly or mildly, they were in a clear minority when one considers that thousands of articles were printed on all kinds of subjects in *The Irish Times* in the years up to 2007.

A sample of *Irish Times* article titles illustrates the flavour of the coverage of the housing bubble years: 'Irish Property Market Has Strong Foundations' (29 October 1999), 'Study Refutes Any House Price "Bubble"' (18 November 1999), 'Bricks and Mortar Unlikely to Lose Their Value' (11 December 2002), 'Prices to Rise as Equilibrium is Miles Away' (18 March 2004), 'House Prices "Set for Soft Landing"' (22 November 2005), 'Property Market Unlikely to Collapse, Says Danske

Chief' (2 February 2006) and 'House Prices Rising at Triple Last Year's Rate' (29 June 2006).[1] Of course, there were some warnings about the bubble, such as those by David McWilliams (1998) and Morgan Kelly (2006, 2007b). However, they constituted minority viewpoints.

The uncritical nature of most articles is understandable if we view their publication through the theoretical framework outlined above and also through the affiliation of their authors. When journalists are excluded, there were 29 articles (out of 165 between 1996 and 2011) by outside writers. Of those, ten were mainstream economists (independent or academic), eight were affiliated with the corporate or financial sectors, four worked for the real estate industry, four were politicians from establishment political parties (e.g. Fine Gael), and three were academics other than economists. That these writers were favourable to the property industry and the establishment explains why they would be supportive of Ireland's economic policies.

A striking aspect of the majority of articles is a lack of analysis, whatever the interpretation presented in the piece. Most commentary is vague or reports scattered facts without bringing them together to support specific claims, or it reports the opinions of 'experts' or the findings of a report, without guiding readers as to what is most and least significant. In short, it would have been virtually impossible for readers of *The Irish Times* to detect the existence of a bubble with any degree of confidence, let alone to understand its likely negative consequences for the economy before it had actually burst.

The search used above was deemed the most appropriate one to assess media coverage of the bubble. In particular, the term 'bubble' was preferred to 'boom' because the latter has positive connotations (a rapidly growing economy) whereas a bubble denotes an unsustainable market by definition. Media references to a 'housing boom' would therefore not necessarily convey the risks faced by the market. Nevertheless, one could ask whether the media used the word 'boom' to warn about an unsustainable housing market without using the word 'bubble'. For example, did any articles state ideas like: 'the housing boom will end abruptly and the ensuing crash will reverberate throughout the economy'? If many such articles existed, one would have to concede that the media did warn about a bubble, albeit without using the word 'bubble'. In order to examine this hypothesis, the same search as above was conducted, but with the term 'boom' instead of 'bubble', as follows:

Search: boom W/s (property OR "real estate" OR hous!) :
At the Start
Duplicate removal: moderate on
Date: 1 January 1996 to 31 December 2011
Source: Irish Times

This search returned a total of 615 articles (off-topic articles were not removed because this search was conducted in a less detailed fashion in order to test the hypothesis quickly). Between 1996 and 2007, 351 articles were returned. A survey of the pieces (without formal coding) identified 15 that could be considered to present a relatively clear warning about the existence of an unsustainable real estate market that was likely to deflate somewhat abruptly. This suggests that the overwhelming majority of pieces were either enthusiastic about the boom or vague about it. Readers rarely received a clear warning about the dangers associated with the market. As stated above, one striking aspect of the coverage was the large amount of brief, descriptive, non-analytical reporting.

Media coverage: austerity

Without doubt, Ireland has been a poster child for austerity in Europe (Borooah 2014). While a number of countries responded to the 2008–09 financial crisis by using Keynesian measures, Ireland reacted immediately with fiscal consolidation. The scale of adjustment has been very large, amounting to 20% of GDP between 2008 and 2015, two-thirds (€20.5 billion) in spending cuts and one-third (€11.5 billion) in tax increases (NERI 2014, 39; Irish Fiscal Advisory Council 2014, p. 9). These measures have affected most negatively those at the bottom of the income scale and ordinary people in general. The deprivation rate has increased from 11.8% in 2007 to 29.0% in 2014, corresponding to 1,390,000 people (CSO 2015). Austerity budgets have hit the poorest harshly, as illustrated in some of the other chapters in this volume. The bottom 10% of the population (on the income scale) suffered larger income losses than all other deciles except for the top decile (Callan *et al.* 2013).

Irish and European elites have strongly supported fiscal consolidation. The media have provided significant ideological support for the strategy since 2008. A systematic study (Mercille 2014, 2015) examined 929 opinion articles and editorials in the five main Irish newspapers (*Irish Independent, Sunday Independent, The Irish Times, Sunday Business Post* and *Sunday Times* (Irish edition)) between 2008 and 2013. It classified them according to whether they were supportive, opposed or neutral towards austerity. It found that 58% of pieces supported austerity and only 11% opposed it (the remainder were neutral). There was no newspaper whose editorial line opposed fiscal consolidation (all were supportive of it).

It is also interesting to take a look at the articles' authorship. Of the 929 pieces, 223 were by outside contributors (i.e. excluding journalists). Of the 223, 29% are mainstream economists, 28% work in the corporate or financial sector, and 20% are officials in the three main political parties that governed Ireland during the economic crisis, and which have implemented austerity (Fine Gael, Fianna Fáil, Labour); of these, only four are from the Labour Party, suggesting that most are from the two centre-right parties that have dominated Irish politics since Independence. The remainder of authors included academics (9%) (excluding mainstream economists), representatives of progressive organisations (7%), and trade union officials (3%). The majority of writers (77%), therefore, were affiliated with elite political or economic institutions, which makes for a conservative authorship.

The media were quite explicit in stating their position at the outset. In November 2008, the editors of *The Irish Times* were uncomfortable with the fact that 'Members of the general public still do not appreciate the possible extent of the economic downturn' because two-thirds of the population believed that the national budget was too tough and only 10% of people wanted it to be even harsher. The editors thus stated that 'the Government will have a major job to do in educating public opinion about unpalatable economic realities and the need for civic discipline'.

Thus, during the crisis, the media assisted the government in presenting its message in a favourable way to the population. A representative example of the media's attitude was provided by the *Irish Independent* when it stated that the 'budgetary danger for the Government this year may be that people will come to think the danger has passed' and begin to question the necessity for austerity. Therefore, the government and the media must drive the message that there is 'no room for complacency as we're still on a knife-edge' (Keenan 2010).

Critically, news outlets have followed the government's priority to reduce spending over raising taxes. This strategy followed that of the 'troika' of the European Commission, International Monetary Fund and European Central Bank. Out of the 929 opinion pieces examined by Mercille (2015), 290 noted the importance of cutting public expenditure, against 127 that asserted that tax hikes were a necessity (the other articles remained neutral or did not outline a clear viewpoint). A *Sunday Independent* (2009a) editorial illustrates the conventional view presented by the media: it asserts that the economic recovery 'will not come from sharp increases in income tax, or from a range of new indirect taxes disguised as "green" taxes. In fact, the Government risks real and lasting damage to this economy if it believes that it can tax it back to health. It cannot. Before it raises a single tax, it must demonstrate a determination to cut its spending and embrace reform of the public sector.'

A recurrent media theme has been to argue for cuts in the public sector—in particular to public servants' pay—while reducing the number of employees as well. The newspapers surveyed by Mercille (2015, pp. 137–138) ran headlines like 'Padded public sector is in need of reality check' and 'Bloated public sector a luxury we can no longer afford'. Other themes included the alleged need for discipline and dedication to austerity, and the claims that there was no alternative to fiscal consolidation, that immediate pain was warranted, and that austerity would restore market 'confidence', with headlines such as: 'Commitment and stamina are required for fiscal consolidation', 'New Budget will prove tough but necessary', 'Only sustained cuts can now keep Ireland afloat', 'We must suffer the pain now—or else we will blight future generations', 'Bill is tough but necessary', 'Tough budget would restore confidence', 'Supplementary budget can begin urgent task of restoring depleted tax revenues' (see Mercille 2015, pp. 137–138).

Just as during the housing bubble, the media's position reflected that of the political establishment and the corporate sector. Austerity as a strategy was determined by the Irish government in coordination with the troika, the latter representing European and global political and economic elites. Irish businesses and employers also strongly endorsed it. For example, IBEC (Irish Business and Employers Confederation), the main employers' association, stated in 2013 that 'IBEC to date has been supportive of the front-loaded fiscal consolidation Ireland has undertaken, believing it to be necessary for returning public finances onto a sustainable footing and re-entering the bond markets' (IBEC 2013, p. 2). Moreover, the organisation has favoured expenditure cuts in the public sector and in welfare over tax increases. In 2009, it recommended to the government that it implement fiscal consolidation to reduce the deficit and that 'the vast bulk of this reduction should be achieved through spending cuts, including pay and social welfare' (IBEC 2009, p. 3). Further, the Irish Chambers of Commerce chief executive, Ian Talbot (2011), wrote that 'the government should be commended for the manner in which it has delivered yet another austerity budget with the minimum dissension from the general public'.

In addition to reducing the government deficit, austerity involved 'structural' adjustments such as privatisation and policies to make labour more 'flexible'. The business community supported such policies. For example, Talbot (2011) stated that 'there have to be vast levels of efficiencies that could be driven via reform of rostering, clamping down on sick leave and modifying bad work practices and rosters that no longer make sense for our society'. The media strongly endorsed such calls. Daniel McConnell in the *Irish Independent* asserted that:

> Everything should be up for change: work practices, contracts of employment, working hours, pensions, organisation, leadership, pay and the numbers employed … Privatisation, forever long-fingered because the trade unions would not consider it, must be rolled out, both to raise money and to breathe life and competitiveness into the economy. December's Budget must be ferocious, painful and seismic … and no amount of grandstanding from union leaders … and the soon-to-be powerless trade unions can be allowed to obscure reality. (McConnell 2010)

News outlets backed employers when workers threatened to strike to resist austerity measures. A *Sunday Independent* article entitled 'Why union blackmail must be faced down' asserted that the 'selfish, sneaky and reckless actions of the public sector unions show how out of touch they are' (Delaney 2010). An *Irish Times* (2009) editorial entitled 'Strikes will solve nothing' added that industrial action 'damages the broad national interest'. In November 2009, trade unions attempted for the first time to organise a national strike during austerity. A *Sunday Independent* (2009b) editorial entitled 'No good can come out of strike' suggested that this was not the correct way to proceed because it would cause disruptions everywhere: 'Schools across the country will be closed, inconveniencing tens of thousands of parents and children, while thousands more must suffer deferred operations as hospitals fall back on reduced staffing levels.' In sum, the editors opined that the 'strike is folly, a visceral but outdated response to a very modern crisis'. In short, the media provided significant ideological support for the policy of austerity.

Conclusion

This chapter has documented the ways in which the media have reported on austerity and the housing bubble that preceded it. News outlets presented a very positive picture of fiscal consolidation while omitting to discuss at length the growing bubble in the property market on the eve of the economic crisis. Media coverage in both case studies can be explained by recourse to the theoretical framework outlined at the beginning of the chapter. The mass media are composed of corporate entities and state-owned news outlets. They therefore share political and economic elite values and this is reflected in the range of opinions that they present to readers and viewers. Advertising and cost pressures further orientate media content towards the interests of the corporate sector.

During the housing bubble years, Ireland's political economy revolved around a stimulation of the economy through speculation in the property market. The financial and construction sectors were fully immersed in this strategy, and the government drew significant tax revenues from it. Irish elites, including the media, thus had a vested interest in maintaining this model of development, at least in the short term. The economic crisis was then used as a pretext to roll out an austerity programme that followed European policy. The troika and Irish elites worked assiduously to implement fiscal consolidation over the next few years in order to deepen neoliberalism and reassert their dominant socio-economic position, supported by the mainstream media. It opposed attempts at resisting austerity and did not regularly present alternative interpretations of the situation and different solutions to address the problems faced. It could be argued therefore that the media have been key players in constraining debate on the bubble and austerity in an Irish context.

Finally, one important issue to examine is: how could the media present more diversified and inclusive viewpoints? The answer lies mostly with what is referred to as the alternative media. The latter are non-corporate and owned and managed democratically, often by relatively smaller firms, non-profits or government entities. In Ireland, the alternative media scene is extremely small compared to, say, in the United States, the United Kingdom and other European countries. Even in the Irish mainstream (mass) media, there is not a single outlet that could be labelled 'centre-left' such as the *Guardian* in Britain or *Le Monde Diplomatique* in France.

It is thus crucial to develop and grow an alternative media if more critical viewpoints are to occupy a more prominent place in public discourse and in the political and economic spheres in general. So far, the only alternative media outlets that exist in Ireland tend to be too small to reach any significant readership, and lack resources to operate conveniently. If public support was provided to start and develop such outlets (print, radio, television), the Irish media landscape would be greatly diversified. For the time being, it seems that social media platforms like Facebook and Twitter have replaced alternative news organisations. But social media's potential is limited in that news and analysis circulated there often tend to be lost and diluted in the flood of other information, and editorial oversight is generally weak. Building an alternative media presence in Ireland may be one of the great challenges of the future.

Notes

[1] Some of those titles are not taken from the formal search conducted above but from other general searches, simply to illustrate the kinds of titles that appeared in *The Irish Times* during the housing bubble.

Part 2: Experiencing austerity

5. Austerity in the European periphery: the Irish experience

Niamh Hardiman, Spyros Blavoukos, Sebastian Dellepiane-Avellaneda and George Pagoulatos

Introduction

Ireland has come to be seen as an exemplary case of the successful practice of austerity, and its experience was in marked contrast with that of the southern European countries with which it had recently been closely linked (Brazys and Hardiman 2015). These outcomes have been attributed to thoroughgoing implementation of the austerity measures required by Ireland's 2010 loan programme, supported by strong continuity in two successive governments' policy stance. In addition, Ireland's experience is taken to indicate that sustained pursuit of fiscal retrenchment need not be politically destabilising. But these inferences would be somewhat misleading. The real story about fiscal adjustments in Ireland is more problematic, the reasons for recovery are more complex, and the political consequences are a good deal more nuanced.

These issues cannot be fully understood without taking account of the wider European context of crisis. Many elements of this story are shared with the other countries in the Eurozone periphery that have been at the epicentre of the crisis, that is, Spain, Portugal and Greece.

As Wren-Lewis suggests in Chapter 1 of this volume, the terms of adjustment were harsher in the periphery than they might have been had a balanced EU-wide macroeconomic policy mix been in place. The severity of the recession varied across the periphery; we see variation both in the impact of austerity measures and in the prospects for recovery. Ireland does indeed show more signs of recovery than the others. But in Ireland as elsewhere, the political consequences of austerity have been far-reaching. Across Europe, the politics of austerity has put representative government under growing pressure.

Austerity in the European periphery

The experience of crisis in the European periphery, including Ireland, cannot be understood independently of the broader political and economic governance of the Eurozone. In this chapter, we set out a contrasting yet complementary analysis to that of Ó Riain (Chapter 14, this volume). The 'varieties of capitalism' approach would indeed put Ireland in a different category from Spain, Portugal and Greece, but we suggest not only that the dynamics of core and periphery within European Monetary Union (EMU) gave rise to similar experiences of austerity, but also that this has altered the political systems of these four countries in perhaps surprisingly similar ways, with long-term consequences that are as yet unknown. The institutional framework governing EMU constrained the repertoire of policy responses available to national governments and intensified the experience of austerity (Wolff and Sapir 2015). Simon Wren-Lewis, in this volume (Chapter 1) and elsewhere, draws a useful distinction between 'ordinary' fiscal consolidation and fiscal adjustments that are tantamount to 'austerity' policies, and defines austerity as:

> fiscal consolidation that leads to a significant increase in involuntary unemployment, or perhaps more formally but less colloquially as leading to a noticeably more negative output gap. (Wren-Lewis 2015)

So why did Ireland, along with the rest of the European periphery, have to experience higher unemployment and a 'more negative output gap' than would have been required by the need to address the fiscal deficit? The story can be traced back to the perverse incentives for the countries of the periphery that followed from EMU. After 2000, they could avail of interest rates well below their historic averages.

Growth potential made them attractive destinations for lending that was unconstrained by any central financial risk assessment. The surge of capital into both public- and private-sector borrowing contributed to driving inflation upwards, yet governments could not raise interest rates to combat this, and were politically constrained in their capacity to control the consequences through fiscal policy alone (Dellepiane and Hardiman 2010). When the crisis struck in 2008, these economies were very exposed to the risks of a 'sudden stop' of financial flows (Merler and Pisani-Ferry 2012; Dellepiane-Avellaneda *et al.* forthcoming). The collapse of economic activity and plummeting revenues pushed Ireland and Spain into serious fiscal difficulties, intensified the public spending problems of the Greek state, and stalled the already low growth performance of the Portuguese economy. The fiscal crisis of the Eurozone was a consequence of the collapse of the banking system, and not itself a primary cause of crisis (Baldwin and Giavazzi 2015).

The 'unfinished architecture' of the Eurozone (Schmidt 2010) resulted in a slow and protracted series of attempts to generate sufficient consent, institutional capacity, and financial reserves to deal appropriately with the situation. The European authorities struggled to respond adequately to the banking sector crisis and its fallout for governments' borrowing capabilities. After Greece, Ireland, and then Portugal ceased to be able to borrow on international markets, the permanent European Financial Stability Mechanism was put in place only in October 2012. An EU framework for resolution of failing banks was not agreed until 2014.

At the same time, the widespread yet misleading diagnosis of the Eurozone crisis as one of fiscal irresponsibility generated a new commitment at official level to control fiscal deficit and debt levels more firmly. From the outset, the euro had been a very lightly governed currency, with no scope for fiscal transfers to member states in response to an asymmetrical shock, no overall lender of last resort to prevent bank system collapse, and (in principle) no possibility of bailout in the event of excessive debt liabilities resulting in a state being cut off from international markets. The intention had been to enforce member states' conformity to broad targets of inflation, deficit, and debt levels, through active manipulation of fiscal policy at national level. Under the foundational legislation governing the euro, the Commission was already empowered to initiate Excessive Deficit Procedures. The Fiscal Compact entered into force in January 2013. But by that time, the existential crisis of the euro had abated—not because of the prospect of stricter fiscal rules, but because of the European Central Bank's (ECB) market-calming assurances in July 2012 that it would 'do whatever it takes' to protect the Eurozone from collapse (De Grauwe and Ji 2013), followed in due course by a programme of monetary expansion or quantitative easing (QE).

This then was the context within which the European authorities became committed to strict enforcement of fiscal rules and strict timetables for deficit reduction. These were, in effect, the only continuous policy instruments in existence within the Eurozone, and this was the policy area in which it proved easiest to introduce stronger central controls. The European authorities were therefore committed to enforcing a rapid reduction in fiscal deficits even in the depths of recessionary conditions, and in the absence of effective policy coordination capable of offsetting the adverse macroeconomic consequences.

Once again, the European periphery countries were locked into policy prescriptions set at EU level. The countries worst affected by the crisis could not respond along the lines of past fiscal adjustments, by devaluing their currencies to gain competitive advantage and generate some new growth prospects, and allowing inflation to rise to reduce the real burden of debt (see Chapters 1 and 2 of this volume). The full force of relative cost adjustment had to be borne through 'internal devaluation', that is, by reducing the living standards within the member states concerned. Pursuing retrenchment proved to be particularly difficult because it was expressed as a ratio, and a shrinking GDP could cause even real gains in fiscal retrenchment to be expressed as deteriorations in the overall deficit targets. Even if some measure of fiscal adjustment were indeed necessary, the absence of counterbalancing growth-promoting policy measures, and the speed with which fiscal retrenchment was required, undoubtedly intensified the experience of austerity (Guajardo *et al.* 2011; IMF 2012).

Asymmetrical macroeconomic policy mix

The countries that were subject to loan programmes—Greece, Ireland and Portugal, and Spain in respect of its banking sector—were subject to tight monitoring of their compliance with austerity measures. To varying degrees, they were also subject to additional 'structural adjustment' requirements, intended to facilitate new growth, in the expectation that supply-side liberalisation and deregulation was all that stood between these countries and renewed growth. These measures proved most destabilising to the groups, especially public-sector employees and welfare recipients, who were already adversely affected by austerity. There was little evidence to support the expectation of significant growth from reforms such as these in the short or even medium term. Yet there were no other mechanisms in place to generate growth: public investments were constrained by the fiscal constraints these countries were required to observe, and private investments were limited due to the incapacity and unwillingness of banks to engage in new lending.

But not all Eurozone member states were subject to these tight constraints. The 'core', northern member states had more fiscal head-room and significantly depressed domestic demand, particularly Germany. If the Eurozone were to be envisaged as a single economic unit, deflation in periphery countries would have warranted inflation levels in Germany and other core economies of well above 2%, in order to produce an aggregate average inflation performance for the Eurozone as a whole of 'close to but below 2%', the ECB's sole target. But German political—and public—opinion was highly resistant to this, and near-deflation persisted in Germany too. German economic performance, ever since reunification in 1990, had been strongly export-led, based on sustained suppression of domestic demand and intensified export orientation. Figure 5.1 shows the consequences.

This depiction of the harmonised competitiveness index based on unit labour costs shows the relationship between productivity and labour costs within each country relative to its own long-term average, over the period between 1995 and 2012. Wage costs are not the only determinant of competitiveness, and the significant deteri-oration in the relative performance of the periphery countries after 2000 was driven primarily by the negative interest rates on borrowing that obtained after entry to EMU. What is significant about Figure 5.1 nonetheless is its reminder that the performance of individual European economies cannot be considered in isolation. Cost repres-sion in Germany meant domestic wages were not rising in response to improved productivity. The surpluses generated, instead of contribut-ing to additional demand across the European economy as a whole, were channelled into savings. These savings fuelled the capital flows that further destabilised the periphery economies.

The sudden collapse of domestic living standards in the periph-ery after 2008 was also an unnecessarily painful experience, seen in a wider European context. In an integrated economy, dearth of demand in one region can be offset by its increase in another, facil-itated by their common currency. But Figure 5.2 shows the highly

Figure 5.1

Competitiveness index

Source: European Central Bank

Harmonised Competitive Index, country average 1995–2012=100

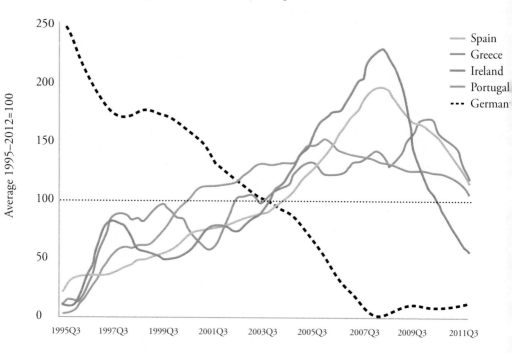

asymmetrical adjustment required of the Eurozone periphery in the absence of increased economic activity in the core.

The current account balance in the periphery deteriorated significantly, firstly in response to the flow of capital from the core to the periphery during the 2000s, and then in the depths of the crisis itself. The change in 2009 reflected the collapse of domestic demand in the periphery, which is apparent from the flat line apparent in the core as a whole, and the positive improvement in Germany's performance, due in part to its greater trade diversification, particularly to China. More generally, indeed, it could be noted that EMU gave Germany an added boost in pursuing its advantages in high-technology, high-value-added production, while there were very few incentives or facilities to stimulate the southern European periphery to break out

Figure 5.2

Asymmetrical macroeconomic adjustment in trade relations

Source: Eurostat

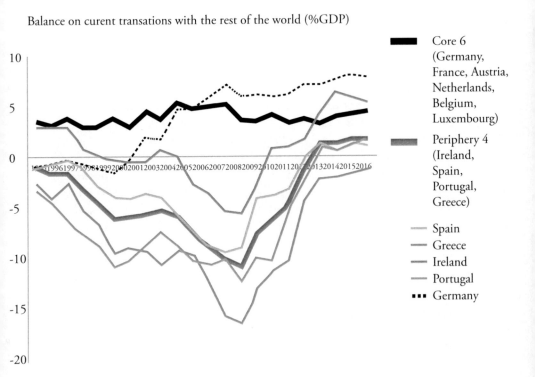

Balance on curent transations with the rest of the world (%GDP)

of its traditional niches of low-end production and a concentration of activity in non-tradable sectors of the economy. The consumption boom and the unproductive housing boom in the periphery during the 2000s, associated with unrestrained lending from the core, had further reinforced these perverse asymmetries.

IMF research showed that the effects of fiscal retrenchment within the Eurozone member states after 2009 had cumulative effects that spread across borders, and that the multiplier effect of austerity was a good deal higher than anticipated in some of the worst-affected cases (IMF 2012). And yet the European Commission's own new Macroeconomic Scoreboard, intended to track dimensions of potentially destabilising economic performance that had hitherto attracted little attention, explicitly permitted a bigger maximum current account surplus (+6%, which Germany consistently exceeded since 2012 anyway) relative to the largest permissible deficit (a threshold of -4%).

Variations in adjustment

The experiences of austerity in the European periphery, although exhibiting a good deal of variation, cannot be understood without understanding their relationship to what was happening in the core. The economic impact of the measures taken depended on a number of factors including the fiscal starting conditions of each country, the configuration of its welfare provisions, an issue raised in the next chapter by Whelan and Nolan, the administrative and implementation capacity of the system, and the recovery capacity of the economy.

The fiscal effort each achieved was considerable. As Figure 5.3 shows, Greece—the poorest of the four Eurozone periphery countries and the one with the biggest problems of political and administrative capacity—implemented the most far-reaching change in fiscal balance between 2009 and 2012.

The preferred adjustment strategy supported by the official lenders favoured spending cuts over tax increases. Cuts in public spending may be considered more tolerable through the lens of prioritising deficit reduction and limiting damage to output potential. But there are disproportionate distributional effects on those who depend on public transfers and public services. Among the consequences was a sharp increase in unemployment. Figure 5.4 shows how dramatically this increased after 2008 from relatively low levels during the years of steady growth that preceded the crash.

In Ireland and Spain, some of the increase was attributable to the shock caused by the initial collapse of the construction sector. But prolonged recessionary conditions, the freeze in bank lending despite extensive recapitalisation, and the burden of private debt on households and on non-financial firms alike, resulted in a sustained period of stagnation across most of the periphery. Youth unemployment typically ran at about twice the average rate in the overall economy; in Spain and in Greece, there is little exaggeration in speaking of a 'lost generation' of youth with restricted employment prospects, limited access to welfare supports, and few prospects of independent living.

In Ireland, the aggregate significance of the measures taken by the Fianna Fáil–Green coalition between 2008 and 2010, then the Fine Gael–Labour coalition from 2011 onwards, is contested. As Whelan and Nolan (Chapter 6, this volume) illustrate, the income losses

Figure 5.3

Scale of fiscal retrenchment, 2009–2012

Source: OECD Economic Outlook, Volume 2012, Issue 2, 17 December 2012.

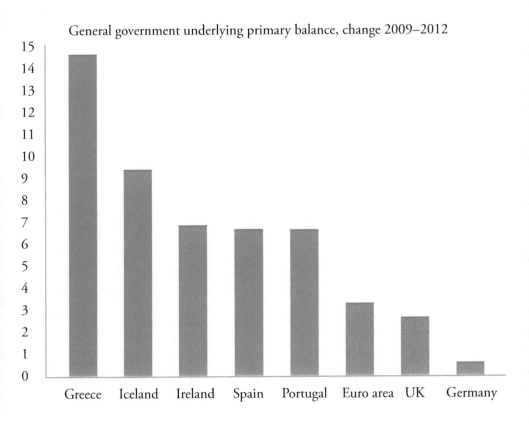

General government underlying primary balance, change 2009–2012

affected all income groups, but economic stress was most pronounced at the bottom, particularly for those dropping into the lowest 10% as a result of job losses.

Ireland's recovery began to become apparent during 2013 and 2014, with an increase in recorded GDP and an expansion in the value of goods and services as a proportion of GDP. This was more than just a feature of the way corporate profits were declared by the foreign direct investment (FDI) sector in order to minimise their tax liabilities under Ireland's internationally low corporate tax regime (FitzGerald 2013; Henigan 2014). Unemployment began to fall as more jobs were created. These indicators led some commentators to believe that

Figure 5.4

Total unemployment rate

Source: Eurostat

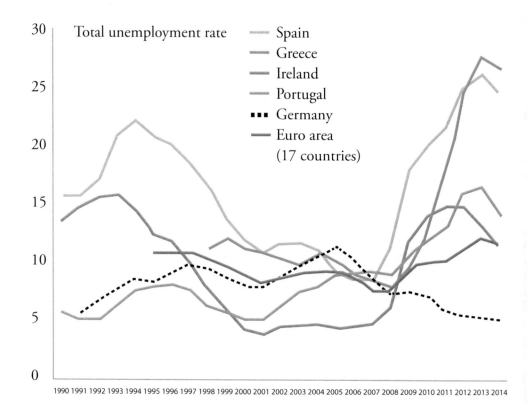

Total unemployment rate

- Spain
- Greece
- Ireland
- Portugal
- ■■■ Germany
- Euro area (17 countries)

the recovery came about as a consequence of austerity policies. This interpretation is fully in line with the European Commission's own diagnosis of the most effective pathway to recovery in the Eurozone. The conditions for a return to economic growth, it is argued, require cutting wage costs to improve competitiveness, which in turn will stimulate the demand for exported goods and services—that is, a replication of the German model of export-driven growth through wage and other cost repression (see Chapters 1, 3 and 4 in this volume).

But the inference that austerity caused recovery is not well grounded in the Irish case—if anything, it could be argued that recovery came about in spite of austerity. It is true, as Figure 5.1 shows, that

Irish competitiveness based on unit labour costs showed some relative improvement during the recession. But the conditions behind this are more complex than the story of a beneficial 'internal deflation' might suggest. Firstly, the relative improvement in competitiveness began in 2007, before the implementation of any austerity measures, with the stalling of the housing boom and the end of the long spell of diverting investments into unproductive assets. Aggregate productivity data improved because of rising unemployment in the relatively low-skilled, low-value-added construction sector.

Secondly, a reduction in the wage rate in the private sector should be one of the principal mechanisms behind better export performance, but this did not happen in Ireland. The exporting sector is highly concentrated in the foreign-owned, high-tech sectors that includes production in information and communications technology and in pharmaceuticals, and internationally traded sectors such as software design, insurance, and other financial services. The principal domestic exporting sectors are agriculture and food products. These sectors did not suffer relative losses in cost competitiveness during the boom; neither did they generally experience pay cuts during the recession (Breathnach 2010; Regan 2015). Employees who experienced pay cuts were mostly in sectors such as the public sector or in construction, all of them non-traded sectors. The rate of investment in Ireland on the part of foreign multinationals increased during the period of recession but the upturn is mainly attributable to mobile US capital made available by QE, incentivised by the continuities in Irish FDI policy rather than by austerity (Brazys and Regan 2015; Regan and Brazys 2017).

Thirdly, it is true that Ireland's real effective exchange rate improved in parallel with the implementation of austerity measures, as Figure 5.5 shows.

Nonetheless, the most convincing explanation does not support the conventional austerity argument that better export performance followed from a combination of private-sector wage-cutting and public-sector cost-cutting. Rather, Ireland's export performance is strongly connected to the fate of the British and US economies. The relative weakness of the euro made Irish exports more competitive without internal price adjustments. Furthermore, while labour costs in the exporting sectors remained stable or increased in Ireland, they increased more rapidly among its trading partners (O'Farrell 2015). Since they had control over their own monetary and fiscal policies, they were not tied into the sluggish performance of the Eurozone economies, so domestic demand in these economies was also more buoyant.

Figure 5.5

Real effective exchange rates

Source: Bruegel Dataset

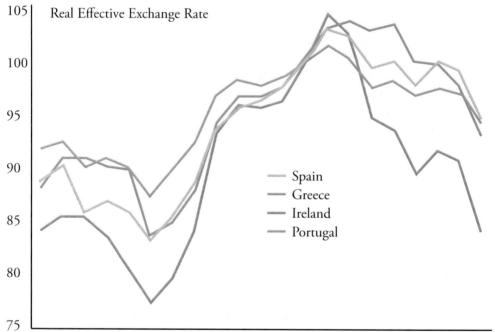

Political effects of austerity

The economic crisis exposed new tensions between the need for unified European-level policy responses and national economic needs that were very diverse. What then were the implications for domestic politics? In the early stages of the crisis, it seemed that left–right politics would continue as usual, with the right benefiting from hopes for stability, and the left resurgent in response to demands for redistribution (Lindvall 2014). The earliest elections held during the crisis resulted in changes of government in which the established opposition party or parties benefited. Those held responsible for implementing unwelcome austerity were punished electorally, in a shift from left to right (as in Spain and Portugal) or from centre-right to centre-left (as in Ireland). There seemed to be 'no general ideological shift in response to the Great Recession' (Bartels and Bermeo 2014, p. 12).

But over the years, established political parties have come under increased pressure. A new kind of politics began to emerge in the European periphery that involved direct mobilisation of disaffected groups, especially young people excluded from the labour market, reflecting a more generalised dissatisfaction with the available policy solutions (Coelho *et al.* 2016). In Spain, this took the form of the party system's fragmentation, as challenger parties Podemos on the left and Ciudadanos on the right took issue with the mainstream parties' perceived corruption and inability to offer an alternative to austerity (Coelho *et al.* 2016). The issue of Catalan independence further divided the parties from each other, so that even after two elections in 2016, Spain was left with a protracted period with limited prospects of stable government formation. Portugal had no new 'anti-politics' challenger party, but the outgoing centre-right coalition of Social Democrats and Christian Democrats lost its majority in 2015 to a leftward surge in support not just for the mainstream opposition Socialists, but in particular for the smaller, far-left parties that had been excluded from government formation until now. As in Spain, no stable majority government could be formed, and the Socialists had to resort to building *ad hoc* coalitions to support policy, one issue at a time. The most dramatic collapse of the party system took place in Greece. The challenger party SYRIZA came from the radical left; it benefited from the all-but-complete collapse in 2012 of the mainstream Social Democratic PASOK and the discrediting of its main rival New Democracy—and from the frustrations of Greek voters with the hardships mandated by the terms of Greece's loan agreements.

So what were the political consequences of austerity in Ireland in this comparative perspective? In broad terms, the trends in Ireland were very similar to those in the other periphery countries. The party system had already suffered a shock after the 2011 general election: the precipitous electoral collapse of Fianna Fáil, from its long-held role as dominant party to a mere 17% of the total vote, is analogous to the implosion of PASOK. Fine Gael and Labour had gained a large bounce from this, but the years of austerity led to their being severely punished at the polls in February 2016. Even though a Fine Gael-led minority government was eventually formed, that party now had only

25% of the vote share, a fall of 11 points. The electorate's punishment of Labour was even more dramatic. From a vote share of 20% in 2011, it now fell to under 7%, and its seat share dropped below 5%. The outcome of the February 2016 election was the most fragmented Dáil ever, and the longest ever government formation period (Little 2016). One of the most dramatic outcomes, though, was the emergence of a sizeable number of independent deputies, and small leftist alliances, accounting for 20% of voters' first preferences. These fragmented challenger parties and candidates in Ireland mobilised much of their support through campaigns of opposition to some of the more contentious taxes and charges introduced during the years of austerity. A profile of party system fragmentation, and the fragmentation of opinion, was in evidence in Ireland as elsewhere.

But perhaps the most dramatic outcome of the election was the shift in the balance of power between the larger parties. The formerly disgraced Fianna Fáil party made a strong comeback (though less convincing than they had hoped), winning 44 seats to their earlier 21. Sinn Féin posed a challenger-party appeal to Labour voters who felt most aggrieved at austerity measures: it displaced Labour as the third largest party for the first time. But Sinn Féin also posed a potentially more serious longer-term threat to Fianna Fáil's attempts at electoral recovery, because it cultivated a similar kind of populist, cross-class appeal, albeit from a more left-leaning starting-point.

The prospects of forming a stable government were deeply uncertain, and Ireland now entered the same uncharted waters as Portugal and Spain. Political divisions in Spain centred on left and right, political corruption, and Catalan independence; in Portugal, the issues were also about left and right, and also between centre-left and far left. In Ireland, the main party divide still ran along the lines of the historic nationalist divisions, but was now complicated by the programmatically very diverse group of independents and 'others'. The logic of numbers suggested that two of the three largest parties would have to form a coalition, but as in Spain, each had excluded the possibility of coalescing with either of the other two. The minority government formed by Fine Gael was heralded as a form of 'new politics', requiring ongoing external support of the government by Fianna Fáil. But the stability and durability of this arrangement was uncertain in a system designed for strong executive government, weak opposition, and a limited role for the legislature. Ireland was not Spain, in that it succeeded in forming a government eventually. But Ireland was no

Denmark either, which had a long tradition of minority government formation supported by a balanced executive and legislature (Müller and Strøm 2000).

These outcomes can only be understood in the context of initial electoral revulsion at the effects of the crisis, followed by widespread electoral revolt at the terms of the programme of austerity. Political dissent, in Hirschman's formulation, can take the form of exit, voice or loyalty. Overt 'voice' was uncommon in Irish politics (Naughton 2015; Pappas and O'Malley 2014). 'Exit' may have contributed to muting open expressions of dissatisfaction, since about 10% of the young population was estimated to have emigrated during the years of austerity (see Gilmartin, Chapter 12, this volume). But this is not the whole story. Ireland certainly had grievances aplenty, mobilisers to act on them, and the opportunity to be heard (Kriesi 2014). After all, the trade union movement had organised large-scale and well-supported street demonstrations in the early phases of the crisis, in protest at direct public-sector pay cuts, transfer payments, and reduced spending on social services (see Hourigan, Chapter 7, this volume). But to forestall continued clashes, they were willing to enter into negotiations with both of the governments that had held power; the ensuing agreements converted 'voice' into a grudging acquiescence, if not actual 'loyalty'. The later waves of protest, organised by radical left organisations, mostly appealed to the sections of the electorate that did not feel represented by the trade unions—whether because they were unemployed or because they perceived the unions' actions and the Labour Party's concerns to be more beneficial to public-sector than to private-sector employees.

The political effects of austerity on Irish politics were therefore in many ways quite similar to those seen in the other periphery countries. But there was one striking point of difference. Unlike the rest of the Eurozone, the Irish economy in 2014 and 2015 showed signs of renewed growth. Protest vote intentions were strongest during the worst of the recession; an improvement in economic performance took some of the heat from the politics of opposition (Louwerse 2015).

However, the recovery was experienced unevenly. The exporting sector bounced back, and many domestic firms proved quite resilient; but investment, especially in public infrastructure, housing and services, starved by austerity, remained low. Many people continue to be angry about the terms of bank recapitalisation in 2010. Yet bank lending remained highly constrained. The sizeable small and medium enterprise (SME) sector continued to suffer from large debt overhang, and over 1,000 businesses closed during 2015. Ireland's dysfunctional housing market developed many new problems (see Lyons, Chapter 8, this volume). Social services were inadequate; health services were in chaos. The capacity of the fragmented leftists to convert dissatisfaction into protest, protest into votes, and votes into seats—let alone seats into bargaining capacity in government formation—was as yet untested. Meanwhile, a fragmented and potentially unstable party system was a striking political legacy of austerity.

Conclusion

Ireland's experiences of austerity cannot be fully understood without recognising that Ireland, along with the other periphery states in the Eurozone, is embedded in a broader European political economy, and that the economic fortunes of the periphery are not independent of what happens elsewhere. Ireland's budgetary policy continued to be shaped by newly tightened European fiscal rules. Ireland began to escape the pervasive stagnation of the southern periphery because its productive activities were more closely integrated into the Anglo-European economy. Nonetheless, its recovery depended on the congruence of favourable conditions whose continuation was beyond the control of national government, such as the appreciation of the dollar and sterling relative to the euro, low interest rates on still very high sovereign debt and private debt, low oil prices and stability in the wider international economy, including China. The destabilising implications of Brexit for economic performance were particularly feared in Ireland.

Across Europe, established party systems have come under pressure in ways that make existing forms of representative government more difficult. The economic crisis certainly intensified these trends. But these trends also had deeper secular roots in the slow decay of party identification among voters (Marsh 2006; Dalton 2000). Established parties were losing support, and the beneficiaries were new, challenger parties avowing a form of anti-politics, offering a new way of organising, and promising a new set of priorities. Austerity brought citizens' trust in established political parties to a low point in most European countries, lower even than their trust in their national governments. The reason appears simple—increasingly, voters seemed to believe that it mattered little for whom they voted, since the policies of the mainstream parties seemed all too similar. Hence the appeal of parties offering an alternative approach to politics.

The economic crisis may therefore have exposed something more fundamental about European politics, which is that political representation and accountability to voters is increasingly at odds with governments' responsibilities toward actors outside the national territory: this is Peter Mair's analysis (Mair 2013, 2014). Governments incur obligations to comply with EU treaties and rules, but the legitimacy of the EU itself depends heavily on good economic performance. If the EU can offer no hope of a better future, Euroscepticism and even far-right nationalism can flourish at the domestic level (Scharpf 2014), an issue of particular import at present. Governments are also obliged to anticipate the responses of international financial markets to their policy choices. Together, these constraints mean that no single government has the capacity to adopt a heterodox policy stance, a lesson that Greece learned to its great cost in 2015 (Dellepiane and Hardiman 2012; Dellepiane-Avellaneda and Hardiman 2015).

Across Europe, the erosion of old party loyalties, combined with an apparent lack of responsiveness of national parties to voter anxieties about unemployment, stagnating incomes and debt, contributed to a growing sense that there was little to choose between parties. All of this fed into a wider disenchantment with and cynicism about politics itself. Political organisations that offered a politics of greater responsiveness to popular concerns, whether from the left or the right, began to do well in the polls. The left challenger parties in the periphery were not hostile to the EU or to EMU. But the rise of the extreme right from France to Greece, and the accession to power of the nationalist right in Hungary and Poland—and indeed the terms of the debate about Britain's referendum on membership of the EU—articulated an alternative view of national interests that would put more member states increasingly at odds with the EU itself. To some, the European democratic project itself was entrapped by the technocratic logic of the market (Offe 2014); 'Social Europe', it seemed, had first been eroded by the Single Market and then comprehensively buried by EMU. It remained to be seen whether European countries, and the EU itself, could 'get the politics right by enabling citizens greater say over decision-making in ways that serve to rebuild trust while counteracting the rise of the extremes' (Schmidt 2015, p. 112).

6. Austerity and inequality in Ireland

Christopher T. Whelan and Brian Nolan

Introduction

In this chapter we focus on the impact of the economic crisis in Ireland on income levels, poverty and inequality, and also on subjectively assessed economic stress. Conventional measures of poverty and inequality may not adequately capture the complexity of the recession and the multiple ways in which different households were affected. Here we incorporate both the distinctive features of income change during the crisis and what can be learned from a multidimensional perspective going beyond income (Nolan and Whelan 2011). Given the distinctive role played by debt up to and through the crisis, we bring the experience of economic stress and its distribution across income classes into the picture. Chapter 10 of this volume provides a complementary analysis of the impact on children.

Ireland represents a particularly interesting case study of the distributional impact of pronounced macroeconomic fluctuations. The Great Recession has accentuated pre-existing concerns relating to income inequality (Piketty 2014) and the negative impact such inequality may have on a variety of social outcomes (Wilkinson and Pickett 2009). However, recent research on longer-term trends in income inequality may not be of much help in understanding the impact of the recent economic crisis and how that varied across countries—as Eichengreen (2015, p. 470) notes, 'Piketty dismisses the crisis as a blip.' It would also be unwise to assume that the subjective impact of the economic crisis is centrally about the effects of income inequality on social psychological mechanisms relating to factors such as status attainment and social capital, of the sort highlighted by Wilkinson and Pickett. Atkinson and Morelli's (2011) comprehensive analysis of the historical relationship between economic crisis and income inequality concludes that there is no hard and fast pattern; crises differ greatly from each other in their causes and outcomes in terms of inequality. Focusing specifically on the impact of the Great Recession, Jenkins *et al*.'s (2013) comparative study showed that the initial distributional effects varied widely across countries, reflecting differences not only in the nature of the macroeconomic downturn but also in the manner in which taxes and transfers cushioned household net incomes from the full consequences of reductions in market incomes.

In countries most severely affected by the Great Recession, considerable debate has emerged as to where the heaviest burden has fallen. In Ireland claims relating to increasing polarisation have been made by a variety of social critics who have argued that the nature of the 'austerity' policies adopted has involved particular sacrifices for the most vulnerable. This debate has been influenced by a tendency to assume that the Irish case can be read off from general international trends relating to income inequality. Further, as we shall see, evidence on the distributional impact of discretionary policy changes implemented in successive budgets must be interpreted with care, and the overall distributional effect of taxation and welfare policy must also be taken into account. While the dominant theme relating to the impact of the economic crisis in Ireland has related to increased income inequality and a failure to protect the 'vulnerable', the general reduction in living standards, the scale of tax increases, debt and negative housing equity as house prices collapsed, public-sector job and pay cuts, and difficulties experienced by the self-employed have meant that the notion of 'middle-class squeeze' has also been prominent (Whelan *et al.* 2016a, 2016c; Whelan and Maître 2014).

In this chapter we will focus first on the impact of the economic crisis on conventional measures of household income levels, relative income poverty and inequality and income mobility. We will then proceed to an analysis of changing patterns relating to the distribution of economic stress across income classes while locating the patterns seen in Ireland in a comparative context. The analysis is based on data from the European Union Statistics on Income and Living Conditions (EU-SILC) survey carried out by the CSO, the key source tracking the evolution of income and broader circumstances for Irish households.

The evolution of income inequality and poverty

We will not attempt to provide here a description of the extent and nature of the macroeconomic shock that the Great Recession represented for Ireland (see for example Whelan 2014 and McHale, Chapter 2, this volume). The immediate contraction in national output and income was greater than in any other OECD country, so that by 2010 GNP per head in real terms was back to levels seen a decade earlier. Details on the nature of the crisis are provided in Chapter 1 of this volume, but the most striking impact was on unemployment, which soared from 5% to 15%. The initial impact on household incomes was less than that on national output, but by 2012 median disposable household income (adjusting for differences in household size and composition) had fallen by 14% in real terms.

We shall focus first on poverty. Figure 6.1 illustrates that the relative income poverty rate, measuring those in households below 60% of median income, actually fell in the early years of recession from 16.5% to 14.1% before rising again in 2012. This was in a context where median income itself was falling sharply, as we have seen, so the income poverty threshold in such a purely relative measure would also decline. Figure 6.1 also shows the poverty rate when the relative poverty line in 2007 is instead held constant in real terms from then onwards, that is, adjusted for consumer price inflation. By contrast, this 'anchored' poverty rate rose sharply, reaching 24% by 2012. Rates of material deprivation (households reporting enforced absence of two or more items from a set of 11) rose even more sharply, from about 13% before the crisis to 30% by 2012. This affected both those falling below the relative income poverty threshold and those above it. Figure 6.1 also shows that the percentage both below that income threshold and reporting such deprivation (referred to as 'consistent poverty') rose from 4% to 8%.

Given the scale of the macroeconomic shock and its impact on average income, summary measures of inequality in disposable

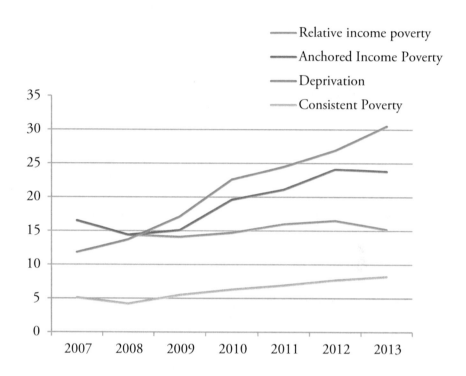

Figure 6.1

Poverty indicators through the crisis

Source: Authors' calculation based on CSO-SILC

Figure 6.2

Decile shares of equivalised disposable income among persons, 2007 to 2013

Source: Authors' calculation based on CSO-SILC

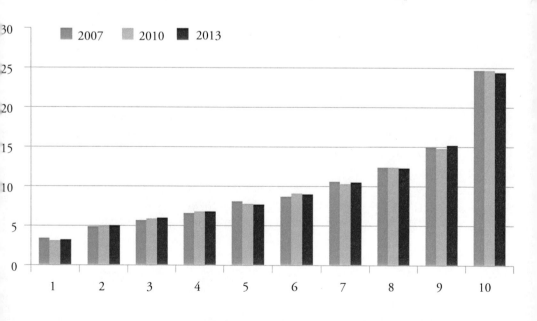

income remained remarkably stable over the recession. The Gini coefficient, the most widely used summary measure of income inequality which ranges from 0 (no inequality) to 1 (maximum inequality), was about 0.31 as the economic boom peaked in 2007, and remained at about that level between then and 2013 apart from 2009, when it fell temporarily to 0.29. Callan *et al.* (2014, 2016) provide some explanation of this given that at the onset of the crisis both effective tax rates and social welfare rates were increased, whereas subsequently cash transfers for working-age recipients were cut. Single summary measures can mask what is happening at different points in the distribution, so Figure 6.2 shows the shares in total disposable income going to each one-tenth (decile) of the distribution before and through the crisis. This also shows considerable stability, although the shares of the bottom and top deciles did fall. As Gornick and Jäntti observe (2013, p. 9), what economists often refer to as the 'middle class' are more accurately described as those in the 'middle' of the income distribution. It is also clear from Figure 6.2 that the shares going to the middle deciles (either deciles 4–6 or 3–7) did not fall, so there was no 'squeeze' of the 'middle' in that sense.

In focusing on 'the middle', an alternative suggested by Atkinson and Brandolini (2013) to examining deciles or quintiles—which by construction relate to equally sized groups—is to look at the numbers in income categories defined as specific percentages of median household income. Here we distinguish 'the income poor', households with incomes below 60% of median equivalised income; those who are 'precarious' or on the 'margins' of poverty, between 60% and 75% of the median; a 'lower middle class' between 75% and 125% of the median; an 'upper middle class' between 125% and 166% of the median; and an affluent class with incomes of 167% of the median or more. Over the recession, the proportion of persons falling into the middle income categories rose modestly, while mean incomes fell sharply for all groups, with the largest declines for the bottom income group, consistent with the decile-based pattern described earlier.

Analysis by Savage *et al.* (2015) sheds further light on what happened to incomes across the distribution over the recession. Average incomes in real terms declined by between 10% and 14% for deciles 2–10, but by 22% for the bottom decile. Such greater losses for the bottom decile are a common feature of the OECD countries worst affected by the crisis, such as Greece and Spain. Outcomes in terms of income levels and distribution were driven by what was happening to incomes from the market, by the way the tax and transfer systems responded 'automatically' to the widespread decline in income from the market, and by the tax and transfer policies adopted in dealing with the fiscal deficit associated with the crisis. Here we do not discuss whether the scale of the tax increases and spending cuts was appropriate (see Chapters 1 and 2 of this volume), but focus on the distributional consequences.

The distributional impact of the policy measures adopted has been the subject of a series of studies by Callan and colleagues using the SWITCH tax-benefit simulation model (see for example Callan *et al.* 2014, 2016; Keane *et al.* 2014; Savage *et al.* 2015). The pattern revealed is that income losses associated with discretionary tax and transfer policy choices were fairly even across the distribution except for the bottom and top deciles, where they were relatively large. Callan *et al.* (2016) show that budgets over the 2009 to 2016 period (including public-sector pay cuts) gave rise to substantial income losses of the order of 8–10% across most of the income distribution, rising to almost 13% for the bottom decile and 14% for the top decile. Savage *et al.* (2015) show that while inequality in market incomes rose sharply, the redistributive impact of the tax and transfer systems taken together also rose substantially, reflecting discrete policy choices made but also the 'automatic stabilisers' which operate through taxes and transfers as household incomes from the market fall.

It is key in interpreting these cross-sectional 'snapshots' that the deciles of the income distribution, or median-based income categories, will not contain the same people from one year to the next. Particularly in such a deep recession, there will be significant re-ranking of individuals throughout the income distribution, so those below the poverty threshold or in the bottom 10% will change from year to year. As Savage *et al.* (2015) show, the fall in average income for the bottom decile was driven by the incomes of those dropping into the bottom 10% rather than located there at the outset. These may include, for example, self-employed suffering major declines in income and falling through the social security safety-net, which in other respects can be seen generally as having provided an effective income floor through the Great Recession. One could be misled into concluding that the greatest income losses were felt by those who were at the bottom of the distribution as the crisis struck.

The changing distribution of economic stress across income classes

In this section, we go beyond income to focus on economic stress and what that reveals about the impact of the crisis in Ireland, put in comparative perspective. Our analysis is based on data from the 2008 and 2012 waves of the EU Survey of Income and Living Conditions (SILC). This choice of years is influenced by the fact that for most countries the income measure in EU-SILC refers to the previous calendar year while in Ireland it refers to the 12 months prior to the interview. We have included 16 economically advanced European countries, comprising the original EU-15 excluding Luxembourg together with Iceland and Norway. Our focus is on individuals residing in households where the Household Reference Person (HRP) is aged 65 or below.

Measuring economic stress

Our measure of economic stress is based on a set of items that are intended to capture debt problems but also capacity to cope with financial demands. Overall we understand the outcome to reflect debt problems directly associated with objective financial circumstances but also with the capacity to adjust to such circumstances and reference groups. Drawing on the items available in EU-SILC, our proposed indicator of economic stress includes items relating to structural arrears, burden of housing costs, and illiquidity in terms of inability to meet unexpected expenses, and adds items relating to debt experiences in the past 12 months and experiencing difficulty in making ends meet. The full set of items is as follows.

1. Households were defined as having a structural problem with arrears where they were unable to avoid arrears relating to mortgage or rent, or utility bills or hire purchase instalments (in the past 12 months). Households experiencing such problems were given values of 1 while the remainder were scored as 0.
2. Illiquidity: Individuals in households indicating that they were unable to cope with unexpected expenses were scored 1 while all others were scored 0.
3. Respondents indicating that housing costs were a 'heavy burden' or 'somewhat of a burden' were scored as 1 while the remaining category was assigned a value of 0.

4. A further indicator of debt was captured by the question 'Has the household had to go into debt within the last 12 months to meet ordinary living expenses such as mortgage repayments, rent, food and Christmas or back-to-school expenses?' A positive answer was scored as 1 while a negative one was assigned a value of 0.
5. Respondents indicating that the household had 'great difficulty' or 'difficulty' in making ends meet were given a value of 1 while the remaining categories were scored as 0.

Each item is weighted by its prevalence in the population, so less frequently experienced stresses (or deprivation) are allocated a proportionately greater weight. The weighted items are then added and this produces a continuous variable that has then been 'normalised' to produce scores ranging from 0 to 1. A score of zero means that the individual is not stressed (or deprived) on any of the items while a score of 1 means that the individual is stressed (or deprived) on all items while intermediate scores reflect the pattern of stress (or deprivation) responses and the prevalence weights at each point in time. The index displays both satisfactory levels of reliability and extremely modest variation across countries (Whelan *et al.* 2016a).

Welfare regimes

The focus in our analysis is on individual countries. However, to bring out the nature of key changes over time we locate results for individual countries in the context of those relating to the welfare regime (Esping-Andersen 1990) to which they are allocated, each of which has its own redistributive logic. We distinguish the following clusters:

- the social democratic regime comprising Sweden, Denmark, Iceland, Finland, Norway and the Netherlands
- the corporatist regime comprising Germany, Austria, Belgium and France
- the liberal regime comprising Ireland and the UK
- the southern European regime comprising Greece, Italy, Portugal and Spain

Economic stress levels by country and welfare regime in 2008 and 2012

In Figure 6.3 we set out the mean levels of economic stress for countries and welfare regimes in 2008 and 2012. The pattern of mean stress levels across countries in 2008, at the beginning of the crisis, was generally in line with what one would expect on the basis of their welfare regime membership. The lowest average level of stress of 0.110 was in the social democratic countries; there was considerable variability within this cluster but all countries in this regime, other than Finland, had lower scores than the other countries in our analysis. The next lowest mean stress level was for the corporatist cluster, with an average of 0.174 and only modest variation across its members, followed by the liberal regime with an average value of 0.208. The highest stress level of 0.282 was observed in the southern European regime, with Italy and Greece at the upper end but within-cluster variance being extremely modest. Overall, stress levels for the corporatist regime were almost 60% higher than for the social democratic cluster; for the liberal group they were twice as high with the mean level for Ireland being 0.225; and for the southern European group almost three times as high.

By 2012, the average stress level for the social democratic regime had increased marginally due to increases in Denmark, the Netherlands and most particularly Iceland, where the mean value increased by over 80% over this short period so it became a clear outlier. For the corporatist regime the mean stress score declined marginally. For the liberal regime the average increased by 0.040, entirely due to an increase of 55% in Ireland, which raised the mean level to 0.349. All of the southern European countries experienced increases in stress levels. For countries other than Greece these ranged from a perhaps surprising low of 4.4% for Portugal to 11.4% for Spain. For Greece the increase was over 50%, which produced a stress level of 0.430, higher than in any of the remaining countries. While average welfare regime scores remained in line with expectations, Iceland, Ireland and Greece, each of which experienced different forms of extreme crisis, exhibited distinctive increases in stress levels so that Ireland and Greece became the countries with the highest stress levels while Iceland rose to equal Portugal.

Income class effects on economic stress for Ireland, Iceland and Greece

At this point we examine the changing impact of income class on economic stress levels in Ireland and provide comparisons with these

Figure 6.3

Mean stress by country, welfare regime and year of survey
(see text for meaning of abbreviations)

Source: Authors' calculations based on EU-SILC

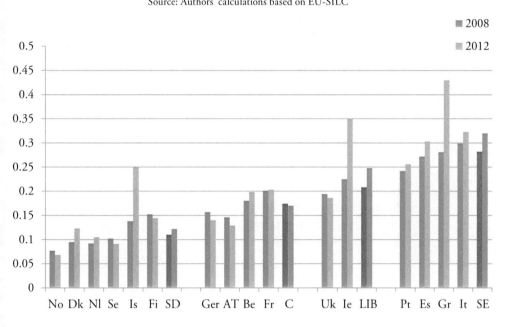

outcomes in Iceland and Greece, each of which has also experienced distinctive overall increases in economic stress levels between 2008 and 2012.

In 2008 Ireland exhibited a hierarchical pattern of income class with differences of 0.309 and 0.329 respectively between the income poor and precarious classes and the most affluent group, with a gradual decline for the remaining categories. Over time stress levels increased for all income class categories. For the income poor group the increase was 0.150, higher than for the precarious class figure of 0.096 and slightly lower than for the lower middle class category, where an increase of 0.159 was observed. For the remaining two higher income classes there was an average additional increase of 0.084. Thus across the board an increase in stress levels was observed but was accompanied by a form of income class differentiation that contrasts the income poor and lower middle class with the upper middle and affluent classes. The precarious class constitutes something of an exception with an observed increase of 0.096, higher than for the two upper classes but a good deal less than for the lower middle class.

The pattern of change for Iceland was somewhat different. In 2008, as in Ireland, there was a clear hierarchical pattern of income class effects, with the stress level for the income poor class being 0.218 higher than for the most affluent income class. In 2012 stress levels increased for all classes in Iceland; however, changes over time in the magnitude of class effects did not display a hierarchical pattern. The largest increase of 0.144 was for the lower middle class category while the next highest increments, of approximately 0.100, were in the adjacent categories, producing a clear curvilinear pattern.

In 2008 stress levels in Greece were somewhat higher than in Ireland. The stress score for the lowest income group was 0.426, which was 0.331 higher than for the most affluent group with the effect displaying a gradual decline across income categories. Over time stress levels increased for all classes, with a pattern of class differentiation closer to the Irish case than the Icelandic one but with a clearer hierarchical element across the three lowest income categories. For the two highest income classes the average increase was approximately 0.100; it was 0.157 for the three lowest classes, with the highest value of 0.185 being observed for the income poor class.

In Figure 6.4 we summarise the changing pattern of income class effects across all three countries. In each case the absolute level of stress increased for the affluent class. However, with the exception of the upper middle class in Greece, in relation to all the remaining classes the relative position of the affluent class improved. Similarly, in all three countries the advantage enjoyed by the upper middle class over the lower middle class increased over time. These effects contribute to a significant degree of class polarisation. However, the overall picture is complicated by other effects. Greece provides the clearest picture of income class polarisation with a significant contrast between increases in stress in the bottom three and top two classes and a clear pattern of hierarchical differentiation within the former. Iceland provides a striking contrast with clear evidence of lower middle class squeeze relative to all other classes and a fairly uniform deterioration in their position relative to the affluent class being observed for the remaining classes.

The Irish case provides a mixed picture. We find evidence of lower middle class squeeze, as in Iceland, but also an increasing disparity between the income poor and all classes other than the lower middle class, as in Greece. However, while changing circumstances and policy

Figure 6.4

Changing income class effects on economic stress between 2008 and 2012

Source:Authors' calculation based on CSO-SILC

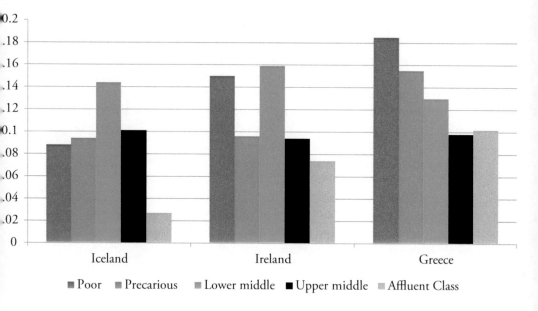

responses exacerbated the position of the income poor, the additional stresses experienced by the precarious class were no greater than for the upper middle class. Thus in the Irish case we observe both polarisation in relation to the income poor and lower middle class squeeze. The differential impact of the crisis across these three countries reflects a variety of factors, including the differing scale and nature of the macroeconomic shock, the role of housing and related debt in Iceland and Ireland, the robustness of the social protection system which was much less developed in Greece, and the external environment which was particularly unfavourable there.

Conclusions

The recession following on the financial crisis had a dramatic impact on incomes in Ireland, with median household incomes down 14% by 2012. The impact on poverty levels, measured *vis-à-vis* relative income thresholds, was much less marked than when a threshold 'anchored' in real terms is used. Deprivation levels rose substantially both for households below and above such income poverty thresholds. Summary measures of income inequality did not increase and the distribution was rather stable, but income losses were most pronounced at the bottom, driven by large income falls for those dropping into the bottom 10% rather than those there at the onset of the crisis.

By 2012 Ireland, Iceland and Greece, which previously fitted predictably into their respective welfare regimes, had become clear outliers in relation to economic stress. All three countries exhibited substantial increases in levels of economic stress associated with the Great Recession. However, in each case the changes in the pattern of income class differentiation were somewhat different. For Ireland the pattern of change over time involved a clear contrast between the income poor and the lower middle classes and the upper middle class and affluent classes. Thus a form of class polarisation coexists with the fact that exposure to significantly higher relative risk of economic stress extended into the lower middle class. In this case income class polarisation does not exclude lower middle class squeeze and is consistent with the pattern of change relating to deprivation. Further analysis focusing on social class is consistent with these findings but reveals the particular difficulties experienced by the non-agricultural self-employed. The situation of the precarious class, which saw its relative position deteriorate significantly less than was the case for the income poor and the lower middle, is a distinctive feature of the Irish pattern and requires further exploration. The Irish experience contrasted with Iceland, where the most substantial increases in stress were around the middle, and Greece, where the three lowest income classes had the greatest increases.

These findings bring out the extent to which the impact of the Great Recession varied even among the hardest-hit countries, and even more so between them and the countries where it represented a less dramatic, though still very substantial, macroeconomic shock. They also serve to highlight the advantages of going beyond reliance on income—in aggregate and at the micro household level—in monitoring and seeking to understand the impact of such a shock.

The fact that the level of income inequality in Ireland was rather stable through the crisis, and the income losses associated with discretionary budgetary measures were broadly proportionate across the income distribution, may seem at variance with much of the commentary about the distributional impact of austerity, with its frequent reference to an inequitable distribution of the burden of fiscal adjustment and failure to protect the vulnerable. This apparent disconnect is itself a topic worth further investigation, but a number of factors may contribute. Clearly there is no straightforward relationship between such distributional outcomes and the manner in which the electorate has experienced and responded to the recession and associated 'austerity' measures. Responses to 'austerity' will have been mediated *inter alia* by the extent to which it was considered unavoidable or misconceived, imposed by the troika versus domestically determined, or reflecting previous policy failures versus neoliberal ideology (as discussed in a number of the earlier chapters). The focus on the costs of bailing out the bank system as opposed to other factors contributing to the fiscal deficit clearly played an important role in framing perceptions and responses.

More broadly, themes of increased inequality, failure to protect the vulnerable and lack of 'fairness' clearly had considerable public resonance. The role played by the welfare and taxation systems in buffering the effects of the crisis does not appear to have been generally appreciated, while budgetary choices about tax and social welfare spending figured prominently in political and popular debates despite the evidence that these were progressive in the immediate response to the crisis and broadly proportional overall. However, it is difficult to account for political and electoral consequences of the economic crisis and the significant legitimacy gap emerging between a large proportion of the electorate and the established parties, as Hardiman *et al.* document in Chapter 5 of this volume, purely in terms of inequality and direct redistribution. Instead, we would argue that it is necessary to focus on how reductions in real living standards, increased debt levels and cuts in public services led to unprecedented increases in levels of economic vulnerability and stress, substantially changing the profiles of those exposed to such outcomes as the association between income and deprivation and economic stress weakened.

Whelan and Maître (2014, p. 483) observed that while up to that point economic contraction and austerity had provoked little in the way of disruption or social conflict, dealing with the political pressures arising from a 'middle class squeeze' while sustaining the social welfare arrangements that have traditionally protected the economically vulnerable presents formidable challenges in terms of maintaining social cohesion and political legitimacy. How formidable those challenges were was revealed in the response provoked by attempts to broaden the tax base through the Universal Social Charge and raise revenue from property taxes and payment for services and utilities. Discussion of these issues goes well beyond the scope of this chapter (see Chapters 5 and 7 in this volume). However, the evidence we have presented in this chapter, together with some of the other contributions, make it clear that simply characterising such responses in terms of opposition to increasing inequality and a neoliberal agenda would be a gross oversimplification.

7. Austerity, resistance and social protest in Ireland: movement outcomes

Niamh Hourigan

Introduction

The varying protest responses of European societies to structural adjustment programmes imposed by the European Union/European Central Bank/International Monetary Fund after the 2008 banking crisis have been one of the most intriguing sociological dimensions of the recent global economic recession. During the early years of the crisis, Ireland and Greece were often portrayed in the international media at opposing ends of a spectrum of protest, with Ireland indeed politically positioning itself in this way (Borooah 2014). The Greeks were characterised as taking to the streets in significant numbers to protest against austerity while Irish citizens meekly accepted their fate. Detailed research on protest in each context demonstrates that this contrast has been overdrawn (Pappas and O'Malley 2014; Power *et al.* 2015; Karyotis and Rudig 2015; Hearne 2015). However, a number of distinctive features of the Irish protest response to austerity merit critical consideration.

This chapter begins by mapping the four overlapping phases of Irish anti-austerity protest between 2008 and 2016, which can be characterised as (1) early single-issue protests, (2) muted protest, (3) popular mobilisation, (4) deepening confrontation leading to political realignment. The achievements of the Irish anti-austerity movement are considered in light of research on social movement outcomes (Gamson 1975; Giugni *et al.* 1999; Amenta *et al.* 2010). Within this literature, the successes and failures of social movements are examined in terms of three key criteria: goal attainment, changes to systems of interest representation, and value transformation. An assessment of the impact of these movements on values will focus particularly on attitudes towards cronyism and corruption that were identified as a contributory factor to the Irish banking crisis (Honohan 2009; Regling and Watson 2010; Nyberg 2011; Ross 2010; O'Toole 2010).

Social movement outcomes

During the mid-twentieth century, social movement theorists tended to portray social protest as the political response of marginalised citizens to grievance. Margit Mayer (1995, p. 172) notes that 'as spontaneous, essentially expressive outbursts social movements are not accorded, in the long run, the capacity to influence societal development or policy outcomes. Only parties, interest groups and leadership strata have this capacity.' However, analysis of the outcomes of social protest in the United States in the post-war period generated increasing optimism about the efficacy of social movements. William Gamson (1975) examined 53 social movements and found that they succeeded in producing significant social and political change. In developing a framework through which 'success' could be measured, he distinguished between 'tangible changes to public policy' and 'changes to systems of interest representation' (Della Porta and Diani 1999, p. 208). Analysts studying European social movements have devoted greater attention to the role that social movements play in generating value transformation (Touraine 1971, 1981; Melucci 1984, 1989). Research on social movement outcomes by these European 'new' social movement scholars has focused on the capacity of social movements to introduce their core ideologies into mainstream public debates (Eder 1996). As well as changing voting patterns and making policy gains, these movements may seek to change the lifestyle and belief systems of ordinary citizens to accord with their values as they believe the 'personal is political' (Scott 1996).

Social movement scholars have more recently focused on the tensions between the three types of social movement outcomes: goal attainment, interest representation and value transformation.

Drawing on Amenta *et al.* (2010), McVeigh *et al.* (2014, p. 1146) note that a social movement that fails to achieve short-term policy change may in fact 'produce significant social change, while a movement that achieves its goals may have only a minimal impact on society at large'. In addition, Giugni *et al.* (1999) have noted that some of the most significant changes wrought by social movements can be the unintended consequences of activism, envisaged neither by social movement activists nor by political elites. Each of these factors will be considered in assessing the outcomes of Irish anti-austerity protests between 2008 and 2016.

Phases of anti-austerity protest

As outlined in the introduction to the chapter, four overlapping phases of Irish anti-austerity protest can be identified since the crisis in the Irish banking system became apparent in 2008.

Phase 1: Early single-issue movements

In 2008, international market unease about the stability of Irish banks coupled with the collapse of major European and American banks contributed to a crisis in the Irish banking system. The government tried and failed to rebuild market confidence with the provision of a blanket guarantee of Irish bank debt (Donovan and Murphy 2013). As outlined earlier in this volume, this was accompanied by significant cuts to public spending including the removal of medical cards from some old age pensioners and increasing third-level tuition fees (Allen and O'Boyle 2013). These early austerity cuts were met with a robust protest response. On 22 October 2008, 15,000 pensioners and 10,000 students converged on Dáil Éireann to express their dissatisfaction with these changes. However, as the scale of the Irish banking crisis became apparent in 2009, levels of protest diminished significantly.

Phase 2: Muted protest

By early 2010 it had become clear that the Irish state would not have the resources to honour its commitment under the 2008 bank guarantee. Rumours of high-level talks about an EU/IMF/ECB bailout began circulating. In November 2010, the Governor of the Irish Central Bank announced on radio that Ireland would have to enter a bailout programme (Donovan and Murphy 2013). The rapidity of the decline of the Irish economy coupled with poor communication from government officials contributed to a level of shock and panic that appeared to have a muting effect on social protest. As the bailout agreement was being signed, 50,000 people protested in Dublin in November. Pappas and O'Malley (2014, p. 1598) note that after this protest 'one union Mandate suggested that it would plan a campaign of civil disobedience and national strike. However, none ever materialized.'

Occupy camps were visible in a number of Irish cities and the small Co. Cork town of Ballyhea began its long-running 'Ballyhea says No' campaign in response to the bailout. However, these protests received nothing like the popular support for resistance to austerity evident in other bailout countries at the time. The Fianna Fáil/ Green coalition experienced one of the worst defeats of any post-war European government at the general election, indicating significant levels of public anger about the bailout (Farrell *et al.* 2011). Hardiman points out in Chapter 5 of this volume that the Fine Gael/Labour coalition that replaced it pursued largely the same policies, supported by the national media which, as Mercille explains in Chapter 4, broadly endorsed the view that there was no alternative to austerity. As the range of cuts and new taxes increased in 2012, it became clear that levels of protest were about to escalate.

Phase 3: Popular mobilisation

The introduction of the Household Charge, an interim property tax, in 2012 changed the dynamic of anti-austerity protest in Ireland. This new tax generated a level of resistance that grew steadily during that year, building popular support for the Irish anti-austerity movement (O'Flynn *et al.* 2013). Half of those liable for the charge did not pay, and in 2013 it was replaced by a centrally collected property tax. If the anti-household charge and property tax campaigns brought more coherence to the anti-austerity movement, the issue of water charges provided the catalyst for much wider levels of protest (Power *et al.* 2015). In 2013 a utility company, Irish Water, was established, taking over the responsibility for water provision from local authorities. The government announced the installation of water meters at every home, 90% of which would be installed by the end of 2014, when water charges would be introduced. The physical installation of water meters in 2014 brought austerity onto the doorstep of thousands of Irish citizens, prompting a robust protest response at local level (Hearne 2015).

The last three months of 2014 witnessed three large-scale national protests which built on support garnered through local community protests against the installation of water meters. On 11 October, the first national day of action, groups organised under the banner 'Right2Water' were expecting about 10,000 to attend their protest in Dublin. The final attendance figure was closer to 80,000. The same day MEP Paul Murphy, who was closely associated with the anti-water charges campaign, won the Dublin South-West by-election. In response, the government announced that Irish Water customers would be entitled to €100 relief on their bills but this concession did little to dampen public anger. On 1 November, the second mass day of action against water charges, over 100,000 protesters turned out. On 6 November the government suffered an embarrassing defeat in the Oireachtas (Irish parliament) when Labour senators backed an opposition motion to decide whether Irish Water should remain in public ownership. In the Dáil (lower house of parliament) on 19 November, the government announced a revised charging structure whereby charges were reduced to two flat rates until the end of 2018. It was hoped that this climb-down would take much of the energy out of the water campaign. While the numbers of protesters were lower at the 10 December march, even official Garda (police) figures estimated an attendance of 30,000 (Hearne 2015).

Phase 4: Deepening confrontation and political realignment

Irish anti-austerity protest entered a fourth distinct phase in late 2014. On 7 November, Minister Leo Varadkar argued that a more confrontational dynamic was emerging within the anti-water charge campaign led by the 'sinister fringe' of the Irish anti-austerity movement. Power *et al.* (2015, p. 15) comment:

> The term 'sinister fringe' (and to a lesser extent 'sinister element') formed a significant part of the state's discursive armoury in the battle for hearts and minds … it was subsequently used routinely by the political elite in their attempts to fragment and undermine the legitimacy of the protests.

A number of incidents intensified this confrontational dynamic between the government and protesters. Tánaiste (Deputy Prime Minister) Joan Burton was trapped in her car for two hours after she attended an event in Jobstown on 15 November 2014. On 20 November, Fine Gael TD Noel Coonan compared water protesters to ISIS and commented that Dublin protesters wanted to 'act like parasites' and 'live off country people'. At the end of January 2015, footage emerged of water protester Derek Byrne calling President Michael D. Higgins a 'midget parasite' because he had signed the water legislation into law. On 23 February 2015, Gardaí (police officers) had to be called to a meeting of Cork City Council after it was invaded by water protesters. In February 2015, more than 20 people believed to have been associated with the detaining of Joan Burton in Jobstown were arrested. While in prison, three of the protesters went on hunger strike. In July 2015, levels of confrontation increased again when water protesters prevented politicians from leaving Dáil Éireann (Brophy 2015).

The mass protests that had been such a prominent feature of the anti-water charge campaign in 2014 did not entirely disappear in 2015. Protests on 27 March and 29 August in Dublin involved over 80,000 participants according to the Right2Water campaign. After the latter protest, groups associated with Right2Water announced that they were establishing a more broadly based political movement called Right2Change. They released a statement:

> Water charges have proven a tipping point, but the hundreds of thousands who have marched since last October—culminating in today's massive demonstration of people power, which saw between 80,000 and 100,000 take to the streets of Dublin—have been marching about much more. From cuts in Lone Parent payments to the homelessness crisis which this summer saw nearly 2,000 adults and over 1,000 children in emergency accommodation in our capital city, it's clear that the economic recovery being trumpeted by the Government is not a people's recovery ... Politics is about choices, and the wrong choices have been made. (www.Right2Change.ie)

They also released a policy document which broadened the agenda of the movement, focusing not just on the right to water but also the right to health, education, housing and work, all of which, they argued, had been undermined by austerity programmes. The Right2Change umbrella became a key focus for political alignment among parties and individuals on the left of the Irish political spectrum in the run-up to the general election in February 2016, though it did not succeed in completely uniting these groups.

As the general election campaign gathered momentum, polls indicated that the water charge issue would have an impact on the outcome (Donnelly 2015). In mid-January, Fianna Fáil leader Micheál Martin pledged to abolish Irish Water if elected, though his party had supported the introduction of water charges in 2010. However, as Niamh Hardiman explains clearly in Chapter 5, the outcome of the 26 February election was indeterminate. The ruling coalition parties, Fine Gael and Labour, lost too many seats to form a majority government. Fianna Fáil didn't gain sufficient seats to form an alternative government, while Sinn Féin remained broadly aloof from government formation negotiations. Ultimately, Fine Gael formed a minority-led government with the support of a number of independent TDs and the Fianna Fáil, who technically remained in opposition. Crucial to securing the support of Fianna Fáil for this administration was an agreement to suspend water charges for a period of nine months while 'an expert commission considers a sustainable model of funding water services' (O'Halloran 2016).

In June 2016, MEP Marian Harkin tabled a parliamentary question to EU Environmental Commissioner Karmenu Vella asking if Ireland's earlier method of paying for water through general taxation, which was in place when Ireland adopted the EU Water Framework Directive in 2003, was still valid. In his response, Commissioner Vella indicated that Ireland has signed up to Article 9(4) of the Framework Directive, which sets down 'strict conditions' related to water charges. He indicated that as the Irish government had introduced the concept of water charges in 2010, it no longer enjoyed 'flexibility' on the water charge issue and would have to instigate some form of water charge regime under the directive (Downing and Doyle 2016). This robust response suggests that the complete abolition of water charges may be a very difficult goal to achieve in the long term. However, the suspension of water charges led to a very significant reduction in the numbers attending anti-water charge protests in 2016.

Protest outcomes

Goal attainment

An overview of the successes and failures of the Irish anti-austerity movement between 2008 and 2016 from a goal attainment perspective suggests that the movement did have some capacity to directly alter public policy. All the major welfare cuts identified in the original agreement with the troika were implemented during this period (O'Flynn *et al.* 2014, Hearne 2015). However, the anti-water charge campaign was more successful in terms of generating specific changes to policy (Power *et al.* 2015). In his cross-country analysis of anti-nuclear movements of the 1980s, Herbert Kitschelt (1986) divided the analysis of social movement policy gains into those that were procedural, substantial and structural. In terms of this division, the Irish anti-water charge movement's policy gains have been substantial so far. Right2Water succeeded in having water charges significantly reduced and then suspended in 2016. The question of whether these policy gains will prove to be structural is, as yet, unclear. While Fianna Fáil and other parties have sought the abolition of Irish Water, the European Commission has maintained a robust stance, insisting that some form of water charge regime must be introduced. Ireland remains locked into the European Water Framework Directive and as Kieran Allen indicates in Chapter 3 of this volume, the Commission along with other European institutions has been successful in imposing a range of top-down austerity measures on the Irish state since 2010.

Changes to systems of interest representation

During the early austerity period in Ireland, politicians themselves appeared to believe that protest responses to austerity were muted because Irish citizens expressed their discontent so forcefully through the ballot box. Labour Minister Ruairí Quinn commented: 'Unlike Greece, Spain and Portugal where there were riots in the streets and all sorts of disruptions, the people held their breaths and waited for the ballot box and dropped the grenade silently into the ballot box' (*Irish Independent* 2014). The general election of February 2011 delivered the sitting coalition one of the worst defeats of any post-war European government (Little 2011). While the new ruling Fine Gael/Labour coalition had a comfortable majority, parties and individual candidates strongly associated with an anti-austerity position also made significant gains. Sinn Féin increased its seats in the Dáil from five to fourteen. Parties gathered under the umbrella of the United Left Alliance won five seats, while nine independent candidates were elected (Farrell *et al.* 2011).

Given the increased levels of activism in 2013 and 2014, the European and local elections of 2014 were a significant test of the impact of the anti-austerity movement on systems of interest representation. At local level, Sinn Féin won 105 additional seats to bring its total local representatives up to 159, making it the third largest party in local government. People Before Profit and the Anti-Austerity Alliance won 28 seats between them, providing a further endorsement of the anti-austerity position. Government parties lost 186 seats between them; Fianna Fáil, which had been largely blamed for the crisis, gained 49 seats. The European election result presents an even more complex picture. Sinn Féin gained three seats, making it the second largest Irish party in terms of European representation, and independent candidates won three. However, Fine Gael retained its four seats while Fianna Fáil lost two (Kavanagh 2015).

The centrality of the water charge issue to anti-austerity politics in Ireland becomes abundantly clear when the results of the 2016 General Election are examined. Fine Gael and Labour, who continued to champion water charges throughout the campaign, lost 42 seats between them. The Labour Party—led by Joan Burton, who, as Minister for Social Protection, had implemented a range of cuts to welfare payments—lost 26 seats, falling to just seven representatives in the parliament. Parties on the left who were associated with the anti-austerity movement all made gains. Sinn Féin gained nine seats, bringing its total to 23, while the Anti-Austerity Alliance/People Before Profit gained two, bringing their total to six. In addition, the majority of rural independent candidates who were elected opposed water charges (O'Regan 2016). However, Fianna Fáil proved more successful at resisting the encroachment of anti-austerity politics from the left. The party ran its campaign on the slogan 'A Fairer Ireland', communicating a subtle anti-austerity message, and announced its intention to abolish Irish Water before the election. Getting Fianna Fáil to alter its position on the water charge issue is regarded by leaders of Right2Water/Right2Change as one of their most significant achievements (Gibney 2016).

The groups and organisations associated with the Right2Water campaign were drawn from across the ideological spectrum of Irish politics, with socialist parties, community organisations and more right-wing groups such as Direct Democracy Ireland coalescing around the water issue. As parties on the left were more consistent in their opposition to water charges, it is not surprising that they may have benefited more from the momentum that gathered around the campaign. However, the unwillingness of the same parties to engage in government formation negotiations after the election limited their impact on a broader system of interest representation in Ireland. Rory Costello (2016) has argued that as Fianna Fáil positioned itself in the centre during the campaign, it should have been in a strong position to open government formation negotiations with parties on the left after the election. However, some form of alliance with centre-right Fine Gael became the only option because parties on the left 'washed their hands of the whole thing' and 'ruled out negotiating with civil war parties [Fianna Fáil and Fine Gael]' in his view. Costello concludes:

> Of course, this may be in the long-term strategic interests of those parties. But it is a clear abandonment of their voters, who elected them based on their policies. Once in opposition, these parties will have little or no influence over government policy, yet this is exactly where they seem to want to be.

In their analysis of the impact of social movements on systems of interest representation, McVeigh *et al.* (2014, p. 1148) note that take-off issues (such as water charges) 'can produce a notable shuffling of social relations and interaction patterns ... Social movements, therefore, may not simply influence individual opinions in the short term—they can also embed people within new social relations that hinge upon support or opposition to a movement and its goals.' Despite its limited impact on government formation, the anti-austerity movement has provided some support for this analysis. The movement has succeeded in eroding support for established political parties, particularly those who didn't support its core goals. Fianna Fáil's *volte-face* on the water charge issue was perhaps the strongest demonstration of the anti-water charge campaign's political influence. Whether the various independent politicians and parties on the left associated with the anti-austerity movement can develop into a more coherent alliance challenging the dominance of the centre-right parties remains to be seen.

Anti-austerity protest and value change in Ireland

In order to assess the impact of Irish anti-austerity protests on value change, it is important to examine the causes of the banking crisis. One would assume that values perceived to have contributed to the economic crash would be the focus of criticism by social movement activists. The Irish government commissioned a series of reports by

Patrick Honohan (2009), Regling and Watson (2010) and Peter Nyberg (2011), which highlighted how weak rules and poor implementation of regulatory systems contributed to the financial crash. At the same time, a number of Irish journalists published books that suggested that strong personal relationships among Irish political, banking and business elites were the basis for a form of cronyism that contributed to the banking crash (Ross 2010; O'Toole 2010). A feature of the 2011 and 2012 period was increased criticism of cronyism by leaders of the anti-austerity movement. Independent TDs Clare Daly, Luke 'Ming' Flanagan, Mick Wallace and Richard Boyd Barrett devoted particular attention to the practice of penalty points for traffic offences being corruptly cancelled by the police. Their actions, along with the statements of Garda whistle-blowers, resulted in the resignations of both the Garda Commissioner and the Minister for Justice in 2014 (Kelly 2014).

In 2015, the theme of cronyism became a direct focus for the Irish anti-austerity movement. Independent TD Catherine Murphy raised questions in the Dáil about the circumstances surrounding the establishment of Irish Water. She focused on the awarding of the contract for the installation of water meters to Sierra Support Services Group, a subsidiary of Siteserv: a company owned by businessman Denis O'Brien, who has close links with Fine Gael. She demanded details of loan agreements between O'Brien and the state bank, IBRC. In May 2015, Denis O'Brien was granted an injunction against the national broadcaster RTÉ to prevent it from disseminating details of his loan agreements. Murphy subsequently repeated details of these agreements in the Dáil under the mantle of Dáil privilege (McGee 2015). Meanwhile the anti-austerity movement focused some of its street protests on O'Brien, featuring his image on placards and using campaign cries of 'Denis the Menace'. The issue tapped into a deep pre-existing anger about cronyism, which Rory Hearne identified in his survey of activists involved in the anti-water charge movement:

> The responses to the survey clearly show that the water protests are an expression of people's anger against the cumulative impacts of austerity, the injustice of the 'socialisation' of the banking debts, inequality, corruption and cronyism, and the 'give-away' of Ireland's natural resources. (Hearne 2015, p. 9)

However, this ideological focus within the Irish anti-austerity movement does not appear to have had significant impact on attitudes to cronyism in the wider Irish population.

Elaine Byrne's (2011) study of corruption in Ireland demonstrated that although Irish citizens have had a keen awareness of corruption since the 1990s, this has not had a significant impact on their voting choices. She cites an MRBI poll conducted in 1991, which found:

> A total of 89 per cent agreed that 'there is a Golden Circle of people in Ireland who are using power to make money for themselves'. Some 81 per cent agreed that the people in this Golden Circle were made up in equal measure of business people and politicians. Some 76 per cent thought the scandals were part and parcel of the Irish economic system rather than one-off events. (Byrne 2011, p. 107)

During the 1990s and 2000s, a succession of tribunals in Ireland investigated corruption. However, individual politicians and political parties who had been involved in corrupt practices received little formal sanction, and parliamentarians such as Michael Lowry TD were re-elected following criticism in tribunal reports.

Data on perceptions of corruption in Ireland underline the continuing complexity of public attitudes. Transparency International lists Ireland on its corruption perception index (CPI), while Eurobarometer has carried out two general surveys on attitudes to corruption in Ireland during the austerity period. Even before the banking crisis, Ireland's ranking in the CPI scale had declined from 11th in 1995 to 17th out of the 180 countries listed in 2007. After the bailout, it appeared that Ireland was perceived as more corrupt, with the country ranking 19th in 2011 and 25th in 2012 after the publication of two tribunal reports. Between 2013 and 2014, when the anti-water charges campaign became more active, Ireland's ranking in the CPI actually improved, returning to 17th in 2014, although the country fell one place to 18th in 2015 (www.transparency.org).

The two Eurobarometer studies, which sample a wider selection of the Irish population, also demonstrate a complex pattern. In 2011, the 'Attitudes of Europeans towards Corruption' study (published in 2012) found that 86% of Irish people thought that corruption was a problem in Ireland, up 1 percentage point from 2009. While 70%

of Irish people did not believe the government was doing enough to combat corruption, there was a 3 percentage point decline in those who believed that corruption existed in national and local institutions. There was a further 4 percentage point decline in those who believed that politicians at local and national levels were taking bribes for personal gain. A second Eurobarometer study, carried out in 2013 when anti-austerity protests had become more visible and published in 2014, indicated that 81% of Irish people believed that corruption was a problem in Ireland, a 5 percentage point decline since 2011. Therefore, anti-austerity protests did not appear to have a substantial impact on attitudes to corruption, although the slippage of one place in the CPI index in 2015 might reflect concerns raised by the IBRC controversy (Leahy 2015).

Conclusion

After the 2010 bank bailout, the Irish public surprised international commentators with its relatively muted protest response to the EU/ECB/IMF fiscal adjustment programme. However, as welfare cuts and new taxes deepened in 2012, levels of protest increased. In terms of goal attainment, the achievements of the Irish anti-austerity movement were relatively limited between 2008 and 2016, with no major reversals to the significant welfare cuts introduced during this period. The anti-water charges campaign has been more successful, with an initial reduction followed by a temporary suspension of water charges in 2016. While this represents a substantial achievement for a social movement, it is important to acknowledge that the scale of water charges is small when compared to the broader spectrum of public service, welfare cuts and new taxes such as the property tax introduced under austerity in Ireland.

In terms of changes in values related to corruption, the outcome of Irish anti-austerity protest is also quite mixed. Perceptions of levels of corruption in Ireland that were very high in 2011 and 2012 appeared to decrease from 2013 onwards, the period when the Irish anti-austerity movement was most active.

The most significant legacy of the Irish anti-austerity campaign may be its impact on the system of interest representation. Since 2011, parties and individuals associated with the Irish anti-austerity movement have had considerable success at local, national and European elections. The anti-water charge campaign has served as a very effective focal point for convergence between independent TDs and parties such as Sinn Féin, People Before Profit and the Anti-Austerity Alliance. It is too early to say whether these linkages will lead to the long-term decline of the so-called 'civil war' divide which has dominated Irish politics since the 1920s (Farrell 1999). Nevertheless, it is clear that the Irish anti-austerity movement has brought a new level of inter-organisational cooperation and political visibility to those on the left of the Irish political spectrum that may have considerable influence on Irish politics for many years to come.

8. Housing and austerity: a two-way street

Ronan Lyons

Context

This volume opens with a chapter by Simon Wren-Lewis on a general theory of austerity. Underpinning it is a desire for policymakers—as well as the social sciences—to learn from the experience of austerity over the past decade. In particular, Wren-Lewis makes the point that austerity was, at a global level, unnecessary. The footnote to this finding is that, in particular countries, austerity at a national level was unavoidable.

Ireland's recent economic history is not only remarkable but also incredibly useful, if policy makers are to learn lessons. The economic journey from 'the poor man of Western Europe' in the late 1980s, through the export-led growth of the 1990s and the credit-led growth of the early 2000s, to the sharp economic contraction in the years after 2007 contains much for other small open economic regions to learn. This is particularly true in the context of a region—Ireland—largely dependent on one city of global significance (Dublin), where that region lacks its own monetary policy and recourse to the traditional levers of trade policy to react to economic shocks. Exposed to global economic tailwinds, and later headwinds, and with an inadequate domestic policy response, two key aspects of the local economy—government spending and housing—bore much of the brunt of Ireland's economic contraction.

With Ireland once again one of Western Europe's fastest growing economies, it is tempting for policy makers locally to assume that lessons have been learned, or perhaps that Ireland was unlucky in its exposure to global shocks. It is the aim of this chapter to show that the poor management of two key domestically focused sectors contributed separately and jointly to the severity of the economic correction in Ireland. In so doing, it hopes to highlight some key themes for policy makers to take away from Ireland's experience of austerity and housing.

The bulk of the chapter is organised around two key relationships. The first is the contribution that the housing sector made initially to the huge expansion in government spending and thus, by corollary, in austerity. Whereas that section focuses on the effect of housing on austerity, the next section focuses on the reverse: the impact austerity has had on the housing sector in Ireland. The penultimate section draws out the policy implications of the preceding analysis, outlining principles that could act as the foundation for housing policy into the future.

From housing to austerity

As of 2007, on the cusp of austerity, Ireland's steady state rate of economic growth was thought to be at least 5% a year. In such a world, permanent increases in public sector spending were not thought serious risks, as over a decade of strong growth had meant almost no net gain in national debt and a fall in debt to national income from over 100% to below 30%. Figure 8.1 shows projected nominal GDP, in billions of euro, from 2004 to 2020, across a range of IMF World Economic Outlook reports from 2007 to 2015. As can be seen, there was a clear downward revision of expected future growth between 2008 and 2009, coinciding with the Global Financial Crisis. Thereafter, there was very little change in the expected size of the economy in the future, for five years. Only in the 2015 World Economic Outlook report was the future growth path of the Irish economy revised upwards again.

What this means in practical terms is that the economy in 2013 was roughly one third smaller than policy makers—local and international—had expected it to be as recently as 2008. In the 2013 forecasts, the economy was only expected to surpass €250 billion in

Figure 8.1

Projected nominal GDP (billions of euro) 2004–2020, from IMF World
Economic Outlook reports 2007–2015

Source: IMF, *World Economic Outlook*, various years

WEO 2015
WEO 2014
WEO 2013
WEO 2012
WEO 2011
WEO 2010
WEO 2009
WEO 2008
WEO 2007

size in 2018, 10 years 'behind schedule' if one compares with the 2007
World Economic Outlook report. This matters because the size of the
economy represents the full base of activity that can be taxed and, in
practical terms, annual output (a flow) is compared to national debt
(a stock), with the rule of thumb being that the latter should be no
greater than the former. Where national debt exceeds annual output,
economic growth must exceed the interest on debt in order for the
debt burden to remain manageable.

The sharp and unexpected contraction in the general economy thus
had a clear impact on the public finances but also an impact directly on
the housing market. As average incomes declined, and as unemployment rose sharply from 5% to 15%, demand for housing contracted.
The direct channel—fewer households can afford the same house

prices—is amplified by the fact that housing is an asset on the household's balance sheet. Work by John Muellbauer (2007) and Jiri Slacalek (2006) outlines the potential for housing to have wealth effects and collateral effects on the real economy, including personal consumption. As housing prices rose, homeowners consumed out of their new housing wealth—but the same holds true in reverse and thus as house prices fell, consumption fell. The importance of this in terms of government capacity to tax and spend was a sustained increase in permanent spending commitments by central government. Between 2000 and 2007, gross public spending more than doubled, from €26bn to €56bn. Much of this increase was in the form of expanded transfer payments and higher salaries to public servants, with significant extra spending committed through an expensive public sector pay benchmarking exercise.

This very substantial increase in spending occurred without any substantial addition to national debt, being funded instead through taxation revenues. This balancing of spending with receipts was a key risk, as it was ultimately just an illusion of fiscal prudence. Much of the tax receipts was temporary in nature, and predicated on an excessive property sector as illustrated by McHale (Chapter 2, this volume). For example, between 2000 and 2006, an estimated €6bn in extra revenues came from three areas directly related to the housing market. The first category is income tax receipts from the construction sector, which grew from fewer than 150,000 workers to more than 250,000. This, combined with increased average earnings, drove direct income tax receipts from construction up from less than €1bn in 2000 to over €2bn in 2006. Excluded from this are other occupations where employment levels grew as a result of the housing boom, including estate agents, financial institutions and related retail, such as furniture.

The second key category of temporary receipts was VAT receipts on newly built homes. Between 2000 and 2007, the number of new homes built roughly doubled, as did their average value. The net result was an increase in estimated VAT receipts from new homes from less than €1bn in 2000 to more than €3.2bn in 2006. The third and final major category of temporary tax revenues was stamp duty receipts, which were measured directly in government accounts and were dominated by transactions in housing and in related goods, such as development land. Between 2000 and 2006, stamp duty receipts rose from €1.1bn to €3.7bn.

Thus, even from just these three direct areas where housing fed in to receipts, it is clear that housing was a key contributor to the increase

Figure 8.2

Revenues from stamp duty, VAT, and income tax, 2000 to 2014

Source: calculations based on Department of Finance figures)

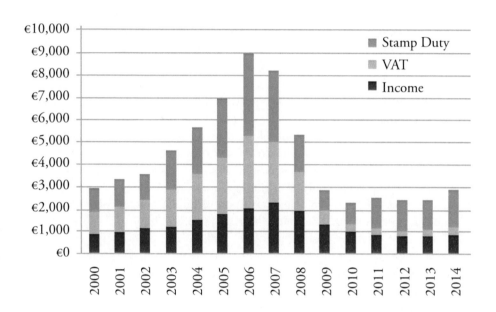

in public spending in the final years before austerity (see also Julien Mercille, Chapter 4, this volume, for the impact of property on revenues in another key sector, the media). The figures presented above, based on Department of Finance publications, suggest that property-related revenues rose from €3bn in 2000 to €9bn in 2006. An overview of revenues from these three sources, from 2000 to 2014, is presented in Figure 8.2.

The sharp decline in economic activity in Ireland after 2007 included an end to the credit-fuelled housing bubble, with a dramatic fall in prices and an even more dramatic fall in construction activity. While prices fell by 55% on average—slightly less for larger properties, and slightly more for apartments—activity in the housing market fell by close to 90%. This is true across a number of measures of activity, including transaction volumes and construction of new homes. As a result, what had become a key component of government revenues evaporated. As shown in Figure 8.2, revenues from income tax, VAT and stamp duty directly related to housing fell from an estimated

€9bn in 2006 to just €2.5bn in 2010. This is a gap that has persisted through to the time of writing (2016).

While as part of various 'austerity measures' (Callan *et al.* 2011), an annual Local Property Tax has been introduced, its revenues are roughly one tenth of the revenues from stamp duties prior to 2006. It is also true that the rate levied in Ireland (at 0.18% of the market value) is significantly below many other developed countries. In many parts of the US, annual property taxes are 1% of the market value or more. Such high property taxes not only provide a sustainable revenue base for local government, they are associated with less volatile housing market cycles, through imposing greater holding costs of property.

The final element of exploring the path from housing to austerity is to note the role played by housing in government spending, rather than government receipts. The extra expenditure by the government was spent roughly proportionately on housing. Public spending on housing comprised about 2.7% of all government spending through-out the period 2004–08. The proportion of public monies spent on housing had increased substantially from 1.6% in 1999 to 3.4% in 2001, before falling back to this level. This meant that, on the eve of austerity, just short of 1% of GDP was being spent annually on housing by the government. The total level of government spending (left-hand scale) and the fraction of government spending and of GDP spent on housing (right-hand scale) for the period 1995–2015 is shown in Figure 8.3. Overall, the link between housing and austerity is probably best highlighted by the aggregate statistics: the €10bn fall in government spending during austerity is in large part accounted for by a €6.5bn fall in property-related government revenues during the same period. In this context, austerity became more or less unavoida-ble, as outlined by John McHale in Chapter 2 of this volume.

A note is worthwhile on the topic of ghost estates and unfinished developments. There has been much public commentary about the number of vacant homes in Ireland, with some conflation of vacant homes and ghost estates. While there were almost 290,000 vacant homes in the 2011 Census, less than 10% of those (roughly 23,000) were vacant and complete homes in the 2,846 unfinished develop-ments surveyed by the government in late 2010 (Department of the Environment, 2010; see also work by Rob Kitchin of Maynooth University). The bulk of the estimated 179,000 units in so-called ghost estates were either complete and occupied (78,000) or merely at planning stage (58,000).

Figure 8.3

The total level of government spending (left-hand scale) and the fraction of government spending and of GDP spent on housing (right-hand scale),1995–2015

Source: calculations based on Department of Finance figures

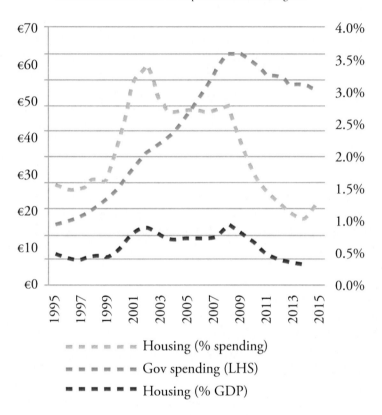

In addition, strong housing demand has seen the number of homes in ghost estates fall dramatically since 2010. The number of ghost estates fell from nearly 2,850 to less than 670 in 2015, with the number of vacant and complete homes down almost 90% in five years, to 2,800. Perhaps surprisingly, while Ireland has a problem with vacant homes – the rate of vacancy is 1.5–2 times higher than in some other European countries—this does not stem from recent over-construction in estates. Other factors, including a lengthy legal and probate system, the Fair Deal Nursing Home Support scheme and a low level of property tax (which limits the penalty for holding property empty for speculative reasons), are likely to contribute to this, although more detailed research is required to understand the relative importance of the various factors.

From austerity to housing

Thus far, this chapter has shown the strong effect that the housing sector had on government spending, both when spending was rising and when austerity took place. This section explores the reverse effect, namely the impact austerity has had on the housing sector. In general, the nature of government receipts has meant that public spending in Ireland since 2000 has been extremely pro-cyclical, with a sharp fall in spending between 2009 and 2014. Not only did the level of government spending fall, spending was also concentrated in three key areas: education, healthcare and social transfers. Of the aggregate fall in government spending of roughly €10bn, capital spending proportionately bore the brunt of the cuts.

This is shown in Figure 8.4. Capital spending, in other words investing to meet future needs, fell from more than 20% of all government spending in 2000 to less than 10% in 2013. Relative to national income, for every €1 earned, over 10 cent was invested in capital spending in the early 1980s. By 2015, that figure had fallen to just 4 cent. Some commentators might argue that this low level of investment was less accidental and more ideological, with housing among the areas of government spending most badly affected by the austerity of the post-2007 period. As shown in Figure 8.3, in aggregate, it fell from roughly 3% of government spending around the year 2000 to approximately 1% 15 years later.

What is the rationale for government spending on housing? The starting point for housing as a component of government spending is the UN Declaration of Human Rights. The first part of Article 25 of the Declaration states that every household has the right to a standard of living adequate for their health and well-being, including food, clothing, housing and medical care and necessary social services. The decline in average incomes and in employment between 2007 and 2010 meant that there was a huge outward shift in the demand for social housing in Ireland. The earlier by Whelan and Nolan (Chapter 6, this volume) describe how austerity affected inequality and those on lower incomes in particular. In the economics of the sector, there were a significantly larger fraction of households with inadequate incomes relative to the cost of their accommodation.

Figure 8.4

Capital spending, 1983–2013

Source: calculations based on Department of Finance figures

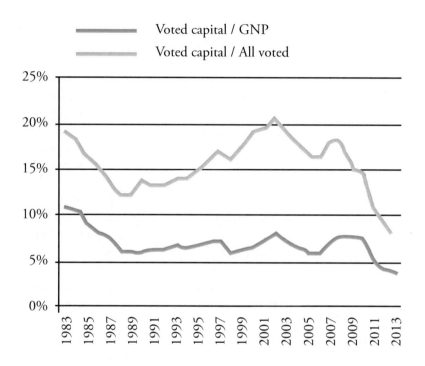

Unfortunately, in the case of Ireland, social housing had effectively been privatised in the decade to 2007. Part V of the Planning and Development Acts 2000–06 meant that the burden for funding new social and affordable housing was placed on those who bought new properties, as 20% of new developments were supposed to be set aside for social and affordable requirements. Newly built properties were bought disproportionately by first-time buyers, and these buyers were on below-average incomes relative to society as a whole (even if not necessarily their own age cohort). This meant that the burden for paying for new homes was regressive in nature. The provision of new social housing was also entirely dependent on the provision of private housing. The underlying assumption of Part V was that private and social housing were complements: when more of one was needed, more of the other was needed also. Of course, this is not the case. For a given population level, private and social housing are clear substitutes. Thus, when private completions fell from over 80,000 units a year to 10,000 a year, any fraction of that total also collapsed.

With a lack of newly built homes in the social housing sector, greater reliance was placed on the private-rented sector to house those on lowest incomes. In principle, this would work provided the subsidies were non-distortive—that is, they did not affect the incentive to work—and varied by need, that is, that those on lowest incomes were given the greatest subsidy. Unfortunately, the nature of subsidy adopted was a fixed-amount rent supplement, rather than an income-varying supplement. This meant that so-called 'welfare tenants' were pitted against 'working tenants' for a fixed pool of rental properties, with rent supplement limits reviewed to ensure recipients were not at an advantage relative to other market participants.

At its most fundamental level, spending on housing is now treated largely as a current account item rather than a capital account one. This goes against best practice in the area of social housing, in other words debt-financed building of homes for those with inadequate incomes to cover the costs of construction themselves. Compounding this, the nature of rent supplement is about subsidies relative to market rents, rather than subsidies relative to the gap between inadequate incomes and construction costs.

To explore this further, let's suppose that a site is to be used for 100 two-bedroom apartments in Dublin. The 2011 Dublin City Council Development Plan has very specific requirements not only about aggregate floor space but also about ceiling heights, balcony depths, basement car parking spaces, the number of lifts per floor, orientation and many other features of the unit. Each of these features brings benefits but also incurs extra costs, including the opportunity cost of lost space. A requirement, for example, to have 'two per core', that is, six lift shafts and six stairwells on a floor with 12 apartments—rather than two lifts and stairs, as would be common in other cities—incurs significant costs upfront, on an ongoing basis as lifts are costly to maintain, but also in opportunity cost, as three times the floor-space is lost for accommodation. Similarly, a requirement unique to Ireland that almost all units be dual orientation—and that none of the single-orientation units be north- or east-facing—renders many sites problematic or even without value.

This matters for social housing because of the need to link construction costs to real household incomes. While there is disagreement about the exact magnitudes, estimates as of 2016 suggest that building 100 two-bedroom apartments in Dublin would typically involve hard costs (labour and materials) of at least €1,800 a square metre. With a minimum of 85 square metres under Dublin City Council rules, and factoring in soft costs, such as a 12.5% profit margin, VAT of 13.5%, local authority levies and other fees (such as professionals' fees), this results in a total up-front cost per unit of roughly €275,000—excluding all land costs.

Allowing for a 5% net yield, with a 20% margin for management and maintenance, this means that the break-even monthly rent required to cover the costs of construction, but not including land, would be nearly €1,400. Realistically, factoring in land costs would mean a break-even monthly rent of at least €1,600 or, depending on the area, closer to €2,000. As of 2016, prevailing market rents for two-bedroom apartments across the country were far below this level. Only in the highest value locations, such as Dublin 2 and Dublin 4, could such rents of roughly €1,800 a month for a two-bedroom apartment be sustained. In cities other than Dublin, average rents for two-bedroom apartments are closer to €700.

It is worth stressing that the figures presented above are meant to be indicative rather than definitive. A transparent government-sponsored audit of the elements of construction costs in Ireland is required, as the figures above rely on information gathered from a variety of sources. Nonetheless, regardless of the exact figure required for building a home, the point remains: the higher the hard construction costs, the less affordable is housing. This hinders housing supply and places greater strain on the social housing sector. In simple terms, if a household with disposable income of €3,000 a month can only sustainably spend €1,000 on housing, what does a monthly budget of €1,000 translate into, in construction terms?

This question shows how it is possible to convert directly from such a break-even rent calculation to the need for housing subsidies by using the income distribution and the rule of thumb for housing affordability, that no more than one third of disposable income should be spent on housing. In other words, to afford a monthly rent of €1,800, a household would need to have monthly disposable income of three times this: €5,400. Allowing for the Irish tax system, this means that only households with a gross annual income of more than €85,000 would be able to afford the minimum allowable unit in Dublin City Council. This corresponds to close to the 90th percentile of the income distribution.

While, in theory, an income-varying subsidy for all those earning less than this amount would restore the principle of access to housing, it is fiscally not feasible for nine-tenths of households to be in receipt of subsidies. As work by Saiz (2010) and Quigley and Raphael (2005) has shown, local policy makers can use housing and land regulations to restrict supply, to the detriment of low-income households. Regulations about housing standards can be viewed as discrimination against those on lower incomes, either intentionally or accidentally. More generally, the point of this section is to highlight the link between construction costs and social housing. If the hard costs of construction are too high relative to real incomes, then for a meaningful right to housing services to exist, society must top up households with inadequate incomes. The higher construction costs are, the greater a fraction of households will need assistance—thus, it is clearly in the interests of the taxpayer to ensure efficiency in construction.

Principles for policy

Once the link between subsidies and construction costs is accepted, this provides a clear policy prescription. The question for voters or policy makers to decide is what fraction of households will be entitled to a housing subsidy related to their income. Leaving aside issues around household composition and the equivalisation of income, if that fraction were a third, then the minimum socially acceptable dwelling should reflect the disposable income of the household at the 33rd percentile.

How might this be achieved? Two areas where Ireland's minimum requirements appear to be out of line with its economic peer group are the hard costs per square metre and the minimum number of square metres allowed for various dwelling types. As outlined above, at €1,800/m^2 and a minimum of 85m^2, the break-even rent of a two-bedroom apartment in 2015 was roughly €1,400, excluding land costs. Were construction costs €1,500/m^2 and if the minimum size of a two-bedroom apartment were 85m^2, the break-even monthly rent would be closer to €800.

The difference for a family of two adults and two children, earning €45,000 a year, is substantial. In the 2015 status quo, the maximum number of square metres they can afford is 62, but the minimum allowed to be built is 85. That family, with an above-average income, would require a subsidy of at least €400 a month (more if land costs are included) just to afford the minimum unit. The scenario presented above means that the minimum would be 60m^2, while lower per-square-metre costs mean the maximum they could afford would be 75m^2.

Note also that such a system of income-varying housing subsidies would blur the distinction between social and market housing at the margin. When a household moved from, say, the 30th percentile to the 35th, due to a new, better-paying job, they would stop receiving the subsidy but would not necessarily have to move accommodation. The same change in reverse, due to an economic downturn, for example, would not result in an eviction, as the nature of the subsidy would offer a for-profit owner excellent collateral.

As mentioned above, the figures presented above in relation to construction costs are meant to be illustrative rather than definitive. And, in large part, the lack of official figures about construction costs prevents any agreed course of action. In late 2015, the National Competitiveness Council committed to benchmarking residential construction costs in Ireland relative to other countries. This exercise would identify which parameters are most out of line compared to our peers, and hopefully create consensus on the topic.

It is not clear, for example, why per-square-metre costs in the Republic of Ireland are so high relative to other locations including Northern Ireland. Some of this may be due to minimum specifications, such as lift and basement car parking requirements. Reynolds (2015) suggests that another important factor is the nature of safety certification. In most developed countries, buildings are certified as fit for occupation by the local authority. In Ireland, during the housing boom, the rate of inspections was well below 10%, leading to situations such as the well-publicised Priory Hall case.[1]

The response was not to move to certification by the local authority, but rather to move to a model of complete self-certification, typically by the architect. Reynolds (2015) highlights that this new system brought significant inefficiencies, with the cost of certification per unit estimated to be roughly €25,000, compared to approximately €250 in Northern Ireland, where a more standard system of official certification is in operation. On the other hand, those involved in the construction of apartments (rather than one-off homes) argue that BER certification is relatively efficient on a per-unit basis. Identifying the actions that would have the biggest impact on construction costs must be the priority for the government if it is to tackle the lack of new housing supply. In short, the cost of building homes must be reduced so that new homes are affordable to those on average incomes, and to those on below-average incomes if appropriately subsidised.

Conclusion

This chapter has explored the relationship between two key domestic economic sectors: government spending and the housing sector. The first direction of the relationship explored, from housing to austerity, highlighted the contribution of housing to greater public receipts. While they were largely temporary in nature, contingent on high levels of economic activity, they helped finance a dramatic increase in public spending. Much of this additional public spending was in the form of permanent (or at least hard-to-reverse) spending commitments, particularly around pay and social transfers. When Ireland underwent a substantial economic correction, such that the level of GDP was at one point 10 years behind IMF predictions, this affected revenues and ultimately spending. Core areas of government spending—health, education and social transfers—were by and large protected, resulting in sharp cuts to other forms of spending, in particular capital spending. This includes housing, which is now treated more as an item of current expenditure than of capital spending.

The shift in housing policy during the Celtic Tiger phase, away from debt-financed social housing and towards fixed-amount rent supplement, was particularly unfortunate as it left the state entirely unable to respond to the huge outward shift in demand for social housing after the downturn. More generally, housing is similar to other areas of government spending in Ireland, with a significant lack of counter-cyclical capacity. Two themes that have arisen in this chapter have been firstly, recognising the importance of capital spending, including housing, on the part of government; and related to this, the importance of shifting government spending from pro- to counter-cyclical.

In terms of reforming policy in relation to housing, one key objective to keep at the heart of housing policy should be giving people freedom of choice—both within housing, allowing trade-offs between size and location, and between housing and other goods, for example where people want to spend a smaller fraction of their income on housing and more elsewhere. If this represents the efficiency motive, the second key objective reflects the equity motive: housing subsidies should assist those with inadequate incomes, and the more inadequate the income, the greater the support should be.

Currently, the system reflects very few of the attributes of best practice. Minimum specifications are completely divorced from their costs and from the real economy, resulting in regulation—including around safety certification—acting as a tool for discrimination against those on lower incomes. If the 2015 Central Bank mortgage market regulations effectively capped house prices relative to incomes, the same now needs to be done with construction costs, to ensure that where demand exceeds supply, there is a supply response and thus affordable accommodation.

The new government in 2016 faced a range of related problems in housing, including a lack of affordable homes for first-time buyers, an extreme shortage of rental accommodation, a student accommodation crisis and the phenomenon of working homeless families living in hotels. Ultimately, these all stem from an inability of supply to respond to greater demand. Until there is consensus about the evidence of why construction costs in Ireland are so out of line with other countries and with incomes locally, these problems will persist.

Notes

[1] Priory Hall is a 65-unit apartment complex in Donaghmede, Dublin. Some 41 households had to vacate their homes in October 2011 after authorities had deemed the buildings unsafe. After the developer failed to undertake the necessary works to make the buildings habitable, Dublin City Council undertook a three-year reconstruction programme at a cost of approximately €30m.

9. Poverty and risk: the impact of austerity on vulnerable females in Dublin's inner city

Emma Heffernan

> I was only getting then me benefit, which is hard to live
> on when you're living on the streets … so a lot of the
> girls that lived in the hostel were on the game.
>
> (Maria, 32, sex worker in Dublin's north inner city,
> July 2010)

Introduction

After the high unemployment and emigration that defined the 1980s and much of the early 1990s, the dawn of the 'Celtic Tiger' was a time of huge social and economic change in Ireland. By 2004, Ireland was ranked as the most globalised nation on the planet (Kearney 2004) and had gone from being one of the poorest states in Europe to one of the wealthiest (Sweeney 2005). One of the most remarkable developments during the Celtic Tiger era was rapid social mobility and expansion of the middle classes (McWilliams 2006). However, even though the burgeoning middle classes saw a dramatic increase in their standard of living, there were still major gaps between the new globally oriented 'cosmopolitan elite' and a 'local underclass' dependent on the social welfare system (Inglis 2008, p. 19).

Eriksen (2007) has argued that in order to understand globalisation in its totality, we must see its beneficiaries as well as its victims, the 'globalisers' and the 'globalised', those who are part of the process and those who are excluded—the human detritus of these transnational economic processes. In Ireland, a small but significant section of the population did not benefit from the newfound success bestowed by the Celtic Tiger. While the poverty gap (the measure of how far below a particular poverty line individuals fall) in Ireland declined from 20% in 2004 to 17% in 2007 (Russell *et al.* 2010, p. 13), EU-SILC (EU Survey on Income and Living Conditions) data estimate that in 2006, at the height of the boom, 6.9% of the Irish population were living in 'consistent poverty,' with almost 33% of these children, as discussed in more detail by Watson *et al.* in the next chapter. Furthermore, 8.8% of people experienced debt in paying for everyday expenses, such as food, clothing and heat (CSO 2007).

In 2008, Ireland experienced its worst economic and labour market crisis since the foundation of the state, which had a profound effect on the standard of living of Irish households (CSO 2013a, 2013b; Maître *et al.* 2014; Whelan 2013; Nolan *et al.* 2012; Savage *et al.* 2015; Whelan and Nolan, Chapter 6, this volume). While most of the chapters in this volume tell the aggregate story of Ireland and the Great Recession, this chapter aims to report the reality of everyday poverty and vulnerability at ground level. Through the use of two case studies, it examines the lives and experiences of one of the most vulnerable populations in Irish society, who even at the peak of the boom were struggling to survive—homeless, drug-using women involved in street-based prostitution in Dublin's inner city. Through ethnographic snapshots, it reflects on how a shift from a moment of prosperity to one of austerity impacted on risk-taking activities of this group of women, further entrenching their vulnerability and social exclusion. The research presented here comes from a larger body of work: an in-depth analysis of female sexual labour in Dublin from 2005 to 2011, which coincided with the peak of the boom and early years of recession.

Recession and the community and voluntary sector

In its first submission to the United Nations Committee on Economic, Social and Cultural Rights, the Irish Human Rights and Equality

Commission argued that austerity measures implemented by the Irish state meant that 'the burden of the crisis and dominant responses to it has fallen disproportionately on those least able to bear its impacts' (2015, p. 8). They argue that austerity policies have resulted in increased poverty and deprivation rates for both adults and children and significantly reduced access to public services, especially in the areas of health, education and social services. Those on lower incomes, the unemployed, the homeless, migrant groups and people with disabilities were particularly impacted.

Access to public services such as health, education and training, and social housing is critical to the functioning of society, as illustrated elsewhere in this volume. Furthermore, social structures and institutions can play a role in alleviating the impact of economic shocks, reducing vulnerability and supporting coping mechanisms to prevent, and provide routes out of poverty. This is especially so in moments of crisis when people, especially those with fewest resources and least ability to cope, become even more dependent on public services (National Economic and Social Council (NESC) 2005, 2013). The voluntary and community sector plays a crucial role, working in tandem with public agencies to provide services to the poorest and most disadvantaged as well as in developing capacity in civil society. Community and voluntary organisations comprise groups working with, but not limited to, health, social policy, employment, housing and homelessness, drugs services, social welfare, allied health services, human rights, people with disabilities, community development and youth work (Acheson *et al.* 2004, 2005). They are often the services people turn to when most in need. While the social welfare system has been relatively successful in ameliorating the worst effects of the crisis, social transfers do not take account of the provision and availability of services and supports, or other factors such as the cost of living, levels of debt or the broader tax and welfare system (NESC 2013). The state's focus on cutting funding to essential public services has had severe social impacts, disproportionately impacting the poor and those most in need, and reducing the ability of the state to function in essential areas of poverty, health, children, education, racism and inter-culturalism, housing and homelessness (Harvey 2012; Burke 2010; Irish Medical Organisation 2012; Society of St Vincent de Paul (SVP) 2012a; NESC 2013; Burke *et al.* 2014; Community Platform 2014; Healy *et al.* 2015; Watson *et al.*, Chapter 10, this volume). Indeed, Harvey (2012, p. 11) questions the government's commitment to protecting the most vulnerable, arguing that the 'role, function and performance' of the community and voluntary sector 'in modern Irish society was gravely undermined by a series of unexpected actions by the state' following the financial collapse, with disproportionate cuts to this sector.

In 2008, the community and voluntary sector comprised approximately 6,100 organizations and employed approximately 53,098 people, with an estimated value to the economy of €6.5bn. It is estimated that between 2008 and 2012, the general fall in government spending across all sectors was approximately 2.8%, while funding to the community and voluntary sector was cut by 35%, leading to loss of employment in the sector and to drastic cuts to service provision. Funding for voluntary social housing fell by 54%, local community development programmes by 35% and drugs initiatives by 29%; funding for the community service programme was down by 18% and for the Family Support agency, which funds Family Resource Centres, was down by 17%. The RAPID programme, which works in disadvantaged urban areas, had its funding cut by 67%, while the CLÁR programme, working in disadvantaged rural areas, was shut down. Funding for community and social inclusion fell by 72%. This reduction in government funding coincided with reductions in disposable incomes and public charitable donations. Community and voluntary organisations were forced to dismiss staff and to close or curtail services (Harvey 2012). At the same time, there was an increase in demand for the same services as recession began to bite and more people, the most disadvantaged individuals and families, sought support. Community and voluntary organisations faced increased demand for cash, food, help with household expenses and clothing. Demands on the SVP rose by 35% in 2011, with 60% of calls for direct assistance from households with children, particularly one-parent families. Furthermore, 65% of callers to SVP offices were in receipt of social welfare (SVP 2012b).

The financial crisis and homelessness

One of the most shocking outcomes of the financial crisis as it played out in Ireland has been an unprecedented increase in homelessness, especially in the capital city. Between December 2014 and December 2015 there was a net increase of 43% in the number of people recorded as homeless (Peter McVerry Trust 2016). Recent figures from the Dublin Region Homeless Executive (2016) indicate that almost

5,500 adults accessed emergency homeless shelters in Dublin in 2015. In January 2016, 769 families with 1,570 dependants were living in homeless accommodation in the Dublin region, a 101% increase in homeless children in the capital since the previous January. A total of 134 families (with 269 children) became homeless in January 2016, the highest ever monthly increase in family homelessness, of which 125 (with 253 children) were 'newly' homeless (Focus Ireland 2016). At the time of writing, there are almost 90,000 households on the social housing waiting list, rents have increased nationally and the number of properties available for rent has sharply declined. Moreover, rent supplement levels are insufficient to meet the cost of renting (Simon Community 2014). It is within this context that the most vulnerable members of society have been forced into even more extreme living and working conditions, with little external support.

In the next section of the chapter, the impact of austerity at the individual level, contrasting with the structural and cohort-driven analysis of previous chapters, is explored through an ethnographic analysis. I introduce Susie and Maria, two vulnerable women working in street-based prostitution, to highlight the impact of social policy cutbacks on some of the most vulnerable citizens in our capital city.[1]

Introducing Susie

I originally met Susie in the women's prison where she was serving time for shoplifting. Susie was born in Dublin's inner city in the 1970s. She had a difficult childhood, most of it spent in the care system. She never knew her father, and her mother died of cancer when she was four years old, leaving her and her siblings alone. Ending up in care, she eventually started stealing and was sent to a centre for young offenders. As she explains:

> I was in a lot of homes and that when I was young, I then started to rob and that when I was young, and I got locked up in the Detention Centre and I was in there for four years, and then when I got out of there on me eighteenth birthday, I was in there when I was fifteen and got out when I was eighteen, got four years but I just done three years, and then when I got out, I started getting into drugs, a few of me friends started smoking [using drugs]. I started smoking gear [heroin] and got to like it

and got strung out on it, and after a few years I was strung out on gear I ended up on coke [cocaine], and then I'd been strung out for a few years when I started banging up [injecting], when I started on the coke I got very bad, and that's why I started going on the game [sex work].

When she was released from prison in 2007, with no money, no family to rely on and no place to live, Susie ended up in emergency accommodation in the city centre. As her drug use worsened she became involved in sex work, selling sex in the north inner city. With the increase in homelessness in the capital since the recession and competition for bed spaces in shelters, securing a bed in a hostel became increasingly difficult. Faced with sleeping on the streets, she began sleeping in an abandoned factory on the north side of the Liffey. With nothing to do all day and nowhere to go, most days she just 'hung around', went to see her key worker or to the drop-in clinic in the local community drug project. However, after cuts to services and when her keyworkers hours were cut to reduce cost, Susie felt increasingly isolated and without support. She tried several times to get into a residential drug rehabilitation unit, 'a place where you can take your methadone and get on a course or something', but with cutbacks in drugs services she lost all hope of getting clean. To supplement her income from social welfare and prostitution, Susie resorted to begging and to stealing on occasion, though she was constantly worried that she would get caught by the police, and end up back in prison. Susie felt that her life was spiralling out of control and did not know where to turn to for help.

Like many women working at the more chaotic end of the sexual services market, Susie's story highlights the limits of personal choice when women are faced with difficult decisions about caring for themselves and their families. Unable to secure any meaningful employment in the formal economy and struggling to survive on welfare, many women are forced to work in the informal economy, often selling drugs, stolen goods or sex, as well as resorting to begging, in order to feed and clothe themselves and their families. Susie is not all that unusual; for many vulnerable women, engaging in prostitution seems like the best option to protect and support their families. Occasions such as communions and confirmations, events such as Christmas and birthdays, school trips or the return of children to school after the summer break increase pressure to provide for their families, as several research participants in the broader study attested:

I've gone out [selling sex] if I've no money for dinner tomorrow, if you need money for the kids swimming or the bus fare the next morning. You can't let your kids starve, can you? (Kathleen, 42, from Tallaght and mother of two children)

Or a school trip comes up and you'd go down [to sell sex] and get €50. (Sandra, 44, from city centre and mother of two children)

I'd pay my rent and then I'd have to buy food, just basically to survive, to be able to give the kids a little treat, so that's how come I got involved in prostitution. (Lorraine, 32, from Ballymun and mother of three children)

I want to give me kid a good a life, and if that means me going down Benburb Street [to sell sex], then that's what I have to do. (Aisling, 30, from Ballymun and mother of one child)

Addiction to drugs such as heroin, cocaine and benzodiazepines as well as alcohol is also part of a survival mechanism for some women engaging in street-based prostitution. Cuts to drugs services have severely impacted the lives of these women, in terms of access to services and supports when they are most in need. Estimates suggest that the Drugs Initiative budget was cut by 37% between 2008 and 2014, forcing essential local drug services on the ground to deal with cumulative cuts of up to 30%. These cuts have affected a wide range of services, including treatment, rehabilitation, aftercare, youth services, education and awareness, childcare as well as community safety (Citywide, 2015). As sex work provides a good income compared with alternative income-generating activities, it can lead to increased drug use, and in turn to even more chaotic lifestyles. Several women reported that their drug use increased when they became homeless and involved in prostitution, which meant they needed more and more money; this became a vicious circle leading to spending more time in prostitution, or engaging in riskier sexual practices. Social services that previously acted as a safety net were cut or no longer available, such as meeting with a key worker or accessing outreach services, often the vital link between drug-using women and the broader health and social care system, including mental health services, housing, and drug services. Many are not sure where to turn to for help; the services that do exist are often difficult to access and it requires a certain amount of social capital to be able to navigate the health and social care system. Susie was devastated when her key worker's hours were cut and she was eventually let go from the community drug project where she provided support to drug-using women

> Me key worker, like she got her hours cut, so she couldn't see me, then she was gone completely. Like there's nothing now, no one, no fucking support at all. I've nowhere else to go, no one to talk to, and I've all this stuff going on in me head.

Many women reported extremely poor mental and physical health and felt their health deteriorated as a result of their drug use, being homeless and engaging in prostitution:

> I get sick a lot, I've got pneumonia a few times from being out in the cold, and like me having HIV like, my immune system is fucked. (Kate)

> It's the fucking cold, some nights are fine but some nights hail rain or snow I'm out there, I'm standing out in the fucking snow, I have no choice, it can get pretty cold out there you know … I get colds a lot. (Lorraine)

Finding employment is difficult for many women with no qualifications and a poor track record of employment. Those who did manage to gain employment in the formal economy were invariably in low-paying, precarious positions. One of my research participants, Maria, had been supplementing her social welfare with part-time work to make ends meet until she lost her job.

Maria

Maria, a 40-year-old mother of three, was born and raised in Finglas. She left school at 15, and with no qualifications found it difficult to find a job. She managed to secure part-time work in a coffee shop to supplement her inadequate social welfare, but as her wages were cut she found it more and more difficult to make ends meet. She eventually lost her job, could not keep up her rent repayments and became homeless. Initially she and her three children slept on the floors of family and friends, but when their generosity ran out she had nowhere else to go and spent her time moving between homeless services, sleeping in an abandoned building and living in her car, with her children:

> I was homeless for seven months with me kids, living in and out of the car, the factory down near Moore Street, it was a burned-out factory, I used to live there, and from B&B to B&B. I got a pain in me face going from B&B to B&B with the kids, you know what I mean like, because they kept saying 'Where are we gonna sleep tonight?'.

To make ends meet Maria became involved in prostitution when introduced by a friend:

> I was only getting then me benefit, which is hard to live on when you're living on the streets ... so a lot of the girls that lived in the hostel were on the game.

Eventually social services became involved and her children were taken into care, leaving Maria alone on the streets. This was a devastating loss for her and was the catalyst for what she describes as her life 'spiralling out of control'. Most nights she managed to get a bed in a hostel, but as her drug habit worsened, she lost her bed in the hostel and began sleeping rough. Adjusting to life on the street was a difficult transition for Maria. One of the most difficult aspects of sleeping rough was not being able to have a place to store her possessions, especially her clothes. Maria describes the difficulty of adjusting to life on the streets:

> I was so hungry, but also I needed new clothes, like I lost all my property, I was living in a hostel in the city centre, and I lost my bed and got kicked out, like you're told to take your clothes with you and that, but I had six black bags of clothes, like, like how are you supposed to? Like I can't walk down the street with six black bags of clothes. I had nowhere to go, so I took three sets of clothes with me, and when you're on the street you have nowhere

to wash, and I didn't know the routines of the streets, like where the launderettes were, and as my clothes were getting dirty, I was throwing them away, and buying new ones, it costs money to do that, so to do that you need money, so it's either shop lifting or prostitution.

Maria found that living in close proximity to other drug users made her own habit worse and contributed to her deterioration:

I ended up in that hostel, it should be shut down, it's a fucking drugs den. Since living there I have just spi-ralled: it wasn't a spiral, it was a straight slope back down, straight back down to the gutter. I ended up back using heroin, cocaine, Valium: you name it, I used it.

For women working in prostitution, being homeless and using drugs often meant taking increased risks. The next section examines the impact of the recession on their risk-taking activities when selling sex on the streets of Dublin.

Sex work, risk and recession

Sexual services markets are usually highly stratified, and often com-prise a mixture of outdoor (street-based) and indoor work venues, such as brothels and escort agencies. Like other industries, the sex industry has relatively privileged and exploitative positions for its workers, and those working in different sectors of the market face different types of risks and operate within different 'risk environments' (Rhodes 2002). Women involved in prostitution face multiple occupational health risks in the their daily lives, including risk of disease, violence, discrimina-tion, exploitation and criminalisation, depending on the social location of the worker and the social context of where the work takes place (Chapkis 1997; Rekart 2005; Sanders *et al.* 2009; WHO 2014; Amnesty International 2016). Street-based prostitution is often associated with higher risks (Brooks-Gordon 2006; Church *et al.* 2001; Kinnell 2006).

Much of the risk associated with sex work can be attributed to the laws that govern the sale of sexual services, the social stigma attached to prostitution, and, to some extent, societal ambivalence to the welfare of sex workers. Many sex workers learn to accept a certain degree of risk associated with their work and adopt a range of strategies for managing this risk, including assessing potential clients, categorising and discriminating between clients, managing the encounter itself, maintaining good relationships with regular clients, working with other girls, exchanging information about 'dodgy' clients, attempting to control their drug use, trusting their intuition, carrying a weapon, and working in a familiar environment.

Managing occupational risks is crucial for sex workers to maintain their personal health and safety. Since the beginning of the recession, many sex workers noticed a reduction in client numbers, leading to increased competition between sex workers in a particular geographical location. They had to drop their prices to secure bookings, or offer services they normally would not, such as unprotected sex, which has a higher premium attached to it. Maria describes how the reduction in clients has meant that women are forced to sell 'riskier' sex:

> I just feel hopeless you know, and even being on the game, it's dangerous and it's scary, and when it comes to it, a lot of the men don't want to use condoms, well they are refusing to use condoms and a lot of the girls are OK with that, 'cause it's getting harder, there aren't as many clients, there's not as many clients as there used to be, and the ones that are there are refusing to use condoms. So yeah, they would offer you more money to do it without a condom.

Women like Maria and Susie were forced to drop their prices to attract this dwindling client population. This coincided with a perception among women that there were more women on the streets selling sex. These factors meant that women needed to work for longer and take on more clients to make enough money. For women, suspending condom use was a contentious issue and caused a lot of stress. Some women felt that they had no option but others were more reluctant, worrying about sexually transmitted infections and the impact it might have on their children:

> Like I'm being honest with you, if I was offered enough I'd do it, like I haven't done it, but that's not like saying I would never do it, it's just I was never offered enough. (Kathleen)

> Well I have. Just for the extra money. (Mandy)

It's not worth it, like with HIV and hepatitis, it's not worth it, I've three kids. (Lorraine)

As women were forced to take on clients they would rather reject, and having to work for longer to maintain an adequate income, many were forced to move out of their familiar working areas to areas that were darker and felt more dangerous, such as along the Liffey quays, towards Islandbridge and the Phoenix Park. Maria fears for her life every times she gets into a car with a client she would rather reject:

The worst is the fear, yeah the fear of being raped or attacked, it's constant like. You know, every time you get into a car, every time. Like when I got raped, it wasn't in a car, I was on foot, yeah, so every time I get into a car I think, is this me last one? Will I see my kids again? Now normally that's gone out of your head within a couple of seconds, by the person, 'cause you know they're all right.

Many of the street-based sex workers I met during my fieldwork had chaotic lifestyles. Many of their life choices were limited by multiple and overlapping social and economic issues such as drug addiction, homelessness, poor physical and mental health, being haphazardly connected to health and social care services, difficult childhoods, poor educational attainment, a poor social support network and a lack of any real opportunities to improve their lives. This was further complicated by the criminal nature of sex work, which forces many to work in dangerous environments. Some women found it difficult to access even the most basic services and supports, with services reported as fragmented, incoherent and often non-existent, even in times of prosperity. For many women in this position, getting out of the poverty trap felt next to impossible, leading to increased feelings of hopelessness, desperation and suicidal ideation. Maria comments on a time she felt close to suicide:

I need support, I've no support, I need support to get me back on my feet. I just felt so lost, I didn't know up from down, which direction for my life to go in, I was starting to have suicidal thoughts. My life is a mess, it's a complete and utter mess.

Cuts to public services and supports compounded these circumstances of poverty, structural violence and social exclusion, pushing many deeper into desperate and often hopeless situations.

Conclusion

Even during boom times, a significant section of the Irish population was living in consistent poverty, struggling to survive and unable to afford everyday expenses. Following the financial crash, austerity policies have pushed people further into poverty, as well as significantly reducing access to essential public services and supports. Access to public services such as health, education and training, and social housing are critical to the functioning of society, but also act as a social safety net, insulating the most vulnerable, both in times of prosperity and in times of austerity.

Individual narratives such as those of Susie and Maria not only bring to light the multiple interconnecting historical, socioeconomic, political and structural processes that shape people's lives, but also highlight the complexity of the challenge ahead if we are to break the cycle of intergenerational poverty and find pathways out of homelessness, out of addiction and out of vulnerability. Tackling poverty requires an integrated cross-sectorial approach that recognises the multiple intersecting causes of poverty, inequality and exclusion. As we reimagine and slowly rebuild our post-crisis society, it is crucial that the most vulnerable are protected through sustainable social protection programmes and policies.

Acknowledgements

This research was funded by Government of Ireland Irish Research Council postgraduate scholarship and a John and Pat Hume scholarship from Maynooth University.

Notes

[1] In order to protect the identity of participants, pseudonyms are used throughout.

10. Child poverty in a period of austerity

Dorothy Watson, Bertrand Maître,
Christopher T. Whelan and James Williams

Introduction

Poverty and economic disadvantage have a range of negative effects on children, including on physical and mental health, educational achievement, and emotional and behavioural outcomes. In this chapter we examine the impact of the Great Recession on the economic well-being of families and the consequences this had for children. We draw on the first and second waves of the Growing Up in Ireland (GUI) study for two cohorts of children. The availability of data for two waves for each cohort allows us to compare the pre-recession and mid-recession situations of families with infant children (ages nine months and three years) and children in middle childhood (ages nine and thirteen years).

Ireland is a particularly interesting case because of the scale of the economic crisis and the fact that it was preceded by an unprecedented boom. Earlier research on the impact of the recession on the population as a whole has concluded that the distinctive nature of the Irish case adds to the need to go beyond relative poverty measures based on current disposable income and adopt a multidimensional perspective

(Whelan and Maître 2014). In this chapter, in addition to reporting changes in relation to income poverty and material deprivation, we focus on the notion of economic vulnerability.

A frequent demand from a wide variety of sources during recent debates on welfare cuts and tax increases has related to the need to 'protect the vulnerable', although it is far from clear that a consensus exists as to who is to be included under this heading. More generally, efforts to develop the notion of economic vulnerability have involved extending the concerns in the social exclusion literature with multidimensionality and dynamics. This involves a shift of focus from current deprivation to insecurity and exposure to risk and shock. Such concerns seem to be particularly salient given the scale of the economic crisis and the manner in which it has been associated with pervasive debt issues (Whelan *et al.* 2014). In this chapter we will seek to take account of the impact of the economic crisis in Ireland not only on levels of vulnerability but also on the character of vulnerability and the changing socio-economic profiles of those experiencing such vulnerability. In so doing we will take account of the timing of GUI cohort interviews relative to the onset of the Great Recession.

Consequences of child poverty

Child poverty is a concern not only because of its immediate consequences for the well-being of children but also because it has potentially long-term negative consequences that persist into adulthood. Duncan *et al.* (2012) summarise a range of evidence from the US relating to the consequences of early childhood poverty for adult labour market outcome. Longitudinal research, particularly in the United States, has shown that childhood poverty is associated with reduced life opportunities and a greater risk of experiencing poverty during adulthood. A review by Brooks-Gunn and Duncan (1997) found that family income is related to children's ability- and achievement-related outcomes as well as to emotional outcomes.

There is clear evidence of negative health outcomes for children born into poverty, including lower birth weight, higher infant mortality and poorer health (Department for Work and Pensions 2007). Focusing on developmental issues, Duncan *et al.* (1994) found that low income and poverty were good predictors of cognitive development and behavioural measures at age five, even controlling for factors such as family structure and maternal education. Other research also points to the importance of the early childhood years for learning skills such as self-regulating attention (Duncan *et al.* 2007; Holzer *et al.* 2007). Many studies have found that long-term exposure to poverty was associated with behavioural problems at school, low self-esteem, problems in peer relations (Bolger *et al.* 1995), and depression and antisocial behaviour (McLeod and Shanahan 1996; Jarjoura *et al.* 2002).

The evidence drawn from these studies also affirms the enduring costs to society associated with these negative outcomes—encompassing health problems, crime, low educational achievement, and welfare dependence (Duncan *et al.* 2012; Waldfogel 2013). The fact that childhood economic disadvantage can have long-lasting consequences has been demonstrated in the Irish longitudinal study on ageing (TILDA), a panel study of adults aged 50 and over which includes retrospective information on childhood experiences. This research has found that growing up in poor households increased the risk of a number of health problems in later life, including cardiovascular disease, lung disease, and mental health issues (McCrory *et al.* 2015).

The persistence of poverty over several years is particularly harmful and the timing of poverty is also important. In particular, income poverty experienced in the early years of childhood can be more consequential for adult employment outcomes than income poverty experienced in later childhood (Duncan *et al.* 2012). Low household income during the early childhood years was also associated with lower rates of high-school completion and high neighbourhood poverty, and poor-quality schooling may exacerbate this effect (Brooks-Gunn and Duncan 1997).

Research from the GUI survey on the 1998 cohort at age nine has already established an association between childhood poverty and outcomes including achievement in maths and reading, social adjustment, behavioural problems, and health (Williams and Whelan 2011). For instance, nine-year-old children from the lowest income quintile were more likely to have emotional and conduct difficulties as well as problems with hyperactivity and peer relationships. These children also had higher levels of absences from school and higher rates of non-completion of homework, and their mothers were more likely to have literacy and numeracy difficulties (Williams *et al.* 2009).

Other research on the GUI data has found that family type is associated with the risk of disadvantage, with lone-parent and cohabiting families at higher risk (Fahey *et al.* 2012; Hannan and Halpin 2014). Results reported by Fahey *et al.* (2012) indicate that poverty and low levels of education are important in accounting for the lower well-being of children in one-parent families. Hannan and Halpin (2014), similarly, point to the significance of pre-existing differences, including socio-economic differences between family types, in accounting for the disadvantage in health and self concept faced by children in lone-parent or cohabiting families.

Our analysis takes advantage of the longitudinal nature of the GUI survey and, taking account of the accumulating evidence on the limitations of focusing solely on income, adopts a multidimensional perspective. Thus, in line with emerging trends in the literature, our approach was both multidimensional and dynamic (Nolan and Whelan 2011; Tomlinson *et al.* 2008).

Data and methods

The GUI survey is a large longitudinal study of children in Ireland. It tracks the development and well-being of two nationally representative cohorts of children: the 1998 cohort and the 2008 cohort. The samples were strict probability samples. The 1998 cohort was selected following clustering at the level of the school, while the 2008 cohort was a random sample selected from the Child Benefit records. Interviews were conducted via Computer-Assisted Personal Interview (CAPI) with the primary care-giver (PCG, usually the mother), the resident secondary care-giver (SCG, usually the father), the teachers of the older 1998 cohort of children at wave one, and the older 1998 cohort children themselves. In the present analysis we rely on data provided by the PCG.

In this chapter, data from the first two waves of both cohorts are used, when the children in the 2008 cohort were nine months and subsequently three years old and those in the 1998 cohort were nine and subsequently 13 years of age. The samples in the study were reweighted or statistically adjusted to ensure that they were nationally representative of the age groups in question, both cross-sectionally and longitudinally. The present analysis includes the 9,793 families who responded in both waves of the 2008 cohort and the 7,423 families who responded in both waves for the 1998 cohort. The large sample sizes, the probability samples and the calibration to ensure representativeness mean that the results can be generalised to the population of children in both cohorts.

Figure 10.1

Timing of the GUI surveys (see text for details)

Source: Central Statistics Office (CSO) for consumer price index and unemployment rate.
Department of Social Welfare Rates Booklets for each year for amount of benefits.

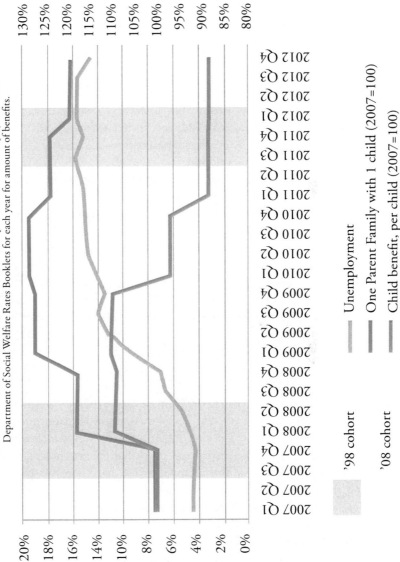

'98 cohort

'08 cohort

—— Unemployment

—— One Parent Family with 1 child (2007=100)

—— Child benefit, per child (2007=100)

The timing of the GUI surveys in relation to the onset of 'the Great Recession' is important (see Figure 10.1). The unemployment rate is graphed against the axis to the left in Figure 10.1. The first wave of the 1998 cohort was conducted with the families of the nine-year-olds between August 2007 and June 2008, slightly before the major shocks of the recession later that year. The second wave, when the children were aged 13, took place between August 2011 and March 2012. This corresponded to the deepest point of the recession, before any growth in employment was evident. The first wave of the 2008 cohort, when the children were aged nine months, occurred a little later: between September 2008 and March 2009, right at the start of the recession when unemployment was rising most sharply. The second wave, when the children were three years old, was from December 2010 to July 2011. At this stage, unemployment was still increasing and GNP was still falling but at a much slower rate.

Figure 10.1 also gives an indication of the timing of changes in some key social protection payments. The axis to the right shows the changes in the value of Child Benefit and One Parent Family Payment (assuming one child) in real terms between 2007 and 2012, with the 2007 value taken as 100%. The universal Child Benefit payment had increased in real terms between 2007 and 2008 by about 10% and it was maintained at that level in 2009 before being cut in 2010 and again in 2011 so that it was below 90% of the 2007 rate by mid-recession. The One Parent Family Payment had been increased by over 15% in real terms for a parent with one child between 2007 and 2008. It was increased further in 2009, reaching almost 30% above the 2007 figure in real terms by 2010. It was then cut in 2011 and again in 2012 but remained almost 20% above the 2007 rate by 2012. Unemployment payments, apart from non-contributory payments to young adults that were cut sharply, followed a similar pattern to those for one-parent families. The cuts in Child Benefit would have affected all families. For families dependent on Social Protection, this would have been balanced by the increase in the basic rates of payment and the rate payable for qualified dependent children, leaving them roughly 15% better off in real terms by 2012 than in 2007.

Given the timing of the GUI fieldwork, we would expect the families of the 2008 cohort to be in the first wave affected by unemployment or concerns about employment loss. For this reason, we might expect that the impact of the recession would be seen most

Figure 10.2

Trends in material deprivation

Source: EU-SILC 2005 to 2013

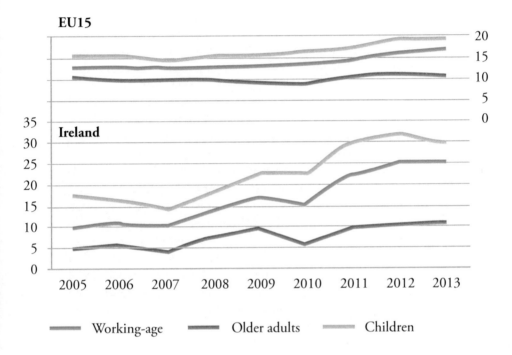

clearly in the 1998 cohort, since the interviewing was substantially completed before the very steep rise in unemployment in the fourth quarter of 2008.

Results

Trends over time

Before turning to the situation of families with children based on the GUI data, we draw on data from the EU Survey of Income and Living Conditions (EU-SILC) to provide some background on how the situation of children has compared to that of older adults since 2004. In Figure 10.2 we focus on trends in material deprivation, which refers to having to do without three or more of nine basic goods and services because the household cannot afford them. Even before the recession, there was a higher risk of material deprivation among children than among adults.

The gap between the age groups is particularly large in Ireland. While older adults were relatively protected during the recession, children suffered most. The level of material deprivation in households with children increased sharply in 2008, as the recession began, and rose again in 2011 following cuts to working-age social welfare payments and Child Benefit in 2010 and again in 2011. At the same time, the levels of the state pensions were maintained. The highest level of material deprivation was in 2013, with a rate of 30% among children compared to 10% among older adults. While the rate is also higher for children than for older adults in the EU-15,[1] the gap is wider in Ireland. In 2012, the rate among children in Ireland was 30%, compared to 25% for working-age adults and just 10% for adults over age 60.

The focus on material deprivation is part of a growing recognition that poverty is not just about money. In the case of children it has also been argued that our measures should take account of the experiences of children themselves (Kerrins et al. 2011). However, Whelan and Maître (2012) and Watson et al. (2012), taking advantage of a special module in the CSO SILC 2009 module, concluded that the children exposed specifically to childhood deprivation were generally a subset of children captured by population indicators. On the other hand, restricting our attention to childhood deprivation would lead us to miss out on a significant number of children residing in households experiencing deprivation but not exposed to deprivation on specifically childhood items. Ridge (2009), in an in-depth qualitative study, found that children showed keen insight into the challenges and demands that poverty generates for their parents. Identifying children in poverty does not necessarily require providing an in-depth account of their experiences, although such accounts are valuable for a variety of purposes including the design of child-appropriate responses.

Economic vulnerability

The indicator of economic vulnerability is designed to measure economic disadvantage by taking account of several dimensions rather than relying solely on income (Grusky and Weeden, 2007; Nolan and Whelan 2007, 2010). The inclusion of several dimensions and

Figure 10.3

Change in the economic vulnerability level of families between the
first and second waves of the GUI surveys

Source: Growing Up in Ireland Survey, 1998 Cohort at ages 9 and 13;
2008 cohort at ages nine months and 3.

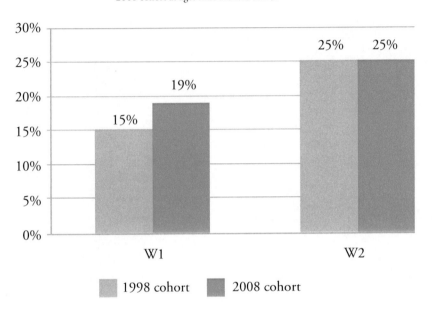

focusing on the notion of latent risk profiles is intended to capture
distinctions that are likely to be more enduring than those based on
current disposable income, or indeed multiple deprivation at a particular point in time (Hanappi *et al.* 2015). In the present analysis,
we identify families that are economically vulnerable by looking at
three indicators—income level, household joblessness, and economic
stress—and using latent class analysis to identify the economically
vulnerable group (see Watson *et al.* 2014 for details).

Figure 10.3 shows change in the economic vulnerability level of
families between the first and second waves of the surveys. Recall that
the data collection for the 1998 cohort in the first wave took place
before the start of the recession while the recession had already begun
by the time interviewing was conducted with the families of the 2008

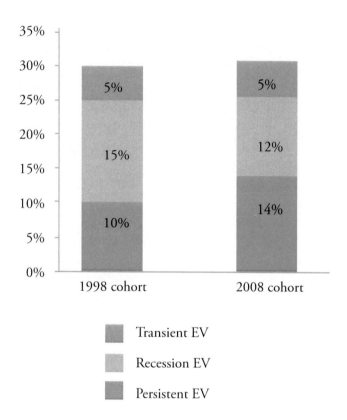

Figure 10.4

Economic vulnerability groups.

Source: Growing Up in Ireland Survey, 1998 Cohort at ages 9 and 13;
2008 cohort at ages nine months and 3.

cohort. As a result, the level of economic vulnerability in the first wave was higher for the 2008 cohort (19% compared to 15%) because the families were already feeling the effects of the recession. By the second wave, which took place in mid-recession for both groups, the rate of economic vulnerability had increased to 25% for both groups.

Economic vulnerability dynamics

With such a substantial increase in economic vulnerability over the period, it is clear that many families that had not been vulnerable in the first wave were drawn into such vulnerability in the recession. However, the longitudinal nature of the data allows us to look at vulnerability dynamics. We can distinguish three groups: persistent vulnerability refers to being vulnerable in both waves; transient vulnerability refers to being vulnerable in the first wave but not in the second wave; and recession vulnerability refers to becoming economically vulnerable in the second wave in mid-recession.

Figure 10.4 shows that there was some persistence of economic vulnerability (10% of the 1998 cohort and 15% of the 2008 cohort), some families drawn into this situation by the recession (15% and 12%, respectively), and also a certain amount of escape from economic vulnerability (5% of both groups). Again, the timing of the first wave has a bearing on the level of persistent and recession vulnerability for both groups. In other words, it is not that the 2008 cohort was less affected by the recession (with 12% vs. 15% entering economic vulnerability as a result of the recession) but that they were already beginning to experience the effects of the recession in the first wave, as we saw in Figure 10.3.

Earlier analyses also showed that the recession had an impact not only on levels of vulnerability, but also on the character of vulnerability (Watson *et al.* 2014). In the first wave, especially for the 1998 cohort where the interviews took place before the start of the recession, the main driver of economic vulnerability was low income. However, by the second wave, economic stress and household joblessness had become much more important. This shows the impact of the recession on the nature of disadvantage, with an increase in the pressure to make ends meet in the context of falling employment levels, increasing debt levels, falling earnings, and reduced social welfare payments as a result of fiscal consolidation and austerity measures.

Consequences for children

As noted above, previous research has pointed to a range of negative consequences that poverty has for children. The GUI data allow us to examine some of these consequences in an Irish context. Of particular relevance from a policy perspective is the question of whether the negative consequences are found mainly for children in families that were persistently economically vulnerable or are also apparent for those in families drawn into economic vulnerability in the recession.

We focus here on children's socio-emotional development as measured by the Strengths & Difficulties Questionnaire (SDQ; Goodman

Figure 10.5

Adjusted risk of socio-emotional problems by economic vulnerability

Source: Growing Up in Ireland Survey, 1998 Cohort at ages 9 and 13;
2008 cohort at ages nine months and 3 (based on results of model shown in Table 10.1).

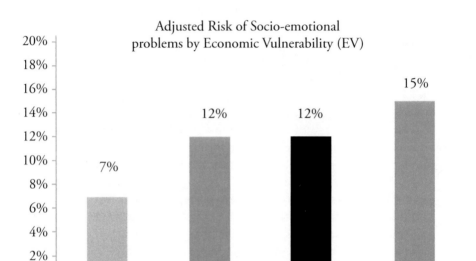

1997). This scale is designed to assess emotional health and problem behaviours among children and young people. It includes indicators of emotional problems, conduct problems, hyperactivity/inattention and peer relationship problems. The questionnaire was completed by the PCG (usually the child's mother). We take the top 10% of scores here as this is the group most likely to experience socio-emotional problems.

A range of other family and child characteristics will also be associated with having a high SDQ score. For instance, high SDQ scores are more common among boys and among children whose parents have lower levels of education. In presenting the results on the relationship between economic vulnerability and the risk of socio-emotional problems, then, we show the 'adjusted risk' in Figure 10.5. This is the percentage we would expect to see with a high SDQ score in each of the four economic vulnerability dynamics categories with other characteristics held constant (calculated from model Table 10.1). The other characteristics are child gender, cohort, family type (lone-parent or couple household by number of children), mother's education, mother's age at child's birth and change in family composition between waves (e.g. separation, additional children).

Figure 10.5 shows that the adjusted risk of socio-emotional problems is 7% for children whose families were economically vulnerable in neither wave; 12% for children in families that were economically vulnerable in one of the two waves and 15% for children in families that were economically vulnerable in both waves. It is clear that economic vulnerability has negative consequences for children's socio-emotional development and these consequences are more marked where the economic vulnerability is persistent. It is also worth noting, though, that although the families drawn into economic vulnerability by the recession had experienced vulnerability for a shorter period, the negative consequences for children were still apparent compared to those vulnerable in neither wave. It may at times have seemed as though economic hardship in the recession was almost the norm. However, the children in families worst affected by the recession suffered, even if they had been in better circumstances before the recession.

A second point worth noting is that even in the families whose economic vulnerability was transient, the negative impact on socio-emotional development of the children was still evident. They may not have been as badly affected as those whose vulnerability was persistent, but they fared worse than those who were not economically vulnerable in either wave.

Other analyses, not shown here, indicated that the impact of economic vulnerability on socio-emotional development was similar for boys and girls and for the two cohorts. In other words, there was no evidence that economic vulnerability had more serious consequences for boys than girls, or vice versa, or that the consequences were more serious for the younger cohort than for the older cohort.

Conclusions and implications

As noted at the beginning of this chapter, poverty and deprivation rates had been higher for children than for adults even before the recession—a pattern that was general in the EU-15, though more marked in Ireland. Drawing on a multi-dimensional indicator of economic disadvantage based on low income, household joblessness and economic stress, we examined the impact of the recession on the economic vulnerability of families. Economic vulnerability increased for families during the recession, reaching 25% for the families of both cohorts by mid-recession.

The longitudinal design of the GUI survey allowed us to examine the extent of persistence or transition in economic vulnerability between the first two waves of the survey. Focusing on the 1998 cohort for whom the first wave of interviews took place before the start of the recession, we found that 10% of families were economically vulnerable in both waves, 15% became economically vulnerable in the recession, and 5% managed to escape economic vulnerability. We noted some differences in the profile of the group drawn into economic vulnerability during the recession. The dimensions of joblessness and economic stress became more important whereas low income had dominated before the recession. In addition, the group that became economically vulnerable in the recession had a less disadvantaged profile than the group that had been vulnerable in the first wave of the survey: the parents in the former families were more likely to have better levels of education and to be couple families. As a result, those entering vulnerability were far less likely to fit the typical profile of those dependent on social welfare in the pre-recession era.

As Nolan and Maître (2017) note, changes in the tax and transfer system resulted in average declines in income for families with children greater than those for other working-age family types, reflecting cuts in Child Benefit and Early Childcare Supplement in particular, although they also note that this occurred in a context where such universal payments for children had increased substantially during the years of the economic boom to the point where child-related transfers were among the most generous in the EU. While the impact of the recession on the incomes of households with children was significantly buffered, judgements differ as to whether there were feasible alternatives that would have more effectively protected children while at the same time dealing with the scale of the fiscal crisis.

In any event, whether we focus on reductions in real income, material deprivation, economic stress or economic vulnerability for households with children, worklessness is central (Watson *et al.* 2012).

Households with children were also hardest hit by the property collapse and exposure to negative equity, mortgage arrears, increased debt levels in general, public-sector wage cuts and cutbacks in public services. The combined impact of these factors ensured that the impact of economic crisis was experienced far more severely by children and their parents than by, in particular, the elderly. Compared with Iceland and Greece—countries that have experienced similar levels of economic upheaval—Ireland emerges as quite distinctive in this respect (Whelan *et al.* 2016b).

Economic vulnerability has negative implications for children. Focusing on child socio-emotional development measured with the Strengths and Difficulties Questionnaire, we identified a group of children in the top decile: those most likely to have socio-emotional and behavioural problems. Children in economically vulnerable families were more likely to have socio-emotional problems even taking into account other characteristics of the child (such as gender) and family (family type; age and education of primary-care giver). After taking account of other characteristics, the adjusted proportion with socio-emotional problems was 7% where the family was not economically vulnerable; 12% where the family had been economically vulnerable in one of the two waves, and 15% where the family was economically vulnerable in both waves.

These findings have a number of implications for policy. Clearly, in order to ensure the healthy development of children, attention to economic vulnerability is warranted. Not only was persistent economic vulnerability a problem, but at the second wave we could still see the negative consequences for children of having been economically vulnerable in the first wave—an effect that persisted for over two years. We could also see the negative consequences of having become economically vulnerable in the recession. Both of these findings point to the importance of taking seriously even a short-term adverse shock to the economic well-being of families.

Another implication is linked to the changing profile of economically vulnerable families. In line with the general findings of Whelan and Nolan (Chapter 6, this volume), a broader group of families was drawn into economic vulnerability in the recession: more couple families and more families with higher levels of education. Tackling economic vulnerability for this more diverse group will require moving beyond the traditional focus in welfare policy on income support, to include a mix of strategies such as those addressing childcare, housing supply and housing costs. The challenge for the future is to find the optimal mix of income support and services to meet the needs of a more diverse group of families at risk of economic vulnerability. Income support will remain important for families whose earning capacity is reduced by low levels of education, disability or having just one parent available to juggle the tasks of carer and breadwinner. Issues such as housing affordability are likely to be more pressing for families at a higher level of income but who are above the eligibility threshold for social housing support. As Ronan Lyons (Chapter 8, this volume) has suggested, this will be challenging as the housing challenge can only be resolved by examining the underlying structures of housing provision in Ireland in order to properly address diverse housing needs. Finally, childcare costs and availability are relevant to most families of young children, except the small number who can afford to have one parent act as full-time carer or have access to support from an extended family.

The Growing Up in Ireland Survey is an incredibly rich source of data on children and families in Ireland, and the analysis here could only draw on a small part of the data. Other research has shown that the impact of economic vulnerability on children can be somewhat ameliorated by family resources such as high levels of parental education or the presence of two parents (Watson *et al.* 2014). Research has also shown that family dynamics—parenting style, maternal depression, marital satisfaction and the parent–child relationship—matter for children's socio-emotional well-being (Nixon 2012). The nature of the impact of the recession on such family dynamics could be explored in greater depth. The importance of these family dynamics and non-monetary resources suggests that services and supports to vulnerable families may be part of the response to the 'recession scarring' of children.

In the first chapter of this volume, Simon Wren-Lewis defines austerity in terms of a fiscal consolidation that leads to significant increases in involuntary unemployment. In this chapter, we traced the impact of rising unemployment and household joblessness on the economic vulnerability of families. Further, we showed the link between such economic vulnerability and an increased risk of socio-emotional problems in children: problems that are already visible in families that became economically vulnerable as a result of the recession and that are still visible in children a number of years after the episode of economic vulnerability. This is all the more regrettable if Wren-Lewis is correct in his assessment that austerity could have been avoided or, at least, the worst impact on unemployment could have been reduced. An important lesson for the future will be the need to factor in the cost of the long-term consequences of child poverty and vulnerability in the calculus underlying politico-economic decisions.

Note

[1] Austria, Belgium, Denmark, Finland, France, Germany, Greece, Ireland, Italy, Luxembourg, the Netherlands, Portugal, Spain, Sweden and United Kingdom

Table 10.1

Relative risk ratios for potentially problematic SDQ by characteristics of child and family

Source: Growing Up in Ireland Survey, 1998 Cohort at ages 9 and 13; 2008 cohort at ages nine months and 3.

		Odds ratios
Gender of Child	Male	(Ref)
	Female	0.738***
Age of primary care-giver at birth of child	Under 25	1.485***
	25-29	1.437***
	30-34	1.096
	35-39	(Ref)
	40+	1.403*
Household Type Wave 1	Lone parent, 1 child	1.334*
	Lone parent, 2+ children	1.077
	Couple, one child	(Ref)
	Couple, two children	0.801**
	Couple, 3+ children	0.680***
Cohabiting in Wave 1?	No	(Ref)
	Yes, cohabiting W1	1.101
Change in carers(s) by Wave 2	No change	(Ref)
	New carer joins	1.122
	One parent died/left	1.795***
More children by Wave 2	No	(Ref)
	Yes, more children	1.049
Primary care-giver education, wave 1	Lower 2nd level or less	2.225***
	Upper 2nd to lower 3rd level	1.473***
	Third level degree or higher	(Ref)
Economic Vulnerability	Neither wave	(Ref)
	Wave 1 only	1.682***
	Wave 2 only	1.678***
Cohort	Both waves	2.227***
	Child born in 2008	(Ref)
	Child Born in 1998	1.149
Constant		0.050***
Observations		17,079

*** $p<0.01$, ** $p<0.05$, * $p<0.1$

11. Resilience: a high price for survival? The impact of austerity on Irish higher education, South and North

Rosalind Pritchard and Maria Slowey

Introduction: austerity and resilience

The response to the international 2008 financial crash, and the subsequent recession, was similar in most developed countries: the imposition of economic austerity. Based on a series of neoliberal economic arguments, austerity policies resulted *inter alia* in fundamental, systemic reductions in public expenditure. While presented as 'neutral' or inevitable, core policies were ideologically driven, as previously discussed in this volume by Allen (Chapter 3) and Mercille (Chapter 4) among others, and associated with the aim to 'shrink the state' (notably commented upon by Nobel Laureates Krugman (2010) and Stiglitz (2012)). In relation to higher education, the extent to which recent austerity policies represent a fundamental change in direction, or rather a logical intensification of several decades of neoliberal policies, is open for debate (Schuetze and Alvarez-Mendiola 2012). The

UK in particular has been at the forefront of a global growth of audit culture and new public management in higher education (Henkel and Little 1999; Deem *et al.* 2007; Shattock 2012).

A cross-border analysis of selected aspects of the impact of austerity on higher education in the Republic of Ireland and Northern Ireland offers an interesting comparative opportunity because, although higher education institutions (HEIs) operate under different political and financial regimes, universities in the two jurisdictions have a shared history, and both parts of Ireland 'have an administrative system heavily influenced by British practice and commitment to public service' (Osborne 1996, p. 3).[1] We draw on the concept of 'institutional resilience' as an analytic tool with which to explore responses to the funding crisis brought about as part of austerity measures. Resilience here is defined as 'the capacity of individuals or social/ technical systems to handle boundary conditions and interpret early warnings and weak signals of change' (Karlsen and Pritchard 2013, p. 1). In this endeavour, two characteristics have been shown to be of importance: the ability to detect potential short- or medium-term threats; and the 'strength of will, determination, perseverance and [...] capacity to act rationally in the face of hardship...' (Välikangas 2010, p. 3).

Our chapter draws on original qualitative accounts (oral or written) provided by some expert observers and senior officers of HEIs, giving a snapshot of 'response resilience' in highly constrained circumstances. We make no claims for generalisability and, as respondents' views are largely from a leadership perspective, evidently they represent one point of view among many competing narratives. This short discussion of inevitably complex issues is organised in four parts: first, a brief summary of higher education funding trends in the Republic and Northern Ireland; second, 'snapshots' illustrating the impact of funding cuts on students and staff; third, issues of governance, leadership and resilience; finally, we reflect on the price of resilience in terms of potential compromising of core values and purposes.

The financial crisis and higher education funding cuts

The public higher education providers on the island of Ireland comprise: (a) seven universities in the Republic and two in Northern Ireland (plus the Open University); (b) Institutes of Technology (IoTs) in the Republic (a number of which in 2016 were seeking recognition as Technological Universities); and (c) in both jurisdictions, Colleges

Table 11.1

Irish universities: Times Higher Education World University Rankings 2015

Source: personal communication to author RP by *THE*, 12 October 2015.

Institution	Rank	No. of FTE students*	Staff–student ratio	International students
Trinity College Dublin (TCD)	160	15,521	18	25%
University College Dublin (UCD)	=176	22,193	24.5	23%
Queen's University Belfast (QUB)	200	17,940	17.9	30%
National University of Ireland, Galway (NUIG)	251–300	14,067	26.8	14%
Maynooth University (MU)	351–400	7.653	28	11%
University College Cork (UCC)	351–400	15,805	22.3	15%
Dublin City University (DCU)	401–500	8,546	22.9	17%
Ulster University (UU)	401–500	19,622	15.8	15%
University of Limerick (UL)	501–600	12,212	19.8	13%

Data extracted from the WUR (2015).

*FTE, full-time equivalent. *Times Higher Education* (*THE*) ensures that income figures provided are converted using Purchasing Price Parity which adjusts for countries' relative prosperities; responses from its reputation survey are calibrated in line with UNESCO listed academic population levels; there is a country adjustment in the citation scores.

of Education, regional Colleges of Further and Higher Education and specialist colleges. The focus of this chapter is predominantly on the university sector, where governance structures are very similar in the two jurisdictions. While the value and validity of international HEI rankings are questionable for many reasons (Hazelkorn 2011), they offer a shorthand way to demonstrate that Irish universities on both sides of the border arguably 'punch above their weight'. For example, in the World University Ranking, four Irish universities are listed in the top 300 and all are in the top 600 (WUR 2015; Table 11.1).

However, the impact of the economic crash on higher education in the Republic has been particularly dramatic. Core state expenditure declined steeply from 2007/08 onwards at a time when student numbers were increasing, resulting in a drop in per-student income of approximately 22% to 2015 (Figure 11.1). There had been a

Figure 11.1

Core (state) income for higher education by total student numbers
Republic of Ireland: 2007/8–2015/16

Source: adapted from: *Expert Group on the Future of Higher Education [Ireland]* (2015a, Figure 2, p. 5)

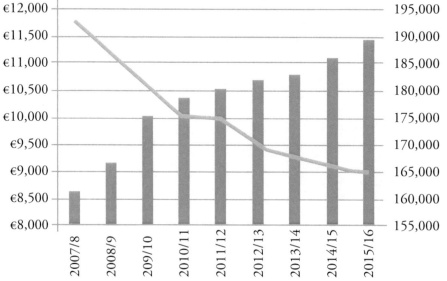

FTE Students
Income per student

decrease of funding per student of 18%, from €11,000 to €9,000 (T. Boland 2015): from a low base, as, for example, it has been estimated (Hazelkorn 2011) that investment per student enrolment in TCD is less than one sixth that of universities with comparable ranking in the USA. As a publication by the Royal Irish Academy (2016a) outlines, the higher education capital budget had been reduced by 85% since 2008 while student numbers increased by 25%, and the staff–student ratio deteriorated from 16:1 to over 20:1, comparing poorly with the OECD average of 14:1. Investment in infrastructure had fallen from over €200m in 2008 to €35m in 2014 (NERI 2014). Employers joined HEIs, the Higher Education Authority, staff and student unions in drawing attention to the detrimental impact of these cuts; the national employer representative body pointed out that Ireland was one of only four OECD countries in which spending on tertiary education had decreased since 2008, resulting in a system that 'is unsustainable and is close to breaking point' (IBEC 2016, p. 23).

The situation in Northern Ireland has been somewhat different. As a post-conflict society it had long relied on transfers from the British Exchequer to fund increases in public expenditure; this led to a large public sector, the size of which was not in proportion to Northern Ireland's tax base. In 2015 about 30% of its workforce was employed in the public sector compared with 18% in the UK as a whole and about 20% in the Republic of Ireland (V. Boland, 2015). The effects of the crisis thus took somewhat longer to manifest themselves in Northern Ireland than in the Republic, and it was not until 2011/12 that they became obvious, as is shown in Figure 11.2.

A comprehensive analysis of the development of higher education in the Republic undertaken by Clancy (2015, p. 245) identified three main factors as contributing to the crisis. While both the political landscape and the funding base for higher education are different, these also carry resonances in Northern Ireland.

- First, the increasing demand from potential students for access to higher education.
- Second, strong competing demands for support from other areas of public service, coupled with a political culture in favour of no increases in taxation, or even reductions in tax levels.
- Third, the fact that the economic boom and bust cycle had placed family households under severe financial pressures.

Figure 11.2

Recurrent grant to universities in Northern Ireland 2007/8 to 2015/2016

Source: Department for Employment and Learning (DELNI) provided at RP's request.

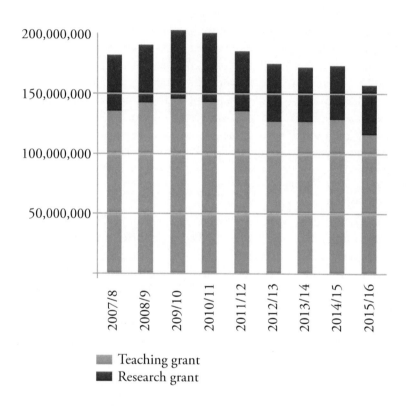

The impact of austerity on higher education

'Cost-sharing'

Our interest here is not in financial detail but rather in the 'austerity' policy momentum on both sides of the border towards 'cost-sharing'. In the Republic, while student fees had been abolished in 1997, by 2016 an initially nominal annual Student Contribution had increased to just under €3,000—perhaps not coincidentally, similar to the initial fee of £3,000 in the UK introduced by the Labour government in 1999. An Expert Group set up in the Republic to identify funding options commenced its work by outlining the central purposes and value of higher education in contemporary Irish society as adding 'to the understanding of, and hence the flourishing of, an integrated social, institutional, cultural and economic life' (Expert Group 2015a, p. iii). By the time the final report was published in 2016, it estimated that additional annual funding of €600 million would be required by 2021 and €1 billion by 2030 'to deliver higher quality outcomes and provide for increased demographics. This will allow an improvement in student:staff ratios, better engagement with students, and improved support services for teachers and students' (Expert Group 2016, p. 7). It was argued that this investment was essential to underpin the quality of undergraduate education, along with a capital investment of €5.5 billion and additional €100 million to deliver a 'more effective system' of student financial aid. The main body of the report outlined a range of international policy approaches that might deliver this level of funding, reflecting different balances between public and private stakeholders including employers; it was fully aware of how controversial decisions might appear when deciding how to share the remaining burden between the student and the State (Expert Group 2016, p. 7).

This was different to the approach taken by the British Conservative government which, in a radical and controversial move in England, not only increased undergraduate fees up to a ceiling of £9,000 (set to rise in line with forecasted inflation and subject to evidence of teaching excellence), but left certain Humanities and Social Sciences subjects without any core ('block') funding apart from fees contingent on student enrolment (Pritchard 2015). Students in Northern Ireland pay lower fees than in England (2016 fees were £3,810), a decision for a time hailed as a triumph for devolution, and intended to facilitate access for less advantaged students. Initially, the NI Executive bridged the deficit between the Northern Irish and English tuition fee rates, but subsequently the disparity between the two funding regimes grew because less money is available for higher education due to overall pressures on public expenditure in Northern Ireland. In 2014/15 the equivalent funding gap between Northern Ireland universities and their English counterparts was over £39 million, or between £1,000 and £2,500 per student depending on subject area. The rate of disinvestment increased in 2015/16 with further cuts of over £16 million (Royal Irish Academy 2016b).

Widening access

An important policy priority shared by both jurisdictions in recent decades is to widen access to students from socio-economic and other groups underrepresented in higher education. While stark inequalities remain (Byrne and McCoy 2013), some progress has been made on both sides of the border. For example, in the UK overall, 32.6% of young full-time first degree entrants were from National Statistics Socio-economic Classifications (NS-SEC) 4 to 7 in 2013/14; this compares with 32.5% at Queen's University Belfast (QUB) and 45.8% at Ulster University (UU) (Department for Employment and Learning 2015). In the Republic, a detailed analysis showed small but steady progress over time in increasing accessibility for those from manual and lower non-manual backgrounds (Clancy and Goastellec 2007). However, while policies North and South seek to mitigate financial pressures through means-tested supports and special access routes, all respondents in our study expressed concerns about the impact of austerity policies on access in the Republic.[2]

> For undergraduate students the recession and budget cuts have meant: increasing student contributions; fewer part-time and summer jobs available; less money in the home to support students; limited ability to borrow (with a credit squeeze). These tend to have disproportionate impact on the poorest families who are less likely to have the resources, and are also less likely to have an expectation of automatic progression to higher education. (R3)

This respondent commented how, in their institution, an annual hardship fund had been entirely spent before the end of the first semester.

Study participants also signalled a high impact on mature, part-time and postgraduate students, precisely the target groups for the lifelong learning approach widely associated with the 'knowledge society' (Slowey and Schuetze 2012). One drew attention to 'swingeing cuts in support for community education and related NGO activity over 2008–12', pointing to a lack of coherence and suggesting that there were 'substantial reductions in those geographical areas known to be most disadvantaged' (R8). Daly (2015) has highlighted in particular the injustice of part-time students being excluded from the Free Fees scheme and ineligible for maintenance grants in contrast to their full-time peers; indeed several interviewees in our study emphasised that for part-time higher education students there has been a very serious contraction of funding opportunities which has 'disproportionately impacted on people in lower socio-economic groups' (R12).

Impact on staff

One of the most obvious, immediate and dramatic effects of austerity policies in Ireland was a real reduction in the income of academic, research and support staff through a combination of salary cuts and increased pension and other levies (Clarke *et al.* 2015). An 'emergency' government-imposed Employment Control Framework (ECF) halted staff appointments (academic, research and support) in HEIs as it did in all public bodies. So even if universities were able to generate income from other sources they could not use this for staff promotions or appointments. This limitation on the ability to manage their own resources not only made it more difficult to extricate HEIs from an extremely challenging situation but, arguably, cut to the heart of institutional autonomy—a point to which we return later. The ECF resulted in 'a drop in salary, reduced promotion opportunities, increase in working hours, more short term contracts, attempts at course rationalisation, early retirements resulting in a depletion in experienced staff in the sector' (R7).

Examining the implications of the dramatic decline in funding per student in the Republic, the Chief Executive of the Higher Education Authority made clear his awareness that the system was struggling to cope with reduced levels of public funding, recognising that staff in the institutions 'responded with resilience and flexibility, well above the norm. But such resilience cannot be sustained indefinitely and morale among many staff is now low, and will sink further if there is no end in sight' (T. Boland 2015, p. 2). With reports of increasing class sizes and concerns about student attendance levels (Slowey *et al.* 2014), the high standing of the Irish higher education system was in considerable jeopardy without 'an injection of investment and a renewed approach to sustaining its capital and recurrent funding needs ... A policy of managed decline, by default if not deliberate, opens up an appalling vista for our future' (T. Boland 2015, p. 11).

In contrast to the situation in the Republic, for a time after the economic crisis universities in Northern Ireland fared reasonably well financially. Thus we read that for QUB 2012/13 was 'another successful year' with a surplus of £10.7m and a net assets position, at 31 July 2013, of £461.4m; total income for the year had increased by 1.2% (QUB

2013). UU's financial results for the 2012–13 year showed a surplus of £14.4 million, a margin of 7.5%, and net cash (assets) of £51m (UU 2013).[3] However, the good times did not last and in 2015, the funding allocation for HEIs fell by 8.2%. QUB announced immediate job cuts of *c*.236 and student cuts of *c*.290 (1,010 over the next three years). Ulster University also intended to cut over 200 jobs and 250 student places in the 2015–16 session (1,200 over the next three years).

As early as 2012, in an analysis of stress factors (University and College Union (UCU) 2012a, 2012b, 2014), both Queen's and Ulster University were placed in a group with below-average well-being and above-average stress levels. Staff were working long hours: at QUB, 40.6% worked more than 50 hours per week, and at UU, the corresponding figure was 43%. Over half of the respondents (53%) in a UU survey of staff stated that they were 'often' or 'always' pressured to work long hours, and one third claimed that they were constantly 'working intensely' (Faulkner 2012). The impact of the most recent cuts on staff has seen a further deterioration in psycho-social welfare.

Austerity policies, governance and resilience

One central manifestation of austerity policies is the impact on governance—specifically, issues of agency—and the extent to which HEIs are in a position to manage their own affairs, for good or bad. Clearly, accountability for public investment is essential. But, as one expert international respondent in our study put it:

> Irish universities are operating with one hand tied behind their backs. I find it extraordinary that the Irish government has imposed these cuts on the one hand, but on the other has not enabled universities to respond to those cuts in an optimal way. (R13)

Drawing from a typology for comparative analysis of governance (de Boer *et al.* 2007), we consider two aspects: state regulation and academic self-governance.

State regulation

As mentioned earlier, the UK was one of the first countries to introduce neoliberalism and new public management (NPM) into higher education, increasing the exposure of the universities to market forces and bringing them more under the direct control of the state, notably through a process of mandatory quality assurance (Pritchard 2011, pp. 1–18, 130; 2013). Broucker *et al.* (2016) have developed a typology of NPM characteristics and by a series of criteria they align ten countries along a continuum of early, medium and late adopters of NPM. England belongs to the early category, as does the USA. Ireland is not among the ten studied, but one could reasonably argue that it is a middle adopter, having begun the neoliberal changes long before late adopters like Hungary or Lithuania. Ireland did not experience the political equivalent of Thatcherism in the 1980s; however, the pace of change accelerated and a comprehensive review of developments in Ireland points to increased centralisation and a 'clear pattern whereby universities have experienced a sharp decline in autonomy in the face of a more interventionist state' (Clancy 2015, p. 270). To take a concrete example, mentioned by most respondents in various ways, institutions were left with little opportunity to manage staff retirements and appointments. Thus, in one institution, a national incentive scheme for early retirement

> resulted in a cohort of the most experienced staff all departing within a short period of time. Departure rates that would, in normal times, take a period of ten years occurred in a 2–3 year period. (R4)

Austerity measures thus resulted in direct 'interference' as

> reduced public funding, increased student numbers, and the curtailment of staff numbers through the governmentally imposed ECF, all ... have constrained the University's freedom to operate. Because of this sharp reduction in unit resource, all universities in Ireland have been forced to increase intake in order to achieve balanced budgets. This is a vicious circle that obviously cannot continue indefinitely. (R1)

One respondent observed that 'the economic imperative has required some hard but appropriate changes to be made' (R2). However, overall it was strongly emphasised that attempts to absorb cuts put institutions under major strain, the cumulative impact being that austerity has allowed the Government to drive an agenda that in its own right may have significant negative impacts. The general interference and micromanagement of activity at one end and the introduction of ill-thought out strategies around clustering and consolidation … are requiring excessive management time for minimal improvement to the system. (R2)

Academic self-governance

With the rise of managerialism in HEIs and the president or vice chancellor as chief executive rather than first among equals, collegial bodies such as the Academic Senate became less powerful and increasingly expected to endorse decisions made at executive levels (Shattock 2012). Associated with this growth in managerialism was an emphasis on quality management: in 1997 the UK established the Quality Assurance Agency, which functioned as a regulator and represented for some 'an attack on academic assumptions of self-regulation' (Henkel 2000, p. 111).

In Ireland, academic and curriculum decisions are the clear responsibility of academic councils (or their equivalent in the case of TCD). However, with a view to 'complying' with the Bologna Process and associated criteria for independence of scrutiny, the Irish universities voluntarily ceded their right to review academic units and quality of teaching to the Irish Universities Quality Board, a jointly administered agency. One direct effect of the financial crisis was a government cost-cutting decision in 2012 to merge this body with three other related agencies into Quality and Qualifications Ireland with, arguably, further loss of autonomy (Government of Ireland 2012).

But perhaps most important is the fact that, increasingly, educational decisions are based on resourcing rather than academic grounds. This is not to slip into some mythical notion of a 'golden age', but all respondents were concerned that the quality of education is being eroded, leaving a dilemma for the system as a whole because

no single institution wants to be the first to suggest that all of this is having a directly detrimental effect on the quality of Irish higher education … however, there can be no doubt that the cumulative effect of these measures we are forced to adopt will impact on quality. (R14)

Any public admission of falling quality could cause a crisis of confidence in Irish HEIs and reduce their rankings.

Resilience: Higher education responds

Sitting alongside critiques of new public management in higher education is a growing emphasis—in difficult times—on the importance of leadership in higher education (Middlehurst *et al.* 2014). Given the impact of austerity policies, perhaps inevitably the first focus of senior officers is on how/where to cut budgets, with opportunities for intellectual leadership curtailed. Respondents described a common range of steps taken, including

> increased class sizes, larger tutorial groups, and reduced access to one-to-one interaction with academics; reduced options and subject streams; academics teaching increasing student numbers (with a consequent impact on research time); reduced library purchasing and opening hours; charges for medical services; reduced support services such as porters, security and building opening hours. (R1)

In the case of the Republic the second main strategy has been to attempt to generate revenue from non-governmental sources including recruitment of international students, borrowing for infrastructure projects, seeking philanthropic funding, establishing spin-off companies and maximising income from commercial activity; the last mentioned, as a respondent points out, 'indirectly impacts on the student experience as we raise money by licensing activities such as food provision, shops, banking, etc.' (R2). The overall result is that by 2015 most Irish universities were generating around 50% of their income from such sources (Expert Group 2015b), representing 'a very significant shift for institutions that are nominally public bodies' (R14).

In Northern Ireland, the economic position of the universities tends to be counter-cyclical. In bad times they may contract less than other enterprises, while in boom times they may not grow as fast (QUB 2013, p. 14). If we consider just the issue of buildings, Ulster University has begun work on a new £250 million city-centre campus to house the transfer of about 15,000 students and staff from Jordanstown to the Cathedral Quarter in Belfast. The project began in 2012/13 and is continuing despite the financial downturn. Queen's wants to move into the top league of global universities, and is investing £205 million within a rolling five-year plan to enhance its estate (QUB 2013). In a press release (UUK, March 2015) UU and QUB show that in 2012/13 they contributed £1.5 billion to the NI economy with over 18,000 jobs created. Their publicity forms part of their fight to demonstrate resilience and their value to the community, though some staff claim that Queen's cares more about buildings than about human beings (UCU 2013).

Concluding comment: survival, but at what price?

Our analysis has shown through a series of short 'snapshots' how the higher education context on the island of Ireland has radically changed in the past decade. But how far do the 'austerity policies' represent a substantial change in policy direction in Ireland or Northern Ireland? Or do they mainly reflect an acceleration of wider international trends characteristic of higher education policy in many states since the 1990s? Scott (2015) points to a number of characteristics of the accentuated global 'neoliberal turn' in higher education, three of which, although they play out somewhat differently, can be readily discerned in Ireland, North and South.

First, and most significantly, the trend towards what is termed 'cost-sharing'—a concept widely promulgated by influential international agencies such as OECD and the World Bank—contributes, some have argued, to a global trend of isomorphism in higher education systems (Meyer et al. 2007) at the expense of addressing the specifics of national environments (Clancy 2016). We certainly see evidence of a focus on 'cost-sharing' on both sides of the border as central to rolling back the impact of recent austerity measures. In the current political climate in the Republic of Ireland this will almost certainly involve charging students upfront or through some deferred repayment system (see RIA 2016a for options). Similarly in Northern Ireland, standards appear hard to maintain unless the HEIs can harvest additional funding to keep them comparable with other parts of the UK, especially England, where maximum fees are charged. The evidence from the UK suggests that while the widening participation agenda for school leavers has not been damaged by the existence of fees, the impact on lifelong learning, in terms of part-time study, has been severe (Callender 2013). Moreover, as Watson et al. (Chapter 10 in the present volume) point out, high financial demands can contribute to a wider climate of insecurity and exposure to risk and shock for the most vulnerable families.

Second, the increasing significance of institutional leadership has transformed organisational culture within higher education institutions. Both North and South, there is evidence of what one of the founders of contemporary sociological study of higher education, Burton Clark (1998), termed the strengthened 'steering core'. Comprising senior leaders and managers, the steering core is presented as a necessary 'rational' organisational response to the complexity of issues with which universities and other HEIs are dealing. Viewed from this perspective, our senior respondents' complaint that their room for manoeuvre is highly constrained by contemporary state policies makes perfect sense. On the other hand, decisions are taken on a daily basis about where cuts might hit or where any possible new investment might be made: decisions that are not 'neutral' but are socially constructed (as shown in empirical studies from Slaughter and Leslie's (1997) work on retrenchment and academic capitalism through to recent analyses of gender in higher education management in the Republic (O'Connor 2014)).

Third, with the increasing importance attached to international rankings by politicians in particular (whether or not this focus is justified), a challenge is posed to national or regional 'systems' of higher education with the growth of (selective) international networks of institutions. In the Republic, largely with a view to increasing efficiency and effectiveness, a national strategy supporting institutional alliances, mergers, networks and regional groupings of various kinds has become part of the policy landscape (Slowey 2013; Clancy 2015). In Northern Ireland discussions continue about generating efficiencies in traditionally divided areas such as teacher education (Borooah and Knox 2015). HEIs on the island of Ireland have much in common and, potentially, reputations for quality can be jointly enhanced or damaged. In these difficult times, perhaps one area for positive development may lie in strengthening developments in north–south HEI collaboration as a form of international network (Clancy 2015, p. 183).[4] However, Brexit may well make it harder for Northern Ireland to establish and sustain international research contacts, networks and mobility; one part of the island of Ireland will be in the EU and the other outside it: hardly desirable conditions for promoting greater synergies.

At their best, HEIs in Ireland are displaying considerable resilience in adverse circumstances—not only generating new revenue sources but seeking to maintain quality and expand access through innovation. However, as Healy (Chapter 16, this volume) points out, economic growth will not solve all problems, and direct action will be required to prevent the emergence of new inequalities. Qualitative material from our small-scale study, set alongside statistical data, points to the incipient danger of 'hollowing out' the core missions of higher education. Already the public/private dimension has become increasingly blurred as HEIs seek to diversify and maintain/enhance their income streams (Marginson 2007).

And here, the single most important point we want to make lies in a fundamental paradox: the more energy that institutions divert into new ventures (generating new sources of income), and the more successful they are at this, the more likely they may be to suffer a crisis of legitimation (Burawoy 2012) in which the public becomes reluctant to view HEIs as serving an important and distinctive intellectual, social and cultural mission. Yes, cities and regions tend to remain genuinely proud of their HEIs, yet somewhere enthusiasm (and, broadly speaking, respect) of the public does not appear to be translated through political structures into funding approaches that adequately support public higher education to meet the often competing objectives ascribed to it in contemporary Irish society.

Acknowledgements

The interviews for this research were conducted by Maria Slowey in autumn 2015. Both co-authors thank the interviewees for the enthusiasm with which they participated. Responsibility for interpretation lies entirely with the authors.

Notes

[1] Official designations—Republic of Ireland (the Republic) and Northern Ireland (NI, a constituent part of the United Kingdom of Great Britain and Northern Ireland)—are used in this chapter; when it is necessary to differentiate between the two jurisdictions, reference is made to the North and South.

[2] Participants are anonymously identified in-text by a distinguishing number (e.g. Respondent 1, R2 ...).

[3] The university bore the name University of Ulster from its inception in 1984 until its rebranding in October 2014 as Ulster University.

[4] Potentially building on work of the Centre for Cross Border Studies (http://crossborder.ie/)

12. Migration patterns, experiences and consequences in an age of austerity

Mary Gilmartin

Introduction

Identifying the start of austerity in contemporary Ireland is a fraught process. For some, it began with the bank guarantee in September 2008, though the warning signs were perhaps apparent earlier. For others, the period of austerity is explicitly linked to the troika deal: the provision of financial support from the IMF, the European Commission and the European Central Bank in November 2010, in exchange for a range of concessions, particularly in relation to reform of public spending. There are also disagreements over the time frame of austerity. While some—particularly government officials—claim that austerity has ended, others argue that austerity persists and will have significant longer-term consequences for Irish society (see Coulter (2015) and Allen (Chapter 3, this volume) for a more detailed discussion).

Debates over the relationship between austerity and migration in contemporary Ireland are similarly charged. Initial reports from the Central Statistics Office suggested that, in 2009, Ireland became a country of net emigration for the first time since 1996. This was marked as a symbolic event: a return to the spectre of forced emigration that had haunted Ireland since the nineteenth century, and that many believed had been banished by the Celtic Tiger (Gilmartin 2015, p. 39). Since that point in 2009, public discourses about migration and austerity have mainly focused on emigration, particularly the emigration of young Irish men and women from Ireland. The loss of young men became a source of particular concern, with regular reports of GAA clubs in rural areas who were unable to field teams because of emigration (Gilmartin 2015, pp. 108–115).

The emotional responses to austerity and to changing patterns of migration have made it difficult to clearly identify and acknowledge the realities of migration in contemporary Ireland. In particular, the publicly articulated narrative of exile, rooted in despair, masks the more complex relationship that exists between austerity and migration in Ireland. This chapter begins by examining patterns of migration flows, to show continuities and changes in the contemporary movements of people from and to Ireland. Secondly it considers the experiences of migrants in an era of austerity, with a particular focus on work. I conclude with a short discussion of the broader relationship between austerity, migration and socio-spatial transformations, in terms of both the present and the implications for the future.

Migration flows: Continuities and changes

In the year to April 2007, almost 105,000 more people immigrated to Ireland than emigrated from the country. This marked the high point of levels of immigration to Ireland, with a total number of immigrants of over 150,000. In the same year, however, the total number of emigrants from Ireland—at just over 46,000—was also higher than it had been in any year since 1990. The average annual flow of immigrants into Ireland in the period from 1996 to 2016 was around 67,500, while the average annual flow of emigrants out of Ireland in the same period was around 50,000. The important point to note is that at the height of the Celtic Tiger era, and before austerity, the levels of annual emigration from Ireland were considerable.

As Table 12.1 shows, though, there have been considerable variations in flows of immigration, emigration and net migration over that period. Certainly, levels of emigration from Ireland increased significantly in the period after the bank bailout in 2008, when unemployment rates soared. But this trend had started earlier, with

Table 12.1

Migration flows to Ireland, 1996-2016 ('000s)

Source: Central Statistics Office, 2015b; 2016

	Immigration to Ireland	Emigration from Ireland	Net immigration/ (emigration)
1996	39.2	31.2	8
1997	44.5	25.3	19.2
1998	46	28.6	17.4
1999	48.9	31.5	17.4
2000	52.6	26.6	26
2001	59	26.2	32.8
2002	66.9	25.6	41.3
2003	60	29.3	30.7
2004	58.5	26.5	32
2005	84.6	29.4	55.2
2006	107.8	36	71.8
2007	151.1	46.3	104.8
2008	113.5	49.2	64.3
2009	73.7	72	1.7
2010	41.8	69.2	(27.4)
2011	53.3	80.6	(27.3)
2012*	52.7	87.1	(34.4)
2013*	55.9	89	(33.1)
2014*	60.6	81.9	(21.3)
2015*	69.3	80.9	(11.6)
2016*	79.3	76.2	3.1

* Estimates
Additional references: Central Statistics Office 2015a Population and Migration Estimates April 2015, 26 August. http://www.cso.ie/en/releasesandpublications/er/pme/populationand-migrationestimatesapril2015/
Central Statistics Office 2016 Population and Migration Estimates April 2016, 23 August. http://www.cso.ie/en/releasesandpublications/er/pme/populationandmigrationestimatesap-ril2016/

Table 12.2

Immigration to and emigration from Ireland by nationality, 2007-16 ('000s)

Source: Central Statistics Office, 2015a, 2016; Gilmartin, 2015, 33-6

Immigrants	2007	2008	2009	2010	2011	2012*	2013*	2014*	2015*	2016*
Irish	30.7	23.8	23	17.9	19.6	20.6	15.7	11.6	12.1	21.1
UK	4.3	6.8	3.9	2.5	4.1	2.2	4.9	4.9	5.0	4.5
Rest of EU-15	11.8	9.6	11.5	6.2	7.1	7.2	7.4	8.7	8.9	10.0
EU-12/13	85.3	54.7	21.1	9.3	10.1	10.4	10.9	10.0	12.8	12.0
Rest of World	19.0	18.6	14.1	6.0	12.4	12.4	17.1	25.5	30.4	31.8
Total	151.1	113.5	73.6	41.8	53.3	52.7	55.9	60.6	69.3	79.3
Emigrants										
Irish	12.9	13.1	19.2	28.9	42	46.5	50.9	40.7	35.3	31.8
UK	3.7	3.7	3.9	3	4.6	3.5	3.9	2.7	3.8	2.6
Rest of EU-15	8.9	6	7.4	9	10.2	11.2	9.9	14	15.6	10.3
EU-12/13	12.6	17.2	30.5	19	13.9	14.8	14	10.1	8.5	12.9
Rest of World	8.2	9	11	9.3	9.9	11.1	10.3	14.4	17.7	18.5
Total	46.3	49	72	69.2	80.6	87.1	89	81.9	80.9	76.2

Rest of EU-15: Austria, Belgium, Denmark, Finland, France, Germany, Greece, Italy, Luxembourg, the Netherlands, Portugal, Spain, Sweden. EU-12/13: Croatia (joined 1 July 2013), Cyprus, Czech Republic, Estonia, Hungary, Latvia, Lithuania, Malta, Poland, Slovakia, Slovenia (joined 1 May 2004), Bulgaria, Romania (joined 1 January 2007).

*Estimates

Additional references: Central Statistics Office 2015a Population and Migration Estimates April 2015, 26 August. http://www.cso.ie/en/releasesandpublications/er/pme/populationandmigrationestimatesapril2015/

annual increases each year from 2005. In fact, 2014 was the first year in a decade where emigration flows were lower than the previous year. Equally, while immigration flows decreased dramatically in 2009 and 2010, they have generally increased every year since then. Immigration flows into Ireland in the year to April 2016 were higher than in 2004, the year of European Union (EU) enlargement when people from the EU accession states—including Poland, Lithuania and Latvia—were granted permission to move to and work in Ireland. The number of people from these newer EU states moving to Ireland has stabilised, at an average of 10,600 per annum between 2010 and 2016. However, the number of immigrants who are not EU nationals has increased from a low of 6,000 in 2010 to almost 32,000 in 2016. Table 12.2 shows immigration to, and emigration from, Ireland by broad national categories for the years from 2007 to 2016. Asylum seekers make up a very small proportion of this immigration flow. In the year to April 2016, just 3.9% of all immigrants to Ireland were asylum seekers (ORAC 2015, 2016). Instead, most of the increase in immigration from the rest of the world has been through a growth in international students, who attend language schools and further and higher education colleges and institutions (see Pritchard and Slowey, Chapter 11, this volume for a brief discussion of the growing importance of international students to the funding position of higher education institutions in Ireland).

Since the onset of austerity measures, there has been a considerable increase in the number of Irish nationals emigrating from Ireland. Over 295,000 Irish nationals have left the country since the bank guarantee in 2008. Of these, 56% were male and 44% were female, and it is estimated that over 70% were in their twenties when they emigrated (Glynn *et al.* 2015, p. 9). The UK remains a very important destination for emigrants from Ireland, with an average of around 19,000 people moving there each year from 2011 to 2016. Canada, Australia and the US are also important emigrant destinations, particularly for those with Irish nationality. Emigration to Canada, Australia and the US is generally through temporary visas, such as Working Holiday programmes. It has been argued that some of these temporary programmes were expanded and specifically targeted Irish migrants because they were predominantly white and middle-class (Helleiner 2015). Because of the way data on emigration from Ireland are gathered, this information is incomplete, and relies on statistics from destination countries such as the UK and Australia about the immigration of Irish nationals. As a result, it is difficult to fully map the extent of migration flows to countries outside the EU and some English-speaking countries. The data also provide very limited information about the extent of onward migration from Ireland by non-Irish nationals. In the same period (2011–16), over 74,000 people from the EU accession states emigrated from Ireland, 56% of whom were male.

There has also been a significant drop in the number of Irish nationals returning to Ireland. As Table 12.2 shows, while over 30,000 Irish nationals immigrated to Ireland in 2007, by 2016 this had dropped by over 30%. Yet overall levels of immigration to Ireland have generally been increasing since 2010. In 2015, the proportion of that immigration flow made up by Irish nationals—17.4%—was at its lowest level in years. Government officials are beginning to develop policies in order to increase the number and proportion of Irish nationals in the annual immigration flow. This harks back to the early years of the Celtic Tiger era, where a significant increase in returning Irish emigrants—many of whom were explicitly targeted by the Jobs Ireland campaign between 2000 and 2002—was associated with rapid economic development. As David Ralph (2009, p. 188) suggests, 'Ireland's graduate returnees [were heralded] as a flagship constituency in catalysing Ireland's recent economic and cultural revival.'

New patterns of migration have also emerged in the period of austerity that are not easily captured by official statistics. The term 'circular migration' refers to 'repeated migration experiences between an origin and destination involving more than one migration and return' (Hugo 2013, p. 2). While circular migration is gaining more significance, there are no statistical data on this issue for Ireland (Quinn 2011). However, a study by David Ralph (2015) provides insights into commuter migration, which is a form of circular migration. Ralph interviewed men and some women who lived in Ireland and commuted to work in Britain, Belgium, France, Germany, Austria, Switzerland, Spain and Sweden. He identified three types of Euro-commuters: survivors, strivers and thrivers. Of these three types, survivors are of most relevance to a discussion of migration and austerity. These are people who feel compelled to commute across borders because of lost income and the need to keep servicing high mortgage payments in the aftermath of the economic crash (Ralph 2015, pp. 37–42).

Public discourses and debates about migration in the period of austerity highlight the increase in levels of emigration from Ireland,

and the return to a period of net emigration. This is certainly the case, with large numbers of people leaving Ireland each year for traditional emigrant destinations such as the UK, Australia, the US and Canada. Many of those are young Irish men and women, and their departure from Ireland has received considerable media and policy attention. For example, the 'Generation Emigration' project in *The Irish Times* newspaper has been running since October 2011, and records the experiences of contemporary Irish emigrants (see Gray 2013 for a detailed discussion). In addition, there have been a number of initiatives in relation to diaspora policy, such as the establishment of the Global Irish Economic Forum and the Global Irish Network (Boyle *et al.* 2013), and the creation of the post of Minister for Diaspora Affairs in 2014. However, the emigration of Irish nationals is just one aspect of contemporary migration in the context of Ireland. People with other nationalities are also emigrating from Ireland, and we know very little about their reasons for leaving the country and the implications of their departure. The focus on emigration from Ireland also obscures some important trends in other migration flows, such as:

1. The ongoing importance of immigration to Ireland, both from countries within the EU and, in recent years, through a marked increase in the flows of people from outside the EU. The resilience of immigration to Ireland has to be understood in connection with the sustained presence of immigrants living in Ireland. Throughout austerity, Ireland has remained a country of immigrants and immigration, despite a widespread assumption that immigrants would leave if the economic state of the country deteriorated. The assumption of temporariness, as in the case of other European countries, has been shown to be inaccurate (Gilmartin 2015, pp. 43–52).
2. The very low level of return migration to Ireland by Irish nationals living outside the country.
3. The emergence of new forms of migration, such as circular or commuter or onward migration, which are not well captured in official statistics.

In the next part of the chapter, I discuss these issues in relation to the experiences of migrants in a time of austerity, in Ireland and elsewhere.

Migrant experiences

When levels of emigration from Ireland began to increase, a number of academic and other researchers sought to explore the reasons for emigration and the experiences of Irish emigrants in their new homes. Interest in the experiences of Irish emigrants was limited during the Celtic Tiger era: a very small range of studies highlighted different aspects of emigration, such as crisis emigration to the UK (Walls 2005), the experiences of Irish and other working holidaymakers in Australia (Allon and Anderson 2010; Clarke 2005), conflicts between recent Irish emigrants and more established diaspora communities (Mulligan 2008), and the difficulties faced by Irish return migrants (Ralph 2009). However, with the rapid increase in levels of emigration, attention turned again to this issue. Earlier work focused on the emigration intentions of tertiary-educated students in Ireland. Cairns (2014), for example, suggested that while there were high levels of mobility intentions among this population cohort, there was no clear link between this and austerity. Instead, he posited that mobility intentions were more closely linked to social class, with students from wealthier backgrounds more likely to express an interest in emigration. This potential for mobility was, in turn, connected to 'family based mobility capital' (Moriarty *et al.* 2015, p. 87).

However, when the wide-ranging Emigre study of recent emigrants from Ireland asked about people's reasons for departure, it was clear that many were in fact leaving precisely because of austerity. Close to 70% of those who left Ireland in 2013 said their reason was work-related, compared to just over 35% in 2008 (Glynn *et al.* 2013, pp. 38-40). Job opportunities and progression were also the key reasons given by recent emigrants to London and Toronto interviewed for a study by the National Youth Council of Ireland (McAleer 2013, pp. 41, 60). Austerity certainly emerges as an important factor in this later research on emigration of Irish nationals from Ireland, but not always in the form of crisis emigration because of job loss or economic shock. Instead, many of the participants in both the Emigre and the NYCI research studies highlighted underemployment, insecure work and lack of job progression—all linked to the deterioration of working conditions under austerity (Fraser *et al.* 2013, pp. 44–47)— as important in their migration decision-making. The public-sector moratorium, introduced in 2009, was a key factor in the deterioration of employment prospects for many people living in Ireland: it imposed a ban on recruitment and promotions in sectors such as education and healthcare, and encouraged early retirement of many experienced public-sector workers (Glynn *et al.* 2015, p. 11). Chapters 3 (Allen) and 5 (Hardiman *et al.*) of this volume provide further discussions of the impacts of austerity on employment more generally and on public-sector employment.

The specific experiences of a particular group of migrants—Irish teachers in Britain—provide important insights into migrant experiences. In a research project, Ryan and Kurdi (2014) surveyed and interviewed Irish migrants who were working as teachers in Britain. Some had qualified in Ireland; others had moved to Britain to train because of the difficulty in getting access to courses or gaining teaching experience in Ireland. In many instances, the research participants compared the ease of getting a job in Britain to the difficulties they had faced or would face in Ireland. Many made explicit reference to the effects of austerity, and its impact on their lives and choices. As Ryan and Kurdi (2014, p. 35) say, they 'were angry about the recession in Ireland and how the opportunities Ireland had enjoyed were squandered and mismanaged by politicians and banks'. While some of the more recent arrivals were unsettled, it was more common for teachers to have extended their stay beyond their original plans, in part because they felt they had better chances for progression and promotion in Britain (Ryan and Kurdi 2014, p. 48).

The Irish teachers who took part in Ryan and Kurdi's research highlighted difficult working conditions in Ireland under austerity. This was also the case for health care professionals who, like teachers, were generally employed in the public sector. Nurses particularly felt the effects of the public-sector moratorium. Between 2009 and 2013, there was a 13% reduction in the total nursing workforce in the health service (Wells and White 2014, p. 567). The number of training places for nurses was reduced, it became very difficult for new nursing graduates to secure employment, and there was anecdotal evidence of between 30% and 40% of newly trained nurses leaving the country each year (Wells and White 2014, p. 568). Equally, immigrant nurses who were recruited to work in the Irish health care sector were also planning to emigrate: one survey suggested that over 70% of immigrant nurses wanted to leave Ireland (Humphries *et al.* 2012, p. 48). For many, this was directly related to the recession, which had 'raised awareness of their status as migrant workers, at the mercy of short-term immigration status and the ever-changing requirements of the health system' (Humphries *et al.* 2012, p. 48).

The experiences of another group of healthcare professionals, doctors, also provide insights into the effects of austerity on migrants. The first issue to highlight is the extent to which the Irish health system had come to rely on foreign-trained doctors. By 2010, 33.4% of all registered doctors in Ireland were trained outside the country, and 75% of those were trained outside the EU (Bidwell *et al.* 2013, p. 39). Many of these doctors were recruited during the Celtic Tiger era. After 2008, there was 'a dramatic (four-fold) fall in the number of non-EU doctors' registering to practise in Ireland (Bidwell *et al.* 2013, p. 36): in part because of the public-sector moratorium on recruitment; in part because of wage reductions and tax increases for public sector workers. Yet Ireland has become reliant on foreign-trained doctors to fill vacancies in the health system of the country, particularly because of the emigration of Irish-trained doctors following qualification. While there are no comprehensive data on the emigration of Irish-trained doctors, there is an indication of substantial levels of emigration (Humphries *et al.* 2015). In a recent survey of doctors who had emigrated from Ireland, Humphries *et al.* summarise their views of working in the Irish and other health services. They say that many see emigration:

> as a means of escaping from difficult working conditions in Ireland, their source country. They describe a lack of respect afforded to health professionals in the Irish health system, particularly in relation to staffing levels and working conditions. Respondents spoke of the superior working conditions in their destination countries, which appeared to both vindicate their emigration decision and complicate the decision to return. (Humphries *et al.* 2015, p. 7)

While some Irish-trained doctors who took part in the research were open to the possibility of returning, most felt that working conditions in the Irish health system were so difficult and stressful as to make return unwise or unattractive. Foreign-trained doctors currently working in the Irish health system face even more difficulties, because they have very limited access to training or to career progression (Humphries *et al.* 2013; Gilmartin 2015, pp. 59–61). As a result, many are planning onward migration from Ireland.

The relationship between migration, austerity and skilled workers—specifically teachers, nurses and doctors—is complex. For

Irish nationals, the difficulties in finding secure work, or in accessing training or career progression—clear consequences of austerity as it has played out in the public sector—have been among the factors in migration decisions. However, the experiences of Irish emigrants at work in other countries have, in many instances, challenged their initial assumptions of emigration as a short-term event. For skilled immigrant workers in Ireland, particularly in the health system, austerity has resulted in a deterioration of working conditions, and has led many to consider the possibility of onward migration. In these instances, the longer-term consequences of austerity are having a marked impact on changing patterns of migration. This loss of skilled labour in the public sector compounds the impact of funding cuts to social care and community work outlined by Heffernan (Chapter 9, this volume).

The experiences of skilled workers who are, or who wish to be, employed in the public sector provide one important insight into the relationship between the lived experience of austerity and migration. Another important insight is evident in the impacts of austerity on the working lives of immigrants living in Ireland. The first point to note is the relationship between immigrant status, employment and unemployment. The Celtic Tiger era in Ireland 'was fuelled by what are often called "immigrant jobs"' (Goodwin-White 2013, p. 221), where the wage gap between Irish workers and immigrant workers was calculated at between 10% and 18% (Barrett *et al.* 2012). The jobs that immigrants held were the first to go when the recession hit, with immigrants losing their jobs before Irish workers in the same industries (Barrett and Kelly 2012; Goodwin-White 2013). The second point to note is the persistence of sectoral concentration in employment in Ireland. Immigrant workers—particularly from the newer EU countries such as Poland, Lithuania and Croatia, as well as from outside the EU—remain concentrated in sectors such as security, home care and domestic work, and restaurant work, where working conditions are more precarious and the potential for exploitation is enhanced (MRCI 2015). There are some exceptions, such as the high proportion of immigrants from outside the EU who are recruited and employed in the health sector or in information technology industries. Overall, though, immigrant workers have experienced similar difficulties at work to their Irish counterparts, which have been exacerbated in some instances by their immigration status.

Conclusion

As the Irish economy begins to show some signs of recovery (see Ó Riain, Chapter 14, this volume for a detailed discussion), the issue of migration is again receiving attention. In particular, the need to attract skilled immigrants to Ireland in order to sustain and expand economic growth has been foregrounded. This has taken place in two ways. The first is a focus on encouraging the return of skilled Irish emigrants. For example, the Nursing in Ireland campaign, launched in July 2015, aimed to recruit 500 Irish nurses and midwives currently working in the UK. The recruitment campaign included a tax-free location package and credit for experience gained outside Ireland. By November 2015, however, only 77 nurses and midwives had been recruited through the scheme (Kenny 2015). A targeted advertising campaign ran in the Christmas 2015 period, with posters at airports encouraging Irish emigrants to return to Ireland, a dedicated website offering job vacancies and other information, and a Twitter hashtag, #hometowork (Department of Foreign Affairs and Trade 2015).

The second example is a revised labour immigration policy. Legislation introduced in October 2014 makes it easier for immigrants from outside the EU with demand-driven 'critical skills' to move to Ireland, to attain permanent residence, and to have their families join them. Currently, people with skills defined as critical include engineers, scientists, ICT professionals, health professionals, accountants, management consultants, experts in big data analytics and international marketing experts (see Department of Jobs, Enterprise and Innovation 2016 for a complete list). Allied to this, a new 'Trusted Partner Initiative' allows employers a fast-track route to apply for permits for potential employees with critical skills.

The emphasis on attracting particular types of skilled immigrants to Ireland serves as a symbolic marker of the end of austerity. However, it also masks the longer-term and grounded effects of austerity. For migrants at work, these include the intensification of sectoral concentration, the ongoing experiences of deskilling for immigrants in Ireland, and the deterioration of working conditions for many workers. This has broader implications, particularly in relation to the ability of immigrants to participate fully in Irish society. While access to residency and citizenship has become easier for many immigrants in Ireland in the period of austerity (Fanning 2015), the conditions of their participation in Irish society remain, in many instances, restricted and difficult. The invisibility of migrants in Irish society is made clear in this volume. Apart from this chapter, the sole mention of immigrants is by Pritchard and Slowey (Chapter 11), who point only to the role of international students as a source of additional revenue. In chapters that discuss issues of housing (Lyons, Chapter 8), inequality (Whelan *et al.*, Chapter 6) and inclusivity (Healy, Chapter 16), the particular issues faced by immigrants in Ireland are not addressed. These include the concentration of some immigrant groups in the private rental sector, leading to insecure tenure; immigrant experiences of sectoral concentration and deskilling at work; and the exclusion of immigrants who are not citizens from voting in most elections in Ireland (Gilmartin 2015). The fact that the post of Minister for Integration in the Irish Government existed only from 2007 to 2011 is another clear sign of the refusal to acknowledge the presence of, and difficulties faced by, immigrants in Ireland. The emphasis on skilled migration also masks the social effects of new forms of austerity-induced migration, such as circular or commuter migration.

More broadly, the effects of austerity are not confined to Ireland. The social transformation that has resulted from global austerity has given rise to new and consolidated patterns of global migration, such as increases in levels of emigration from countries directly and indirectly affected by austerity, and the intensified efforts of other countries to limit both immigration and the rights of many immigrants. The effects of those new patterns and processes of human mobility— for immigrants, for emigrants, and for countries like Ireland—will intensify in the years to come. In his introductory chapter, Simon Wren-Lewis describes austerity as 'right-wing opportunism'. Our failure to acknowledge the realities of migration and migrant experiences in this age of austerity make migrants a more likely target of right-wing opportunism in an uncertain future.

13. The austerity myth: parenting and the new thrift culture in contemporary Ireland

Fiona Murphy

Introduction

A young girl dressed in baggy pants and an oversized shirt presents me with a cup of coffee as I sit waiting to interview the manager of one of Cork's newest flea markets. With a lyrical Cork accent, she starts to tell me about her excitement at having procured a job serving coffee in the market. As a college student in University College Cork, she said this part time job offers her the opportunity to be more 'green' and 'sustainable'. Her younger colleague, also a student, tells me that when her peers ask her where she works, they all become very interested and 'join in the debate about how to be green'. Clearly passionate about the topic of sustainability, I ask the girls whether there is a shift in the mindsets of their peers. In response, the younger girl starts to snap her fingers while bursting into song, 'Hey, Macklemore! Can we go thrift shopping? …I'm gonna pop some tags. Only got twenty dollars in my pocket. I'm hunting, looking for a come up, this is fucking awesome'. Together, the girls snap their fingers and laugh out loud, their joviality is stirring. 'Have you seen how many hits this song has had on YouTube? Of course there is a change in how people see things,' the younger girl insists. As the market starts to buzz, the girls run off to serve coffee and pastries to hungry Saturday shoppers whilst a band begins to play in the corner (Field notes, 2013).

Flea markets, charity shops, swap shops, baby goods markets, community gardens, a TV show called 'Díol É' (Gaelic for 'for sale'), barter projects in scenic towns such as Clonakilty in West Cork and Killarney in County Kerry, books about recession Ireland, the sharing economy and collaborative consumption practices (the list could go on); all of these have evolved and proliferated since the beginning of Ireland's economic crisis. 'Austerity Ireland', where men in suits stand in charity shops buying suits, looks radically different to 'Celtic Tiger Ireland'.

This chapter examines Ireland's transition from an affluent society known as the Celtic Tiger to a relatively impoverished one deeply impacted by global recession and austerity measures (see Moore-Cherry, McHale and Heffernan, Introduction, and Whelan and Nolan, Chapter 6, this volume; Coulter and Nagle 2015), with a particular focus on the relationship between parenting, thrift culture and sustainability values. This chapter utilizes 'thrift culture' as a conceptual frame in which to explore broader socio-cultural change in an Irish context. Such an analysis has value because we live in a moment where economic crisis and environmental crisis have become intersecting discourses (see Klein 2014) to the extent that some commenters believe that we might well be moving towards what Peter Wells (2010) has called an age of 'eco-austerity'. This chapter explores whether better environmental ethics (particularly in the context of consumption practices) could prove to be a pathway out of austerity or whether such 'eco-austerity' practices might merely be a new form of austerity governance (Foucault 2007). The flea market referred to in the opening field notes—a site of colour, of jumble and paraphernalia, of collector's items, coffee and music—is one example of how Irish consumption spaces during the economic crisis have started to change. Ireland's rising unemployment and emigration levels, coupled with increasing crime rates and a decline in mental health, has left the country in a crisis deeply anchored in discourses of loss, failure, and indeed, nostalgia. This politics of nostalgia has led to an embrace of the old, of thrift, even frugality, as an alternative lifestyle approach in the context of economic malaise. Ultimately, this chapter discusses the emergence of alternative lifestyles and the evolution of new social relations, solidarities and mutualities in the context of austerity.

Through an ethnographic analysis of the proliferation of baby goods markets (i.e. second-hand markets selling goods for babies and young children) alongside the growth of moral discourses around the nature of Irish parenting, this chapter examines whether citizen-consumers (such as parents) see their relationship with this new thrift culture as transitional or as a new way of 'being' in austerity Ireland. It also questions whether the scapegoating of single parents (see Allen, Chapter 3, this volume), cuts to maternity payments and the re-imaginings of 'parents' and the 'family' through austerity—as key agents in both economic decline (poor parenting, spendthrift-overconsumption, spoilt children, social debt) and as the solution to recovery (good parenting, the stay at home mother, frugal)—have changed the way Irish parents see both their roles and consumption practices. This chapter argues that the politics of austerity, like the politics of finance capital, are reliant on a powerful mythology (see Keohane and Kuhling 2014). Visions of austerity are harnessed through the 'myth/s' of an 'authentic' past, one that ordinary citizens are asked to return to. As such, the myths generated by austerity politics have created new cultural formations wherein notions of the good life, value and well-being have accrued a revalorized potency, which for some Irish parents have become embedded in sustainability values and for others mark a mere shift to more pragmatic consumption practices.

Austerity myths and thrift culture

Austerity Ireland has seen widespread deficit-cutting, reduction of benefits, income inequality (see Whelan and Nolan, Chapter 6, this volume), cuts to public services (see Pritchard and Slowey, Chapter 11, this volume), tax increases (but not on the corporate sector), emigration (Chapter 12, this volume) and an overall reduction in general spending (see Wren-Lewis, Chapter 1, this volume; Coulter and Nagle, 2015). As McHale (2017) notes, Ireland's economic crisis was precipitated by what he calls 'three interacting bubbles—a property-price bubble, a credit bubble, and a construction bubble' (McHale, Chapter 2, p. 38; see also Lyons, Chapter 8, this volume). Austerity, as Mark Blyth (2013, p.10) puts it, is a 'zombie economic idea' that has further entrenched societal inequalities, as described by Heffernan (Chapter 9, this volume) and Watson *et al.* (Chapter 10, this volume), and has been widely critiqued as a failed remedial action with questions of sovereignty remaining at its core. But austerity is also happening at a critical juncture where the environmental crisis is proving more urgent than ever (see Klein 2014).

The intimate coupling of austerity politics with environmental politics evinces the way in which austerity works as an important nodal point for the intersection of right and left politics. As a potent, even hegemonic myth, austerity harnesses myriad tropes, images and narratives that reanimate more conventional readings of both economic and environmental crisis (see Bramall 2013). This is a myth with sacrifice as its central trope. It is a myth that in its ritual re-enactments produces a creative tension between the act of imagining a 'sustainable', debt-free future and the re-examination of a recent past riddled with overconsumption and debt. The symbolism of this simple, potentially more austere and yet somehow better life appeals in particular to sustainability politics, as many authors have illuminated (Bramall 2013; Hinton and Redclift 2009; Jensen 2013). The return to 'frugality' and 'thrift' in the context of austerity has been posited by more hopeful environmental advocates as a potential route to a more sustainable way of life. Commentators such as Simms (2001) argue that reconfiguring the current global crisis as the 'environmental debt economy' can potentially open a space wherein human well-being globally can be improved. Others, however, such as Evans (2011) do not posit such a neatly interwoven relationship between practices of thrift in austerity and a more sustainable future.

Austerity, when considered through the lens of sustainability politics, acts as both a charter for social action and a foundational narrative that urges a return to nature, and to frugal and simple living. However, while its mythic properties remain visible, austerity continues to be a site of discursive struggle (Brammall 2013), particularly for those concerned with the inequities it generates. Austerity's discursive repertoire emanates from the notions of 'blame' and 'irresponsibility', thereby presenting ordinary citizens as 'wasteful', 'greedy', 'vulgar', and as such, responsible in no small part for the economic crisis. Large developers and banks notwithstanding, it is ordinary citizens who need to suffer, to 'share in the pain', in order to move out of crisis. While many Irish citizens are aware of the contradictions inherent in this pan-European austerity myth, income cuts and taxation levies have seen a high percentage of the population struggling to live on a daily basis. Indeed, in spite of the centrality of the family in the Irish constitution, we have seen a number of cuts directed at families: to one-parent family benefits, maternity payments, child benefit as well as widespread emigration of the young and educated. The cohort of people in their mid-30s to mid-40s, the age most impacted on by the economic crisis (see ESRI 2013), are also the same group of people who tend to have younger children, thereby tending to have higher expenditures and costs. Writing of austerity in Britain, Jensen (2013, p.10) argues that:

> The austerity narrative perhaps coalesces more substantively and intensively around the institution of the family and parenting than any other site. The current austerity regime—a lattice of reduced public spending, welfare benefit restrictions and sanctions, together with precarity and escalating living and housing costs—is effecting an economic squeeze on families, and particularly on families with low incomes, single-parent families, families with disabled children, large families and families who are precariously housed.

Jensen's argument resonates very closely with austerity Ireland, where we have seen a number of substantive attacks on the family. She argues that feckless/bad parenting is set up as a form of scapegoating for both economic and moral decline, while good parenting (in the form of sacrifice) is constructed as the solution to the current crisis.

Austerity means that belt-tightening has become a moral imperative as well as a real necessity, especially for families. As Mark Blyth (2013) highlights, the problem is not necessarily belt-tightening as such, it is simply that we are not all wearing the same trousers. What Clarke and Newman (2012, p.300) call the 'alchemy of austerity' produces new cultural formations that are embedded in ideas of the authentic, 'who we once were' before events like the Celtic Tiger and its associated links with greed and corruption changed the society we live in. Within these limitations, the trope of the 'authentic' past, of the 'good life' so convincingly seeded by the myth of austerity, has been widely adopted. Ireland's broad acceptance of austerity and lack of protest politics (with the recent exception of the water charge protests; see Hourigan, Chapter 7, this volume) has been questioned, with some commentators positing the belief that Catholic values of austere living have been regenerated (Kenny 2012). Since 2008, Irish society has seen the rise of a revitalized thrift culture with the proliferation of second-hand markets, charity and second-hand clothing stores, community gardens and the grow-it-yourself movement. Some of this has evolved out of necessity, some of it from the austerity 'myth,' making thrift culture into a fashion, a reasoned state of 'austerity chic'. The benefits of this new thrift culture are widely lauded: it makes us more authentic, more 'green and sustainable' and improves our overall well-being. While some of this could be deemed 'magical thinking', there are, however, numerous positives to the emergence of this new thrift culture. Soper (2013, p.249) argues that austerity Ireland now has the space to 'denounce the puritanical and socially conservative aspects of traditional cultures of resistance to modernity, and argue for the importance of associating avant-garde social policy with a post-consumerist politics of prosperity', all with the potential to forge a new pathway to sustainable living.

The mainstreaming of a 'make, mend and do' culture should, of course, also ignite real concerns about who is being asked to simplify their lives and for what ends. Clarke and Newman (2012) question the ideological reworking of austerity for different ends, but the sustainability interpretation of austerity focuses on the value of thrift and frugality as a generative model for sustainable consumption and living. However, as Daniel Miller (1998, p.25) argues 'thrift' is open to multiple interpretations and often signifies the ability to buy 'more with less,' thereby ultimately being a 'ritual transformation of shopping from the fantasy of spending to the fantasy of saving', and not necessarily conducive to sustainable living. Coupled with the proliferation of second-hand shops and community gardening in Irish society in recent years, we also see the rise of stores such as Primark and Dealz (Poundland) as well as discount supermarkets such as Aldi and Lidl (with a visible, rapid expansion). Kim Humphrey (2010, p.188) argues that the global recession 'does not simply confirm anti-consumerist critique, nor unproblematically move us towards anti-consumerist goals'. Nonetheless, the austerity myth's rhetorical persuasiveness has seen new articulations of value, quality and worth in Irish consumption spaces. One of my research participants, a flea market stall holder and shop owner, puts it thus:

> Out with the old, in with the new, the Celtic Tiger was nothing but a 'throw-away culture,' now we have this resurgence of thrift, everywhere people looking for value (Interview, 2013).

The resurgence of such a diverse array of second-hand consumption spaces in Irish society might confirm this, but why is this happening? Constrained financially and perhaps motivated to live differently, are Irish parents and families turning towards the new thrift culture for purely economic reasons? Or will these changes have a lasting impact on how Irish families understand and practice sustainable consumption practices?

Thrift and parenting

> I sell nostalgia products; you know, the games or toys you would have played with when you were a child yourself. I see parents coming to the market now more and more looking for toys for their children, the same ones they used to play with themselves. I guess that's what happens during a recession, we all want a bit of the past. (Interview with seller, Cork, March 2013)

> I only wear second-hand and vintage. Second-hand markets and vintage stores somehow disappeared during the Celtic Tiger. In the 1980s there were quite a number dotted around Dublin, but for a long period I had to find everything online or when I went to Britain, I would hit the second-hand stores. Post-Celtic Tiger, I am delighted to say that this is all starting to change. I think it's all for

the better. (Interview with Annette, March 2013, writer and second-hand shopper)

In the proliferation of second-hand consumption spaces in Ireland during the economic crisis, the growth of second-hand baby goods markets has become quite apparent. Since 2010, ARÍS (the Irish word for 'again') started to operate and trade in second-hand baby goods. ARÍS, which is modelled after the British National Childcare Trust second-hand markets for baby goods, enables parents to sell and buy second-hand baby goods, particularly clothes and equipment. Since ARÍS opened its doors in Dublin, a number of other second-hand markets for baby goods have started in the South and West of Ireland, as well as a number of large 'competitors' in the Leinster region. As part of a larger project, I interviewed the operators of all of these baby goods markets and conducted ethnographic research at four of the markets. What is most striking about these markets is the broad demography of the sellers and buyers, and the widespread success of the model, in spite of numerous successful online operators such as BabyBay. The operator of ARÍS explains it thus:

> There is a cultural thing of 'passing on' in Ireland, which is totally acceptable—but with friends and families—not strangers. When I had the boys even though it was in the Celtic Tiger, I didn't fall into the trap of buying everything new. I just want safe and clean, I don't care what version of bugaboo Gwyneth Paltrow is wheeling down Notting Hill. I don't like the online markets for baby goods because for babies it is all about touch, feel, smell. It is such a personal thing. The online baby goods shopping is not a model that works for me. When I set this market up in 2010, it was the first one in Ireland. I based it on the British National Childcare Trust model; initially the idea was met with a somewhat muted response from people. (Interview with founder of ARÍS, Dublin, April 2013)

Similarly, the operator of one of the newer markets says:

> When I was pregnant, I had no intention of buying everything new. I shopped around online, but it is a

pain, like you want everything in the one place, just walk in and see what's there and buy it. It didn't exist in this area so I just set it up. (Interview with a baby-market operator, Cork, March 2013)

What many of the operators point to is the affective dimension of these second-hand markets, the buying and selling of baby goods (above many other kinds) is articulated as deeply sensory:

> Sellers, particularly, get very emotional—emptying out your attic is such an emotionally laden process. I see mothers who perhaps have had difficulty having their child and they can't believe that part of their lives is all behind them as they sell on the goods. You see some parents delighted, 'no more babies, no more babies', and others who can't believe that part of their life is over. (Interview with a baby-market operator, Dublin, May 2013)

In addition to the sensory aspects of the trade of second-hand baby goods, a number of the market operators indicated a shift in the kinds of individuals attending the markets in conjunction with the deepening of the economic crisis:

> You can see that the profile of the sellers in particular has changed. When we first set up, the sellers were people who knew and understood market culture, people who were interested in sustainability et cetera, but as the crisis worsened, you would see people rock up who were selling because they really needed the money. I would tend to treat these sellers a little differently to the other types, you have to be sensitive, but you can see from the goods and the 2005 jeep that they arrive in what they used to have. I pay attention to these kinds of things. (Interview with baby goods market operator, Dublin, May 2013)

> We are booked out months in advance with our stalls, and the demand seems to be getting greater all the time. You can see the quality of stuff people are selling, it is

great. But people are needing to sell this stuff more and more, you can see, and it's sometimes surprising the kinds of people who show up. (Interview with a baby goods market operator, Cork, March 2013)

Attending the markets and speaking to both buyers and sellers, one becomes cognisant of the diverse motives for attending the markets. In my discussions with the sellers in particular, economic motives seem primary:

I do a lot of these markets, it's increasingly about value, I mean look around—do you see the quality of the stuff? People are here because it is a recession and they can get good value for their money. I've never heard any of the sellers or buyers give other reasons. Sustainability certainly isn't ever mentioned. (Interview with a seller, Dublin, April 2014)

This is my first time attending one of these. I am into recycling; I'd never throw anything out. I would give it away if I can first, and then I heard about these markets and said why not? Why not try to make some money from everything I have stored in my attic? (Interview with a seller, April 2014)

We are both major clothes lovers; during the boom we would have only bought the best. We are both single mothers, and even though we would have had excellent jobs during the boom, we are no longer working. We decided to give this market a go and see how it goes. I think it is better than online as you can see what you are getting straight away. We are also both into up-cycling and are environmentally aware, but we are primarily here for the cash. (Interview with a seller, March 2013)

The markets are a hive of activity, some providing entertainment for kids and trial classes for baby massage or information booths on breastfeeding. Sellers, buyers and market operators all point to the pressures that the contemporary Irish parent is under due to austerity.

It's all this pressure, no money, big mortgages; in the Celtic Tiger people went mad, it was all new, new, new, especially for babies. You wouldn't have dreamt of saying you bought something second-hand a while back. I think we are going back to better times now. Things are a little simpler. (Buyer, Dublin, April 2014).

I'm here because I can get value for money. Have you seen some of the stuff in here? There is a Trunki over there for thirteen euro and a bugaboo down there like new. I came here because my boss was here a while back and he got a load of stuff, and he is not badly off. (Buyer, Dublin, April 2014).

I think I would have probably been too embarrassed to admit to being somewhere like a second-hand market, especially for your children, during the boom, now it's all different. Penneys? no problem, second-hand? no problem. I think we are all different and maybe even though we find ourselves quite stretched, we are some-what more appreciative of what's important in life. (Buyer, Dublin, April 2014)

In my conversations with buyers, sellers and market operators, the words 'sustainability' and 'environmental' are only ever mentioned in a secondary capacity to monetary concerns. All of the market operators have a keen awareness of the sustainable impact of what they are trying to do, but they see the model in an Irish context as having a finite lifespan. Nonetheless, sellers and buyers continue to return to the markets in different capacities, with some customers claiming that they are now inspired to shop for second-hand goods in other domains. Parents are shopping in second-hand baby goods markets predominantly because they are seeking value for money in a world where they are under great financial pressure. Some, however, see a societal redefinition or shift in this move towards second-hand, particularly in the context of baby goods. Moral understandings of societal change are posited in the desire to return to a better, simpler past, and some of my research participants articulate this as a recon-stitution of the individual, the parent and indeed, Irish society. 'We are better for it', one of my research participants puts it, but this has become something of a catch-cry in certain sectors of Irish society; the notion that we will somehow emerge from this crisis as better people no longer beleaguered by the excesses of the Celtic Tiger. Is this the successful workings of a subject-making, morality-imposing, stigmatizing austerity myth? Can we truly say that an Ireland post-crisis will be any different?

Conclusion

The island of Ireland is a land disenchanted by the all-pervasive myth of austerity (see Coulter and Nagle 2015). It is also, however, a nation seeking transformation (Keohane and Kuhling 2014). Examining new articulations of parenting, thrift-culture and sustainability through the lens of the austerity myth highlights the tensions between the mythology of the market economy and the failures therein. As Jensen (2013) suggests, the austerity myth has been important in Ireland in recent years in interpellating ordinary citizens into thrifty consumers. Whether these idioms of thrift and frugality will bring lasting benefits, either in our role as parents or citizen-consumers in the context of recovery, is not so clear. Such uncertainty reinforces the need for cross-sectoral and partnership approaches in implementing sustainability policies, and embedding them as habitual, in an Irish context. Cronin (2011, p.64) argues that the green agenda cannot be truly envisioned without recourse to 'a robust sense of social justice', but whether this sense of social justice will be forthcoming is debatable, particularly when one looks at an austerity Ireland steeped in inequality. Seán Healy (Chapter 16, this volume) highlights the challenges in creating a more just society as Ireland moves into recovery mode.

When examined in the context of sustainability politics, it could be argued that the austerity myth is working to achieve some new-found respect for notions of 'thrift' and 'frugality' that coalesce with forms of sustainable consumption, and are thus broadly positive in thrust. However, this is a thrift culture created by the rolling back of important welfare and institutional supports, and grounded in deep societal inequities. Unmoored from the premises of social justice—with justice, rights and equality at its heart—the evidence presented here suggests this is not a progressive form of sustainability politics. Notwithstanding its limitations, it might present an opportunity to think about what a 'human economy' (Hart, 2010) might look like in post-crisis Ireland and what steps we might need to put in place in a context of 'uneven recovery' (Chapters 5 and 14, this volume) to arrive at such a transformation.

Acknowledgements

This research was part of a larger Irish Research Council project working with Dr Pierre McDonagh and Dr Sofia Lopez on sustainable consumption in economic crisis. The second-hand baby goods markets stood out as potentially interesting sites of research in the context of the relationship between parenting, austerity and sustainability.

Part 3: Beyond austerity?
From crisis to recovery

14. Ireland's recovery: explanation, potential and pitfalls

Seán Ó Riain

Introduction

Ireland is apparently in the midst of a remarkable recovery after one of the deepest crises in contemporary capitalist economies. The country, however, seems politically and culturally uncertain about this recovery; many feel caught between a deep suspicion that this recovery is temporary and/or narrowly based on a series of relatively optimistic prognoses of an increased 'fiscal space' to fund measures to compensate for the losses of recent years (whether those be tax cuts, pay increases, public services, capital investment or other measures). This uncertainty is not surprising given that the only feature of Ireland's economic history more striking than its ability to recover from a series of crises is to just as quickly move from each recovery into a new form of crisis. Can Ireland break out of this cycle of boom and bust for the first time in its history? The answer is further complicated by debates about the economic and social effects of austerity policies, the mix of tax increases and (particularly) spending cuts that Ireland pursued with some vigour between 2008 and 2015. Is Ireland's recovery the crucial piece of evidence in support of austerity policies?

In contrast with the previous chapters in this volume that sought to outline how various different individuals, groups and society more generally experiences austerity, this chapter explores the dynamics of Ireland's recovery through austerity. First, it returns to some of the arguments outlined in Part 1 of the book, examining the meaning of austerity and distinguishing two different austerity projects in Europe, with very different implications for future policy, societal and economic development. While Ireland's rhetoric is largely mobilised around the continental European version, its practice is closer to 'liberal austerity'. Second, the paper briefly reviews Ireland's recovery and some unusual features of the recovery. It explains how Ireland's recovery is not a break with past practices but is in many ways—for better and for worse—continuous with key historical features of its economy. These include high inequality linked to property and other assets, flexible labour markets, the mobilisation of foreign investment and a tentatively emerging domestic business class across a range of sectors supported by public agencies. Third, the chapter argues that Ireland will once more face important choices previously faced in the late 1990s and late 1970s. It argues that there are potential sources of reconstruction in the current situation that could be built upon. However, the belief in 'internal devaluation' and 'market orthodoxy' as the source of the recovery could threaten the recovery itself, undermining the investment and public action required to sustain and deepen it.

Recovery to what? Two worlds of 'austerity'

It is now a byword of Irish politics that future governments must be 'prudent' and not repeat the mistakes of the mid-2000s, when the public finances were left vulnerable to external shocks in ways that greatly increased the effect of the financial crisis of 2008 on public debt, and on the society. There is significant room for different views on what prudence might consist of, as illustrated in pre-general election debates in 2016 about the size of the 'fiscal space' available to future governments. The new politics consists of 'technical' disagreements about budget balances and the room for expansion, but always within 'moral' rhetorics of fiscal responsibility and conservatism. We can, however, look more deeply at what a post- austerity future might look like.

This future is not as obvious as it may appear. A variety of analysts link austerity directly to economic liberalism, primarily through the dominant emphasis within austerity policies on reducing public spending and therefore almost inevitably shrinking the size of the state, but also through permanent disciplining of demands for wage increases. However, when we examine the responses to the economic crisis since 2008, the strongest focus on austerity, both in terms of the practical policies advocated and the rhetoric of the moral and economic need to 'live within the state's means', has been in Northern Europe, apparently the least liberal and the most coordinated and 'social' of all the capitalisms (Hall and Soskice 2001; Ó Riain 2014).

Table 14.1 allows us to examine this apparent paradox more closely—showing indicators of the degree of financialisation, fiscal conservatism, welfare effort and 'high road' production in the different 'worlds of capitalism' (Esping-Andersen 1999). The Nordic and Continental economies—the most 'coordinated' and 'social' of the capitalisms—are the least likely to run fiscal deficits (whether actual or 'structural'). While clearly more fiscally conservative, they also have the largest states—whether that is measured in terms of contemporary social protection and services or social investment in the future (including active labour market policy, education, research and so on). Fiscal conservatism and large states go hand in hand in practice, immediately contradicting the 'austerity' prescription. Looked at from the Liberal political economy vantage point, smaller states have difficulty maintaining fiscal discipline.

This sheds a different light on the political choices around 'austerity' dissected by Simon Wren-Lewis in Chapter 1 of this volume. Austerity is not simply a project of right-wing opportunism but is consistent with many strands in the political and policy practices and discourses of the 'left-wing' national models in Europe. Furthermore, the combinations of fiscal, monetary and other policies in those countries are in places quite different from those that Wren-Lewis argues could have driven recovery without the same impact on unemployment. Given the long recoveries of Finland and Sweden from their 1990s recessions, it is likely that Wren-Lewis' arguments hold, but the politics of implementing them in post-crisis Europe were not simply due to right-wing opportunism but also to their lack of appeal to institutionalised 'left elites'. The 'ideological project' of austerity as described by Kieran Allen (Chapter 3, this volume) could be linked discursively to left-wing projects of building the state as well as to right-wing projects of shrinking it.

Table 14.1

Fiscal balance, social contracts and production regimes in Europe

	Average 'Structural' Fiscal Balance 1999–2007	Social Spending, 2002 (% GDP)	'Social Investment', 2000 (% GDP)	Banks as % of all Profits in the Economy	Average Business R&D Investment 1999–2007 (% GDP)	% 'Learning' Organisation of Work, 2000 (Holm et al. 2010)
Nordic Social Democracies	0.3	36.6	11.3	4.7	2.26	53
Continental Christian Democracies	-1.7	32.5	9.6	5.5	1.42	47
Liberal (UK & Ireland)	-2.5	27.5	8.1	11.9	0.97	29
Mediterranean	-4.0	26.6	7.0	6.3	0.40	24

The contradictions of 'austerity' go deeper, however. The three right-hand columns of Table 14.1 give more information on the organisation of private finance and business in Europe. The percentage of corporate profits in the economy that go to banks is an indicator of the 'financialisation' of that economy—the extent to which financial actors dominate economic activity (Krippner 2011). The liberal economies stand out here as the most financialised. However, this is not associated with strong investment in the upgrading of production as liberal economies have weaker business investment in research and development as well as a much smaller percentage of workers in workplaces centred on 'learning' (including high rates of training, extensive worker decision-making autonomy, and so on).

The alternative to austerity as a strategy for recovery was typically presented as some version of Keynesian stimulus policy, that would drive recovery through expansion of the economy rather than direct consolidation of the debt and that would repudiate the 'liberal' policy of austerity. Despite ongoing debates about the self-defeating nature of 'austerity' at the European level, EU elites have resisted what they see as the siren call of Keynesianism. However, the analysis here suggests that we need to revisit the place of Keynesianism in contemporary debates. While Keynes is often read as an advocate of counter-cyclical spending (as described by Lyons, Chapter 8, in this volume) and quantitative easing, this relies purely on a reading of Keynes as macro-economic manager. Keynes also emphasised a more general role for government, particularly in securing social protection and investment and generally managing the economy and ensuring appropriate level of investment and other long-term economic requirements. While most commentators associate the social democratic worlds of capitalism with Keynesianism, in practice it is this more general argument of Keynes for social investments and long range planning and management that is most characteristic of the social democratic and Christian democratic countries. The Keynes who advocated counter-cyclical spending and macro-economic reflation to escape from crisis is in practice more widely favoured in liberal political economies, as seen in the persistently higher deficits run in such economies.

This points to a crucial distinction between austerity and fiscal conservatism: northern European countries historically combine their higher levels of social spending (an antipathy to 'austerity') with an aversion to budget deficits (a deep commitment to 'fiscal prudence'). Fiscal discipline has less to do with German cultural memories of the inflation of the 1930s than with the general logics of these models of political economy (see Ó Riain 2014). In the 'social market' economies, fiscal prudence has historically been associated with the protection of the state and the public sector from the cycles of capitalism rather than with shrinking the state to respond to those fluctuations and pressures.

Barnes and Wren (2012) argue that Ireland and the UK face the choice of a return to the form of 'Privatised Keynesianism' that dominated in the 2000s (with demand stoked by loose financial markets) or the turn to a more 'European' strategy of export-oriented competitiveness. This analysis suggests that such a choice involves a much deeper transformation—one that anchors a strategy of competitiveness in investment in both organisations and society, in empowerment of employees, in curbing the dominance of finance and wrapping all this in a blanket of fiscal prudence. The European 'social contract' is clearly at the heart of this mix of institutions and policies. Mathematically, the balancing of a budget is possible with either low tax and spend or high tax and spend. In practice, however, the comparative evidence suggests that a developed social model and high investment economy is crucial to the ability to sustain fiscal prudence.

None of this is to suggest that the 'European' fiscal model is unambiguously superior; after all, it appears that this instinctive fiscal conservatism has greatly prolonged the recession in Europe and beyond. Furthermore, Haffert and Mahrtens (2015) point out that austerity can become a self-fulfilling prophesy as the political actors supporting austerity and the institutions charged with implementing it internalise these policy routines as part of their everyday operation and 'common sense'. This dynamic may have changed the comparative logic of political economies as they find that even the Nordic economies have deepened fiscal consolidation and have favoured spending cuts over tax increases. Nonetheless, the fundamental point that these are political and social choices still stands—even if on a very rocky terrain.

Inside Ireland's recovery: first steps on the road to (the next) crisis?

What are we to make of Ireland's recovery in the context of these different combinations of fiscal, social and economic policy mixes? Ireland has clearly not pursued a Keynesian stimulus; while it has continued to run a budget deficit, there has been significant fiscal consolidation including tax increases and (especially) cuts in spending. There have been significant wage cuts in the public sector (discussed in Chapters 3, 11 and 12 of this volume), and incomes among non-professional workers in the private sector also declined (although not for many professionals and managers). Ireland has largely followed a strategy of 'internal devaluation', shrinking the state as well as the share of national income going to wages.

In the process, Ireland has walked a tightrope of debt management. Unlike Greece and arguably some other peripheral European economies, Ireland at the time of the 2008 crisis was poised on the precipice of a debt burden that was conceivably repayable. This has led to a complex dance of Irish and European political actors, sticking to a rigid doctrine of debt repayment while fudging the issue in certain practical respects, mixing compromise with very significant coercion. Cuts in spending and tax increases gradually reduced the debt ratio even as GDP stagnated. The EU helped to reduce borrowing costs by introducing some low profile re-financing of debt through trading debt over time as well as through Mario Draghi's 2012 declaration that he would back the Euro to whatever extent necessary. Domestically, the largely state-owned banks were slow to repossess houses where mortgages were significantly in arrears, allowing the government to avoid the political costs of evicting homeowners while allowing the banks to avoid locking in their losses on such debts (and ensuring new long-term streams of revenue). Ireland finessed its way through a debt minefield—but at the cost of diminished public services, rewarding the holders of Ireland's debt, and facilitating a burgeoning crisis of housing supply, rising rents and growing family homelessness (discussed in other chapters in this volume).

What then of Ireland's recovery? Ireland appears to have emerged alone from the economic wreckage of the European periphery, with rapid economic growth and, more significantly, substantial employment growth. Assessing the Irish recovery is made difficult by the usual issues that plague the observer of Irish economic fortunes—data on growth, trade and productivity is exceptionally difficult to understand given the distortions introduced by the accounting practices of foreign firms located in Ireland (indeed, even GNP, once a trusted figure, has been rendered suspicious in recent years). However, it is clear that there has been an improvement in the fortunes of the Irish economy, most reliably observable in an improved employment performance. This chapter focuses most closely on employment trends in providing its characterisation of the Irish recovery.

Table 14.2 shows the basic outline of Ireland's exceptionally strong employment growth since 2012, the low point of employment after the crisis. While there are controversial aspects to the figures, the large majority of this employment growth is real—and, after early growth in part-time, temporary and flexible hour work, nearly all of the past three years' growth is in full-time, non-temporary employment. Furthermore, as Figure 14.1 shows, investment in the Irish economy has shifted from the crisis era, with investment in dwellings collapsing and growing investment in research and development (R&D) and software now outstripping non-residential building and roads, respectively.

However, we should not interpret this growth as a wide-ranging recovery based on renewed confidence and improved incomes—the sectors with the least growth are those most sensitive to the general level of activity and demand. Instead, we need to look more closely at three key sectors that have led the recovery: industry and information and communications technology (forming an export-oriented growth cluster); construction; and accommodation and food. By looking at these more detailed sectoral dynamics, we can examine how Ireland's employment recovery might fit into the comparative picture of European capitalisms, and, crucially, ascertain whether it is driven by improved competitiveness due to internal devaluation, or by investment and organisational upgrading.

Information and communications have grown steadily through the crisis period and in recent years there has been a broader-based growth in industry. The Annual Business Survey of Economic Impact shows that this employment growth is mainly among the export-oriented firms that are clients of the IDA and Enterprise Ireland, the state agencies that attract foreign firms and develop domestic enterprises. More surprising, however, is that two thirds of the employment growth is in Irish firms, spread across medium-tech manufacturing, food and business services as well as the software sector where foreign firm employment is concentrated. More striking still is that more R&D workers are now employed in Irish firms than in foreign firms (Figure 14.2). These sectors have seen little or no reduction in wages; instead, their growth is the outcome of a long-standing process of development of an export sector, consisting of both domestic firms and higher profile foreign companies, and supported by the activities of a 'developmental network state' consisting of public agencies supporting enterprise development and science and technology investment (Ó

Persons in Employment, 2008–15 (000s, Quarter 3, Seasonally Adjusted)

Source: CSO, *Quarterly National Household Survey*

	2008	2009	2010	2011	2012	2013	2014	2015	2012–15
Agriculture	113	96	90	82	86	111	110	113	27
Industry	297	256	246	239	231	242	239	252	21
Construction	236	153	116	109	101	105	112	127	26
Wholesale and retail	310	279	278	277	273	273	275	274	1
Transport	96	97	93	97	90	88	88	90	0
Accommodation & Food	136	131	129	121	123	138	140	140	17
Information and Communication	72	74	76	77	78	82	79	84	6
FIRE	106	111	101	99	102	102	103	100	-3
Professional Services	113	101	97	97	100	111	117	123	22
Administrative Services	78	70	62	69	67	65	65	68	1
Public Admin	107	105	104	99	100	96	98	101	2
Education	140	139	149	137	141	141	144	147	6
Health	222	236	240	244	245	244	250	253	8
Other	105	99	98	96	102	100	102	105	3
Not stated	8	8	8	4	3	..	6	7	4
Total	2136	1954	1886	1846	1841	1899	1927	1983	142

Figure 14.1

Capital Investment in Ireland, 1995–2014 (current prices)

Source: CSO, National Income and Expenditure

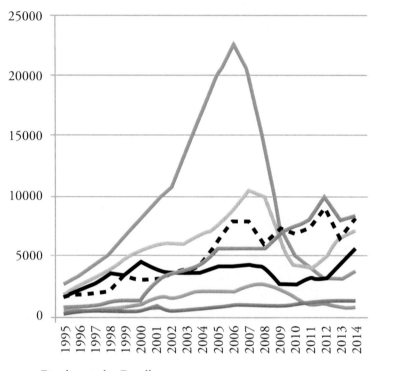

- ━━━ Fixed capital – Dwellings
- ━━━ Fixed capital – Roads
- ━━━ Fixed capital – Other building and construction (including land rehabilitation etc.)
- ▪▪▪▪ Fixed capital – Transport equipment
- ━━━ Fixed capital – Other machinery and equipment
- ━━━ Fixed capital – Software
- ━━━ Fixed capital – Research and development

Riain 2004, 2010). Without the real estate and finance bubble of the 1990s to divert resources into speculation, growth in these sectors has once more taken off.

It is interesting, therefore, that the other major sector leading job growth is construction itself. Construction investment in recent years has been primarily in non-residential building, with much of

Figure 14.2

R&D staff employed by Irish and foreign firms

Source: CSO, *Business Expenditure on Research and Development*

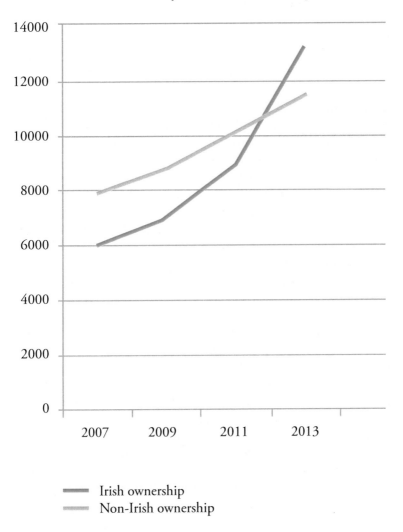

— Irish ownership
— Non-Irish ownership

this driven by the growth in industry and information and communications technology. While office construction has increased rapidly in recent years, the vacancy rate of office space has also declined, indicating that this round of construction is linked more closely to the overall economy than the bubble of the 2000s (Savills 2015; Ó Riain 2014, Chapter 3). This building activity has been heavily influenced by government action. This has been led by the National Asset Management Agency (NAMA), a controversial agency that has a mandate to obtain the best return for the state on the distressed loans it took on from developers and banks after the crisis of 2008. However, in practice, NAMA has played a very significant role in reshaping property development and the urban environment in a form of 'Asset-Price Keynesianism' (Byrne forthcoming; Norris and Byrne 2015). NAMA has effectively remade the market, all the while denying it is playing any such role. The agency has control over the large majority of development sites and has managed the rate at which such sites come on the market, the bundles of assets that are sold together (and their price), the buyers (and therefore developers) coming into the market and the locational dynamics of investment. All this has been supported by a variety of other measures, including a range of financing mechanisms through NAMA itself and government policies and legislation, such as enabling the formation of Real Estate Investment Trusts (REITs) (Byrne and Norris 2015). One area that has changed relatively little is wages, which remained largely flat in the post-crisis era.

Ironically perhaps, the strategy adopted in construction has been based upon one long-used in export-oriented sectors—using Ireland's many international ties to mobilise capital to take advantage of carefully constructed resources and opportunities (Ruane 2010). Just as the domestic momentum in export sectors has quietly grown, construction is increasingly dominated by international players. The growth in the construction sector has been actively created through public policy—for better or worse—and all the while with the various actors involved maintaining the illusion of a 'natural' market when in practice this is being clearly and actively constructed.

Third, and finally, there is the accommodation and food sector. What makes this sector interesting is that it did not grow as a part of a general increase in demand—if it had, then we would have expected wholesale and retail trade to lead the way, although they remained stagnant until 2015. The growth of accommodation and food services in the context of overall stagnant demand seems to reflect a number of key aspects of demand in Ireland. Until 2012 at least, it appears that much of the demand for these services came from the business sector, with turnover recovering fastest between 2008 and 2012 in the events and catering sub-sector (CSO, Business and Distribution Services). Tourism has boomed in recent years, boosting the accommodation and food sector, with some anecdotal evidence that the classic weaknesses of poor product development that bedevilled the industry (O'Brien 2010, 2011) are beginning to be addressed. Furthermore, demand seems likely to be skewed towards such discretionary items, as 47% of the income gains of the recovery have been held by the top 10% in the income distribution (and particularly those who are self-employed and/or hold property) (Taft 2016).

While macroeconomic stabilisation no doubt played a role in Ireland's employment recovery, an explanation focused on 'internal devaluation' is incomplete at best. Looking at the three drivers of growth we have examined, wages grew in information and communications technology, were largely stable in construction and declined somewhat in accommodation and food. While a moderated approach to wage growth can certainly help competitiveness, there is little evidence that it was central to Ireland's employment growth, which is now showing signs of boosting private demand and tax revenues (Regan 2015). More crucial were two other factors: the weakening of the distorting factors that sucked resources into financialised speculation in the 2000s, and the role of public action in promoting the export, construction and tourism sectors.

Deepening or destroying recovery?

One of the largest austerity policies in recent world economic history was undertaken in response to the Irish crisis (Whelan 2010). Wage competitiveness improved and domestic demand stagnated. Public finances improved as public services were weakened. The government promised significant tax cuts even as the foundations of public finances remain shaky. Nonetheless, more than six years after its crash, Ireland's economy is now showing signs of a significant recovery. In particular, employment is growing and tax revenues are increasing, while budget deficits are narrowing.

However, Ireland's most intractable contemporary economic and political dilemmas remain and are evident in debates that seem unable to address the core of the issue, let alone resolve it. Let us briefly note four of these dilemmas. First, while Ireland brings in significant monies from the international economy, its ability to turn this into productive investment is weak, diminishing the current account balance over time; this is largely due to the relative weakness of domestic enterprise. Second, economic debates are caught in a bind between the need to increase a wide band of relatively mediocre wages while improving competitiveness, emphasising the need for enhanced productive investment and greater innovation. Third, distributional politics are caught between a persistent inequality in market incomes and an effective but controversial redistribution system using cash transfers; Ireland's comparatively high inequality in market incomes means there is a 'missing middle' in the income distribution. Fourth, Ireland's public finances rest on a narrow base with employer contributions exceptionally low while an unusually high percentage of workers are outside the tax net. Yet both these poorer households and the smaller firms face difficulties in paying these contributions.

These dilemmas promise to remain intractable without further progress on Ireland's developmental project, and not just enhanced competitiveness. Can a 'new middle' of productive indigenous firms providing good employment to empowered employees be constructed? Our examination of the sources of Ireland's employment recovery suggests that not only is such progress realistic, it has also been central to the aspects of Ireland's recent recovery that are genuine and sustainable. However, this progress remains somewhat precarious.

There are some interesting new developments in financing, enterprise and innovation policy. The business-lending expertise that exists among private institutions is at least as developed in the public agencies. Indeed, quite early in the course of the economic crisis, officials from Enterprise Ireland were sent to advise staff in the banking organisations on business lending (NESC 2012). The engagement between state industrial development agencies and export-oriented businesses over a period of some decades has resulted in significant organisational learning (Ó Riain 2004).

After the crisis, a wide range of public schemes provided financing for longstanding as well as newly developed enterprises. These schemes included increasing efforts to create investment funds for different classes of firms in Ireland (including small start-ups, larger firms and distressed firms). The broad thrust of the approach has been to sidestep the difficulties of the banks and to seek out non-bank sources of financing for enterprise. Alongside this, and sometimes entangled with it, has been a policy programme (in the Programme for Government) for developing a State Investment Fund, which became the basis in 2014 of a new (and hotly contested) state investment bank, the Strategic Banking Corporation.

There are also efforts to create institutions that can tackle major gaps in the network of enterprise supports including Enterprise Ireland's extension of its mandate to additional firms, the integration of Enterprise Ireland and the Local Enterprise Offices to engage with smaller domestic firms, and the reform of vocational education committees to enhance the link between regional enterprise and education policy regimes. The 'footprint' of Enterprise Ireland has extended in important and interesting ways but the required supports in financing and innovation may not be present and the local capacity to develop this system is still in question.

Finally, some interesting developments are emerging in innovation policy itself. Under the cloak of 'industry relevance', the organisational model has shifted from the commercialisation of research outputs through an intellectual property framework to an organisational structure that creates innovation centres with (mainly foreign) industry partners and universities—and that will place greater emphasis on ongoing dialogue in a semi-public sphere (as Lester and Piore 2004 suggest). More generally, a new strategy for science and innovation—Innovation 2020—was published in late 2015 and the political negotiations over this, within the innovation and economic policy worlds, revealed a surprisingly wide ranging and somewhat successful coalition for a broader concept of innovation and greater focus on breadth of research and education. However, this broader coalition faces an uphill battle given both its disparate character and the challenges of the current funding regime for higher education as discussed by Pritchard and Slowey (Chapter 11, this volume).

In a time of significant austerity and apparent re-floating of some financial bubbles, the politics of finance, enterprise and innovation appears more open than might be expected. The institutional resources exist within the Irish political economy to support a high investment, high productivity path within capitalism—similar to that which characterises the successful small open European economies. Table 14.1 showed that this path is also generally associated with greater fiscal prudence and sustainable public finances, in part because of the economic benefits of investment but also because of the underlying societal contract that is based on a collective investment in the future.

However, these promising signals and institutional resources also existed in some form at the end of the 1990s but were quickly undermined by a set of policy decisions that promoted financial boosterism and undermined the public finances, even as the high level indicators in the economy looked good. Ireland in 2016 looks very similar. Despite the strengths underlying the recovery, Ireland's ability to move forward is still threatened by the same trends that contributed to its crash. While banks are not lending as recklessly as they once did, they have provided little credit to productive businesses. Both finance and property are once again being boosted as growth sectors, and rising rents and prices are putting pressure on households and small businesses. Key investments in education, training, enterprise development, infrastructure and more are being threatened by the very significant cutbacks of recent years. A rush to promise tax cuts undermines the ability to make the investments that will be essential to avoiding the mistakes made at the end of the 1990s, when society was taken down a path of speculation rather than the sustained egalitarian investment that would have put Ireland in a quite different position in 2008, and today. Fortunately, the opportunity exists in 2016 to revisit those decisions and the following two chapters provide some pointers to how this might be achieved.

15. Resources available for public services: how does Ireland compare now and how might we prepare for the future?

Seamus Coffey

Introduction

Government revenue as a proportion of gross domestic product (GDP) is lower in Ireland than in most other European Union (EU) countries. This raises concerns that the Irish government does not have sufficient resources to provide a level of public services comparable to our EU peers, especially given that government spending in Ireland is significantly below most other EU countries as a proportion of GDP. What are the underlying causes for this difference? The first reason is that the use of GDP in the denominator overstates Ireland's national income while the biggest factor within government spending itself is expenditure on old-age social protection. Once these factors are accounted for, Ireland actually spends more as a proportion of national income than almost all EU countries on the provision of public services.

The enforced austerity in Ireland since 2008 has shown the importance of preparing for downturns before they arrive. Ireland has successfully closed a huge budget deficit, and the final part of this chapter proposes a way of reducing the probability of such measures being necessary in the future. One way to do this is to run surpluses in times of growth and expansion. This chapter contains a proposal for a 'stability fund' with contributions based on corporation tax receipts from the multi-national corporate (MNC) sector in Ireland and withdrawals based on projections of employment growth. Such a fund would provide surpluses and accumulated savings that can be used to mitigate the fiscal and economic consequences of downturns in the economic cycle. However, before turning this proposal, the chapter examines the role of foreign-controlled companies in the Irish economy.

The contribution of foreign-controlled companies to the Irish economy

The direct employment and investment benefits to Ireland from foreign direct investment (FDI) are immense and this is particularly evident in the case of companies from the United States. The business economy in Ireland from 2008 to 2012 is summarised at an aggregate level in Table 15.1 with a breakdown by country of the ultimate owner of companies operating in Ireland.

The table shows that during the early years of the crisis and austerity (2008–12) an annual average of €86.5 billion of gross value added was generated by enterprises in the business economy in Ireland. Of this 47% was generated by Irish-owned enterprises with 53% coming from foreign-owned enterprises. Ireland is the only country in the EU where the value added of foreign companies exceeds the value added of domestic companies. In the EU, an average of 28% of the gross value added in each country comes from foreign-owned companies.

Across the overall business economy in Ireland, 47% of value added is devoted to personnel costs. This labour share—the share of national income going to workers in the form of wages and salaries—is the third lowest in the EU. However, the overall figure masks a significant division. The labour share for Irish-owned companies is 68%, which is the second-highest labour share for domestically owned companies in the EU, and is well above the EU mean of 58%. On the other hand, the labour share for foreign-owned companies in Ireland is just 28%, which is the lowest in the EU by some distance and around half the EU mean of 54%. The labour share for US companies in Ireland is lower again at just 19%. This would suggest that at an aggregate level the foreign-controlled sector in Ireland is 'low pay' but, as can be seen in Table 15.1, the average annual personnel cost per person employed in foreign-owned companies is over €50,000 compared to around €31,500 for Irish-owned companies.

Between 2008 and 2012, there was an average of 1.13 million people employed by enterprises in the business economy in Ireland. Of these, just over 77% were employed by Irish-owned enterprises. The United States make the largest contribution (8.7%) to employment among foreign-owned business economy enterprises in Ireland. The proportion of personnel costs that comes from US-owned companies is even greater at 14.6%, which reflects the average annual personnel cost per person employed in these companies of almost €60,000.

The deduction of personnel costs from gross value added results in gross operating surplus (GOS) can be used to proxy the corporate income tax base. In Ireland more than 70% of the gross operating surplus generated in the business economy comes from foreign-owned companies. This is by far the highest proportion of the EU and the Irish case is a reverse of the EU mean. This outcome means that foreign companies are the dominant source of corporation tax revenues in Ireland.

The gross operating rate (GOR)—a measure of profitability—is 14% in Ireland, the highest in the EU. Again, however, this masks a significant difference between domestic and foreign companies. As shown in Table 15.1, the gross operating rate of Irish-owned companies is just 8% and is the sixth lowest for domestic firms across the 28 countries of the EU. In contrast, for all foreign-owned companies operating in Ireland, the GOR is 19%; for the subset of that which are US-owned companies operating in Ireland the GOR is 22%. Under existing rules, it is clear that US companies have a substantial amount of profit that is subject to corporation tax in Ireland.

Table 15.2 shows the contribution of US-owned companies to the business economy of the 28 countries of the EU. The data, which are annual averages for the period from 2008 to 2012, show the over-performance of Ireland in relation to the attraction of investment from the United States. As noted above, over the period from 2008 to 2012, 8.7% of people employed by enterprises in the business economy in Ireland were with US-controlled companies. This is the highest in the EU (the UK is next at 6.1%, followed by Luxembourg at 5.3%) and more than three times greater than the EU mean of 2.3%.

Table 15.1

The business economy in Ireland, annual averages 2008–12

Source: Eurostat [fats_g1a_08]

Item	All Enterprises €million	Irish-Owned €million
Production value	220,804	91,091
Purchases of goods & services purchased for resale in the same condition as received	104,053	64,233
Turnover	324,862	155,378
Total purchases of goods & services	-232,031	-109,761
Gross value added at factor cost	86,519	40,752
Personnel costs	-40,478	-27,586
Gross operating surplus	**46,042**	**13,166**
Number of enterprises	153,943	150,668
Number of persons employed	**1,133,143**	**877,030**
Labour share, %[1]	**47%**	**68%**
Average personnel cost per person employed, €	35,722	31,454
Simple wage adjusted labour productivity,%[2]	214%	148%
Gross operating rate,%[3]	**14%**	**8%**
Gross investment in tangible assets, €million	**12,966**	**7,042**
Investment per person employed, €	11,443	8,029
Investment rate,%[4]	28%	53%
As a % of Business Economy		
% of persons employed	100.0%	77.4%
% of turnover	100.0%	47.8%
% of value added	100.0%	47.1%
% of personnel costs	100.0%	68.2%
% of gross op. surplus	100.0%	28.6%
% of gross investment	100.0%	54.3%

[1] The labour share is the percentage of gross value added that is devoted to personnel costs

[2] The simple productivity measure is value added as a percentage of personnel costs

[3] The gross operating rate is gross operating surplus as a percentage of turnover

[4] The investment rate is gross investment as a percentage of gross operating surplus

Foreign-Owned €million	Of which:	United States €million	United Kingdom €million	Other EU €million	Rest of the World €million
129,713		95,191	9,302	16,149	9,071
39,820		20,519	7,885	6,869	4,548
169,484		115,602	17,236	22,967	13,679
-122,270		-83,203	-12,658	-16,955	-9,454
45,767		31,859	4,212	5,884	3,812
-12,892		-5,919	-2,554	-2,746	-1,673
32,875		**25,940**	**1,659**	**3,138**	**2,139**
3,275		817	1,103	834	521
256,113		**99,042**	**72,434**	**52,503**	**32,134**
28%		**19%**	**61%**	**47%**	**44%**
50,336		59,764	35,255	52,300	52,065
355%		538%	165%	214%	228%
19%		**22%**	**10%**	**14%**	**16%**
5,924		**2,964**	**617**	**1,301**	**1,042**
23,132		29,924	8,524	24,779	32,436
18%		11%	37%	41%	49%
22.6%		8.7%	6.4%	4.6%	2.8%
52.2%		35.6%	5.3%	7.1%	4.2%
52.9%		36.8%	4.9%	6.8%	4.4%
31.8%		14.6%	6.3%	6.8%	4.1%
71.4%		56.3%	3.6%	6.8%	4.6%
45.7%		22.9%	4.8%	10.0%	8.0%

Table 15.2

Contribution of US-controlled enterprises to the business economy in EU countries, 2008–1?

Source: Eurostat [fats_g1a_08]

	Gross Value Added	Gross Operating Surplus	People Employed in the Business Economy
	%Total	%Total	% Total
Belgium	7.5%	7.5%	3.6%
Bulgaria	2.4%	2.1%	0.9%
Czech Republic	5.1%	4.4%	3.1%
Denmark	4.1%	4.7%	2.4%
Germany	4.1%	4.2%	2.2%
Estonia	2.7%	2.2%	2.4%
Ireland	**36.8%**	**56.3%**	**8.7%**
Greece	1.3%	0.9%	0.5%
Spain	2.4%	2.0%	1.4%
France	4.6%	4.1%	2.6%
Croatia	0.5%	0.4%	0.3%
Italy	3.3%	2.6%	1.7%
Cyprus	0.6%	0.6%	0.2%
Latvia	1.4%	1.3%	0.8%
Lithuania	2.0%	2.1%	0.7%
Luxembourg	8.7%	11.3%	5.3%
Hungary	10.1%	13.1%	3.4%
Malta	2.4%	2.5%	1.4%
Netherlands	7.5%	8.8%	3.4%
Austria	2.9%	2.7%	1.7%
Poland	3.7%	3.8%	2.3%
Portugal	2.9%	2.8%	1.2%
Romania	2.4%	1.9%	1.5%
Slovenia	1.4%	1.5%	0.7%
Slovakia	2.3%	1.5%	1.7%
Finland	2.9%	2.8%	2.0%
Sweden	4.4%	3.7%	3.3%
United Kingdom	9.9%	11.0%	6.1%
MEAN for EU28 (Ex IRE)	3.8%	3.9%	2.1%

Personnel Costs in the Business Economy	Average Personnel Cost per Person Employed	Gross Investment in Tangible Assets in Business Economy	Investment in Tangible Assets per Person Employed	Gross Investment in Tangible Assets
% Total	€	% Total	€	%GDP
7.5%	82,300	3.7%	17,600	0.4%
2.7%	12,000	2.8%	13,800	0.7%
5.7%	22,000	3.0%	5,600	0.4%
3.7%	68,300	1.9%	11,300	0.2%
4.0%	58,500	3.5%	11,200	0.2%
3.0%	16,900	1.2%	3,200	0.1%
14.6%	**59,800**	**22.9%**	**29,900**	**1.7%**
1.6%	48,800	0.5%	5,600	0.0%
2.7%	48,400	1.8%	8,400	0.1%
4.8%	74,900	1.2%	6,900	0.1%
0.6%	24,800	0.4%	7,000	0.0%
3.8%	52,600	3.1%	12,900	0.2%
0.6%	52,700	0.3%	7,600	0.0%
1.5%	14,100	0.5%	3,800	0.1%
1.9%	18,600	0.9%	4,700	0.1%
6.9%	59,000	6.0%	10,700	0.3%
7.2%	20,800	4.9%	6,600	0.6%
2.1%	18,700	1.7%	14,500	0.3%
6.5%	60,400	4.1%	10,100	0.3%
3.1%	64,800	2.8%	20,700	0.3%
3.5%	18,900	2.8%	7,000	0.2%
2.9%	33,500	1.5%	9,300	0.2%
3.1%	11,700	2.4%	11,400	0.5%
1.4%	34,300	0.8%	7,600	0.1%
3.1%	20,600	1.4%	6,100	0.2%
3.0%	56,000	1.7%	8,300	0.1%
4.7%	59,500	2.0%	7,400	0.2%
9.0%	42,100	7.6%	9,400	0.5%
3.7%	40,600	2.4%	9,200	0.2%

In Ireland, US-controlled companies contribute 14.8% of personnel costs paid by enterprises in the business economy; again, this is the highest in the EU by some distance. It can also be seen in Table 15.1 that US-controlled companies contributed nearly one-quarter of gross investment in tangible goods by enterprises in the business economy in Ireland. This is the highest investment in the EU by US companies per person employed (nearly €30,000 per person employed per annum) and is equivalent to 1.7% of Irish GDP—this is nearly six times greater than the EU mean. Table 15.3 complements this and provides the distribution across the business economy of EU of the profits, employment and investment of US-owned companies.

Across the five measures shown in Table 15.3, Ireland attracts a proportion about six times greater than would be implied by GDP. While there is some over-performance in relation to employment and personnel costs, and a somewhat larger out-performance in relation to investment in tangible assets, the standout figure is the amount of profits (as measured by gross operating surplus) that is attributed to the Irish operations of US companies in the EU. Although Ireland is only 1.3% of EU GDP, it can be seen that 16.8% of the €155 billion average annual gross operating surplus (excluding financial and insurance activities) of US companies in the EU is sourced from Ireland. This is greater than the gross operating surplus of US companies in all EU countries bar the UK.

Each year US-owned companies (excluding those in financial and insurance services) pay an average of around €6 billion of personnel costs into the Irish economy. Between 2008 and 2012, gross investment in tangible goods by these companies averaged €3 billion per year. In addition, a portion of the goods and services purchased by the companies would be sourced in Ireland. Although precise figures are not available, this spending is likely to be in the region of €3 billion to €4 billion per annum. In this context, it is clear that the direct contribution of US-owned companies to the Irish economy is in excess of €12 billion per year, and this excludes second-round and multiplier effects.

Between 2008 and 2012, US-owned companies generated around €26 billion of gross operating surplus in Ireland each year. This is hugely significant when it comes to assessing the tax contribution of these companies to the Irish Exchequer. Walsh (2011) assesses the overall tax revenues accruing to the Exchequer from the activities of US-owned companies in Ireland and provides a detailed breakdown of tax payments for 2008. He shows that in 2008, US companies contributed €2 billion of corporation tax revenues that was 40% of the overall total collected under that tax heading. Significant contributions were also made under the other tax headings. In subsequent analysis, Piggott and Walsh (2014, iv) explore the distribution and concentration of corporation tax payments and one of their conclusions is that 'foreign owned multinational companies account for three quarters of corporation tax paid between 2008 and 2012. In 2012 alone, foreign multinationals paid over 79% of Corporation Tax'.

In total, it is likely that the contribution of US companies to the Irish economy is around €15 billion every year. We now turn to how those resources that make their way to the government sector are spent.

Government expenditure: Ireland is not 'low-spend'

In 2014, government revenue for the 28 countries of the EU was equivalent to an average of 43.3% of GDP. If we consider the EU15 as a contiguous block, government revenue was equivalent to 45.7% of GDP. For Ireland, the 2014 figure was 34.4%, which was the lowest of the EU15 countries with only Lithuania and Romania recording lower figures across the entire EU.

The main reasons for Ireland's below-average government revenue are indirect taxes, which were three percentage points of GDP below the EU mean, and social contributions received, which were six percentage points of GDP below the EU mean. If compared to the EU15 as a whole, government revenue in Ireland is eight percentage points of GDP lower. Ireland is above the EU mean for direct taxes on household and corporate income and on wealth, and at 13% of GDP is in line with the outcome for the EU15 as a whole.

However, our primary concern initially is not how Ireland generates resources for public services but how it uses them. With the onset of the crisis in 2008, Ireland began to run substantial deficits. Even though expenditure on public services exceeded the amount of revenue raised, Ireland's government expenditure relative to GDP remained significantly below the EU mean. In 2013, government expenditure in Ireland was equivalent to 40.6% of GDP. This was the lowest in the EU15, with only five countries across the entire EU having a lower level. Relative to GDP, Ireland is below the aggregate figure for the combined EU28 for health, education and social protection. The largest difference is for social protection, where Ireland is four percentage points of GDP below the figure for the EU28. If we

Table 15.3

Distribution of US companies' profits, employment and investment in the EU, 2008–12

Source: Eurostat [fats_g1a_08]

	EU Gross Domestic Product	Gross Value Added*	Gross Operating Surplus*
	€12,474bn	€333.0bn	€154.7bn
Belgium	2.9%	4.1%	3.8%
Bulgaria	0.3%	0.1%	0.1%
Czech Republic	1.2%	1.3%	1.2%
Denmark	1.9%	1.4%	1.3%
Germany	20.2%	16.1%	13.7%
Estonia	0.1%	0.0%	0.0%
Ireland	**1.3%**	**9.5%**	**16.8%**
Greece	1.7%	0.2%	0.1%
Spain	8.4%	3.5%	2.4%
France	15.7%	12.4%	6.9%
Croatia	0.4%	0.0%	0.0%
Italy	12.5%	6.3%	4.9%
Cyprus	0.1%	0.0%	0.0%
Latvia	0.2%	0.0%	0.0%
Lithuania	0.2%	0.1%	0.1%
Luxembourg	0.3%	0.5%	0.5%
Hungary	0.8%	1.4%	1.9%
Malta	0.1%	0.0%	0.0%
Netherlands	4.7%	6.8%	7.5%
Austria	2.3%	1.4%	1.0%
Poland	2.9%	1.6%	1.8%
Portugal	1.4%	0.7%	0.6%
Romania	1.0%	0.4%	0.3%
Slovenia	0.3%	0.1%	0.1%
Slovakia	0.5%	0.2%	0.1%
Finland	1.5%	0.7%	0.6%
Sweden	2.8%	2.4%	1.5%
United Kingdom	14.2%	28.8%	32.6%
Total	**100.0%**	**100.0%**	**100.0%**

*From US-controlled companies in the EU

Persons Employed*	Personnel Costs*	Gross Investment in Tangible Assets*
3,568,024	€179.2bn	€36.7bn
2.7%	4.4%	4.6%
0.5%	0.1%	0.7%
3.1%	1.4%	1.7%
1.1%	1.5%	1.2%
15.6%	18.2%	17.1%
0.2%	0.1%	0.1%
2.8%	**3.3%**	**8.1%**
0.3%	0.3%	0.2%
4.5%	4.4%	3.8%
11.4%	17.0%	7.4%
0.1%	0.0%	0.0%
7.3%	7.6%	9.2%
0.0%	0.0%	0.0%
0.1%	0.0%	0.0%
0.2%	0.1%	0.1%
0.3%	0.4%	0.4%
2.4%	1.0%	1.5%
0.0%	0.0%	0.0%
5.1%	6.2%	5.1%
1.3%	1.6%	2.5%
3.5%	1.3%	2.4%
1.1%	0.7%	1.0%
1.7%	0.4%	1.8%
0.1%	0.1%	0.1%
0.6%	0.2%	0.4%
0.8%	0.9%	0.7%
2.7%	3.2%	2.0%
30.4%	25.6%	28.0%
100.0%	**100.0%**	**100.0%**

combine defence, public order, environment, housing and recreation into a single category, Ireland is two percentage points of GDP below the EU28 figure with approximately half of this difference accounted for by defence.

Across the EU28, government expenditure on social protection was equivalent to 19.9% of GDP in 2013. The corresponding figure for Ireland was 15.7% of GDP, ranking Ireland eighteenth of the EU28 and lowest of the EU15. Just over half of all social protection expenditure in the EU is allocated to old-age social protection (mainly the provision of public pensions). The equivalent of 10.4% of GDP is spent on old-age social protection across the EU, compared to an equivalent of 4.1% of GDP for such expenditure in Ireland.

If we exclude old-age expenditure from overall social protection expenditure, it can be seen that Ireland has the third-highest level of social protection spending on sickness and disability (seventh), survivors (fifteenth), family and children (fourth), unemployment (third) and housing (second) in the EU. Excluding old-age only Denmark (16.8% of GDP) and Finland (12.9% of GDP) spend more than Ireland (11.6% of GDP) on social protection.

There are two reasons why Ireland is a low spender on old-age social protection. The first is demography; Ireland has the lowest proportion of its population aged 65 and over in the EU. For the overall EU, 17.4% of the population is aged 65 and over; in Ireland the proportion is 12.2%. More than 20% of the populations of Greece, Italy and Germany are aged 65 and over, with other countries close to that level. The second reason why Ireland is a low spender on old-age social protection is the flat-rated nature of public pension benefits in Ireland. State pensions are related to the number and duration of contributions rather than size of the contributions made. In most EU countries, people who make larger social insurance contributions receive larger public pensions. This is not the case in Ireland where the maximum payment is capped through flat-rated payments.

If Ireland collected and spent the equivalent of an additional 5% of GDP on public pensions to mimic the 'average' EU system, then government revenue and expenditure figures would be closer to the EU average. For 2014, Ireland would move to 40% of GDP versus the EU average of 45% of GDP for government revenue, and to 46% of GDP versus EU average of 49% of GDP for government expenditure. Social welfare pensions, more than anything else, account for the 'low-tax' and 'low-spend' monikers that are sometimes applied to Ireland. Ireland has fewer pensioners and has a system of social welfare pensions that involves less revenue and expenditure than in other EU countries.

Rather than recommend what changes, if any, should be introduced to our public pension system, all we want to highlight here is the impact expenditure of old-age social protection expenditure has on our government finance aggregates. To do this, we will make two adjustments to government expenditure. First we will strip out old-age social protection expenditure, which is lower in Ireland for the reasons outlined above. We will also omit expenditure on capital transfers, which makes up a small proportion of overall government expenditure for most countries. However, in 2013 both Greece and Slovenia provided substantial capital injections to their ailing banks, which inflated their expenditure figures for that year. Second, we will adjust the national income. For most countries the difference between gross domestic product (GDP) and gross national product (GNP) is insignificant. However, this is not the case for Ireland, as profits from the presence of multinational corporations (MNCs) boosts GDP does not contribute to GNP (apart from the corporation tax that is collected) because the profit accrues to non-resident shareholders. The adjustment that is applied is equal to GDP/ (GNP + 0.5(GDP - GNP)). The adjustments are shown in Table 15.4.

In 2013, Ireland was ranked twenty-third of the EU28 for government expenditure as a proportion of GDP. If we make the same comparison, but exclude old-age social protection expenditure and capital transfers, Ireland's spending (35.9% of GDP) ranks thirteenth in the EU. If we consider expenditure as a proportion of adjusted national income, then Ireland ranks tenth in the EU28 and seventh in the EU15.

Outside of old-age social protection, Ireland does not spend a low proportion of national income on public services and supports. In Chapter 16 of this volume, Healy argues that '[i]t is past time for Ireland to recognise that in order to fund the public services and infrastructure that are required the total tax take must rise towards the European average.' However, if there are problems with the level of public services and supports, the evidence suggests that it is not because Ireland does not spend enough money, but rather the level of services that this money buys.

Table 15.4

Adjusted general government expenditure, % national income (ESA2010), 2013

Source: Eurostat, author's calculations [data ranked by last column]

Country	Government Expenditure, % GDP		minus 'Old Age' Social Protection Expenditure, % GDP	and Capital Transfers, payable, %GDP
Denmark	57.1	4	8.3	0.3
Finland	57.8	3	12.0	0.3
Belgium	54.4	6	8.8	1.9
France	57.1	5	13.5	1.0
Sweden	53.3	7	12.1	0.3
Hungary	49.7	11	8.0	1.6
Croatia	47.0	12	6.0	1.1
Slovenia	59.7	1	10.3	10.4
Netherlands	46.8	13	6.9	0.8
Ireland	**40.6**	**23**	**4.1**	**0.6**
Portugal	50.1	10	11.9	0.9
Austria	50.9	8	12.9	1.2
Luxembourg	44.3	17	11.4	1.1
United Kingdom	45.5	14	8.6	0.8
Italy	50.8	9	14.0	1.2
Spain	44.3	16	8.8	1.0
Slovakia	41.0	22	6.5	0.5
Czech Republic	42.0	20	7.9	1.0
Germany	44.3	15	9.1	0.9
Cyprus	41.4	21	5.4	2.4
Malta	42.3	18	8.3	1.3
Poland	42.2	19	9.3	0.5
Greece	59.2	2	14.4	12.8
Estonia	38.9	24	6.8	1.0
Lithuania	35.5	27	5.8	1.3
Latvia	36.1	26	7.5	0.4
Bulgaria	38.3	25	9.9	0.5
Romania	35.2	28	8.8	1.1
MEAN	**46.6**		**9.2**	**1.7**

equals **Adjusted Government Expenditure, % GDP**		multiply **National Income Adjustment**	equals **Adjusted Government Expenditure, % 'National Income'**	
48.5	1	1.00	48.5	1
45.5	2	1.00	45.4	2
43.7	3	1.01	43.9	3
42.6	4	1.00	42.6	4
40.9	5	1.00	40.9	5
40.1	6	1.01	40.7	6
39.9	7	1.01	40.3	7
39.0	9	1.00	39.1	8
39.1	8	1.00	39.1	9
35.9	**13**	**1.08**	**38.8**	**10**
37.3	10	1.00	37.5	11
36.8	11	1.00	36.8	12
31.8	22	1.15	36.6	13
36.1	12	1.00	36.3	14
35.6	14	1.00	35.6	15
34.5	15	1.00	34.5	16
34.0	17	1.01	34.3	17
33.1	19	1.04	34.3	18
34.3	16	1.00	34.3	19
33.6	18	1.02	34.1	20
32.7	20	1.02	33.5	21
32.4	21	1.00	32.4	22
32.0	22	1.00	32.0	23
31.1	24	1.01	31.5	24
28.4	25	1.01	28.8	25
28.2	26	1.00	28.3	26
27.9	27	1.00	27.9	27
25.3	28	1.00	25.3	28
35.7		**1.01**	**36.2**	

Figure 15.1

Health, education and social welfare

Source: Eurostat (COFOG)

Public expenditure on Health (GF07), Education (GF09) and Social Welfare (GF10) excluding Old-Age Social Protection (GF 1002), % GDP, 2013

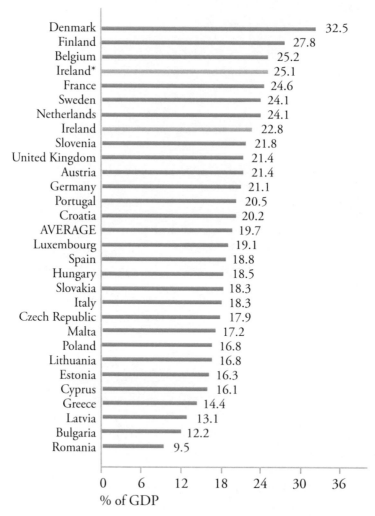

Country	% of GDP
Denmark	32.5
Finland	27.8
Belgium	25.2
Ireland*	25.1
France	24.6
Sweden	24.1
Netherlands	24.1
Ireland	22.8
Slovenia	21.8
United Kingdom	21.4
Austria	21.4
Germany	21.1
Portugal	20.5
Croatia	20.2
AVERAGE	19.7
Luxembourg	19.1
Spain	18.8
Hungary	18.5
Slovakia	18.3
Italy	18.3
Czech Republic	17.9
Malta	17.2
Poland	16.8
Lithuania	16.8
Estonia	16.3
Cyprus	16.1
Greece	14.4
Latvia	13.1
Bulgaria	12.2
Romania	9.5

% of GDP

*Hybrid GDP for Ireland = GDP -0.5 (GDP–GNP)

Figure 15.1 shows that if we look at the 'big three' areas of government expenditure—health, education and social protection (albeit excluding old-age social protection)—Ireland was the seventh highest spender as a proportion of GDP. If we make a national income adjustment to these figures, Ireland ranks fourth behind only Demark, Finland and Belgium. Expenditure will rise as demographics dictate—the key is having the resources to meet it. Even after a period of austerity, Ireland does not lack the spending to pay for public services. Ireland could raise additional revenue to spend now but perhaps it would be best advised to begin raising revenue to cover the inevitable pension-related expenditure that will arise in the future. The final section looks at a proposal to set aside resources to help alleviate the boom-bust nature of the business cycle that impacts on government revenue in Ireland.

Government resources: is it time to save for the 'rainy day'?

Ireland entered the 2008 financial crisis with public finances that appeared to be in a sound state. However, the crisis revealed the fragility that was under the surface, and by 2010 an underlying deficit (that is, excluding the banking-related measures that were also a feature of the time) equivalent to around 11% of GDP had opened. The measures introduced since then—and the recent economic growth—have helped to close this deficit, and in 2017 the public finances are likely to return to balance for the first time in a nearly a decade.

But is this enough? Ireland's fiscal rules require that the government run a balanced budget in structural terms, which will probably be achieved in 2018, but there are no additional formal requirements once the budget is maintained. A balanced budget gives some buffer to accommodate increased borrowing in the event of a downturn but, as our recent experience shows, the extent of the cyclical swings of the Irish economy mean that a balanced budget does not guarantee protection against a downturn.

One of the most notable features of the economic recovery has been the near 50% increase in corporation tax receipts in 2015. In 2014, corporation tax contributed €4.6 billion of revenue to the Irish exchequer; while the figure for 2015 was €6.9 billion. As discussed above around 80% of corporation tax comes from foreign-owned companies. The profit that this tax revenue is derived on is included in Ireland's GDP, but because it accrues to non-resident shareholders it is not part of Ireland's GNP. It is for this reason that this is a substantial gap between Ireland's GDP and GNP.

In light of this, it may be more appropriate to assess Ireland's fiscal ratios in terms of GNP rather than GDP. The employee pay, purchases of goods and services, fixed capital investment and tax paid by MNCs are included in GNP, but the profit on their operations is excluded. The gap between GDP and GNP is a measure of the gross added value that takes place in Ireland, but that does not accrue to Irish residents. Taking GNP as the base for fiscal ratios is a better, but not perfect, reflection of the resources available in Ireland.

Using GNP as the base would have limited impact on the government target to achieve a balanced budget as it will be balanced whether it is measured in terms of GNP or GDP. Using GNP would also have a limited impact on the amount of 'fiscal space' available under the expenditure benchmark component of the fiscal rules. From the point of view of fiscal ratios, the biggest impact of using GNP as the base would be using a lower level of debt as a benchmark of 60% of GNP, which would be around one-fifth lower than the current benchmark set at 60% of GDP.

However, removing MNC profits from the national income base used in the fiscal arithmetic is really only a first step. If GNP is to become the base for fiscal ratios, then the tax revenue collected from the gap between GNP and GDP should also be excluded. Measuring ratios in terms of GNP using revenues not fully derived from GNP would give misleading ratios, especially on the revenue side and given the potential risks to the revenue currently collected from the GNP-GDP gap as it currently exists.

The proposal here is that, as well as excluding MNC profits from the income base, Ireland should exclude MNC profits from the fiscal arithmetic and aim for a balanced budget on that basis. One possibility is to set aside funds equivalent to 5% of the gap between GNP and GDP and target compliance with the fiscal rules excluding this money. The choice of figure corresponds to around half the effective tax rate on the MNC profits that comprise the GDP-GNP gap. If there is expected to be a €30 billion gap between GNP and GDP, this would mean moving beyond a balanced budget and setting aside up to €1.5 billion. The exclusion of these funds would mean budgeting in times of growth for an overall surplus, which could be saved in a type of 'stability fund'. The key benefit of this is that it creates more fiscal space in the event of an economic downturn. Ireland has some previous experience with a sovereign savings fund through the national pensions reserve fund (NPRF) that was established in 2001. Under its original guise, the NPRF was designed so that 1% of GNP was contributed each year. However, there was no provision that this money was to come from savings. Budget documents from 2002 to 2007 show that the targeted position was for a general government deficit in four of these six years. As part of the general government sector, the Exchequer transfers to the NPRF had no impact on the general government balance. With few planned surplus, it was intended that the funds to be put into the NPRF would be borrowed.

The fiscal outturns from this period exceeded the budget day targets as economic growth and, in particular, tax revenues from property and construction, were greater than expected. Even with this, the cumulative position of the general government sector from 2002 to 2007 was a deficit, albeit small, of €0.7 billion. This means that the contributions to the NPRF were made with borrowed money; the 1% of GNP that was supposed to be injected into the funds was never taken out of the fiscal arithmetic. From 2002 to 2007, the contributions to the NPRF totalled €7.7 billion. At the same time, the general government debt rose from €40.1 billion at the start of 2002 to €47.1 billion at the end of 2007. This rise of €6.6 billion over a five-year period essentially represented the contributions to the NPRF. However, the NPRF was not a savings fund; it was a leveraged investment fund.

Using the framework of the fiscal rules, a balanced budget must ensure that surpluses are run in times of growth and fiscal stability. Once a balanced budget is achieved, contributions and withdrawals could be assessed in terms of an economic indicator, such as projected annual employment growth. If there is a balanced budget, the government should make the contributions to the 'stability fund' (5% of the gap between GNP and GDP) if employment growth in budget day macroeconomic forecasts is expected to exceed 1.5%. If employment growth is expected to be less than 1.5%, then contributions to the fund would have to be frozen. Furthermore, if employment growth is expected to fall below 0.5%, then withdrawals from the fund would be allowed. In the event of an economic downturn, the fiscal space is created first by eroding the surpluses and second by spending the accumulated savings.

This fund would have to comply with the package of fiscal rules that Ireland has adopted—the most relevant being the expenditure benchmark that anchors the growth rate of government expenditure to a long-run potential growth rate of the economy. However, within this there is greater flexibility for capital investment with a four-year moving average of investment expenditure used when assessing compliance with the rule. Thus, if there is an increase in investment expenditure in any given year, only one quarter of it is included when compliance with the expenditure benchmark is being assessed.

If managed correctly, such a stability fund would give an increased buffer to the inevitable downturns that a small economy such as Ireland's is open to while also providing funds for investment at a time when employment growth has slowed and value for money may be greater.

Conclusion

The Irish economy of the last fifteen years has shown the dangers of macroeconomic imbalance. Although Ireland has experienced significant austerity, the resources available for the provision of public services as a proportion of national income compares favourably to our EU peers. When taken relative to GDP, government expenditure in Ireland in 2013 on health, education and social protection (excluding old-age) was the seventh highest in the EU. If an adjusted measure of national income is taken, accounting for the GNP-GDP gap, then Ireland is the fourth highest spender in the EU. Any perceived inability to provide adequate public services by EU norms would not seem to arise from a lack of spending, but rather with the level of services actually purchased with that spending.

A major source of resources for the Irish economy comes from the multinational sector and, for reasons of higher risk and the benefits of macroeconomic stability, a portion of the corporation tax receipts from the MNC sector should be set aside to ensure that Ireland moves to a position of budget surpluses rather than just balanced budgets as required under the fiscal rules. This may not be enough to fully offset the negative consequences of future downturns but would give some space to reduce the possibility of austerity and mitigate some of the consequences detailed in earlier chapters.

16. Towards an inclusive and just recovery

Seán Healy

Introduction

Looking at Ireland almost a decade after the financial crash of 2008, one could conclude that all is well and that the future looks bright. Economic growth has been dramatic and the very challenging fiscal targets set have, in fact, been exceeded. Employment is growing. Unemployment is falling. Exports are growing and this growth has been strongly supported by the weakness of the euro. Interest rates are at an historic low.

On the other hand, one could look at Ireland's current situation and come to a very different conclusion. Poverty and social exclusion persist despite economic growth. Deprivation has risen dramatically with new groups falling into poverty, as Whelan and Nolan (Chapter 5, this volume) have shown. The continuing very high levels of public and private debt are deeply worrying. The high level of long-term unemployment and the failure to reverse many of the austerity measures imposed on the vulnerable since the crash of 2008 paint a different picture. The high levels of emigration and youth unemployment raise serious questions that challenge any benign interpretation of how Ireland has succeeded in addressing the consequences of the economic crash.

As has been clear throughout all of the preceding chapters, austerity policies were at the core of the Irish government's response to the extensive challenges it faced when the banking, fiscal and economic crisis happened. It is clear, however, that the social impact of these austerity policies was not considered from the beginning. The main focus was on securing economic recovery on the understanding that once the economy recovered, other issues could be addressed. This approach failed to grasp the fact that services and infrastructure need to be addressed together with economic recovery as all of these are interdependent and all are required if there is to be a fair and inclusive recovery. Looking back on the decisions that were made, a strong case can be argued that government could have achieved its fiscal targets in a way that was fairer and more inclusive, that gave greater protection to the vulnerable and had a less negative impact in areas such as employment.

Simon Wren-Lewis (Chapter 1, this volume) argues that for the world as a whole, austerity could have been avoided. He also concludes that while some austerity was inevitable in a few Eurozone countries, unemployment could have been kept much lower. Ireland's population suffered inordinately from the imposition of an inflexible and rapid austerity response to the crisis.

A recent study published by the Levy Economics Institute examines the relationship between changes in a country's public sector fiscal position and inequality at the top and bottom of the income distribution during the age of austerity (Schneider *et al.* 2015). The study finds that countries that made larger fiscal adjustments in the name of austerity in the period from 2006 to 2013 also saw larger increases in inequality at the top. The study also finds that inequality at the bottom may have decreased in the face of bigger fiscal adjustments, though this effect is not statistically significant despite its notable magnitude. The authors argue that 'whatever reasons were given for the adoption of austerity measures in many European countries, their impact was regressive across the board.' They conclude that 'this will only embolden the critics of austerity who have long suspected that it really represented policy on behalf of the elites at the cost of workers (Bougrine 2012; Peet 2011; Zezza 2012)'. This is a theme also addressed in the chapters by Allen (Chapter 3) and Whelan (Chapter 5) in this volume.

The failure to restructure the Eurozone's design did not help the Irish government in its efforts to address the major challenges emerging from the crash. Neither did the European Commission and the European Central Bank's decisions to persist with policy frameworks that have resulted in the monetary union's spectacularly poor performance. The continuing refusal to recognise that creditors as well as debtors are responsible for their actions has made the situation even more difficult for Ireland.

As Ireland reflects on the legacy of the crisis, there is a widespread desire not to repeat the mistakes that created the crash in the first place. There is also a widespread concern, some of which is articulated by Ó Riain (Chapter 14, this volume), that decision-making may revert to the failed patterns of the past. This chapter sets out to show how Ireland can ensure it does not repeat the mistakes of the past. It complements the economic focus of the previous chapter by providing a guiding vision for a just and inclusive society and a policy framework that would deliver a just and inclusive future for all. If such a future is to emerge, then Ireland has to answer a number of interrelated questions:

- Where does Ireland want to be in 2025?
- What infrastructure and services are required?
- How are these to be delivered?
- How are these to be financed?
- How are decisions on these issues to be made?
- How is progress on these issues to be measured?
- How can a vibrant and sustainable economy be secured throughout this process?

In this volume, Ó Riain (Chapter 14) addresses some of the policy implications that flow from answers to these questions provided by different countries with divergent political philosophies in the EU. So how might Irish policymakers and society more generally answer these questions and what does that mean for a future vision of the country?

A guiding vision

In seeking answers, Ireland should be guided by a vision of becoming a just society in which human rights are protected, human development is facilitated and the environment is respected. The core values of such a society would be human rights, dignity, equality, solidarity, sustainability and pursuit of the common good.

If Ireland was guided by such a vision, it would become a nation in which all women, men and children have what they require to live life with dignity and to fulfil their potential: they would have sufficient income; access to the services they need; and active inclusion in a genuinely participatory society. These outcomes reflect the aspirations of the majority of Irish citizens. To deliver such a just and inclusive society, I suggest a five-part policy framework aimed at securing:

- A vibrant economy
- Decent services and infrastructure
- Just taxation
- Good governance
- Sustainability

A vibrant economy

If Ireland is to have long-term macroeconomic stability and a vibrant economy, then a reduction in the country's debt burden is required, together with a substantial increase in the level of public investment. While Ireland's economy has seen dramatic recovery and has out-performed most of its global competitors, it remains very vulnerable to external developments. Ireland's macroeconomic policy is likely to be severely constrained if the current fiscal rules and parameters are maintained. Healy *et al.* (2015, pp. 22–23) have previously argued that:

> Serious care is required to ensure that the investment required to produce a well-functioning economy, to develop inclusive labour markets, to secure adequate income support and to ensure that access to high-quality services for all is not impeded by the requirements of the SGP, which were developed for a different purpose. The EU has had a major focus on its economic concerns in recent years but paid far too little attention to the social impacts of the decisions made and the initiatives it took. Ireland did not address the social impacts of the bailout measures from the beginning, with very unfair consequences. Now there is an urgent need to rebalance the economic and social aspects of Irish society.

To ensure a vibrant economy in the long run, Ireland needs to tackle its infrastructure deficits in areas such as broadband, social housing, water infrastructure and primary care facilities. This would require a substantial increase in the current level of investment, but within the current fiscal rules, the necessary level of investment will not be secured. Ireland needs a change in the EU's fiscal rules or else the development of an off-balance sheet capital investment programme on the scale required to have a real impact on the current infrastructure deficits.

In this context, economic growth is not an end in itself; rather it is a means to an end, that is, the building of a just, fair and inclusive society. While this is often dismissed as being so obvious that it does not need to be stated, in practice a great deal of discussion on Ireland's best policy pathways, as well as much of the commentary on government decisions, fail to grasp this reality. Government approaches and initiatives are justified on the basis that they will generate economic growth, but there is no discussion on whether or not the type of growth being proposed is likely to address Ireland's deficits and/or build a more just and inclusive society. For example, Coffey (Chapter 15, this volume) outlines a proposal for a new stability fund for Ireland, but does not explain what this fund would be spent on, or how it would be distributed. Are there capital priorities that could be funded to help deliver a more inclusive future?

Decent services and infrastructure

Between the crash of 2008 and the budget of 2015, the Irish government took more than €30 billion out of the economy. Two thirds of this was achieved through cuts in expenditure, while the other third was made up of tax increases. This emphasis on expenditure cuts over tax increases meant that all five budgets between 2012 and 2016 were regressive (Social Justice Ireland 2015; Callan 2015). Many of the expenditure cuts had socially destructive impacts on those who were most vulnerable, as outlined by Heffernan (Chapter 9, this volume) and Watson *et al.* (Chapter 10, this volume) and deprivation grew dramatically in this period.

Examination of the most recent results of the Survey on Income and Living Conditions in Ireland (SILC) conducted by the Central Statistics Office (CSO) shows that 1.3 million people in Ireland are experiencing deprivation, an increase of 650,000 in five years. This means that almost 30% of Ireland's population are deprived of basic essentials. Over 440,000 of these people are children, and about 85,000 are pensioners. Almost one in five children under 18, and roughly one in ten people aged over 65, experienced deprivation (CSO 2015).

The argument that greater priority should be given to providing decent services and infrastructure is strengthened by Ireland's changing demographic situation. Although Ireland's population is young in comparison to those of other European countries, we need to recognise that by 2031 almost one million people in Ireland will be over 65, with 136,000 being over 85 (Social Justice Ireland 2015). Although Irish people are living longer, which is a positive development, Ireland currently has no plans in place for how to care for these people in old age. The barriers to securing sufficient investment must be eliminated.

Ireland also faces major challenges in the areas of homelessness and social housing. While the government's social housing strategy (Department of Environment 2014b) is welcome, it goes nowhere near what is required to address the housing and homelessness crisis. The provision of substantial additional social housing is an urgent requirement. John McHale (Chapter 2, this volume) and Ronan Lyons (Chapter 8, this volume) in this volume have addressed both the key role housing played in the development of the crisis and the challenges currently being faced in relation to adequate and affordable provision. Similar challenges face Ireland in areas such as healthcare, disability services, education, rural development, social protection and pensions, to name but a few. The importance of securing sufficient investment to ensure that deficits in these and other areas are addressed adequately, and without delay, has already been noted.

In addressing these issues it is important that Ireland develop a rights-based approach to social, economic and cultural issues. Social Justice Ireland has presented one such set of proposals in which they argue that seven basic rights need to be acknowledged and recognised (Social Justice Ireland 2015: 31). These are the rights to sufficient income to live life with dignity; meaningful work; appropriate accommodation; relevant education; essential healthcare; cultural respect and real participation in society. To be vindicated, these rights will require greater public expenditure and provision of services.

Adopting a rights-based approach provides challenges and has implications for public policy. Some of these were explored in the NESC Strategy report 'An Investment in Quality: Services, Inclusion and Enterprise' (2003, pp. 355–371). In particular, that analysis suggested: (1) social and economic rights do not always provide the simplicity and clarity that is often seen as their main attraction (cutting through the compromises and messiness of political and administrative processes); (2) securing economic and social rights requires deep public sector reform in order to create effective systems of policy making, delivery of tailored capacitating services, monitoring and revision. For a rights-based approach to be effective, several other elements of the five-part policy framework set out here would have to be delivered, particularly decent services and good governance.

It is also important that no group be left behind if there is to be a just and inclusive recovery. It would be a great mistake for Ireland to repeat the experience of the late 1990s when economic growth mostly benefited those who were employed while others, such as people depending on social welfare pensions and unemployment payments, slipped further and further behind. This situation was rectified for the most part in the years from 2005 to 2007, but the problem has been happening again in recent years. Policy should provide equity in social welfare rates, particularly across genders, and there should be adequate payments for children as well as higher payments for those with disabilities to meet their higher costs.

Finally, in this context, the goal of universal provision for all must remain. This is of particular importance in areas such as healthcare, which still contains profound inequalities between people who are insured and those without insurance cover. The introduction of user charges and the growing conditionality of access to medical cards will see these inequalities deepen.

Just taxation

If Ireland is to address deficits in social services and infrastructure, the question of how this is to be paid for must be considered, which brings us to the issue of just taxation. One of the constraints that Ireland's policy system will face is the requirement under the 'six-pack' rules that additional discretionary expenditure must be funded by additional discretionary revenue. The current trajectory of government policy is for a reduction in total expenditure, including interest repayments, and a reduction in total revenue—of which tax revenue is by far the largest component—in the years to the end of the decade. These projections are set out on a no-policy change basis in the government's budget documents and annual spring statements.

Figure 16.1

Total revenue and total expenditure as a percentage of GDP, 2005–21.*

Source: Eurostat (2015); Department of Finance (2015).

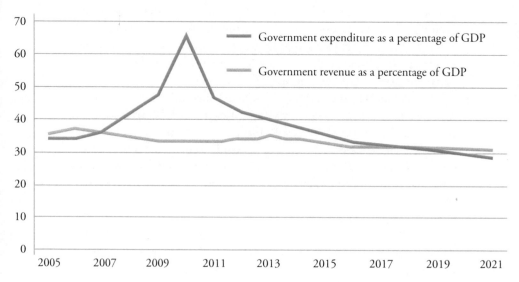

* Note that figures to 2013 are taken from the AMECO database; the cost of re-capitalisation of banking institutions has been removed; figures from 2014 to 2021 are taken from Budget 2016, table A2.2.)

Figure 16.1 shows projected total government revenue and expenditure as a percentage of GDP between 2005 and 2021.

These Department of Finance data show that on a no-policy change basis, government is projecting total revenue will fall to 30.9% of GDP and total expenditure to 28.4% of GDP. By comparison, the most recent data show that the EU was estimated to have a total revenue of 45.3% of GDP and total expenditure of 47.9% of GDP in 2013 (Eurostat 2015).

Can Ireland provide high quality public services to all while allowing total expenditure to fall as a percentage of GDP (or as a percentage of a more appropriate indicator if such can be agreed)? How can Ireland provide social services and infrastructure at an EU average level, which is what most Irish people seem to want, while reducing revenue to levels that are already dramatically below the EU average?

It is not possible to provide European levels of infrastructure and services with US levels of taxation. Ireland can have one or the other, but cannot have both. Ireland simply will not address its infrastructure and social provision deficits if it continues to collect substantially less tax than what is required by other EU countries (see Healy *et al.* 2015, chapter 4 for a more detailed discussion of the issues involved). In order to fund the necessary public services and infrastructure, the total tax take in Ireland must rise towards the European average. To ensure value for money in this process, new criteria for policy evaluation are also required.

To ensure that Ireland's total tax take grows in a fair and just manner, a key medium-term priority must be the re-conceptualisation of the role of the Irish corporation tax regime. In recent years, controversial loopholes in the Irish corporate tax system have been removed after strong pressure was applied, particularly from the Organisation for Economic Co-operation and Development (OECD). However, other loopholes are available, or are being made available, which are likely to lead to further accusations of unfairness. Ireland should move quickly to establish a minimum effective corporate tax rate and to introduce a financial transactions tax. An honest and coherent public debate on corporation tax is urgently required. The need for such a debate is obvious after the Apple ruling on August 30, 2016, in which the European Commission concluded that Ireland gave illegal tax benefits worth up to €13 billion to Apple.

Among the reforms that should be undertaken in the income tax system would be the introduction of refundable tax credits that would benefit those in low-paid jobs. Tax breaks should also be reformed, particularly by standard rating both the pension tax credit and the non-pension discretionary tax breaks; reform of the research and development tax credit also requires attention. Furthermore, there are behavioural taxes and environmental taxes that could and should be introduced. Finally, there is further scope for widening the tax base in areas such as the online betting tax and a windfall gains tax.

Good Governance

Events and investigation have shown that Ireland's governance was not at the required standard in certain areas prior to the economic crash of 2008. This is particularly true in the area of financial regulation. In the years following the crash, government made decisions that subsequently were seen to be very damaging. These decisions, some financial and some budgetary, were made in haste and did not involve any meaningful consultation with major sectors of Irish society. Decision-making in the context of the bank guarantee was especially catastrophic. Reforming governance and getting much broader participation in decision-making are essential if Ireland is to have a just and inclusive future. Three areas that would help such an outcome emerge have been identified.

The first of these is the need for government to move towards a more deliberative process of democracy. Our current decision-making structures see people being chosen in elections to represent the wider population. However, there is widespread agreement that these structures do not provide genuine participation for most people. Their lack of participative structures produces apathy and disillusionment with the political process. The side-lining of the political process is exacerbated by the primacy given to the 'market' by a large majority of analysts, commentators, policy makers and politicians. These see the market as solving most of society's problems. A great many people feel their views are ignored or dismissed despite the evidence they provide to support their position. Engaging people in a genuinely participative process is much easier thanks to modern tools of communication and information sharing that are widely available and easily accessible. A process of deliberative democracy could engage a much larger proportion of society in genuine ongoing dialogue about the shape of society's future, the pathways to be followed to reach that future and the financing of the actions that are decided upon. A recent paper by this author and others states:

> Deliberative democratic structures enable discussion and debate to take place without any imposition of power differentials. Issues and positions are argued and discussed on the basis of the available evidence rather than on the basis of assertions by those who are powerful and unwilling to consider the evidence. Such debate produces evidence-based policy and ensures a high level of accountability among stakeholders. Deliberative participation by all is essential if society is to develop and in practice to maintain principles guaranteeing satisfaction of basic needs, respect for others as equals, economic equality, and religious, social, sexual and ethnic equality. (Healy *et al.* 2015b, 87).

Deliberative democratic processes have a profound and enduring appeal. This set of ideas and approaches was, at certain times at least, evident in the social partnership system that was in place from 1987 to 2008. There is a need to marry deliberative processes with enduring political processes of bargaining, rhetoric and use of expertise. There is also a need to recognise that sometimes experimental action (often by social and environmental NGOs) can precede the kind of conscious deliberation advocated here. In this regard, deliberation is as much about understanding and improving practice as about seeking a prior evidence-based shared understanding.

Two recent government initiatives could be seen as initial steps towards the development of an effective deliberative democratic process. At a national level, the government involved all major sectors of society in the national economic dialogue in mid-2015. At a local level, the development of public participation networks (PPNs) provided a mechanism for effective engagement with all organisations in the community and voluntary, social inclusion and environmental sectors at a local authority level (Department of Environment 2014a). The development and strengthening of these initiatives could encourage engagement with all sectors of society in a process of social dialogue on issues that must be addressed if Ireland is to have a just and inclusive future.

Not every community has the capacity or the infrastructure to engage meaningfully in a process of social dialogue. This is where the community and voluntary sector has a key role to play in informing, engaging with and providing local communities with the skills to participate in and contribute to governance. The community and voluntary sector has also been playing a key role in providing services, advocacy and support for people from childhood to working age to retirement. It also provides detailed up-to-date analysis of the current situation and the impacts government policy is having, especially on those who are vulnerable. The sector's capacity to perform these roles effectively has been drastically reduced due to funding reductions far in excess of the cuts experienced by other sectors in society (Harvey 2012; Heffernan Chapter 9, this volume). In the period after 2011, it appeared that government was treating the community and voluntary sector simply as a cheap version of the private sector or a cheap version of the public sector. Both of these perspectives miss the core of what the community and voluntary sector is all about. The sector has a major contribution to make to improving Ireland's governance and the unfair cuts it has experienced should be reversed.

Evaluation as a tool for ongoing learning should be a part of all government initiatives. While government has taken some welcome steps to increase their research and evaluation capacities in recent years much more could be done. A good starting point might be the development of a genuinely transparent budgetary process.

Sustainability

The fifth and final section of the policy framework to develop a just and inclusive society set out in this paper is the area of sustainability. Development is sustainable when it meets the needs of the present without compromising the needs of future generations (World Commission on Environment and Development 1987). Consequently, financial, environmental, economic and social sustainability are all key objectives of this framework.

In recent years there has been a growing realisation of climate change and climate justice as critical concerns (IPCC 2014). Commitments made at the COP21 (United Nations, 2015) conference in Paris in 2015 were based on the growing realisation that our environment is finite—a fact that had often been ignored in the past. It is essential that public policy be consistent in promoting climate justice and protecting the environment. Without such consistency the very existence of human life on this planet is threatened. This provides Ireland with special challenges as it seeks simultaneously to prioritise a type of agricultural development that will have negative impacts on the environment.

In addressing these challenges, Ireland must focus on putting a sustainable model of development into place. This requires balanced regional development. The need for a balanced socio-economic approach to development was recognised in the National Spatial Strategy 2002–2020. This strategy, however, was undermined by actions taken subsequently by the government that had introduced the strategy in the first place, most notoriously the programme of decentralisation introduced in the budget of 2003 (Meredith and van Egeraat 2013). Direct action is required to prevent the emergence of a two-tier recovery with the gap between urban and rural Ireland widening steadily (Healy *et al.* 2015a, 294). Spatial justice will thus be a key issue in building a more inclusive society and has been addressed in detail by Kearns, Meredith and Morrissey (2014).

If sustainability is to be effectively placed at the core of public policy development, then new indicators of progress are urgently required. GDP alone is an unsatisfactory measure of progress as it only includes the monetary value of gross output, income and expenditure in an economy. The work done by Nobel Prize-winning economists Amartya Sen and Joseph Stiglitz has set a benchmark in this regard (L'Observatoire Français des Conjonctures Économiques 2009). They pointed out that new indicators are required to measure both environmental and financial sustainability while also measuring well-being and happiness.

In its report, titled 'Well-being Matters' (2009) Ireland's National Economic and Social Council suggested that measures of well-being could be constructed that capture data on six domains of people's lives that contribute to well-being including: economic resources; work and participation; relationships and care; community and environment; health; and democracy and values. This set of Satellite National Accounts, incorporating such indicators, should be developed alongside current national accounting measures. The OECD Global Project on Measuring the Progress of Societies has recommended the use of such indicators to inform evidence-based policies (Morrone 2009: 23).

Reflections, implications and responsibilities

Table 16.1 summarises the five-part policy framework set out in the chapter.

If there is to be an inclusive and just recovery, all five of these policy areas must be developed in an integrated and sustainable manner. Priority must be given to long-term outcomes. To this end, multiannual budgeting is essential, as is a constant focus on medium to long-term policy goals. Substantial investment over a protracted period is required if Ireland's social and physical infrastructure deficits are to be addressed, and this might be a key role of the stability fund proposed by Coffey (2017). Such investment is also required given the demographic changes the country faces in the coming decades as the population grows and ages. The policy challenges that Ireland faces in the coming decades require an integrated framework such as the one set out here if they are to be addressed in a sustainable manner.

It is crucial that the political system adopts the long-term approach these challenges require. This would require that policymakers move away from the current dominant view that economic growth will solve all problems and consequently should be prioritised over all other areas of policy. Instead, the interconnections between the

Table 16.1

Five policy areas to deliver a just and sustainable society.

Note: earlier versions of this have been developed in Healy *et al.* (2015) and in Healy *et al.* (2014)

Vibrant economy	Decent services and infrastructure	Just taxation	Good governance	Sustainability
Fiscal and financial stability and sustainable economic growth	Secure services and social infrastructure	Bring Taxes towards EU average	Deliberative democracy and PPNs	Promote climate justice and protect the environment
Adequate Investment programme	Combat unemployment & under-employment	Increase taxes equitably and reduce income inequality	Social dialogue – all sectors in deliberative process	Balanced regional development
A more just economic model	Ensure seven Social, Economic and Cultural rights are achieved	Secure fair share of corporate profits for the State	Reform Policy Evaluation	New indicators of progress and new Satellite National Accounts

various policy areas identified here should be recognised, and it should be acknowledged that balanced development between these areas is essential if there are to be fair and just outcomes. One noteworthy move in this direction was the enactment of the Well-being of Future Generations (Wales) Act 2015 by the National Assembly of Wales that embeds something similar in their legal system. In practice this challenges politicians to ensure that the rising political power of corporate and financial elites is not allowed to overpower decision-making processes. It is crucial that the increasing concentration of political power in a corporate and financial elite, which has been able to influence the rules by which the economy runs, should be resisted (Reich 2015).

Other external developments are also cause for concern. Europe is witnessing an unprecedented influx of refugees caused by the crises not far from its own shores. This situation is even more problematic when viewed in the context of divergent economic prospects and sky-high youth unemployment in the countries on Europe's periphery. The ongoing failure of the fiscal rules to deal fairly and effectively with the consequences of the crisis adds to concerns that the situation in the European Union may worsen rather than improve. The UK's decision to leave the European Union (Brexit) adds an additional challenge to this reality. Effective actions are required if these concerns are not to lead to an unfair and unjust future in which those who suffered most from austerity policies are again left behind.

If these challenges are to be addressed, then various participants in the policy-making process need to take responsibility to ensure the required actions are taken. These are some suggested areas:

- Political parties have a responsibility to be explicit about their vision and values and to specify what criteria for success they would be judged by in the future.
- Media commentators have a responsibility to hold political parties to account in terms of their substantive policy commitments and capacity.
- Social science research funding should prioritise the analysis of societal problems, many of which have been identified in this paper.
- Think tanks and the National Economic and Social Council should develop a division of labour to ensure that the scarce resources available are used to bring accurate analysis and international comparators to bear on informing policy development across a sufficiently broad agenda.
- The Department of Public Expenditure and Reform should adopt a holistic national framework to inform evaluation and policy development.
- Oireachtas Committees should be resourced to scrutinise policy and expenditure by reference to a strategic framework, as well as on discrete project criteria.

These are simply some of the key areas in which action is required if there is to be a genuinely just and inclusive recovery in, and future for, Ireland.

Conclusion
Progressing debates on austerity in Ireland

John McHale, Niamh Moore-Cherry and Emma Heffernan

> Austerity is not part of the European treaties; democracy and the principle of popular sovereignty are. (Alexis Tsipras, Greek Prime Minister)

> People are increasingly frustrated that decisions taken further and further away from them mean their living standards are slashed through enforced austerity or their taxes are used to bail out governments on the other side of the continent. (David Cameron, former Conservative British Prime Minister)

For an economic concept to evoke such visceral reactions is unusual, but perhaps that is because 'austerity' in the contemporary lexicon has become code for so much more than fiscal consolidation in a recession. Whether understood in this narrow way, or more broadly as outlined in the Introduction chapter of this volume, Ireland's recent history is awash with stories about austerity and its impacts. As recently as 10 October 2016, on the eve of Budget 2017, an entire page of *The Irish Times* was devoted to opinion pieces on the negative impacts of austerity on particular groups and what the budget should do to remedy some of the most hard-hitting effects. In this volume, we have attempted to bring together a range of authors from diverse disciplinary, conceptual and ideological backgrounds to explore these issues. We attempt to draw out areas of agreement and convergence, but also highlight the remaining and significant divergences in understanding about the experiences that Ireland and the Irish people have come through in the last decade. All of the authors in this volume argue that austerity is a difficult and harmful thing, and that it can be avoided in the future through better contemporary decision-making. At stake is the very legitimacy of our democracies and social solidarity. Indeed many would argue that the crisis of legitimacy currently affecting the European Union, manifested in the recent UK Brexit vote and the rise in popularity of right-wing nationalist political parties in Austria and France, has been driven in part by the European austerity response to the global financial crisis. The similarity in the quotes above from politicians on radically opposite sides of the political spectrum highlight the almost universal understanding that enforced austerity produces poor societal outcomes.

While this may be accepted, much of the debate in Ireland has been ideologically charged—albeit not to the same extent as in countries such as Greece and Spain—and has been characterised by those with differing perspectives talking past each other. For historic reasons, Ireland's political culture has traditionally been much less ideologically polarised in terms of a left-right wing divide compared to other European countries, but the recent period of crisis, austerity and the path to recovery, has elevated the significance of this axis of difference within the Irish political system. Within that changing context, this volume has attempted to sow the seeds for an evidence-based dialogue about austerity in Ireland. Indeed it is rare to bring such a range of disciplines—anthropology, economics, geography, sociology, education, political science and social policy—together around a common theme. The book has also deliberately embraced multiple conceptual frameworks; there is reference to neoliberalism, keynesianism, ordo-liberalim, social justice, sustainability and democratic legitimacy. By design, it is multi-disciplinary and multi-viewpoint, and at times there may appear to be stark contradictions on how data and events are to be read. The goal of this book therefore has been to situate and foreground the diversity of perspectives on a contested topic, outline the societal impacts of recent experiences in Ireland, and lay out the key considerations for successfully moving into a post-austerity context. Of course, much of this discussion is highly subjective. How we look back and forward is fundamentally shaped by how we perceived and actively experienced the last decade of transformation. How Ireland's recent history will be recorded and who records it are major questions that will shape how this recent period becomes etched into our long-term history and national memory.

The austerity paradox

Untangling the nature of decision-making and public policy-making is no easy task, particularly in a context as complex as the Irish situation since 2008/09. The chapters in this volume document the extremely difficult post-crisis austerity experience in Ireland from a variety of perspectives. Austerity—government spending cuts and tax increases in the teeth of recession—is on its face sharply at odds with the advice of modern macroeconomics. Good countercyclical management calls for stimulus, not contraction in a severe downturn. Moreover, given the difficulties of adjusting to cuts in spending and disposable incomes, there are good arguments for phasing necessary measures over as long a period of time as possible. But with limited fiscal capacity in the face of a huge adverse shock to the economy, policymakers were forced to pursue austerity to fend off the risk of even deeper cuts if borrowing capacity vanished and default deepened the recession. This is the austerity paradox: austerity was needed to limit the risk of even more catastrophic austerity.

As Simon Wren-Lewis observes (Chapter 1, this volume), the situation facing large countries with full control over their currencies such as the UK and the US is quite different: the power to print money to cover deficits and debt rollovers makes the probability of default very low. This safeguard was not available to Ireland as a small member of the (now) 19-country Eurozone. Of course, as Wren-Lewis also notes, this power was available to the Eurozone as a whole—and the Outright Monetary Transactions programme may show some latter willingness to use it. However, the willingness of stronger members to put themselves at risk of making transfers to weaker members is limited, reflecting in turn the limits of solidarity in an incomplete monetary union and the relative power imbalances that underpin the European project. As the experience from 2010 to 2012 shows, the fragility of Ireland's creditworthiness was not hypothetical. A default, most likely coming at the end of the troika programme, would almost certainly have added a further vicious twist to the adverse feedback loops between the banking system, the fiscal system and the real economy that were driving the crisis, increasing the importance of making the programme a success. As harmful as the austerity was, concerted fiscal austerity was needed to meet the programme targets and to limit the risk of even deeper austerity. While things might have been different with alternate policies at a European level, Irish policymakers had to deal with the situation as it was and to calibrate the austerity to achieve the least worst outcome.

Needless to say, this resolution of the austerity paradox would not be universally shared and this is one of the key divergences within the book. Kieran Allen (Chapter 3, this volume) alerts us to the importance of identifying unstated ideological assumptions of the 'austerity experts', mainly mainstream macroeconomists. There is little doubt that some embraced austerity as a means to shrink the size of the state, and to deepen an already pervasive neoliberalism of public policy in Ireland (Fraser *et al.* 2013; Mercille and Murphy 2015). This was made possible by the lack of counter-argumentation put forward in the mainstream commercial and state broadcast media, discussed by Julien Mercille (Chapter 4, this volume), leading to a pro-austerity bias in coverage. But arguably mass market media must also have resonance with the listening, viewing and reading public. Complaints about austerity and the treatment of Ireland by its official creditors certainly captured the public mood. During the height of the crisis, the leading circulation Sunday newspaper ran hard-hitting editorials disparaging 'dumb austerity' and also published strongly worded complaints of mistreatment by Germany. Recognising the evident harms caused by austerity, the merits of the policy course followed were certainly debatable. However, given that Ireland had a massive borrowing requirement and, at the height of the crisis, no access to market credit requiring difficult budgetary adjustments, how intense that debate could actually be is itself a matter for discussion and further examination.

Varieties of harm

The need for and extent of austerity has been widely debated in a number of fora, but a less explored aspect has been the many ways in which the impact of austerity has played out at the experiential level.

The situation is much more nuanced that some commentators would lead us to believe. Although by no means comprehensive, this volume provides numerous descriptions and analyses of the multifaceted harms caused by the interactions of austerity and recession at multiple scales—the societal, familial and individual levels—and across multiple spatial dimensions. The harms examined range through economic vulnerability, fragmentation of political systems, access to housing, drug use, child poverty, education funding, and emigration. Our authors have illustrated how exposure to increased risk and vulnerability has been occurring simultaneously in the public spaces of the city (Heffernan), the home (Lyons; Watson *et al.*) and in working lives (Gilmartin) and ranges from those already marginalised in society (Watson *et al.*) to more mainstream social groups (Murphy; Pritchard and Slowey; Whelan and Nolan). The responses have also been variable (Hardiman *et al.*; Hourigan), with Ireland seen by many as an anomaly compared with the more public and vocal responses in places such as Greece, Portugal and Spain.

Austerity was the medicine used to treat the crisis situation that Ireland found itself in by 2010, but whether or not it was progressive or regressive is a key point of contention and debate. The difficulties in making this judgement are highlighted by Callan *et al.* (2012), who suggest that depending on the evidence used and methodologies employed, very different conclusions can be reached. Whelan and Nolan (Chapter 6, this volume) highlight how in Ireland, at a broad distributional level, aggregate measures of social inequality such as the Gini coefficient remained remarkably stable. However, measures of deprivation rose dramatically, reflecting a recession—and an austerity-induced drop in average living standards. A distinctive feature of the Irish case has been the extent of the burden of economic stress borne by lower-middle class households commonly referred to as the 'squeezed middle' (Hourican 2016). Indeed, one of the most enlightening aspects of their analysis is the vulnerability experienced by those falling into—rather than beginning in—the lowest income classes during the crisis. Downward social mobility is thus a very real harm that has been a product of recent social and economic change, raising questions about place, identity and aspiration that have yet to be explored by social scientists.

The importance of adopting a multidimensional focus that goes beyond examinations of incomes is central to the writing of many of our authors. Dorothy Watson and colleagues (Chapter 10, this volume) stress the importance of looking beyond traditional measures of income and deprivation to a measure of economic *vulnerability* based on low income, household joblessness and economic stress. Using data from two waves of the Growing up in Ireland survey, they find that economic vulnerability increased substantially during the recession and that the incidence of socio-emotional problems for children has risen in line with this. Even short-term spells of vulnerability have lasting impacts, but there is evidence to suggest that non-income household resources such as parental education and the presence of two parents could ameliorate the harm. This challenges policymakers to think beyond monetary resources—and the traditional targeting of welfare policies and income supports—to consider more holistic and creative approaches. Whether or not this is likely to happen or is indeed achievable largely depends on the type of politics and political system that emerges from this period and the demands placed by citizens on those in power.

Reading public life and civic action in Ireland in recent years, one might think that a potential positive to emerge from unpopular austerity measures has been a more engaged citizenry. For example, in her examination of the implications for politics and political engagement, Niamh Hourigan (Chapter 7, this volume) suggests that one outcome of austerity-induced protest movements was a hardening of attitudes towards cronyism and corruption. However, in her temporal study, these initially negative attitudes towards corruption and cronyism were followed by a softening just as the protest movements—particularly around the issue of water charges—appeared to be at their strongest. Why this occurred is worth further exploration, but she argues that the more lasting legacy of the anti-austerity movement may be a greater degree of inter-organisational cooperation on the left of the Irish political spectrum, as more community-based, grassroots activists take to the national political stage. This shift may have been motivated by the disillusionment of voters with mainstream parties, with citizens believing that it matters little in terms of policies pursued which mainstream party is supported. While much less evident in Ireland than elsewhere in Europe, this has led—in addition to disenchantment with politics more generally—to a rise in support for extremist parties. While understandable, the long-term implications of this extreme fragmentation of political systems are as yet unknown but it could lead to political paralysis in reversing the worst impacts of the crisis and austerity years. A specific example of this is evident in Dublin City Council, where 63 local authority seats are split across 10 political parties and 11 Independent councillors. This political fragmentation has, at times, hindered Dublin City Council from functioning effectively and making the important decisions that would help improve quality of life in the city.

But beyond these direct impacts of austerity, one of the most interesting issues raised by various authors in different ways is that the harm that resulted from austerity was so intense in particular domains because of the earlier withdrawal of the state from various activities. This 'roll-back neoliberalism' (Peck and Tickell 2002) is illustrated by Ronan Lyons (Chapter 8, this volume) on the two-way links between austerity and dysfunctions in the housing market. He argues that even prior to the recession, the provision of social housing was effectively privatised through the 'Part V system', and the state has in fact removed itself from the direct provision of social housing. As the need for this type of housing grew, a collapse in private development, a lack of local authority building capacity and cuts to capital budgets effectively meant that no new social housing was built during the recession. Greater demands for social housing were instead met through the rent supplement system, with those on the lowest incomes being disadvantaged by the fixed nature of the supplements—payments that have proved increasingly inadequate given the rising level of market rents. This contributed to a rise in homelessness and a reliance on emergency accommodation provided by the state and its various agencies for those most in need of protection. Similarly, Emma Heffernan (Chapter 9, this volume) provides us with a striking illustration of the harm caused by the combination of cuts to social supports and recession for female sex workers in Dublin. She documents how cuts to drug treatment programmes and recession-induced increases in competition among sex workers led to spirals of increasingly risky behaviours, accentuating the deprivation and desperation of some of society's already most marginalised individuals. These cuts also had significant implications for those working within the social and community care sector, as illustrated by Mary Gilmartin (Chapter 12, this volume) in her discussion of migration and austerity. Cuts to the size of the public sector workforce and public sector wages, along with worsening working conditions, were contributing factors to the rise in emigration, especially for health and teaching professionals. This in turn led to a significant 'brain-drain' with economic, social, cultural and spatial implications. Few social groups were left untouched by the impact of austerity, including immigrants who had, prior to the recession, already been concentrated in more precarious and low-wage occupations. Their relative position worsened further as a result of the crisis, which deepened inequality and created new tensions and polarisations.

What is particularly challenging is that in post-austerity Ireland, the traditional policy responses will not be enough to ameliorate the effects of almost a decade of harm. The social and political dynamics have now substantially changed, there is a more fuzzy narrative around who is vulnerable and how. The multiple challenges facing social mobilities are further complicated by the multi-speed recovery that is occurring and being experienced in a socially and geographically stratified manner.

Repair, resilience and learning

While we may have experienced two successive post-austerity budgets, the legacies of recession and eight austerity budgets remain with us, including higher debt, lower incomes, diminished public services, and postponed investments. Although far from comprehensive, this volume highlights important instances of damages done and desperately needed repairs. These include higher child poverty, a severe housing crisis and underfunded education systems. The new system of fiscal rules and institutions should help create more fiscal capacity in the face of a future adverse shock, but the limits on deficit financing and expenditure growth do constrain the near-term repair effort. Once the medium-term objective of a close to balanced budget is reached, expenditure growth (net of tax changes) should be allowed to grow in line with the underlying potential output growth of the economy, increasing the budgetary room available. How we use the available resources will be critical to whether we address the numerous post-crisis challenges faced by Irish society.

For example, in their analysis of higher education, Rosalind Pritchard and Maria Slowey (Chapter 11, this volume) examine how austerity has affected higher education institutions in both the Republic of Ireland and Northern Ireland. Austerity has accelerated moves towards increased cost sharing, managerial dominance and institutional alliances. While institutions have shown notable resilience in the face of these pressures, generating new revenues but also striving to maintain quality and access through innovation, there is a paradox: 'the more institutions divert energy into new ventures, generating new sources of income—and the more successful they are at this—then perhaps the less the public is likely to view them as serving an important and distinctive intellectual, social and cultural mission' (p. 190). Notwithstanding this resilience, an enduring harm from public underfunding may be the compromising of core value and purposes—and ultimately societal support. While an additional €36.5 million has been provided for the further and higher education sector in Budget 2017, this goes little way towards addressing the €400 million funding gap identified by the Cassells Report in early 2016. At a time when the economy desperately requires highly educated professionals with particular skills sets in order to take advantage of new opportunities, the impacts of severe cuts to education over successive budgets are all too clear. This draws into focus the need to learn from recent experiences and develop new mechanisms or structures to ensure that spending in areas critical to longer-term economic growth is maintained during any future crisis.

As policymakers use available resources to repair the damage done by the crisis and build a fairer and more prosperous society, a key challenge is to ensure we do not repeat our recent experiences. A key lesson relates to recognising and building resilience within the Irish economy; how can we enhance resilience by ensuring sufficient fiscal capacity to deal with the inevitable adverse cyclical shocks in a small and highly internationally integrated economy like Ireland's? Seamus Coffey (Chapter 15, this volume) examines Irish government spending and taxation patterns in a comparative European context, and argues for greater effectiveness of public service delivery and spending. He suggests that policymakers and civil society need to pay more attention not only to how much is spent but how it is spent. This focus on spending patterns and sustainability is a theme raised in a different context by Fiona Murphy (Chapter 13, this volume). She critiques the thrift culture that has emerged in Ireland in recent years and argues that a true shift to a sustainable consumption model—whether at the level of the household or national budget—cannot be achieved without a robust sense of social justice,

The second axis of learning is more structural and related to how we might reduce our overall vulnerability to adverse shocks. Seán Ó Riain (Chapter 14, this volume) notes the numerous post-crisis challenges that Ireland faces, including insufficient public investment, high inequality in market incomes and a narrow tax base. He sees many of these problems as being intractable without further progress on Ireland's development project—progress that goes beyond just improved competitiveness and addresses some fundamental questions about the structure of the Irish economy and society. Seán Healy (Chapter 16, this volume) clearly identifies the key policy challenges Ireland faces and the choices that we must make as a society if we are to heal and repair some of the harm inflicted by austerity. Healy sets out proposals that would ensure the development of a vibrant economy, decent services and infrastructure, just taxation, good governance and sustainability. However, in order to achieve this, we must reflect on, and learn from, the recent past. While no stakeholder would wish to repeat the mistakes that produced the trauma of the last decade in Ireland, real change has arguably been hampered by the type of political system and fragmentation that the austerity years have bequeathed to us.

Towards an agenda for the social sciences in post-austerity Ireland

Given the focus of this volume—generating debate on some of the most fundamental transformations in Irish society since the foundation of the state—what are the prospects for and value of social science in Ireland? This is a difficult question, but undoubtedly social science researchers have a key role to play in raising questions about our path to recovery and providing an evidence base to inform better and more just policymaking. After a decade of change, entrenchment of old divisions and the creation of new axes of polarisation, Ireland has been left a more divided society. How we move forward will shape the life chances and experiences of generations to come and social scientists have a key role to play in interrogating the perhaps less visible or unintended consequences of public policy. For example, in her chapter, Fiona Murphy argues that one impact of austerity has been the emergence of a thrift culture that has produced more sustainable consumption patterns. This might initially be considered a positive outcome, but if this is built on the back of social inequity and hardship, can we really argue that the end (sustainability) justifies the means?

Another key issue emerging from some of the chapters is related to issues of social capital. In their study, Watson *et al.* argue that the worst excesses of socio-economic vulnerability among children can be mitigated in circumstances where there is significant social capital within the household. But as the chapters by Whelan and Nolan,

Pritchard and Slowey, Gilmartin and Heffernan illustrate social and cultural capital has been significantly eroded in recent years. More attention needs to be paid to the effects of austerity on civic life and social capital to capture the complexity and intersections of risk and resilience within Irish society.

Challenging public discourse is a key responsibility. The state reform agenda that accompanied austerity and resulted in public sector pay cuts, job losses, new work practices and the shifting of responsibilities, created an illusion that the crisis was the creation of the public sector and state rather than a failure of the market. It is critical that these types of power dynamics are properly understand if a more progressive form of politics is to emerge. The value of an interdisciplinary approach to this kind of work is that these dynamics can be understood alongside the economic facts and human experience. Creating meaningful dialogues across disciplines and between the academy and a range of publics is vital. In twenty-first-century Ireland, social science has never been as challenged or as essential.

Appendix 1

Results

1.	Housing boom has Central Bank fearful of inflation *The Irish Times*, May 3, 1996, City Edition, Business This Week; Economic Comment; Pg. Supplement page 2, 676 words, by Cliff Taylor
2.	Spiraling House Prices *The Irish Times*, May 12, 1997, City Edition, Editorial Page; Letters To The Editor; Pg. 13, 266 Words, from Paul Robinson
3.	Bathtime In Budapest *The Irish Times*, May 31, 1997, City Edition, Weekend; Pg. Supplement Page 11, 1204 Words, by Angela Long
4.	Irish economy mirrors Asia's before the bust Unless Ireland learns that previously sacrosanct numbers such as the budget deficit, the debt/GDP ratio or the trade surplus are yesterday's acid tests, the huge asset boom which is fuelling massive borrowing will steer Ireland to a January 2000 like Asia's January 1998 *The Irish Times*, January 16, 1998, City Edition, Business & Finance; Pg. 54, 1367 words, by David McWilliams
5.	Housing boom is driven by imminence of euro previously, the Central Bank would have intervened, but interest-rate control has already been lost and policymakers' chief weapon disarmed *The Irish Times*, February 13, 1998, City Edition, Business This Week 1; Pg. 55, 939 words
6.	Bank claims interest rates will tumble *The Irish Times*, March 14, 1998, City Edition, Business & Finance; Pg. 18, 562 words, by Jane Suiter, Economics Reporter
7.	Dublin's Housing Boom *The Irish Times*, March 18, 1998, City Edition, Editorial Page; Editorial Comment; Pg. 15, 579 words
8.	Cooling The Housing Boom *The Irish Times*, April 2, 1998, City Edition, Editorial Page; Editorial Comment; Pg. 17, 530 words

9.	Are we blowing it? If inflation speeds up and the economy slows down, we could be sleep-walking to disaster, writes Denis Coghlan, Chief Political Correspondent *The Irish Times*, April 20, 1998, City Edition, News Features; Pg. 6, 1156 words
10.	Coalition aims to take some steam out of housing market Frank McDonald, Environment Correspondent, on the government's response *The Irish Times*, April 24, 1998, City Edition, News Features; Pg. 14, 1203 words
11.	Vernon puts Green in enviable position Five years ago, Green Property was hobbling along. Now it is worth (pounds) 400 million-plus and the Trafford deal will take it further, writes Bill Murdoch *The Irish Times*, July 17, 1998, City Edition, Business This Week 1; The Friday Interview; Pg. 55, 815 words
12.	Business On Television *The Irish Times*, October 2, 1998, City Edition, Business & Finance; Pg. 58, 414 words, by Alva Mac Sherry
13.	NCB report offers good news for homeowners study provides little reassurance for people trying to get a foothold on the property ladder with house prices predicted to increase further *The Irish Times*, February 12, 1999, City Edition, Business & Finance; Economics; Pg. 55, 921 words, by Jane Suiter
14.	Irresponsible Lending *The Irish Times*, March 13, 1999, City Edition, Editorial Page; Editorial Comment; Pg. 17, 589 words
15.	Budget tax cuts warning issued by IMF *The Irish Times*, August 21, 1999, City Edition, Front Page; Pg. 1, 311 words, by Cliff Taylor, Finance Editor
16.	Bubbles without toil or trouble *The Irish Times*, September 11, 1999, City Edition; Weekend; Wine; Pg. 73, 923 words, by Mary Dowey
17.	Managing our Prosperity *The Irish Times*, October 14, 1999, City Edition; Editorial Page; Editorial Comment; Pg. 17, 614 words
18.	Preparing for the worst The economy remains vulnerable to shocks from both home and abroad, reports Jane O'Sullivan *The Irish Times*, October 14, 1999, City Edition; Millennium +5; Economic And Social Research Institute Medium -Term Review: 1999-2005; Pg. 73, 856 words

19.	To be or not to be generous with tax concessions, that is the question damned if they do, damned if they don't: the ESRI has handed the government a poisoned chalice, writes Denis Coghlan, Chief Political Correspondent *The Irish Times*, October 14, 1999, City Edition; Millennium +5; Economic And Social Research Institute Medium -Term Review: 1999-2005; Pg. 74, 1128 words
20.	Study refutes any house price 'bubble' *The Irish Times*, November 18, 1999, City Edition; Business & Finance; Pg. 20, 402 words, by Jane Suiter, Economics Correspondent
21.	Another strong year likely despite fears of economic 'bubble' There is no sign of the record growth ending in an uncomfortable crash - it is the boom which just goes on and on and is based on stable economic foundations, writes Cliff Taylor, Finance Editor *The Irish Times*, December 30, 1999, City Edition; Business 2000; Pg. 50, 903 words
22.	Conference emphasises need for quality housing *The Irish Times*, January 6, 2000, City Edition; Home News; Pg. 9, 234 words
23.	Starter home prices rise by over 16% Shortage of supply pushes up prices. Jack Fagan, Property Editor, reports *The Irish Times*, February 10, 2000, City Edition; Property; Trends; Pg. 50, 759 words
24.	Stay within your limits As interest rates rise, homebuyers should be cautious, writes Jane Suiter *The Irish Times*, February 17, 2000, City Edition; Property; Pg. 59, 634 words
25.	Eurocrats put on the squeeze *The Irish Times*, March 2, 2000, City Edition; Property; Around The Block; Pg. 52, 258 words
26.	Bank in warning against any drift from PPF *The Irish Times*, March 30, 2000, City Edition; Front Page; Pg. 1, 279 words, by Jane Suiter, Economics Correspondent
27.	Bank shows uncommon optimism *The Irish Times*, March 30, 2000, City Edition; Business & Finance; Pg. 18, 493 words, by Jane Suiter, Economics Correspondent
28.	Don't be last one left with fool's stock *The Irish Times*, May 19, 2000, City Edition; Business This Week 1; Observer; Pg. 55, 902 words, by John Teeling
29.	Soft landing looks good *The Irish Times*, May 25, 2000, City Edition; Property; Around The Block; Pg. 55, 92 words

39.	Goodbody warns of housing bubble risk *The Irish Times*, March 26, 2003, City Edition; Business And Finance; Pg. 18, 495 words, By Cliff Taylor, Economics Editor
40.	Why property bubble not likely to burst *The Irish Times*, April 3, 2003, City Edition; Residential Property; Around The Block; Pg. 53, 229 words
41.	Feedb(at)ck *The Irish Times*, April 5, 2003, City Edition; Business And Finance; Pg. 19, 175 words
42.	'Investor' not a four-letter word *The Irish Times*, April 10, 2003, City Edition; Residential Property; Around The Block; Pg. 54, 255 words
43.	Capital rule change leads to fear of property bubble *The Irish Times*, April 30, 2003, City Edition; Business And Finance; Pg. 16, 305 words
44.	Ireland's property bubble *The Irish Times*, June 11, 2003, City Edition; Editorial Page; Letters to the Editor; Pg. 17, 271 words
45.	Opportunities on the horizon, for the careful investor Despite some uncertainty, low interest rates and a recovering economy give hope to investors, says John Beggs *The Irish Times*, June 12, 2003, City Edition; Property; Talking Property; Pg. 53, 896 words
46.	Stockbrokers forecast fall in housing prices over 18 months *The Irish Times*, June 26, 2003, City Edition; Business And Finance; Pg. 14, 419 words, by Gretchen Friemann
47.	IMF points to 'significant risk' of overvaluation on house prices The Irish property market may be in "bubble territory". Or then again maybe it's not. Even the IMF can't make up its mind, writes Cliff Taylor, Economics Editor *The Irish Times*, August 7, 2003, City Edition; Business And Finance; Pg. 16, 623 words
48.	That Friday feeling *The Irish Times*, August 16, 2003, City Edition; Weekend; On The Town; Pg. 57, 191 words, by Olivia Kelly
49.	Housing market more resilient than others There is little fear of a downward and lasting fall in house prices as they are less susceptible to "bubbles" and other factors that contribute to volatility *The Irish Times*, October 17, 2003, City Edition; Business And Finance; Economics; Pg. 54, 762 words, by Dan Mclaughlin

50.	Hope for the future from those in finance Amid the doom and gloom, some financial voices are offering shoots of optimism, says Michael McAleer *The Irish Times*, November 19, 2003, City Edition; Motors; Motors News; Pg. 59, 758 words
51.	Prices likely to rise by 6% to 8% in 2004 The second-hand market is in good shape as we head into 2004, writes Paul Murgatroyd. Meanwhile, Ronan O'Driscoll predicts frantic activity in the new homes market with price rises of about 5 per cent *The Irish Times*, January 8, 2004, City Edition; Property; Pg. 25, 877 words
52.	Prices to rise as equilibrium is miles away It is amazing that people will go to jail over bin taxes (only a few hundred euro), when thousands of euro are sought from house-buyers in exorbitant levels of stamp duty, writes Eunan O'Carroll *The Irish Times*, March 18, 2004, City Edition; Residential Property; Talking Property; Pg. 53, 731 words
53.	World is investors' oyster but pearls are a rare find Global property hunters risk making mistakes in chasing sparkling returns, writes Laura Slattery *The Irish Times*, April 2, 2004, City Edition; Business And Finance; Pg. 60, 1296 words
54.	Housing market continues to confound all Concern grows as house prices rise against a backdrop of record housing supply and falling rents *The Irish Times*, April 16, 2004, City Edition; Business And Finance; Economics; Pg. 54, 832 words, by Dan Mclaughlin
55.	Datalex's Wilson reaps benefit of trophy house *The Irish Times*, April 16, 2004, City Edition; Business And Finance; Current Account; Pg. 54, 250 words
56.	IMF issues warning over house prices *The Irish Times*, April 22, 2004, City Edition; Business And Finance; Pg. 18, 216 words, by Una McCaffrey
57.	Good times are here to stay *The Irish Times*, June 10, 2004, City Edition; Residential Property; Around The Block; Pg. 53, 177 words
58.	Banning of the hookah keeps social life under tight control *The Irish Times*, July 1, 2004, City Edition; World News; Letter From Tehran; Pg. 13, 683 words, by Ramita Navai

59.	No sign of a pin to burst our housing bubble Rates may be rising in the US and UK, but the sluggish euro zone is happy to maintain the status quo *The Irish Times*, July 16, 2004, City Edition; Business And Finance; Economics; Pg. 54, 976 words, by Cliff Taylor
60.	Warning of house price crash in Britain *The Irish Times*, July 31, 2004, City Edition; Business And Finance; Pg. 20, 371 words, (Reuters)
61.	House prices resemble 'dotcom bubble' *The Irish Times*, September 17, 2004, Finance; Pg. 2, 450 words, John McManus
62.	Speculation has inflated bubbles in Irish property and oil markets *The Irish Times*, September 2, 2005, Finance; Personal Finance; Pg. 8, 894 words, Chris Johns
63.	Property bubble cushioning US economy *The Irish Times*, September 23, 2005, Finance; Business Opinion; Pg. 5, 1055 words, Jim O'Leary
64.	Bank of England's pragmatism helps housing market pick-up *The Irish Times*, November 9, 2005, Finance; Other Stories; Pg. 21, 757 words
65.	Bubble intact despite high house prices *The Irish Times*, November 18, 2005, Finance; Business Opinion; Pg. 5, 903 words, Sheila O'Flanagan
66.	What's next? Experts give their views *The Irish Times*, December 31, 2005 Saturday, News Features; Other Stories; Pg. 3, 536 words
67.	Property market unlikely to collapse, says Danske chief *The Irish Times*, February 2, 2006 Thursday, Finance; Other Stories; Pg. 18, 270 words, Una McCaffrey
68.	Investors feel financially Shanghaied with the bursting of the Chinese property bubble *The Irish Times*, March 2, 2006 Thursday, Property; Overseas Property; Pg. 24, 995 words
69.	Rising bond yields a risk to property bubble *The Irish Times*, April 21, 2006 Friday, Finance; Personal Finance; Pg. 8, 949 words, Chris Johns
70.	Reality Bites *The Irish Times*, May 13, 2006 Saturday, Magazine; Róisín Ingle; Pg. 3, 749 words

84.	Keeping EMU rules an acceptable price to pay for economic benefits *The Irish Times*, September 19, 2008 Friday, Finance; Agenda; Pg. 7, 865 words, Brendan Lynch
85.	Burst housing bubble may mean slow recovery for wider economy - report *The Irish Times*, October 1, 2008 Wednesday, Finance; Pg. 22, 501 words, Jamie Smyth in Brussels
86.	Handling of seismic events was good for Irish politics *The Irish Times*, October 4, 2008 Saturday, OPINION; Opinion; Pg. 15, 1046 words
87.	Economics *The Irish Times*, October 6, 2008 Monday, Innovation; Innovation Opinion ; Pg. 18, 957 words
88.	We squandered long before we were squeezed *The Irish Times*, November 1, 2008 Saturday, Opinion; Pg. 14, 1016 words
89.	Sombre mood at shopping centre conference *The Irish Times*, November 19, 2008 Wednesday Correction Appended, Commercial Property; Pg. 24, 1076 words, Jack Fagan
90.	No room for doubt in developers' world view *The Irish Times*, December 2, 2008 Tuesday, Opinion; Pg. 12, 835 words
91.	Construction halt leads to wide-ranging staff cuts *The Irish Times*, December 4, 2008 Thursday, Property; Architecture; Pg. 8, 1607 words
92.	Property prices in uncertain times *The Irish Times*, December 12, 2008 Friday, FINANCE; Personal Finance; Pg. 9, 863 words, Dominic Coyle
93.	Government must detail real plan to take us out of crisis *The Irish Times*, January 12, 2009 Monday, Opinion; Pg. 13, 1014 words
94.	Japan set for another plunge on economic rollercoaster *The Irish Times*, January 16, 2009 Friday, Opinion; Pg. 14, 1177 words
95.	Facing up to crisis in the public finances *The Irish Times*, February 13, 2009 Friday, Letters; Pg. 17, 1265 words
96.	Myths of the good old days don't stand up to scrutiny *The Irish Times*, February 28, 2009 Saturday, Opinion; Pg. 13, 1053 words

110.	Vendors still slow to lose belief in the hype *The Irish Times*, June 11, 2009 Thursday, Property; New to the Market; Pg. 5, 659 words
111.	Underwater mortgages: a guide to survival *The Irish Times*, June 26, 2009 Friday, Finance; Personal Finance; Pg. 9, 1685 words
112.	Cowen defends role as minister for finance *The Irish Times*, June 27, 2009 Saturday, Ireland; Other Stories; Pg. 6, 627 words, Stephen Collins and HARRY McGee
113.	TCD professor admits being wrong about housing bubble *The Irish Times*, June 30, 2009 Tuesday, Ireland; Other Stories; Pg. 3, 524 words, Harry McGee, Political Staff
114.	Prudent public spending *The Irish Times*, June 30, 2009 Tuesday, Letters; Pg. 15, 103 words
115.	An insight into difficulties and misery caused by bursting of property bubble *The Irish Times*, July 1, 2009 Wednesday, Finance; Business Today; Pg. 17, 692 words, Colm Keena
116.	Brought to our knees by bankers and developers *The Irish Times*, July 3, 2009 Friday, Opinion; Pg. 13, 1741 words, Morgan Kelly
117.	Keeping hope alive in Zimbabwe no easy task despite new unity government *The Irish Times*, July 6, 2009 Monday, World; Other World Stories; Pg. 10, 920 words
118.	Our process of making decisions is flawed *The Irish Times*, July 7, 2009 Tuesday, Opinion; Pg. 14, 873 words
119.	Learning from the credit crunch *The Irish Times*, July 10, 2009 Friday, Finance; Personal Finance; Pg. 9, 1615 words
120.	Taking the healthy option *The Irish Times*, July 14, 2009 Tuesday, Health; The Back Page; Pg. 20, 838 words
121.	Nama not to pay 'bubble' prices, says Lenihan, as Bill published *The Irish Times*, July 31, 2009 Friday, Front Page; Pg. 1, 720 words, Stephen Collins, Political Editor
122.	Country's future mortgaged on sloppy, confused legislation *The Irish Times*, August 1, 2009 Saturday, Opinion; Pg. 14, 1008 words

123.	A vigorous analysis of how the world might look when remade in China's image *The Irish Times*, August 19, 2009 Wednesday, Opinion; Pg. 13, 626 words, Clifford Coonan
124.	Property Investor *The Irish Times*, August 27, 2009 Thursday, Property; New to the Market; Pg. 2, 687 words
125.	The success of Nama is not based on any assumption of a return to the recent 'bubble' prices for property *The Irish Times*, September 1, 2009 Tuesday, Ireland; NAMA debate; Pg. 6, 3276 words
126.	Nama will distort market and is economic nonsense *The Irish Times*, September 2, 2009 Wednesday, Opinion; Pg. 14, 1488 words, Seán Barrett
127.	Property investor *The Irish Times*, September 3, 2009 Thursday, Property; New to the Market; Pg. 2, 701 words
128.	Economic downturn highlights wide division in legal profession *The Irish Times*, September 14, 2009 Monday, Ireland; Other Stories; Pg. 8, 643 words, Carol Coulter, Legal Affairs Editor
129.	Greens faced with ethical dilemma over Nama plan *The Irish Times*, September 14, 2009 Monday, Opinion; Pg. 12, 1159 words
130.	What it means for the banks *The Irish Times*, September 17, 2009 Thursday, Ireland; Nama Bill; Pg. 10, 2648 words
131.	Mixed blessings of more migration and fall in adult population *The Irish Times*, September 18, 2009 Friday, Finance; Business Agenda; Pg. 4, 975 words, Jim O'Leary
132.	Bord Plean·la warns on relaxing planning rules *The Irish Times*, October 15, 2009 Thursday, Ireland; Other Stories; Pg. 9, 630 words, Frank McDonald, Environment Editor
133.	Munich is best of the bunch in European property investment *The Irish Times*, October 15, 2009 Thursday, Property; International; Pg. 15, 872 words, Derek Scally
134.	Chinese cities still booming a year later *The Irish Times*, October 22, 2009 Thursday, Property; International; Pg. 11, 1231 words, Clifford Coonan in Beijing

135.	Financial regulation *The Irish Times*, October 23, 2009 Friday, Opinion; Pg. 17, 422 words
136.	The landed class who blew the bubble *The Irish Times*, October 24, 2009 Saturday, Weekend; News features; Pg. 3, 2102 words
137.	Spacious doer-upper on a fine redbrick road in D6 *The Irish Times*, October 29, 2009 Thursday, Property; New to the Market; Pg. 3, 354 words, Bernice Harrison
138.	Fine Gael government could break up banks, Bruton warns *The Irish Times*, October 30, 2009 Friday, Front Page; Pg. 1, 457 words, Stephen Collins and Mary Minihan
139.	Cork's Elysian is a 'Mary Celeste' adrift in the recession *The Irish Times*, October 31, 2009 Saturday, Weekend; News features; Pg. 2, 755 words
140.	Bank on Bootle *The Irish Times*, November 6, 2009 Friday, Innovation; Banking; Pg. 41, 1219 words
141.	Finally facing up to issue of under-taxation *The Irish Times*, November 21, 2009 Saturday Correction Appended, Opinion; Pg. 16, 930 words
142.	Ich bein ein property investor: is now right time to buy in Berlin? *The Irish Times*, November 26, 2009 Thursday, Property; International; Pg. 9, 1457 words
143.	Time for visionary planning *The Irish Times*, December 4, 2009 Friday, Features; Pg. 17, 1254 words
144.	Cantillon *The Irish Times*, December 8, 2009 Tuesday, Finance; Business Today; Pg. 21, 1071 words
145.	Irish banks face 'very substantial arrears and losses', warns debt rating agency *The Irish Times*, December 16, 2009 Wednesday, Finance; Business Today; Pg. 21, 359 words, Simon Carswell
146.	Sharing the pain of economic crisis *The Irish Times*, December 22, 2009 Tuesday, Letters; Pg. 13, 670 words
147.	New culture of openness needed to get us on track *The Irish Times*, December 22, 2009 Tuesday, Opinion; Pg. 11, 1258 words

148.	Chinese leader aims to avert bubble in property market *The Irish Times*, December 28, 2009 Monday, Finance; Business Today; Pg. 18, 285 words
149.	Silver lining to the gloom *The Irish Times*, December 28, 2009 Monday, Price Watch; Pg. 17, 1196 words, Conor Pope
150.	IMF says Ireland must cut wages *The Irish Times*, December 30, 2009 Wednesday, Finance; Business Today; Pg. 20, 250 words
151.	Opposition parties must tell electorate hard truths *The Irish Times*, January 2, 2010 Saturday, Opinion; Pg. 15, 1454 words
152.	Blowing Up The Bubble *The Irish Times*, January 8, 2010 Friday, Innovation; Pg. 13, 1611 words
153.	Personal equity *The Irish Times*, January 16, 2010 Saturday, MAGAZINE; Pg. 12, 2632 words, Words: Michael Freeman Illustrations: Dermot Flynn
154.	At the risk of oversimplifying, the worst appears to be over *The Irish Times*, January 22, 2010 Friday, Finance; Agenda; Pg. 4, 1016 words, Marian Finnegan
155.	Inquiry needed into how economy lost competitiveness *The Irish Times*, January 23, 2010 Saturday, Opinion; Pg. 16, 998 words
156.	Focus on pay necessary to restore competitiveness *The Irish Times*, January 30, 2010 Saturday, Opinion; Pg. 18, 929 words
157.	Where the heart is *The Irish Times*, January 30, 2010 Saturday, Magazine; Magazine Features; Pg. 14, 1293 words
158.	Oh Canada: should we sell our house there? *The Irish Times*, February 25, 2010 Thursday, Property; Around the block; Pg. 4, 155 words
159.	Bankers played property right through the boom *The Irish Times*, March 1, 2010 Monday, Finance; Pg. 21, 1306 words
160.	Soros says . . . *The Irish Times*, March 5, 2010 Friday, Innovation; Other Stories; Pg. 23, 1795 words
161.	Policing the banking sector *The Irish Times*, March 13, 2010 Saturday, Opinion; Pg. 15, 518 words

162.	How do you protect your home from repossession? *The Irish Times*, March 22, 2010 Monday, Price Watch; Pg. 20, 975 words, Fiona Reddan
163.	Taxpayer is casualty of conflict of interest *The Irish Times*, March 26, 2010 Friday, Opinion; Pg. 16, 1084 words, Colm Keena
164.	Popular thinking on crisis swept aside *The Irish Times*, April 13, 2010 Tuesday, Opinion; Pg. 14, 845 words
165.	Recklessness of banks greater than we know *The Irish Times*, April 15, 2010 Thursday, Opinion; Pg. 13, 911 words
166.	A useful tool for the uninitiated and a refresher course for the experienced *The Irish Times*, April 19, 2010 Monday, Finance; Business Today; Pg. 21, 722 words
167.	Need for shift away from 'age of me' to 'age of we' *The Irish Times*, April 23, 2010 Friday, Opinion; Pg. 14, 1166 words, Geoff Mulgan
168.	Lenihan accepts wind-down of Anglo *The Irish Times*, April 29, 2010 Thursday, Finance; Business Today; Pg. 21, 420 words, Barry O'Halloran and Marie O'Halloran
169.	Property investor *The Irish Times*, May 6, 2010 Thursday, Property; New to the Market; Pg. 2, 675 words
170.	Taoiseach defends his handling of economy before crash *The Irish Times*, May 14, 2010 Friday, Front Page; Pg. 1, 689 words, Stephen Collins and Simon Carswell
171.	Chinese housing market a big threat *The Irish Times*, June 1, 2010 Tuesday, Finance; Business Today; Pg. 19, 297 words, Geoff Dyer in Beijing
172.	Crisis result of property bubble and weak rules *The Irish Times*, June 10, 2010 Thursday, Ireland; Banking Reports; Pg. 10, 579 words, Ciarán Hancock Business Affairs Correspondent
173.	Case of 'too little too late' as growth surged *The Irish Times*, June 10, 2010 Thursday, Ireland; Banking Reports; Pg. 10, 365 words, Caroline Madden
174.	Cantillon *The Irish Times*, June 10, 2010 Thursday, Finance; Business Today; Pg. 23, 985 words

175. The causes of the banking crisis *The Irish Times*, June 10, 2010 Thursday, Opinion; Pg. 19, 520 words

176. Carr steering Mazars *The Irish Times*, June 11, 2010 Friday, Finance; Business Agenda; Pg. 4, 1193 words, Colm Keena

177. Crisis was three-quarters home-grown, says Honohan *The Irish Times*, June 15, 2010 Tuesday, Finance; Pg. 18, 409 words, Suzanne Lynch

178. More to FF poll slump than unpopular cuts *The Irish Times*, June 17, 2010 Thursday, Opinion; Pg. 16, 934 words, Frank McDonald

179. Property Investor *The Irish Times*, June 17, 2010 Thursday, Property; New to the Market; Pg. 2, 659 words, Jack Fagan

180. Return to Commuterland *The Irish Times*, June 19, 2010 Saturday, Weekend; Pg. 1, 2537 words

181. Watch out for the canaries in the coal mine *The Irish Times*, June 19, 2010 Saturday, Weekend; Arts; Pg. 9, 1074 words, Aidan Dunne

182. Department says it warned of property bubble *The Irish Times*, June 24, 2010 Thursday, Front Page; Pg. 1, 454 words, Carl O'Brien, Chief Reporter

183. Is He Getting The Right Advice? *The Irish Times*, June 25, 2010 Friday, Innovation; Economics; Pg. 16, 1424 words

184. China can handle its property bubble *The Irish Times*, July 16, 2010 Friday, Finance; Business Investments; Pg. 9, 957 words, Charlie Fell

185. Timeline of a crisis laid bare in documents *The Irish Times*, July 17, 2010 Saturday, Finance; Banking guarantee documents; Pg. 17, 473 words, Colm Keena

186. The future of Arnotts *The Irish Times*, July 29, 2010 Thursday, Opinion; Pg. 17, 420 words

187. Planning must be built on sustainable foundations *The Irish Times*, July 30, 2010 Friday, Opinion; Pg. 14, 1202 words

188. Populist petty confiscations will not cure economic ills *The Irish Times*, August 16, 2010 Monday, Finance; Business Today; Pg. 18, 871 words, John Collins

189.	Small Print *The Irish Times*, September 1, 2010 Wednesday, Features; Other Features; Pg. 12, 632 words
190.	Evidence shows no benefits from prescription charges *The Irish Times*, September 4, 2010 Saturday, Opinion; Pg. 12, 883 words
191.	China's pre-emptive strike at growing bubble anxiety *The Irish Times*, September 13, 2010 Monday, Finance; Business Today; Pg. 17, 1254 words
192.	Words of the wise: 'I remember the first property bubble' *The Irish Times*, September 14, 2010 Tuesday, Features; Pg. 13, 1726 words
193.	The limits, the failings and the uses of economics after the crash *The Irish Times*, September 17, 2010 Friday, Finance; Business Agenda; Pg. 4, 1032 words
194.	One more thing *The Irish Times*, September 24, 2010 Friday, Finance; Back Page; Pg. 16, 1047 words, Ciarán Hancock
195.	EU seeks tougher sanctions if budget rules flouted *The Irish Times*, September 30, 2010 Thursday, Finance; Pg. 22, 638 words, Arthur Beesley, European Correspondent in Brussels
196.	Losses and taxes for little people *The Irish Times*, September 30, 2010 Thursday, Letters; Pg. 19, 115 words
197.	Property investor *The Irish Times*, September 30, 2010 Thursday, Property; New to the Market; Pg. 2, 680 words
198.	Why future planning must be practical not political *The Irish Times*, October 4, 2010 Monday, Opinion; Pg. 11, 1802 words, Brendan Gleeson
199.	Whiter than white? *The Irish Times*, October 9, 2010 Saturday, Weekend; Book Reviews; Pg. 11, 961 words
200.	We built our businesses and we will do so again, insists Shovlin *The Irish Times*, October 15, 2010 Friday, Finance; Business Agenda; Pg. 5, 750 words, Colm Keena
201.	A legacy of ghost estates *The Irish Times*, October 23, 2010 Saturday, Opinion; Pg. 15, 507 words
202.	Short-sharp medicine may damage the patient *The Irish Times*, October 25, 2010 Monday, Finance; Business News; Pg. 18, 870 words, John McManus

203.	Rehn's Finnish lesson for Irish on beating recession *The Irish Times*, November 9, 2010 Tuesday, OPINION; Opinion; Pg. 12, 835 words
204.	Boom and bust: how to beat a recession *The Irish Times*, November 13, 2010 Saturday, Weekend; News features; Pg. 4, 1535 words
205.	What is unforgivable is Ireland's shameless status as Europe's greatest tax haven, helping to cheat tax from the world's treasuries for decades *The Irish Times*, November 24, 2010 Wednesday, Opinion; Pg. 15, 1138 words
206.	Whistle in the dark *The Irish Times*, November 26, 2010 Friday, Innovation; Other Stories; Pg. 24, 941 words, Derek Scally
207.	Áras candle in the window *The Irish Times*, December 2, 2010 Thursday, Letters; Pg. 19, 71 words
208.	A tale of two crises *The Irish Times*, December 17, 2010 Friday, Innovation; Pg. 22, 1491 words
209.	China raises key interest rates again in an effort to slow down inflation *The Irish Times*, December 27, 2010 Monday, Finance; Pg. 18, 606 words
210.	First chance of growth amid struggle to avoid going under *The Irish Times*, December 31, 2010 Friday, Finance; Pg. 1, 1505 words
211.	Value of Montrose Hotel written down by 80% *The Irish Times*, January 20, 2011 Thursday, Finance; Business News; Pg. 19, 384 words, Colm Keena, Public Affairs Correspondent
212.	Is China a bubble? And what if it bursts? *The Irish Times*, January 22, 2011 Saturday, News Features; Pg. 4, 2319 words, Clifford Coonan in Shanghai
213.	Build it and they will come *The Irish Times*, January 28, 2011 Friday, Innovation; Pg. 18, 1126 words
214.	Constitutional protection needed for statutory inquiry bodies *The Irish Times*, January 31, 2011 Monday, Ireland; Law Matters; Pg. 20, 1057 words
215.	A food crisis on our doorstep *The Irish Times*, January 31, 2011 Monday, Letters; Pg. 17, 246 words

216. Campaign Trail *The Irish Times*, February 7, 2011 Monday, Ireland; Election 2011; Pg. 6, 991 words

217. Planning reform one of several major achievements *The Irish Times*, February 15, 2011 Tuesday, Ireland; Election 2011; Pg. 8, 735 words

218. Is it too late to switch to a fixed mortgage? *The Irish Times*, February 21, 2011 Monday, Price Watch; Pg. 17, 1326 words, Conor Pope

219. The need for stability *The Irish Times*, February 24, 2011 Thursday, Opinion; Pg. 19, 493 words

220. Cold comfort from Europe *The Irish Times*, March 10, 2011 Thursday, Letters; Pg. 17, 61 words

221. Property Investor *The Irish Times*, March 10, 2011 Thursday, Property; The Market; Pg. 2, 691 words, Jack Fagan

222. Celebrating St Patrick's Day *The Irish Times*, March 17, 2011 Thursday, Opinion; Pg. 19, 519 words

223. Preventing a further bubble *The Irish Times*, April 18, 2011 Monday, Letters; Pg. 15, 67 words

224. 'Relentless attention to property' *The Irish Times*, April 20, 2011 Wednesday, Ireland; Nyberg Report; Pg. 7, 241 words, Laura Slattery

225. Average house prices could still be overvalued by up to 30% *The Irish Times*, April 25, 2011 Monday, Opinion; Pg. 14, 1913 words, Martin Walsh

226. Measures to avoid a further property disaster *The Irish Times*, April 26, 2011 Tuesday, Opinion; Pg. 14, 1154 words, Martin Walsh

227. A fabled city defaced by stag parties and a property bubble *The Irish Times*, April 27, 2011 Wednesday, World; Other World Stories; Pg. 12, 752 words

228. Averting another property disaster *The Irish Times*, May 2, 2011 Monday, Letters; Pg. 17, 241 words

229. Preventing another property bubble *The Irish Times*, May 4, 2011 Wednesday, Letters; Pg. 15, 134 words

230.	Kelly's route out of economic crisis is itself a road to ruin *The Irish Times*, May 10, 2011 Tuesday, Opinion; Pg. 16, 1021 words, John Bruton
231.	The other side of Cyprus *The Irish Times*, May 21, 2011 Saturday, Travel; Pg. 15, 1446 words
232.	Herding is detrimental in the world of investment *The Irish Times*, May 27, 2011 Friday, Finance; Investments; Pg. 11, 982 words, Charlie Fell
233.	Is this China's building bubble? *The Irish Times*, May 27, 2011 Friday, Innovation; Asian Economies; Pg. 25, 1431 words, Clifford Coonan in Beijing
234.	Man sentenced for importing cannabis *The Irish Times*, May 28, 2011 Saturday, Ireland; Regional News; Pg. 2, 95 words
235.	A tax on text *The Irish Times*, June 14, 2011 Tuesday, Letters; Pg. 15, 96 words
236.	Sell, sell, sell policy lands BoI with vast rents *The Irish Times*, June 16, 2011 Thursday, Property; Around the block; Pg. 4, 246 words
237.	Cantillon *The Irish Times*, June 23, 2011 Thursday, Finance; Business Today; Pg. 19, 707 words
238.	Banks wrestle with customer relations *The Irish Times*, July 25, 2011 Monday, Price Watch; Pg. 14, 1410 words
239.	Sale of council homes down 90% *The Irish Times*, August 11, 2011 Thursday, Property; Pg. 29, 371 words, Neil Callanan
240.	We can defeat the crisis and emerge stronger *The Irish Times*, August 30, 2011 Tuesday, Opinion; Pg. 14, 1014 words
241.	Fees may have come down but are they low enough? *The Irish Times*, September 20, 2011 Tuesday, Ireland; Other stories; Pg. 8, 834 words, Conor Pope, Consumer Affairs Correspondent
242.	How low can house prices go? *The Irish Times*, October 6, 2011 Thursday, Letters; Pg. 21, 102 words
243.	Nama may be forced to deliver on social housing *The Irish Times*, October 10, 2011 Monday, Ireland; Pg. 3, 520 words, Carl O'Brien, Chief Reporter

244. The 'truth' about public sector pay *The Irish Times*, October 14, 2011 Friday, Letters; Pg. 19, 162 words

245. Plan to deal with mortgage debt *The Irish Times*, October 15, 2011 Saturday, Letters; Pg. 15, 111 words

246. Rumblings in the background were quietly ignored *The Irish Times*, October 15, 2011 Saturday, Ireland; Other stories; Pg. 8, 610 words, Harry McGee

247. Questions remain surrounding Gallagher's financial affairs *The Irish Times*, October 25, 2011 Tuesday, Ireland; Race for the Aras; Pg. 7, 762 words, Colm Keena, Public Affairs Correspondent

248. State investment bank can shift focus from property *The Irish Times*, October 31, 2011 Monday, Opinion; Pg. 16, 1135 words, Seán Ó Riain and Michael O'Sullivan

249. Spanish property bubble fallout continues with evictions, debt and fear of homelessness *The Irish Times*, November 14, 2011 Monday, World; Euro Crisis; Pg. 10, 657 words, Caelainn Hogan in Barcelona

250. Economic indicators for China reveal robust activity *The Irish Times*, November 18, 2011 Friday, Finance; Business Today; Pg. 2, 421 words, Clifford Coonan in Beijing

251. Cantillon *The Irish Times*, November 29, 2011 Tuesday, Finance; Business Today; Pg. 21, 958 words

252. Reaction to Budget 2012 *The Irish Times*, December 8, 2011 Thursday, Letters; Pg. 15, 1072 words

253. Bubble bursts for investors in Celtic Tiger dream property deal *The Irish Times*, December 9, 2011 Friday, Finance; Business News; Pg. 3, 844 words, Colm Keena

254. Will the financial crisis get a new epicentre in China? The Irish Times, December 20, 2011 Tuesday, Finance; Business News; Pg. 16, 798 words, Paul Krugman

255. Time to end the groveling to EU and be assertive The Irish Times, December 21, 2011 Wednesday, Opinion; Pg. 14, 840 words

Appendix 2

Articles Coded

Article #	Out/in	Bubble?	Consequences?	Date
1	in	3	3	1996
2	out			
3	out			
4	in	1	1	1998
5	in	1	3	1998
6	in	1	3	1998
7	in	1	3	1998
8	in	1	3	1998
9	in	1	3	1998
10	in	1	3	1998
11	out			
12	out			
13	in	1	3	1999
14	in	1	1	1999
15	in	1	1	1999
16	out			
17	in	3	3	1999
18	in	1	1	1999
19	in	1	1	1999
20	in	2	2	1999
21	in	1	2	1999
22	in	1	3	2000
23	in	1	3	2000
24	in	1	1	2000
25	in	1	3	2000
26	in	2	2	2000
27	in	2	2	2000
28	in	1	2	2000

Article #	Out/in	Bubble?	Consequences?	Date
29	in	1	2	2000
30	out			
31	in	1	2	2000
32	in	1	1	2000
33	out			
34	out			
35	in	1	1	2002
36	out			
37	out			
38	out			
39	in	1	1	2003
40	in	1	2	2003
41	out			
42	in	3	2	2003
43	out			
44	out			
45	in	2	2	2003
46	in	2	2	2003
47	in	3	3	2003
48	out			
49	in	2	2	2003
50	out			
51	in	2	2	2004
52	in	2	2	2004
53	out			
54	in	2	2	2004
55	out			
56	in	1	1	2004
57	in	3	2	2004
58	out			
59	in	1	3	2004
60	out			
61	in	3	2	2004
62	in	1	2	2005
63	out			
64	out			

Article #	Out/in	Bubble?	Consequences?	Date
65	in	3	3	2005
66	out			
67	in	2	2	2006
68	out			
69	out			
70	out			
71	out			
72	in	3	3	2006
73	in	1	3	2007
74	out			
75	in	3	3	2007
76	out			
77	in	1	1	2008
78	out			
79	in	1	3	2008
80	out			
81	out			
82	in	1	2	2008
83	out			
84	in			2008
85	in			2008
86	in			2008
87	out			
88	in			2008
89	in			2008
90	in			2008
91	in			2008
92	out			
93	in			2009
94	out			
95	out			
96	in			2009
97	in			2009
98	out			
99	in			2009
100	in			2009

Article #	Out/in	Bubble?	Consequences?	Date
101	out			
102	in			2009
103	in			2009
104	in			2009
105	out			
106	in			2009
107	in			2009
108	in			2009
109	out			
110	out			
111	in			2009
112	in			2009
113	in			2009
114	out			
115	in			2009
116	in			2009
117	out			
118	in			2009
119	in			2009
120	out			
121	in			2009
122	in			2009
123	out			
124	in			2009
125	in			2009
126	in			2009
127	in			2009
128	out			
129	in			2009
130	in			2009
131	in			2009
132	in			2009
133	out			
134	out			
135	in			2009
136	in			2009

Article #	Out/in	Bubble?	Consequences?	Date
137	in			2009
138	in			2009
139	in			2009
140	in			2009
141	in			2009
142	out			
143	in			2009
144	in			2009
145	in			2009
146	out			
147	in			2009
148	out			
149	out			
150	in			2009
151	in			2010
152	in			2010
153	out			
154	in			2010
155	in			2010
156	in			2010
157	in			2010
158	out			
159	in			2010
160	out			
161	in			2010
162	in			2010
163	in			2010
164	in			2010
165	in			2010
166	out			
167	in			2010
168	in			2010
169	in			2010
170	in			2010
171	out			
172	in			2010

Article #	Out/in	Bubble?	Consequences?	Date
173	in			2010
174	in			2010
175	in			2010
176	out			
177	in			2010
178	in			2010
179	in			2010
180	in			2010
181	out			
182	in			2010
183	in			2010
184	out			
185	in			2010
186	in			2010
187	in			2010
188	in			2010
189	out			
190	out			
191	out			
192	out			
193	in			2010
194	out			
195	in			2010
196	out			
197	in			2010
198	in			2010
199	in			2010
200	in			2010
201	in			2010
202	in			2010
203	in			2010
204	in			2010
205	in			2010
206	in			2010
207	out			
208	in			2010

Article #	Out/in	Bubble?	Consequences?	Date
209	out			
210	in			2010
211	in			2011
212	out			
213	out			
214	out			
215	out			
216	out			
217	in			2011
218	in			2011
219	in			2011
220	out			
221	in			2011
222	in			2011
223	out			
224	in			2011
225	in			2011
226	in			2011
227	out			
228	out			
229	out			
230	in			2011
231	out			
232	in			2011
233	out			
234	in			2011
235	out			
236	in			2011
237	in			2011
238	in			2011
239	in			2011
240	in			2011
241	out			
242	out			
243	in			2011
244	out			

Article #	Out/in	Bubble?	Consequences?	Date
245	out			
246	in			2011
247	in			2011
248	in			2011
249	out			
250	out			
251	in			2011
252	out			
253	in			2011
254	out			
255	in			2011

Notes

In = article kept;
Out = article rejected from the analysis because off topic or letters to the editor
Bubble? 1:yes; 2:no; 3:vague/neutral
Consequences? 1:bad; 2:fine; 3:vague/neutral

Bibliography

Acheson, N., Harvey, B. and Williamson, A., 2005 'State welfare and the development of voluntary action: the case of Ireland, north and south', *Voluntas* 16(2), 181–202.

Acheson, N., Harvey, B., Kearney, J. and Williamson, A., 2004 *Two Paths, One Purpose – Voluntary Action in Ireland, North and South.* Dublin: Institute of Public Administration.

Allen, K. and O'Boyle, B., 2013 *Austerity Ireland: The Failure of Irish Capitalism.* London and Chicago: Pluto Press and University of Chicago Press Economics Books.

Allen, K., 2009 *Ireland's Economic Crash: A Radical Agenda for Change.* Dublin: Liffey Press.

Allon, F. and Anderson, K., 2010 'Intimate encounters: the embodied transnationalism of backpackers and independent travellers', *Population, Space and Place* 16, 11–22.

Amenta, E., Caren, N., Chiarello, E. and Su, Y., 2010 'The political consequences of social movements', *Annual Review of Sociology* 36, 287–307.

Atkinson, A. and Brandolini, A., 2013 'On the identification of the middle class', in J.C. Gornick and M. Jäntti (eds), *Income Inequality: Economic Disparities and the Middle Class in Affluent Countries.* Stanford, CA: Stanford University Press, 77–100.

Atkinson, A.B. and Morelli, S., 2011 *Economic Crises and Inequality*, Human Development Research Paper 2011/06. Background paper for the Human Development Report 2011. New York: UNDP/UN.

Baldwin, R. and Giavazzi, F., (eds) 2015 *The Eurozone Crisis: A Consensus View of the Causes and a Few Possible Solutions.* London: CEPR Press.

Barnes, L. and A. Wren, 2012 'The Neo-Liberal model in (the) Crisis: Continuity and Change in Great Britain and Ireland' In N. Bermeo and J. Pontusson (eds), *Coping with Crisis: Government Responses to the Great Recession.* New York. Russell Sage Foundation.

Barnes, S. and Smyth, D., 2013 *The Government's Balance Sheet After the Crisis*, Working Paper, Irish Fiscal Advisory Council, Dublin.

Barrett, A. and Kelly, E., 2012 'The impact of Ireland's recession on the labour market outcomes of its immigrants', *European Journal of Population* 28(1), 99–111.

Barrett, A. and Wall, C., 2006 *The Distributional Impact of Ireland's Indirect Tax System*. Dublin: Combat Poverty Agency.

Barrett, A., McGuinness, S. and O'Brien, M., 2012 'The immigrant earnings disadvantage across the earnings and skills distributions: the case of immigrants from the EU's new member states', *British Journal of Industrial Relations* 50, 457–481.

Bartels, L.M. and Bermeo, N., 2014 'Mass politics in tough times', in L. M. Bartels and N. Bermeo (eds), *Mass Politics in Tough Times: Opinions, Votes and Protest in the Great Recession*. Oxford: Oxford University Press, 1–39.

Bidwell, P., Humphries, N., Dicker, P., Thomas, S., Normand, C. and Brugha, R., 2013 'The national and international implications of a decade of doctor migration in the Irish context', *Health Policy* 110(1), 29–38.

Boland, V., 'Northern Ireland braces for austerity', *Financial Times*, 2 March 2015.

Bolger, K.E., Patterson, C.J., Thompson, W.W., and Kupersmidt, J.B., 1995 'Psychosocial adjustment among children experiencing persistent and intermittent family economic hardship', *Child Development* 66, 1107–1129.

Borooah, V. and Knox, C., 2015 *The Economics of Schooling in a Divided Society*. Basingstoke, UK: Palgrave Macmillan.

Borooah, V., 2014 *Europe in an Age of Austerity*. Dordrecht: Springer.

Bougrine, H., 2012 'Fiscal austerity, the great recession and the rise of new dictatorships', *Review of Keynesian Economics* 1(1), 109–125.

Boyle, M., Kitchin, R., and Ancien, D., 2013 'Ireland's diaspora strategy: diaspora for development?', in M. Gilmartin and A. White (eds), *Migrations: Ireland in a Global World*. Manchester: Manchester University Press, 80–97.

Bramall, R., 2013 *The cultural politics of austerity: Past and present in austere times*. Dordrecht: Springer; Basingstoke: Macmillan.

Brazys, S. and Hardiman, N., 2015 'From "Tiger" to "PIIGS": Ireland and the use of heuristics in comparative political economy', *European Journal of Political Research* 54(1), 23–42.

Brenner, N., Peck, J. and Theodore, N., 2010 'Variegated neoliberalization: geographies, modalities, pathways', *Global Networks* 10, 182–222.

Brooks-Gordon, B., 2006 *The Price of Sex: Prostitution, Policy and Society*. Cullompton, UK: Willan.

Brooks-Gunn, J. and Duncan, G.J., 1997 'The effects of poverty on children', *Future of Children* 7(2), 55–71.

Broucker, B., De Wit, K. and Leisyte, L., 2016 'Higher education reform: a systematic comparison of ten countries from a New Public Management perspective', in R.M.O. Pritchard, J. Williams and A. Pausits (eds), *Positioning Higher Education Institutions: From Here to There*. Rotterdam: Sense, pp. 19–40.

Burawoy, M., 2012 Featured review essay of *The Great American University: Its Rise to Pre-eminence, Its Indispensable National Role, Why It Must Be Protected* by Jonathan R. Cole. *Sociology* 41(2), 139–149.

Byrne, D. and McCoy, S., 2013 'Identifying and explaining hidden disadvantage within the non-manual group', *Comparative Social Research* 30, 293–315.

Byrne, E., 2011 *Political Corruption in Ireland 1922–2010: A Crooked Harp.* Manchester: Manchester University Press.

Byrne, M., forthcoming. 'Asset price urbanism and financialization after the crisis: Ireland's National Asset Management Agency' International Journal of Urban and Regional Research.

Cairns, D., 2014 '"I wouldn't stay here": economic crisis and youth mobility in Ireland', *International Migration* 52, 236–249.

Callan T., Keane C. and Savage, M., 'Austerity was top-loaded in earlier budgets', *Irish Times*, December 7, 2012.

Callan, T, Savage, M., Nolan, B. and Colgan, B., 2013 'The Great Recession, austerity and inequality: evidence from Ireland,' *Intereconomics* 48 (6), 335–38.

Callan, T., 'Budget 2016: Changes will have little impact on poorest in society', *Irish Times*, 14 October 2015.

Callan, T., Colgan, B., Logue, C., Savage, M. and Walsh, J.R., 2016 'Distributional impact of tax, welfare and public service pay policies: Budget 2016 and Budgets 2009–2016', Special Article, *Quarterly Economic Commentary*. Dublin: Economic and Social Research Institute.

Callan, T., Keane, C., Savage, M. and Walsh, J.R., 2013 'Distributional Impact of Tax, Welfare and Public Sector Pay Policies: Budget 2014 and Budgets 2009–14' Dublin: Economic and Social Research Institute.

Callan, T., Nolan, B., Keane, C., Savage, M. and Walsh, J.R., 2014 'Crisis, response and distributional impact: the case of Ireland', *IZA Journal of European Labour Studies* 3(9), 1–17.

Callan, T., Savage, M.,Nolan, B. and Colgan, B., 2013 'The Great Recession, austerity and inequality: evidence from Ireland,' *Intereconomics* 48 (6), 335–38.

Callender, C., 2013 'The funding of part-time undergraduate students', in D. Heller and C. Callender (eds), *Student Financing of Higher Education: A Comparative Perspective.* London: Routledge, 115–136.

Calmfors, L. and Wren-Lewis, S., 2011 'What should fiscal councils do?', *Economic Policy* 26, 649–695.

Cardiff, K., 2015 'Witness Statement: Kevin Cardiff', Joint Committee of Inquiry into the Banking Crisis, Dublin.

Central Statistics Office 2007 *EU Survey on Income and Living Conditions (EU-SILC).* Dublin: CSO.

Central Statistics Office 2010 *Quarterly National Household Survey: Health Status and Health Service Utilisation.* Dublin: CSO.

Central Statistics Office 2013 *Survey on Income and Living Conditions.* Dublin: CSO, Table A.

Central Statistics Office 2013a *Quarterly National Household Survey: Effect on Households of the Economic Downturn Quarter 3 2012.* Dublin: CSO.

Central Statistics Office 2013b *Survey of Income and Living Conditions (SILC) 2011 and Revised 2010 Results.* Dublin: CSO.

Central Statistics Office 2015 *Survey on income and living conditions*, Dublin: CSO.

Central Statistics Office 2015 *Quarterly National Household Survey.* Time Series. Dublin: CSO, Table 1A.

Central Statistics Office 2015 *Survey on Income and Living Conditions (SILC) 2013 Results*. Dublin: CSO.

Central Statistics Office 2015b *Statistical Tables: Annual Population Estimates – PEA15*.

Chapkis, W., 1997 *Live Sex Acts: Women Performing Erotic Labour*. London: Cassell.

Church, S., Henderson, M. and Barnard, M., 2001 Violence by clients towards female prostitutes in different work settings: questionnaire survey. *British Medical Journal* 322(7285), 524–525.

Clancy, P. and Goastellec, G., 2007 'Exploring access and equity in higher education: policy and performance in a comparative perspective', *Higher Education Quarterly* 61(2), 136–154.

Clancy, P., 2015 *Irish Higher Education: A Comparative Perspective*. Dublin: Institute of Public Administration.

Clancy, P., 2016 'Isomorphism in higher education policy: the incorporation of supranational perspectives into Irish national policy', *Journal of the European Higher Education Area* 2, 1–26.

Clark, B. R., 1998 *Creating Entrepreneurial Universities: Organizational Pathways of Transformations*. Oxford: Elsevier.

Clarke, J. and Newman, J., 2012 'The alchemy of austerity,' *Critical Social Policy* 32 (3), 299–19.

Clarke, M., Kenny, A. and Loxley, A., 2015 *Creating a Supportive Working Environment for Academics in Higher Education: Country Report Ireland*. Dublin: Irish Federation of University Teachers and Teachers' Union of Ireland.

Clarke, N., 2005 'Detailing transnational lives of the middle: British working holiday makers in Australia', *Journal of Ethnic and Migration Studies* 31(2), 307–322.

Coelho, H., Galindo, H., Leon, S. and O'Malley, E., 2016 *State of the Left: Spain, Portugal, Ireland*. London: Policy Network.

Comptroller and Auditor General 2015 'Cost of banking stabilisation measures as of end-2014', Chapter 3 of *Report of the Accounts of the Public Service 2015*. Dublin.

Coulter, C. and Nagle, A., (eds), 2015 *Ireland under austerity, neoliberal crisis, neoliberal solutions*. Manchester. Manchester University Press.

Coulter, C., 2015 'Ireland under austerity: an introduction to the book', in C. Coulter and A. Nagle (eds), *Ireland under Austerity: Neoliberal Crisis, Neoliberal Solutions*. Manchester: Manchester University Press, 1–43.

Cronin, M., 2012 *The expanding world: towards a politics of microspection*. Washington. Zero Books.

Dalton, R.J., 2000 'The decline of party identification', in R.J. Dalton and M.P. Wattenberg (eds), *Parties Without Partisans: Political Change in Advanced Industrial Democracies*. Oxford: Oxford University Press, 19–36.

De Boer, H., Enders, J. and Schimank, U., 2007 'On the way towards new public management? The governance of university systems in England, the Netherlands, Austria, and Germany', in D. Jansen (ed.), *New Forms of Governance in Research Organizations: Disciplinary Approaches, Interfaces and Integration*. Dordrecht: Springer, 135–152.

De Grauwe, P. and Yuemei Ji, 2013 *Panic-Driven Austerity in the Eurozone and Its Implications*. London: CEPR.

Decoster, A., Loughrey, J., O Donoghue, C. and Verwerft, D., 2010 'How regressive are indirect taxes? A microsimulation analysis for five European countries', *Journal of Policy Analysis and Management* 29(2), 326–350.

Deem, R., Hillyard, S. and Reed, M., 2007 *Knowledge, Higher Education and the New Manageralism*. Oxford: Oxford University Press.

Delaney, E., 'Why union blackmail must be faced down', *Sunday Independent*, 21 March 2010.

Della Porta, D. and Diani, M., 1999 *Social Movements: An Introduction*. London: Blackwell.

Dellepiane, S. and Hardiman, N., 2010 'The European context of Ireland's economic crisis', *Economic and Social Review* 41(4), 471–498.

Dellepiane-Avellaneda, S. and Hardiman, N., 2015 'The politics of fiscal effort in Spain and Ireland: Market credibility versus political legitimacy', in G. Karyotis and R. Gerodimos (eds), *The Politics of Extreme Austerity: Greece Beyond the Crisis*. London: Palgrave Macmillan, 198–221.

Dellepiane-Avellaneda, S., Blavoukos, S., Hardiman, N. and Pagoulatos, G., (forthcoming) 'Economic vulnerability in the Eurozone periphery: an emerging-market perspective', *Studies in Comparative International Development*.

Department for Employment and Learning, 2015 *Performance Indication in Higher Education: Northern Ireland Analysis 2013/14 (Part 1)*. Belfast. DEL, Publication Issue 5, Table 1.

Department for Work and Pensions 2007, *Opportunity for All*. London: DWP.

Department of Environment, Community and Local Government (2014a), Report of the Working Group on Citizen Engagement with Local Government. Dublin: Stationery Office.

Department of the Environment, 2010 *National Survey of Ongoing Housing Developments*, October. Dublin: DoE.

Deutsche Bundesbank, 2011 'Requirement regarding the new cyclical adjustment procedure under the new debt rule', *Monthly Report,* January.

Donovan, D. and Murphy, A., 2013 *The Fall of the Celtic Tiger: Ireland and the Euro Debt Crisis*. Oxford: Oxford University Press.

Downing, J. and Doyle, K., 'There is no going back on water charges – EU', *Irish Independent*, 27 June 2016.

Drudy, P. J., and Collins, M. L., 2011 'Ireland: from boom to austerity', *Cambridge Journal of Regions, Economy and Society* 4, no. 3, 339–354.

Dublin Region Homeless Executive, 2016 *Dublin Region Families Who Are Homeless*. 2016. Infographic. Dublin: Dublin Region Homeless Executive.

Duncan G.J., Brooks-Gunn, J. and Klebanov, P.K., 1994 'Economic deprivation and early childhood development', *Child Development* 65, 296–318.

Duncan, G.J., Ludwig, J. and Magnuson, K., 2007 'Reducing poverty through pre-school interventions', *Future of Children* 17, 143–160.

Duncan, G.J., Magnuson, K., Kalil, A. and Ziol-Guest, K., 2012 'The importance of early childhood poverty', *Social Indicators Research* 108, 87–98.

Economist, 'Castles in hot air', 31 May, 2003.

Economist, 'Special report: Going through the roof—house prices', 30 March 2002.

Eder, K., 1996 'The institutionalisation of environmentalism: ecological discourse and the second transformation of the public sphere', in S. Lash, B. Szerszynski and B. Wynne (eds), *Risk, Environment and Modernity*. London: Sage, 203–223.

Eichengeen, B., 2015 *Hall of Mirrors: The Great Depression, the Great Recession, and the Uses and Misuses of History*. Oxford: Oxford University Press.

Enterprise Strategy Group 2004 *Ahead of the Curve: Ireland's Place in the Global Economy*. Dublin: Enterprise Strategy Group.

Eriksen, T., 2007 *Globalization*. Oxford: Berg.

Esping-Andersen, G., 1990 *The Three Worlds of Welfare Capitalism*. Princeton, NJ: Princeton University Press.

Esping-Andersen, G., 1999 *Social Foundations of Postindustrial Economies*. Oxford. Oxford University Press.

Eurostat, 2010 *Structure of Earnings Survey*. Luxembourg: Eurostat.

Eurostat, 2015 'Euro area and EU28 government deficit at 2.4% and 2.9% of GDP respectively'. News Release. Luxembourg: Eurostat.

Eurostat, 2016 General government gross debt annual data. Luxembourg: Eurostat.

Eurostat, Foreign Control of Enterprises by Economic Activity and a Selection of Controlling Countries (fats_g1a_08).

Eurostat, Government Finance Statistics: General Government Expenditure by Function (COFOG) (gov_10a_exp).

Evans, D., 2011 'Thrifty, green or frugal: reflections on sustainable consumption in a changing economic climate,' *Geoforum* 42 (5), 550–57.

Expert Group on Future Funding for Higher Education, 2015a *The Role, Value and Scale of Higher Education in Ireland. Discussion Paper 2*. Dublin: Expert Group on Future Funding for Higher Education.

Expert Group on Future Funding for Higher Education, 2015b *Optimising Resources in Irish Higher Education. Discussion Paper 2*. Dublin: Expert Group on Future Funding for Higher Education.

Expert Group on Future Funding for Higher Education, 2016 *Investing in National Ambition: A Strategy for Funding Higher Education*. Dublin: Expert Group on Future Funding for Higher Education.

Fahey, T., Keilthy, P. and Polek, E., 2012 *Family Relationships and Family Well-Being: A Study of the Families of Nine Year Olds in Ireland*. Dublin: Family Support Agency.

Fahy, D., O'Brien, M. and Poti, V., 2010 'Combative critics or captured collaborators? Irish financial journalism and the end of the Celtic Tiger', *Irish Communications Review* 12, 5–20.

Fanning, B., 2015 'Immigration, the Celtic Tiger and the economic crisis', *Irish Studies Review* 24(1), DOI:10.1080/09670882.2015.1112995.

Farrell, D., 1999 'Ireland: A party system transformed', in D. Broughton and M. Donovan (eds), *Changing Party Systems in Western Europe*. London: A & C Black, 30–47.

Farrell, S., Murphy, G., Meehan, C. and Rafter, K., 2011 'Assessing the Irish general election of 2011', *New Hibernia Review* 15(3), 36–58.

Faulkner, L., 2012 *Survey of UCU Members: Stress at Ulster*. London: UCU, December.

Finn, D., 2011 'Ireland on the turn? Political and economic consequences of the crash', *New Left Review*, (67), 5–39.

FitzGerald, J., 2010 'The Irish economy today: albatross or phoenix?', *World Economy* 34 (10).

FitzGerald, J., 2013 *Research Notes: The Effect of Redomiciled PLCs on GNP and the Irish Balance of Payments.* Dublin: ESRI.

Focus Ireland 2016 *Focus Ireland says the homelessness crisis must be a top priority for the next government.* Press release. Dublin: Focus Ireland.

Foucault, M., 2007 *Security, Territory, Population. Lectures at the Collège de France, 1977–78.* New York. Palgrave.

Fraser, A., Murphy, E. and Kelly, S., 2013 'Deepening neoliberalism via austerity and "reform": The case of Ireland.' *Human Geography* 6, 38–53.

Gamson, W., 1975 *The Strategy of Social Protest.* Homewood, IL: Dorsey.

Gibney, D., Personal interview with author, 27 July 2016, Dublin.

Gilmartin, M., 2015 *Ireland and Migration in the Twenty-First Century.* Manchester: Manchester University Press.

Giugni, M., McAdam, D. and Tilly, C., (eds) 1999 *How Social Movements Matter.* Lanham, MD: Rowman & Littlefield.

Glynn, I., Kelly, T. and Mac Éinrí, P., 2015 *The Re-emergence of Emigration from Ireland: New Trends in an Old Story.* Washington, DC: Migration Policy Institute.

Goodbody Stockbrokers, 2006 *Irish Economic Commentary*, December. Dublin: Goodbody Stockbrokers.

Goodman, R., 1997 'The Strengths and Difficulties Questionnaire: a research note', *Journal of Child Psychology and Psychiatry* 38, 581–586.

Goodwin-White, J., 2013 'Context, scale, and generation: the constructions of belonging', in M. Gilmartin and A. White (eds), *Migrations: Ireland in a Global World*. Manchester. Manchester University Press, 213–227.

Gornick, J. and Jäntti, M., 2013 'Introduction', in J.C. Gornick and M. Jäntti (eds), *Economic Disparities in the Middle Class in Affluent Countries.* Stanford, CA: Stanford University Press.

Government of Ireland 2012 *Qualifications and Quality Assurance (Education and Training Act) No. 28 of 2012.* Dublin. Government Publications.

Gray, B., 2013 '"Generation Emigration": the politics of (trans)national social reproduction in twenty-first-century Ireland', *Irish Studies Review*, 21(1), 20–36.

Grusky, D.B. and Weeden, K.A., 2007 'Measuring poverty: the case for a sociological approach', in N. Kakawani and J. Silber (eds), *The Many Dimensions of Poverty*. Basingstoke, UK: Palgrave Macmillan.

Guajardo, J., Leigh, D. and Pescatori, A., 2011 *Expansionary Austerity: New International Evidence.* Washington, DC: IMF.

Haffert, L. and Mahrtens, P., 2015 'From Austerity to Expansion? Consolidation, Budget Surpluses, and the Decline of Fiscal Capacity', *Politics and Society* 43, 1, 119–148.

Hall, P. A., and Soskice, D. W., (eds) 2001 *Varieties of Capitalism: The Institutional Foundations of Comparative Advantage.* Oxford. Oxford University Press.

Hanappi, D., Bernardi, L. and Spini, D., 2015 'Vulnerability as a heuristic for interdisciplinary research: Assessing the thematic and methodological structure of empirical life-course studies', *Longitudinal and Life Course Studies* 6(1), 59–87.

Hannan, C. and Halpin, B., 2014 'The influence of family structure on child outcomes: evidence for Ireland', *Economic and Social Review* 45, 1–24.

Hart, K., 2010 *The Human Economy*. UK. Polity Press.

Harvey, B., 2012 *Downsizing the community sector. Changes in employment and services in the voluntary and community sector in Ireland, 2008–2012*. Dublin: Irish Congress of Trade Unions Community Sector Committee.

Harvey, D. 2007 *A Brief History of Neoliberalism*. Oxford: Oxford University Press.

Hazelkorn, E., 2011 *Rankings and the Reshaping of Higher Education: The Battle for World-Class Excellence*. Basingstoke, UK: Palgrave Macmillan.

Healy, S. and Reynolds, B., (eds) 2015 *Measuring Up? Ireland's progress: past, present and future*. Dublin: Social Justice Ireland.

Healy, S., Delaney, A., Leahy, A. Murphy, M., Reynolds, B. and Robinson, J. 2015 'Health', in *Towards a Just Society: Securing Economic Development, Social Equality and Sustainability*. Dublin: Social Justice Ireland.

Healy, S., Murphy, M. and Reynolds, B., (2015) 'What should Ireland do now?', in S. Healy and B. Reynolds, (eds) *Measuring Up? Ireland's progress: past, present and future*. Dublin: Social Justice Ireland.

Healy, T. 2013 'Private Bank Debts and Public Finances: Some Options for Ireland', *NERI WP* 1.

Healy. S., Delaney, A., Leahy, A., Murphy, M., Reynolds, B. and Robinson, J., 2015 'Towards a Just Society: Securing economic development, social equity and sustainability'. Dublin: Social Justice Ireland.

Helleiner, J. 2015 'Recruiting the "culturally compatible" migrant: Irish Working Holiday migration and white settler Canadianness', *Ethnicities*, DOI: 10.1177/1468796815610354.

Henkel, M. and Little, B., (eds) 1999 *Changing Relationships between Higher Education and the State*. London: Jessica Kingsley.

Henkel, M., 2000 *Academic identities and policy change in higher education*. London. Jessica Kingsley.

Hinton, E. and Redclift, M., 2009 *Austerity and sufficiency: the changing politics of sustainable consumption*. London. King's College London.

Holm, J.R., Lorenz, E., Lundvall, B.Å. and Valeyre, A., 2010 'Organizational learning and systems of labor market regulation in Europe' *Industrial and Corporate Change*, 19, 4, 1141–1173.

Holzer, H.J., Duncan, G.J. and Ludwig, J., 2007 'The economic costs of poverty in the United States: Subsequent effects of children growing up poor', Madison, WI: Institute for Research on Poverty, Discussion Paper no. 1327-07.

Hourican, E., 'The unmaking of the middle class', *Irish Independent*. 18 July 2016.

Humphery, K., 2010. 'The simple and the good: ethical consumption as anti-consumerism,' in T. Lewis, and E. Potter (eds) *Ethical consumption: A critical introduction*, 40–53. London. Routledge.

Humphries, N., Brugha, R., and McGee, H., 2012, 'Nurse migration and health workforce planning: Ireland as illustrative of international challenges', *Health Policy* 107, 44–53.

Humphries, N., McAleese, S., Matthews, A. and Brugha, R., 2015 '"Emigration is a matter of self-preservation. The working conditions ... are killing us slowly": qualitative insights into health professional emigration from Ireland', *Human Resources for Health* 13(35). DOI 10.1186/s12960-015-0022-6

Humphries, N., Tyrrell, E., McAleese, S., Bidwell, P., Thomas, S., Normand, C. and Brugha, R., 2013 'A cycle of brain gain, waste and drain—a qualitative study of non-EU migrant doctors in Ireland', *Human Resources for Health* 11(1), 1–21.

Inglis, T., 2008 *Global Ireland: Same Difference*. London: Routledge.

Intergovernmental Panel on Climate Change, 2014 Fifth Assessment of Climate Change-Synthesis Report. New York: UN.

International Monetary Fund Independent Evaluation Office, 2014 *IMF Response to the Financial and Economic Crisis*. Washington, DC: IMF.

International Monetary Fund, 2012 *The Good, the Bad, and the Ugly: 100 Years of Dealing with Public Debt Overhangs*. Washington, DC: IMF.

Irish Business and Employer Council, 2016 *Budget 2016: Invest Ambitiously*. Dublin: IBEC.

Irish Human Rights and Equality Commission 2015 *Ireland and the international Covenant on Economic, Social and Cultural Rights*. Dublin: Irish Human Rights and Equality Commission.

Irish Independent 'Ireland was a shipwreck ... we had to do things we did not want to do – Labour's Pat Rabbitte', 25 May 2014.

Irish Medical Organization 2012 *Position Paper on Health Inequalities*. Dublin: Irish Medical Organization.

Irish Times 'Focus on prime locations and bargains', 28 November 2007.

Irish Times 'Ireland is ranked third in "Economic Freedom" Index', 6 November 2000.

Irish Times 'Public attitudes to the budget', 18 November 2008.

Irish Times 'Strikes will solve nothing', 2 November 2009.

Jarjoura, G.R., Triplett, R.A. and Brinker, G.P., 2002 'Growing up poor: Examining the link between persistent childhood poverty and delinquency', *Journal of Quantitative Criminology* 18, 159–187.

Jenkins, S.P., 2011 *Changing Fortunes: Income Mobility and Poverty Dynamics in Britain*. Oxford: Oxford University Press.

Jenkins, S.P., Brandolini, A., Micklewright, J. and Nolan, B., 2013 *The Great Recession and the Distribution of Household Income*. Oxford: Oxford University Press.

Karlsen, J.E. and Pritchard, R.M.O., (eds) 2013 *Resilient Universities: Confronting Challenges in a Changing World*. Bern: Peter Lang.

Karyotis, G. and Rudig, W., 2015. 'Protest participation, electoral choices and public attitudes towards austerity in Greece', in G .Karyotis and R. Gerodinos (eds), *The Politics of Extreme Austerity: Greece in the Euro-zone Crisis*. London: Palgrave, 502–528.

Kavanagh, A. 2015 'The May 2014 local and European elections in the Republic of Ireland: second order or austerity voting?', *Representation* 51(2), 239–252.

Keane, C., Callan, T., Savage, M., Walsh, J.R. and Colgan, B., 2014 'Distributional impact of tax, welfare and public service pay policies: Budget 2015 and Budgets 2009–2015', *Quarterly Economic Commentary*, Winter. Dublin: Economic and Social Research Institute.

Kearney, A., 2004 'Measuring globalization: economic reversals, forward momentum', *Foreign Policy*, March/April.

Kearns, G., Meredith, D. and Morrissey, J., 2014 *Spatial Justice and the Irish Crisis*. Dublin. Royal Irish Academy.

Keenan, B., 'No room for complacency as we're still on a knife-edge', *Irish Independent*, 6 January 2010.

Kelly, F., 'Political system shocked by Callinan resignation', *Irish Times*, 25 March 2014.

Kelly, M., 2006 'How the housing corner stones of our economy could go into a rapid freefall', *Irish Times*, 28 December.

Kelly, M., 2007a *On the Likely Extent of Falls in Irish House Prices*. UCD Centre of Economic Research Working Paper series 2007, WP07/01, February.

Kelly, M., 2007b 'Banking on very shaky foundations', *Irish Times*, 7 September 2007.

Kelly, M., 2010 *Whatever Happened to Ireland?* Discussion Paper No. 7811, May. London. Centre for Economic Policy Research.

Kenny, C., 2015 'HSE scheme recruits just 77 Irish nurses from abroad', *Irish Times*, 10 November.

Keohane, K. and Kuhling, C., 2014 *The political, domestic and moral economies of post-Celtic Tiger Ireland*. Manchester. Manchester University Press.

Kerrins, L., Greene, S. and Murphy, S., 2011 *Going Without: Measuring Child Poverty and Social Exclusion in Ireland*. Combat Poverty Agency Working Paper 11/08. Dublin: Department of Social Protection.

King, M., 1995 'Commentary: Monetary policy implications of greater fiscal discipline given at Federal Reserve Bank of Kansas City Symposium on Budget Deficits and Debt: Issues and Options.'

Kinnell, H., 2006 'Murder made easy: the final solution to prostitution', in R. Campbell and M. O'Neill (eds), *Sex Work Now*. Cullompton, UK: Willan.

Kinsella, S., 2012 'Is Ireland really the role model for austerity?', *Cambridge Journal of Economics* 36 (1), 223–235.

Kitschelt, H., 1986 'Political opportunity structures and political protest: anti-nuclear movements in four democracies', *British Journal of Political Science*, 16, 57–85.

Klein, N., 2014 *This Changes Everything*. New York. Simon and Schuster.

Kose, M.A., Loungani, P. and Terrones, M.E. 2013 *Why Is This Global Recovery Different?* VoxEU.org, 18 April.

Kriesi, H., 2014 'The political consequences of the economic crisis in Europe: electoral punishment and popular protest', in N. Bermeo and L.M. Bartels (eds), *Mass Politics in Tough Times: Opinions, Votes, and Protest in the Great Recession*. Oxford: Oxford University Press, 297–333.

Krippner, G., 2011 *Capitalizing on Crisis*. Cambridge, MA. Harvard University Press.

Krugman, P., 'Eating the Irish', *New York Times*, 26 November, 2010 A37.

Leahy, P., 'Exclusive Red C poll: Kenny's rise continues', *Sunday Business Post*, 21 November 2015.

Lester, R.K. and Piore, M., 2004 *Innovation—The Missing Dimension*. Cambridge. Harvard University Press.

Levi-Strauss, C., 1995 *Myth and Meaning*. New York. Schocken Books.

Lindvall, J. 2014 'The Electoral Consequences of Two Great Crises', *European Journal of Political Research* 53(4), 747–765.

Little, C. 2011 'The general election of 2011 in the Republic of Ireland: all changed utterly', *West European Politics* 34(6), 1304–1313.

Little, C. 2016 'The Irish general election of February 2016: towards a new politics or an early election?', *West European Politics* 40(2), 479–488.

Lyons, R. 2017 'Housing and Austerity: A Two-Way Street', in E. Heffernan, J. McHale and N. Moore-Cherry (eds) *Debating austerity in Ireland: crisis, experience and recovery*, Dublin: Royal Irish Academy.

Mair, P., 2013 'Smaghi versus the parties: representative government and institutional constraints', in A. Schaefer and W. Streeck (eds), *Politics in the Age of Austerity*. Cambridge: Polity Press, 143–168.

Mair, P., 2014 *Ruling the Void: The Hollowing-Out of Western Democracy*. London: Verso.

Maître, B., Russell, H. and Whelan, C., 2014 *Trends in economic stress and the Great Recession in Ireland. An analysis of the CSO Survey of Income and Living Conditions (SILC)*. Technical Paper No. 5. Dublin: Department of Social Protection.

Marginson, S., (ed.) 2007 *Prospects of Higher Education: Globalization, Market Competition, Public Goods and the Future of the University*. Rotterdam: Sense.

Marsh, M., 2006 'Party identification in Ireland: an insecure anchor for a floating party system', *Electoral Studies* 25(3), 489–508.

Mayer, M., 1995 'Social movement research in the United States: a European perspective', in S. Lyman (ed.), *Social Movements: Critiques, Concepts and Case Studies*. London: Macmillan, 168–195.

McAleer, M.C., 2013 *Time to Go? A Qualitative Research Study Exploring the Experience & Impact of Emigration on Ireland's Youth*. Dublin: National Youth Council of Ireland.

McArdle, P., 2012 *The Euro Crisis: The 'Fiscal Compact' and Fiscal Policy*. Dublin: Institute of International and European Affairs.

McChesney, R., 2004 *The Problem of the Media: US Communication Politics in the 21st Century*. New York: Monthly Review.

McConnell, D., 'Lenihan's last chance to save us', *Sunday Independent*, 7 November 2010.

McCrory, C., Dooley, C., Layte, R., and Kenny, R.A., 2015 'The lasting legacy of childhood adversity for disease risk in later life', *Health Psychology* 34(7), 687–696.

McDonagh, P., Dobscha, S. and Prothero, A., 2011 'Sustainable consumption and production: challenges for transformative consumer research,' in D. Mick, D., Pettigrew, S., Pechmann, C. and Ozanne, J.L. (eds), *Transformative Consumer Research For Personal and Collective Well-Being: Reviews And Frontiers*, 263–27. UK. Routledge.

McGee, H., 'IBRC inquiry's work set to be delayed for months', *Irish Times*, 9 November 2015.

McHale, J., 2012 'An overview of developments in the Irish economy over the last ten years', *The World Economy*, 35(10), 1220–1238.

McLeod, J.D. and Shanahan, M.J., 1996, 'Trajectories of poverty and children's mental health', *Journal of Health and Social Behavior* 37, 207–222.

McVeigh, R., Cunningham, D. and Farrell, J., 2014 'Political polarization as a social movement outcome: 1960s Klan activism and its enduring impact on political re-alignment in Southern counties, 1960 to 2000', *American Sociological Review*, 79(6), 1144–1171.

McWilliams, D., 'Irish economy mirrors Asia's before the bust', *Irish Times*, 16 January 1998.

McWilliams, D., 2006 *The Pope's Children: Ireland's New Elite*. Dublin: Gill & Macmillan.

Melucci, A., 1984 'An end of social movement?', *Social Science Information*, 23, 819–835.

Melucci, A., 1989 *Nomads of the Present: Social Movements and Individual Needs in Contemporary Society*. Philadelphia: Temple University Press.

Mercille, J. and Murphy, E., 2015 *Deepening neoliberalism, austerity, and crisis: Europe's treasure Ireland*. Springer; London: Palgrave.

Mercille, J. and Murphy, E., 2016 'Conceptualising European privatisation processes after the Great Recession', *Antipode* 48(3), 685–704.

Mercille, J. and Murphy, E., 2017a 'The neoliberalization of Irish higher education under austerity', *Critical Sociology,* 43(3): 371–387.

Mercille, J. and Murphy, E., 2017b 'What is privatization? A political economy framework', *Environment and Planning A*, 49(5): 1040–1059.

Mercille, J., 2013 'European media coverage of Argentina's debt default and recovery: distorting the lessons for Europe', *Third World Quarterly* 34(8), 1377–1391.

Mercille, J., 2014a 'The role of the media in sustaining Ireland's housing bubble', *New Political Economy* 19(2), 282–301.

Mercille, J., 2014b 'The role of the media in fiscal consolidation programmes: the case of Ireland', *Cambridge Journal of Economics* 38(2), 281–300.

Mercille, J., 2015 *The Political Economy and Media Coverage of the European Economic Crisis: The Case of Ireland*. London. Routledge.

Meredith, D. and van Egeraat, C., 2013 'Ten Years On: Revisiting the NSS', *Administration*, 60:3–13. Dublin: IPA.

Merler, S. and Pisani-Ferry, J., 2012 *Sudden Stops in the Euro Area*. Brussels: Bruegel Institute.

Meyer, J.W., Ramirez, F.O., Frank, D.J. and Schofer, E., 2007 'Higher education as an institution', in P.J. Gumport (ed.), *Sociology of Higher Education: Contributions and Their Contexts*. Baltimore: Johns Hopkins University Press, 187–221.

Middlehurst, R., Goreham, H., and Woodfield, S., 2014 'Why research leadership in higher education? Exploring contributions from the UK's Leadership Foundation for Higher Education', *Leadership* 5 (3), 311–329.

Migrant Rights Centre Ireland ,2015 *All Work and Low Pay: the Experiences of Migrants Working in Ireland*. Dublin: Migrant Rights Centre Ireland.

Miller, D., 1998 *A theory of shopping*. UK. Cornell University Press.

Moriarty, E., Wickham, J., Daly, S. and Bobek, A., 2015 'Graduate emigration from Ireland: navigating new pathways in familiar places', *Irish Journal of Sociology* 23(2), 71–92.

Morris, S. and Shin, H.S., 2006 'Catalytic finance: when does it work?', *Journal of International Economics*, 70, 161–177.

Morrone, A., 2009 'The OECD Global Project on Measuring Progress and the challenge of assessing and measuring trust', in B. Reynolds and S. Healy (eds) *Beyond GDP: what is progress and how should it be measured*. Dublin: Social Justice Ireland.

Muellbauer, J. 2007 'Housing, credit and consumer expenditure', in *Housing, Housing Finance, and Monetary Policy, a Symposium Sponsored by the Federal Reserve Bank of Kansas City*, Jackson Hole, Wyoming, 267–334.

Müller, W.C. and Strøm, K., (eds) 2000 *Coalition Governments in Western Europe*. Oxford: Oxford University Press.

Mulligan, A., 2008 'Countering exclusion: the "St Pats for all" parade', *Gender, Place & Culture* 15(2), 153–167.

National Competitiveness Council, 2015 *Ireland Competitiveness Scorecard 2015*. Dublin: National Competitiveness Council.

National Economic & Social Council, 2012 Promoting Economic Recovery and Employment. Dublin: NESC.

National Economic and Social Council, 1982 *A Review of Industrial Policy*. Dublin: NESC.

National Economic and Social Council, 2003 An Investment in Quality: Services, Inclusion and Enterprise. Dublin: National Economic and Social Council.

National Economic and Social Council, 2005 *The Developmental Welfare State*, No. 113. Dublin: National Economic and Social Council.

National Economic and Social Council, 2013 *The Social Dimensions of the Crisis*. No. 134. Dublin: National Economic and Social Council.

Naughton, M., 2015 'An interrogation of the character of protest in Ireland since the bailout', *Interface* 7(1), 289–308.

Newman, A., 2012 'Austerity and the End of the European Model' *Foreign Affairs, 1*.

Nixon, E., 2012 *Growing up in Ireland: How Families Matter for Social and Emotional Outcomes of 9-Year-Old Children*. Dublin, Department of Health and Children.

Nolan, B. and Maître, B., 2017 *Children of the Celtic Tiger during the Economic Crisis: Ireland*, in B. Cantillon, Y. Chzhen, S. Handa and B. Nolan (eds), *Children of Austerity, Impact of the Great Recession on Child Poverty in Rich Countries*, 146–169. Oxford: Oxford University Press.

Nolan, B. and Whelan, C.T., 2007 'On the multidimensionality of poverty and social exclusion', in J. Micklewright and S. Jenkins (eds), *Poverty and Inequality: New Directions*. Oxford: Oxford University Press.

Nolan, B. and Whelan, C.T., 2010 'Using non-monetary deprivation indicators to analyse poverty and social exclusion in rich counties: Lessons from Europe?', *Journal of Policy Analysis and Management* 29(2), 305–323.

Nolan, B. and Whelan, C.T., 2011 *Poverty and Deprivation in Europe*. Oxford: Oxford University Press.

Nolan, B., Maître, B., Voitchovsky, S. and Whelan, C.T., 2012 *Inequality and Poverty in Boom and Bust: Ireland as a Case Study*. GINI discussion papers 70. Amsterdam: Amsterdam Institute for Advanced Labour Studies.

Norris, M. and Byrne, M., 2015 'Asset Price Keynesianism, Regional Imbalances and the Irish and Spanish Housing Booms and Busts' *Built Environment*, 41 (2).

O Riain, S., 2000 'The Flexible Developmental State: Globalisation, Information Technology and the "Celtic Tiger"', *Politics & Society*, 28(2), 157–93.

Ó Riain, S., 2004 *The Politics of High Tech Growth: Developmental Network States in the Global Economy*. New York/Cambridge. Cambridge University Press.

Ó Riain, S., 2010 'The Developmental Network State under Threat: Markets and Managerialism in the Irish Innovation System' In Block, F., and Keller, M. R. (eds) *State of Innovation: Perspectives on U.S. Innovation Policy 1969–2009*. Boulder, CO. Paradigm.

Ó Riain, S., 2014 *The Rise and Fall of Ireland's Celtic Tiger: Liberalism, Boom and Bust*. Cambridge. Cambridge University Press.

O'Brien, A., 2011 *The Politics of Tourism Development*. Basingstoke. Palgrave.

O'Brien, D., 'Media played little role in inflating property bubble', *Sunday Independent*, 29 March 2015.

O'Callaghan, C., Boyle, M. and Kitchin, R., 2014 'Post-politics, crisis, and Ireland's "ghost estates"', *Political Geography* 42, 121–133.

O'Connor, P., 2014 *Management and Gender in Higher Education Management*. Manchester: Manchester University Press.

O'Farrell, R., 2015 'Wages and Ireland's international competitiveness', *Economic and Social Review* 46(3), 429–458.

O'Flynn, M., Monaghan, L. and Power, M., 2014 'Scapegoating during a time of crisis: a critique of post Celtic Tiger Ireland', *Sociology* 48(5), 921–937.

O'Flynn, M., Power, M., McCabe, C. and Silke H., 2013 *Class Politics in Post-boom Ireland: A Burgeoning Business*. University of Limerick Working Paper Series WP2013-04.

O'Halloran, M., 'Billing of water charges to be suspended next week', *Irish Times*, 24 June 2016.

O'Regan, M., 'Election 2016: the relentless rise of the independents', *Irish Times*, 28 February 2016.

O'Toole, F., 2009 *Ship of fools: How Stupidity and Corruption Sank the Celtic Tiger*. London: Faber and Faber.

Offe, C., 2014 *Europe Entrapped*. London: Polity Press.

Organisation of Economic Co-operation and Development, 2015 *Employment Outlook 2015*, Statistical Annex, Tables O and I. Paris: OECD

Osborne, R.D., 1996 *Higher Education in Ireland North and South*. London: Jessica Kingsley.

Pappas, T.S. and O'Malley, E., 2014. 'Civil compliance and "political luddism": explaining variance in social unrest during crisis in Ireland and Greece', *American Behavioral Scientist* 58(12), 1592–1613.

Pappas. T. and O'Malley, E., 2014 'Civil compliance and political Luddism: explaining variance in social unrest during crisis in Ireland and Greece', *American Behavioural Scientist* 58(12), 1592–1613.

Peck, J., 2012 'Austerity urbanism: American cities under extreme economy', *City*, 16(6), pp.626–655.

Peck, J., and Tickell, A., 2002 'Neoliberalizing space', *Antipode* 34, 3: 380–404.

Peet, R., 2011 'Inequality, crisis and austerity in finance capitalism', *Cambridge Journal of Regions, Economy, and Society* 4, 383–399.

Peter McVerry Trust, 2016 *Facts and Figures*. Dublin: Peter McVerry Trust.

Piketty, T., 2014 *Capital in the 21st Century*. Cambridge, MA: Harvard University Press.

Power, M., Haynes, A. and Devereux, E., 2015 *Reasonable People v the Sinister Fringe: Interrogating the Framing of Ireland's Water Charge Protesters through the Media Politics of Dissent*. University of Limerick Working Papers Series WP2015-01.

Pritchard, R. and Slowey, M., 2017 'Resilience: A High Price for Survival? Cross-border Perspectives on the Impact of Austerity on Irish Higher Education', in E. Heffernan, J. McHale, and N. Moore-Cherry (eds) *Debating austerity in Ireland: crisis, experience and recovery*, Dublin: Royal Irish Academy.

Pritchard, R.M.O., 2011 'Government power in British higher education', in R.M.O. Pritchard, *Neoliberal Developments in Higher Education: The United Kingdom and Germany*. Bern: Peter Lang, 127–147.

Pritchard, R.M.O., 2013 'Higher education in a competitive world: the new British regime', in J.E. Karlsen and R.M.O. Pritchard (eds), *Resilient Universities: Confronting Challenges in a Changing World*. Bern: Peter Lang, 115–147.

Pritchard, R.M.O., 2015 'Academic values and English higher education', in P. Zgaga, U. Teichler, H. G. Schuetze and A. Wolter (eds) *Higher Education Reform: Looking Back – Looking Forward*. Frankfurt am Main: Peter Lang, pp. 195–214.

Public Health Policy Centre, 2007 *All Ireland Policy Paper on Fuel Poverty and Health*. Dublin: Institute of Public Health.

Queen's University Belfast, 2011 *Corporate Plan 2011–2016*. Belfast: QUB.

Queen's University Belfast, 2013 *Consolidated Financial Statements 2012/13*. Belfast: QUB.

Quigley, J.M. and Raphael, S., 2005 'Regulation and the high cost of housing in California', *American Economic Review* 95(2), 323–328.

Quinn, E., 2011 *Temporary and Circular Migration: Ireland*. Dublin. Economic and Social Research Institute.

Ralph, D., 2009 '"Home is where the heart is"? Understandings of "home" among Irish-born return migrants from the United States', *Irish Studies Review* 17(2), 183–200.

Ralph, D., 2015 *Work, Family and Commuting in Europe: The Lives of Euro-commuters*. Basingstoke, UK: Palgrave Macmillan.

Regan, A. and Brazys, S., 2017 *Celtic Phoenix or Leprechaun Economics? The Politics of an FDI Led Growth Model in Europe*. Geary Institute for Public Policy. Dublin: UCD Geary Institute Working Paper WP2017/01.

Regling, K. and Watson, M., 2010 *A Preliminary Report on the Sources of Ireland's Banking Crisis.* Dublin: Government Publications, Prn A10/07000.

Regulating Better: Government White Paper Setting out Six Principles of Regulation 2004. Dublin: Stationery Office, 20–21.

Rekart, M., 2005 'Sex-work harm reduction', *The Lancet* 366, 2123–2134.

Report of the Expert Group on Resource Allocation and Financing in the Health Sector 2010. Dublin: Government Publications.

Reynolds, M., 2015 *Is Red Tape Killing Our Housing Sector? Building Control Regulation Costs for Multi-unit Housing.* Dublin Economics Workshop Annual Conference.

Rhodes, T., 2002 'The "risk environment": a framework for understanding and reducing drug-related harm', *International Journal of Drug Policy* 13, 85–94.

Ridge, T., 2009 *Childhood Poverty and Social Exclusion.* Bristol: Policy Press.

Ross, S., 2010 *The Bankers: How the Banks Brought Ireland to Its Knees.* Dublin: Penguin Ireland.

Royal Irish Academy, 2016a *Advice Paper No. 8 on the Future Funding of Higher Education in Ireland.* Dublin: Royal Irish Academy.

Royal Irish Academy, 2016b *Advice Paper No. 10 on the Sustainability of the Northern Ireland Higher Education Sector.* Dublin: Royal Irish Academy.

Ruane, J., 2010 'Ireland's Multiple Interface-Periphery Development Model: Achievements and Limits' in M. Bøss (ed.) *The Nation-State in Transformation: The Governance, Growth and Cohesion of Small States under Globalisation.* Aarhus. Aarhus University Press.

Rüdig, W. and Karyotis, G., 2014 'Who protests in Greece? Mass opposition to austerity', *British Journal of Political Science,* 44(03), pp.487–513.

Russell, H., Maître, B. and Nolan, B., 2010 *Monitoring Poverty Trends in Ireland 2004–2007. Key Issues for Children, People of Working Age and Older People.* Dublin: Economic and Social Research Institute.

Ryan, L. and Kurdi, E., 2014 *Young, Highly Qualified Migrants: The Experiences and Expectations of Recently Arrived Irish Teachers in Britain.* London: Social Policy Research Centre, Middlesex University.

Saiz, A., 2010 'The geographic determinants of housing supply', *Quarterly Journal of Economics* 125(3), 1253–1296.

Sanders, T., O'Neill, M. and Pitcher, J., 2009 *Prostitution: Sex Work, Policy and Politics.* London: Sage.

Savage, M., Callan, T., Nolan, B. and Colgan, B., 2015 *The Great Recession, Austerity and Inequality: Evidence from Ireland.* ESRI Working Paper No. 499. Dublin: Economic and Social Research Institute.

Savills, 2015 'Dublin Office Market in Minutes'. Dublin. Savills.

Scharpf, F.W., 2014 *No Exit from the Euro-Rescuing Trap?* Cologne: Max Planck Institute for the Study of Societies.

Schmidt, V.A., 2010 'The unfinished architecture of Europe's economic union', *Governance* 23(4), 555–559.

Schmidt, V.A., 2015 'The forgotten problem of democratic legitimacy: "governing by the rules" and "ruling by numbers"', in M. Matthijs and M. Blyth (eds), *The Future of the Euro.* Oxford: Oxford University Press, pp. 90–114.

Schuetze, H.G. and Alvarez-Mendiola, G., (eds) 2012 *Higher Education Reform: Market and the State*. Rotterdam: Sense.

Scott, A., 1996. *Ideology and New Social Movements*. London: Sage.

Scott, P., 2015 'Mass to market higher education systems: new transitions or false dawn?', in P. Zgaga, U. Teichler, H. G. Schuetze and A. Wolter (eds),*Higher Education Reform: Looking Back – Looking Forward*. Frankfurt am Main: Peter Lang, pp. 195–214.

Shattock, M., 2012 *Making Policy in British Higher Education: 1945–2011*. Maidenhead, UK: Open University Press.

Simms, A., 2001 *An environmental war economy*. UK. NEF Foundation.

Simon Community, 2014 *Making the Right Choices – Simon Communities in Ireland Pre-Budget Submission 2015*. Dublin: Simon Community.

Slaughter, S. and Leslie, L.L., 1997 *Academic Capitalism: Politics, Policies and the Entrepreneurial University*. Baltimore: Johns Hopkins University Press.

Slowey, M. and Schuetze, H.G., 2012 'All change – no change? Lifelong learners in higher education', in M. Slowey and H.G. Schuetze (eds), *Global Perspectives on Higher Education and Lifelong Learners*. London: Routledge, pp. 3–22.

Slowey, M., 2013 'Institutional alliances: passing policy fad or new organizational model?', in P. Axelrod, R.D. Trilokekar, T. Shanahan and R. Wellen (eds), *Making Policy in Turbulent Times: Challenges and Prospects for Higher Education*. Kingston, Canada: McGill University Press, pp. 359–380.

Slowey, M., Kozina, E. and Tan, E., 2014 *Voices of Academics in Irish Higher Education: Perspectives on Professional Development*. Dublin: All Ireland Society for Higher Education.

Smith, J.Z., 1988 *Imagining religion: from Babylon to Jonestown*. USA. University of Chicago Press.

Social Justice Ireland, 2015 National Social Monitor 2015. Dublin: Social Justice Ireland. http://www.socialjustice.ie/content/publications/national-social-monitor-2015 (11 December, 2015)

Society of St Vincent de Paul, 2012a *The Human Face of Austerity*. Dublin: SVP National Office.

Society of St Vincent de Paul, 2012b *2011 Annual Report*. Dublin: SVP National Office.

Soper, K., 2013 'The dialectics of progress: Irish "belatedness" and the politics of prosperity,' *ephemera* 13(12), 249–67.

Stewart, K., 1998 'Poesis: The generativity of emergent things,' in N. Denzin and Y. Lincoln (eds), *The SAGE Handbook of Qualitative Research*, 3rd Edition, 1027–42. USA. Sage Publications.

Stiglitz, J., 2012 *The Price of Inequality: How Today's Divided Society Endangers Our Future*. London: Allen Lane.

Summers, L., 2014 'U.S. economic prospects: secular stagnation, hysteresis, and the Zero Lower Bound', *Business Economics* 49(2).

Sunday Independent, 2009a 'State spending must be slashed', 5 April 2009.

Sunday Independent, 2009b 'No good can come out of strike', 22 November 2009.

Sweeney, E., 2005 Ireland's economic environment: The SCM context. *Technical Focus in Logistical Solutions: The Journal of the National Institute for Transport and Logistics* 8(4), 9–10.

Talbot, I., 'Croke Park agreement is designed to underachieve', *Sunday Business Post*, 11 December 2011.

The VOICE Group (Davies, Andrea, Susan Dobscha, Susi Geiger, Stephanie O'Donohoe, Lisa O'Malley, Andrea Prothero, Elin Brandi Sorensen, Thyra Uth Thomsen), 2010 'Buying into motherhood? Problematic consumption and ambivalence in transitional phases,' *Consumption, Markets and Culture* 3 (4), 373–97.

Tomlinson, M., Walker, R. and Williams, G., 2008 'Measuring Poverty in Britain as a Multidimensional Concept, 1991 to 2003', *Journal of Social Policy* 37(4), 597–620.

Tonkiss, F., 2013 'Austerity urbanism and the makeshift city', *City, 17*(3), pp.312–324.

Touraine, A., 1971 *The Post-industrial Society*. New York: Random House.

Touraine, A., 1981 *The Voice and the Eye: An Analysis of Social Movements*. Cambridge: Cambridge University Press.

Transparency International, 2015 *Corruption Perception Index*.

Turner, V., 1982 *From ritual to theatre: The human seriousness of play*. New York. Performing Arts Journal Publications.

Universities UK, 2015 *Cuts to Higher Education Threaten £1.5 Billion Contribution to Northern Ireland Economy*. London: UUK.

University and College Union , 2013 *Strike on 31st October: Trade Union Response to Management Claims*. London: UCU.

University and College Union, 2012a *National Occupational Stress Survey*. London: UCU.

University and College Union, 2012b *Occupational Stress Survey: The Demands Stressor*. London: UCU.

University and College Union, 2014 *UCU Survey of Work-Related Stress 2014*. London: UCU.

University of Ulster, 2013 *University of Ulster Annual Report and Financial Statements for the Year to 31 July 2013*. Belfast: UU.

Välikangas, L., 2010 *The Resilient Organisation: How Adaptive Cultures Thrive Even When Strategy Fails*. New York: McGraw-Hill.

Waldfogel, J., 2013 'Socio-economic inequality in childhood and beyond: an overview of challenges and findings from comparative analyses of cohort studies', *Longitudinal and Life Course Studies*, 4(3), 268–275.

Walls, P., 2005 Still Leaving. Recent, Vulnerable Irish Emigrants to the UK: Profile, Experiences & Pre-departure Solutions. Dublin: Department of Foreign Affairs.

Walsh, K., 2011 The Economic and Fiscal Contribution of US Investment in Ireland. Journal of the Statistical and Social Inquiry Society of Ireland, Vol. XL, 33–51.

Watson, B., Maître, B. and Whelan, C.T., 2011 *Childhood Deprivation in Ireland*. Dublin: Department of Social Protection and ESRI.

Watson, B., Maître, B. and Whelan, C.T., 2012 *Work and Poverty*. Dublin: Department of Social Protection and ESRI.

Watson, D., Maître, B. Whelan, C.T. and Williams, J., 2014 *Growing Up in Ireland: Dynamics of Child Economic Vulnerability and Socio-Emotional Development – An Analysis of the First Two Waves of the Growing Up in Ireland Study*. Infant and Child Cohorts Report No. 1. Dublin. Department of Children and Youth Affairs.

Watson, D., Whelan, C.T., Maître, B. and Williams, J., 2017, 'Child Poverty in a Period of Austerity', in E. Heffernan, J. McHale, and N. Moore-Cherry (eds) *Debating austerity in Ireland: crisis, experience and recovery*, Dublin: Royal Irish Academy.

Weber, M., 1978 *Economy and Society,* Vol. 1 Berkeley: University of California Press.

Wells, J. and White, M., 2014 'The impact of the economic crisis and austerity on the nursing and midwifery professions in the Republic of Ireland – "boom", "bust" and retrenchment', *Journal of Research in Nursing* 19(7–8), 562–577.

Wells, P.E., 2010 *The automotive industry in an era of eco-austerity*. Cheltenham, Edward Elgar.

Whelan, C.T. and Maître, B., 2012 'Identifying childhood deprivation: How well do national indicators of poverty and deprivation perform?', *Economic & Social Review* 43, 251–272.

Whelan, C.T. and Maître, B., 2014 'The Great Recession and the changing distribution of economic vulnerability by social class: the Irish case. *Journal of European Social Policy* 24(5), 470–485.

Whelan, C.T., Nolan, B. and Maître, B., 2016a 'Polarization or "squeezed middle" in the Great Recession? A comparative European analysis of the distribution of economic stress', *Social Indicators Research*, DOI 10.1007/s11205-016-1350-1.

Whelan, C.T., Russell, H. and Maître, B., 2014. *Trends in Economic Stress and the Great Recession in Ireland: An Analysis of the CSO Survey on Income and Living Conditions (SILC)*. Dublin: Department of Social Protection.

Whelan, C.T., Russell, H. and Maître, B., 2016c 'Economic stress and the Great Recession in Ireland: polarization, individualization or middle class squeeze?', *Social Indicators Research*, 126, 503–526.

Whelan, K., 2010 'Policy Lessons from Ireland's Latest Depression' *Economic and Social Review*, 41. 225–254.

Whelan, K., 2012 'ELA, Promissory notes and all that: the fiscal costs of Anglo Irish Bank', *The Economic and Social Review*, 43(4), 653–673.

Whelan, K., 2014 'Ireland's economic crisis: the good, the bad and the ugly', *Journal of Macroeconomics*, 39, 424–440.

Wherry, F., 2012 Ritualized markets: The culture and economics of budgeting and consumer demand, available at: http://faculty.chicagobooth.edu/workshops/org-smarkets/past/pdf/Ritualized%20Markets%20Manuscript%20v2.pdf, (August 13, 2015).

Wilkinson, R. and Pickett, K., 2009 *The Spirit Level: Why Equality is Better for Everyone*. London: Penguin Books.

Williams, J. and Whelan, C.T., 2011 'Prevalence of relative income poverty and its effect on outcomes among 9-year-olds', Paper presented at *Growing Up in Ireland Annual Conference*, Dublin, 1 December.

Williams, J., Greene, S., Doyle, E., Harris, E., Layte, R., McCoy, S., McCrory, C., Murray, A., Nixon, E., O'Dowd, T., O'Moore, M., Quail, A., Smyth, E., Swords, L. and Thornton, M., 2009 *Growing Up in Ireland: The Lives of 9-Year-Olds*. Dublin: Office of the Minister for Children and Youth Affairs.

Wolf, M., 2014 *The Shifts and the Shocks: What We've Learned and Have Still to Learn from the Financial Crisis*. London: Allen Lane.

Wolff, G.B. and Sapir, A., 2015 *Euro-Area Governance: What to Reform and How to Do It*. Brussels: Bruegel.

World Commission on Environment and Development 1987. Our Common Future. Oxford: Oxford University Press.

World Health Organisation, 2014 *Consolidated Guidelines on HIV Prevention, Diagnosis, Treatment and Care for Key Populations*. Geneva: WHO.

World University Rankings 2015 *Times Higher Education*, 13 January 2016. https://www.timeshighereducation.com/world-university-rankings/2016/world-ranking#!/page/0/length/25.

Wren-Lewis, S., 2015 *The Knowledge Transmission Mechanism and Austerity*, IMK Working Paper, forthcoming.

Wren-Lewis, S., 2017 'A General Theory of Austerity', in E. Heffernan, J. McHale, and N. Moore-Cherry (eds) *Debating austerity in Ireland: crisis, experience and recovery*, Dublin: Royal Irish Academy.

Wright, R., 2010 *Strengthening the Capacity of the Department of Finance: Report of Independent Review Panel*. Dublin: Government Publications.

Zezza, G., 2012 'The impact of fiscal austerity in the eurozone', *Review of Keynesian Economics* 1(1), 37–54.

Websites

Amnesty International 2016 *Amnesty International Policy on State Obligations to Respect, Protect and Fulfil the Human Rights of Sex Workers*. https://www.amnesty.org/en/documents/pol30/4062/2016/en/ (accessed May 2 2017).

Boland, T., 2015 *A dialogue on the future funding of higher education in Ireland*. Speech by Tom Boland, Chief Executive of the Higher Education Funding Council, Royal Irish Academy, 23 September 2015. http://www.hea.ie/news/%E2%80%98speech-tom-boland-chief-executive-hea-higher-education-funding-royal-irish-academy-23rd (accessed May 2 2017).

Brazys, S. and Regan, A., 2015 'These Little PIIGS Went to Market: Enterprise Policy and Divergent Recovery in the Eurozone', Dublin: UCD Geary Institute for Public Policy. http://www.ucd.ie/geary/static/publications/workingpapers/gearywp201517.pdf (accessed May 2 2017).

Breathnach, P., 2010 'Ireland's export competitiveness: myths and facts. Part 3: Alternative approaches to the measurement of export competitiveness', *Ireland After NAMA* blog, 26 May. https://irelandafternama.wordpress.com/ (accessed May 2 2017).

Brophy, D., 2015 'The story of no ... 15 moments that have defined the Irish water protest movement', http://www.thejournal.ie/irish-water-protests-timeline-1963363-Aug2015/ (accessed May 2 2017).

Burke, S., 2010 Boom to bust: its impact on Irish health policy and health services. *Irish Journal of Public Policy* 2 (1). http://publish.ucc.ie/ijpp/2010/01/burke/08/en (accessed 2 May 2017).

Burke, S., Thomas, S., Barry, S. and Keegan, C., 2014 *Measuring, Mapping and Making Sense of Irish Health System Performance in the Recession.* A working paper from the resilience project in the Centre for Health Policy and Management, School of Medicine, Trinity College Dublin. http://www.medicine.tcd.ie/ health-systems-research/assets/pdf/pubs/Resilience-working-paper-March-2014. pdf (accessed May 2 2017).

Callan, T., Leventi, C., Levy, H., Matsaganis, M., Paulus, A. and Sutherland, H., 2011 *The Distributional Effects of Austerity Measures: A Comparison of Six EU Countries.* EUROMOD Working Paper, No. EM6/11, http://hdl.handle. net/10419/64872 (accessed May 2 2017).

Central Statistics Office 2016 *Population and Migration Estimates April 2016*, 23 August. http://www.cso.ie/en/releasesandpublications/er/pme/populationand- migrationestimatesapril2016/ (accessed 2 May 2017).

Central Statistics Office, 2015 Survey on Income and Living Conditions (SILC). http://www.cso.ie/en/releasesandpublications/er/silc/surveyonincomeandliving- conditions2014/ (accessed 21 December 21 2015).

Central Statistics Office, 2015a *Population and Migration Estimates April 2015*, 26 August. http://www.cso.ie/en/releasesandpublications/er/pme/populationand- migrationestimatesapril2015/ (accessed 2 May 2017).

Citywide 2015 *Citywide Drugs Crisis Campaign. Manifesto for Election 2016 – Tackling Ireland's Drug Problem.* http://www.citywide.ie/download/pdf/gener- al_election_2016_manifesto_citywide.pdf (accessed May 2 2017).

Community Platform 2014 Now You See Us: the Human Stories behind Poverty in Ireland. http://communityplatform.ie/nowyouseeus.pdf (accessed May 2 2017)

Convention on the Constitution 2014 Eight Report of the Convention on the Constitution: Economic, Social and Cultural (ESC) Rights. https://www. constitution.ie/AttachmentDownload.ashx?mid=5333bbe7-a9b8-e311-a7ce- 005056a32ee4 (14 December, 2015).

Costello, R., 2016 'Which government best reflects the "will of the people"?', https://politicalreform.ie/2016/03/01/which-government-best-reflects-the-will- of-the-people/ (accessed May 2 2017).

Daly, M., 2015 'Why should part-time students have to pay fees that full-timers do not?', thejournal.ie, 15 August. http://www.thejournal.ie/author/mary-daly/ (accessed May 2 2017)

Dellepiane, S. and Hardiman, N., 2012. *The New Politics of Austerity: Fiscal Responses to the Economic Crisis in Ireland and Spain.* Dublin: UCD Geary Institute for Public Policy. http://www.ucd.ie/geary/static/publications/work- ingpapers/gearywp201207.pdf (accessed May 2 2017).

Department of Environment, Community and Local Government 2014b Social Housing Strategy 2020: Support, Supply and Reform, available online at: http://www.environ.ie/en/Publications/DevelopmentandHousing/Housing/ FileDownLoad,39622,en.pdf (accessed 14 December 2015).

Department of Finance 2015 National Economic Dialogue, available online at: http://www.finance.gov.ie/search/node/National%20Economic%20Dialogue (accessed 15 December 2015).

Department of Finance (n.d.) http://www.finance.gov.ie/what-we-do/eu-interna- tional/irelands-programme-eu-imf-programme (accessed 28 September 2016).

Department of Foreign Affairs and Trade 2015 *Coming Home.* https://www.dfa.ie/global-irish/coming-home/ (accessed May 2 2017).

Department of Jobs, Enterprise and Innovation 2016 *Highly Skilled Eligible Occupations List.* https://www.djei.ie/en/What-We-Do/Jobs-Workplace-and-Skills/Employment-Permits/Employment-Permit-Eligibility/Highly-Skilled-Eligible-Occupations-List/ (accessed May 2 2017).

Donnelly, L. 2015 'An historic general election coming in Ireland in early 2016?', http://www.irishcentral.com/opinion/others/An-historic-general-election-coming-in-Ireland-in-early-2016.html (accessed May 2 2017).

Economist 2015 *Fiscal policy: What is Austerity?* 20 May 2015. Available at: http://www.economist.com/blogs/buttonwood/2015/05/fiscal-policy. [Accessed 21 September 2016].

Eurobarometer 2012 *Special Eurobarometer 374: Corruption.* Brussels: European Commission. http://ec.europa.eu/public_opinion/archives/ebs/ebs_374_en.pdf (accessed May 2 2017).

Eurobarometer 2014 *Special Eurobarometer 397: Corruption.* Brussels: European Commission. http://ec.europa.eu/public_opinion/archives/ebs/ebs_397_en.pdf (accessed May 2 2017).

European Commission 2016 State aid: Ireland gave illegal tax benefits to Apple worth up to €13 billion, available online at: http://europa.eu/rapid/press-release_IP-16-2923_en.htm (accessed May 2 2017)

Forfas. 2013 The Annual Survey of Business Impact. Available from http://www.djei.ie/publications/strategicpolicy/2015/ABSEI_2013_report.pdf

Glynn, I., Kelly, T. and MacÉinrí, P. 2013 *Irish Emigration in an Age of Austerity*, available at: www.ucc.ie/en/media/research/emigre/Emigration_in_an_Age_of_Austerity_Final.pdf (accessed 2 May 2017).

Hearne, R. 2015 *The Irish Water War, Austerity and the 'Risen People'.* https://www.maynoothuniversity.ie/sites/default/files/assets/document/TheIrishWaterwar_0.pdf (accessed May 2 2017).

Henigan, M., 2014 'The idiot/eejit's guide to distorted Irish national economic data', *FinFacts*, http://www.finfacts.ie/irishfinancenews/article_1028148.shtml (accessed May 2 2017).

Honohan, P. 2009 'Why is Ireland's tax collapse so severe?' *Irish Economy.ie* blog, 5 January. http://www.irisheconomy.ie/index.php/2009/01/05/why-is-irelands-tax-collapse-so-severe/ (accessed 2 May 2017).

Honohan, P. 2009 *The Irish Banking Crisis: Regulatory and Financial Stability Policy 2003–2008.* A report to the Minister for Finance by the Governor of the Central Bank. Available at www.socialjustice.ie (accessed May 2 2017).

Honohan, P. 2010 The Irish Banking Crisis; Regulatory and Financial Stability Policy 2003–2008. A report to the Minister for Finance by the Governor of the Central Bank. http://www.bankinginquiry.gov.ie/ (accessed May 2 2017).

http://www.hea.ie/sites/default/files/ria_tb_funding_speech_v2_002.pdf (accessed 16 August 2016).

http://www.hea.ie/sites/default/files/ria_tb_funding_speech_v2_002.pdf (accessed 16 August 2016).

http://www.transparency.org/research/cpi/overview (accessed 2 May 2017).

Hugo, G. 2013 'What we know about circular migration and enhanced mobility', *Migration Policy Institute Policy Brief* No. 7, September, http://www.migration-policy.org/pubs/Circular-Migration.pdf (accessed 2 May 2017).

IBEC (Irish Business and Employers Confederation) 2009 'Pre-budget submission 2010', October. http://www.finfacts.ie/biz10/IBEC_Pre-Budget_Submission_2010.pdf (accessed 2 May 2017).

IBEC 2013 'Budget 2014 submission', June, http://oldwww.finance.gov.ie/documents/prebudgetsubmissions2013/ibec.pdf

Irish Fiscal Advisory Council 2014 'Pre-budget 2015 statement', September. http://www.fiscalcouncil.ie/wp-content/uploads/2014/09/PreBudget_220914_Final.pdf (accessed May 2 2017).

Jensen, T., 2013 'Tough love in tough times,' Studies in the Maternal 4 (2), available at: http://www.mamsie.bbk.ac.uk/articles/abstract/10.16995/sim.35/ (January 19 2016).

Kennedy, G. 2015 *Appearance before the Committee of Inquiry into the Banking Crisis.* 26 March. https://inquiries.oireachtas.ie/banking/hearings/geraldine-kennedy-former-editor-the-irish-times/ (accessed 2 May 2017).

Kenny, M., 'Ireland faces a choice between lucre and liberty,' *The Guardian*, May 25 2012, available at: http://www.theguardian.com/commentisfree/2012/may/25/ireland-faces-choice-lucre-liberty-eu (accessed 13 August 2015).

L'Observatoire Français des Conjonctures Économiques, 2009 The Measurement of Economic Performance and Social Progress Revisited. http://www.ofce.sciences-po.fr/pdf/dtravail/WP2009-33.pdf (accessed 11 December, 2015).

Louwerse, T. 2015 'Irish polling indicator: good autumn for Fine Gael', *Irish Politics Forum* blog, 5 December, http://politicalreform.ie/2015/12/05/irish-polling-indicator-good-autumn-for-fine-gael/ (accessed 2 May 2017).

National Assembly of Wales 2015 Well-being of Future Generations (Wales) Act 2015 http://gov.wales/topics/people-and-communities/people/future-generations-act/?lang=en (accessed 4 October 2016).

National Treatment Purchase Fund Figures. http://www.ntpf.ie/home/pdf//2015/04/nationalnumbers/out-patient/National03.pdf (accessed 2 May 2017).

NERI (Nevin Economic Research Institute), 2014 *Quarterly Economic Observer*, Autumn. http://www.nerinstitute.net/research/quarterly-economic-observer-autumn-2014/ (accessed 2 May 2017).

NERI—Nevin Economic Research Institute 2014 *We Need to Talk about Higher Education*, NERI working paper 2014/no. 14, http://www.nerinstitute.net/download/pdf/we_need_to_talk_about_higher_education.pdf (accessed 2 May 2017).

Nyberg, P. 2011 *Commission of Investigation into the Banking Sector in Ireland.* Available at www.bankinginquiry.gov.ie. (accessed 2 May 2017).

O'Brien, A. 2010 'Reconstructing the Tourism Economy' Progressive Economy Blog, http://www.progressive-economy.ie/2010/05/guest-post-by-anne-obrien.html (accessed May 2 2017).

ORAC 2015 'Annual Report – 2015', http://www.orac.ie/website/orac/oracwebsite.nsf/page/orac-stats_15-en (accessed 2 May 2017).

ORAC 2016 '2015 Stats – April Monthly Statistics', http://www.orac.ie/website/orac/oracwebsite.nsf/page/orac-stats_16-en (accessed 2 May 2017).

Piggot, V and Walsh, K., 2014 Corporation Tax—A Note on the Context and Concentration of Payments. Available from http://www.budget.gov.ie/Budgets/2015/Documents/Corporation_Tax_Context_Concentration_Corporation_Tax_Payments_Revenue.pdf (accessed 2 May 2017).

Regan, A. 2015 'What Explains the Irish Recovery?' Dublin European Institute Blog, http://europedebate.ie/what-explains-the-irish-economic-recovery/ (accessed 2 May 2017).

Regan, A. and Brazys, S., 2017 *Celtic phoenix or leprechaun economics? The politics of an FDI-led growth model in Europe.* Dublin: UCd Geary Institute for Public Policy.

Reich, R. 2015 'Why We Must End Upward Pre-Distribution To The Rich', *Social Europe Journal* 1 October 2015. http://www.socialeurope.eu/2015/10/why-we-must-end-upward-pre-distribution-to-the-rich/ (10 December 2015).

Right2Change 2015 *Right 2 Change: Equality, Democracy, Justice.* http://www.right2change.ie/sites/default/files/media/Right2Change%20Policies.pdf (accessed 2 May 2017).

Schneider, M.P.A., Kinsella, S. and Godin, A., 2015 Redistribution in the Age of Austerity: Evidence from Europe, 2006–13. Levy Institute Working Paper 856. http://www.levyinstitute.org/publications/redistribution-in-the-age-of-austerity-evidence-from-europe-2006-13 (accessed 21 December 2015) .

Slacalek, J. 2006 *What Drives Personal Consumption?: The Role of Housing and Financial Wealth.* DIW Berlin Discussion Papers, No. 647, German Institute for Economic Research. http://EconPapers.repec.org/RePEc:diw:diwwpp:dp647 (accessed 2 May 2017).

Social Justice Ireland 2015, Budget 2016 Analysis & Critique. Dublin: Social Justice Ireland http://www.socialjustice.ie/sites/default/files/attach/publication/4051/sjibudget2016analysis.pdf (accessed 11 December 2015).

Taft, M. 2016 'Clogging Up the Trickle Down' Unite's Notes on the Front Blog, http://notesonthefront.typepad.com/politicaleconomy/2016/01/clogging-up-the-trickle-down.html (accessed 26 January 2016).

United Nations 2015 United Nations Framework Convention on Climate Change. http://unfccc.int/resource/docs/2015/cop21/eng/l09r01.pdf (accessed 21 December 2015).

Whelan, K. 2013 *Ireland's economic crisis the good, the bad and the ugly.* Paper presented at Bank of Greece conference on the Euro Crisis, Athens, 24 May, http://www.karlwhelan.com/Papers/Whelan-IrelandPaper-June2013.pdf (accessed 2 May 2017).

Index

social protection expenditure, 246–51
Spain
    austerity measures, 84–90
        political response, 95
    fiscal crisis, 83–4
Spatial Justice and the Irish Crisis, 6
St Vincent de Paul Society, 146–7
Stability and Growth Pact, 40, 50
    Excessive Deficit Procedure, 46
Stiglitz, Joseph, 175, 267
Strategic Banking Corporation, 232
'structural deficit', 56–7, 251
Structure of Earnings Survey, 65
Sunday Business Post
    stance on austerity, 75
Sunday Independent
    stance on austerity, 75, 76, 77–8
Sunday Times (Irish edition)
    stance on austerity, 75
Survey on Income and Living
    Conditions, 65
sustainability politics, 12, 207, 215,
    266–7
    COP21 conference, 266
    National Spatial Strategy 2002–
        2020, 266

SWITCH tax-benefit simulation
    model, 105
SYRIZA, 95

T
Talbot, Ian, 77
Taxation (Ireland), 58–9, 62–3
    construction sector, 132
    corporation tax, 237, 242–3, 251–2
    fair and just, 261–3
    Household Charge, 118
    indirect, 63, 243
    Local Property Tax, 134
    'Six Pack' rules, 54, 261
    Stamp duty, 132
    SWITCH tax-benefit simulation
        model, 105
    Universal Social Charge, 114
    US-controlled companies, 242–3
    VAT on new homes, 132

Thatcher, Margaret, 62
thrift culture, 205–6, 215–16
    second-hand markets, 211–15
    sustainable living, 209–10
TILDA study, 159
Treaty on Stability, Coordination and
    Governance (Fiscal Compact
    Treaty), 54
'troika' programme, 38, 45, 50, 191
Turnbull, Lord, 32
Twitter, 79

U
UK
    Brexit, 98, 189, 269, 271
    economic recovery, 20
UN Declaration of Human Rights, 136
unemployment, 21
United Left Alliance, 122
USA
    economic recovery, 20

V
Varadkar, Leo, 119
Vella, Karmenu, 121

W
Wallace, Mick, 125
water charges, 9, 63, 118–19, 121,
    127–8
    campaign against, 122
Weber, Max, 54
Weimar Republic, 29
World Bank, 188
World Commission on Environment
    and Development, 266
World War Two, 24
Wright Commission, 56

Z
zero lower bound problem, 19, 20, 35

4